IN
THE SHADOW
OF
THE
RISING SUN

IN THE SHADOW OF THE SHADOW OF THE RISING SUN

The
Political Roots
of
American Economic
Decline

William S. Dietrich

The Pennsylvania State University Press
University Park, Pennsylvania

Library of Congress Cataloging-in-Publication Data

Dietrich, William S.
    In the shadow of the rising sun : the political roots of American economic
decline / William S. Dietrich.

        p.   cm.
    Includes bibliographical references and index.
    ISBN 0-271-00765-6. — ISBN 0-271-00766-4 (pbk.)
    1. United States—Foreign economic relations—Japan. 2. Japan—Foreign eco-
nomic relations—United States. 3. Industry and state—Japan. 4. Industry and
state—United States. 5. Competition, International. I. Title.
HF1456.5.Z4J33   1991
338.973—dc20   91-7668

It is the policy of The Pennsylvania State University Press to use acid-free paper for
the first printing of all clothbound books. Publications on uncoated stock satisfy the
minimum requirements of American National Standard for Information Sciences—
Permanence of Paper for Printed Library Materials, ANSI Z39.48–1984.

To the Memory of My Parents

Marianna Brown Dietrich
1910–1983

Kenneth P. Dietrich
1907–1984

This time it vanished quite slowly,
beginning at the end of the tail, and
ending with the grin, which remained some
time after the rest of it had gone.
    —Lewis Carroll (Alice in Wonderland)

The Moving Finger writes; and, having writ,
Moves on: nor all thy Piety nor Wit
Shall lure it back to cancel half a Line,
Nor all thy Tears wash out a Word of it.
    —The Rubáiyát of Omar Khayyám

CONTENTS

PREFACE

As we enter the last decade of the twentieth century, we in the United States have much to be thankful for. Long-term world prospects for peace and prosperity (recent events in Iraq and Kuwait notwithstanding) never looked better. During the Gorbachev era, international developments have proceeded at a mind-numbing pace. Fortunately, from our present vantage point—well into this political and economic sea change—we can envision the result in reasonably clear outline. Marxian ideology, single-party systems, centrally managed economies, and all other defining elements of what we have come to know as the Communist world will be washed away by a floodtide of free-market capitalism and liberal democracy. Communism failed in most areas, but its critical shortcoming was economic. State-owned enterprises operating in nonmarket, centrally directed economies failed to deliver the goods.

Unfortunately, there are ominous clouds on the horizon. The dangers they represent offer unsettling parallels to the aftermath of World War II. Winston Churchill wrote about that period in a volume entitled *Triumph and Tragedy*. The words in that title are apt words for today too. In 1990 there are still a great many people who remember well the exhilaration Americans felt at the defeat of the Axis Powers. But our joy was short-lived, for the Soviet Union soon confronted us with massive armed forces in Europe and nuclear weapons that for the first time threatened destruction on American soil.

Today we face a new challenge. It is not a military challenge, but it threatens our way of life and ultimately our freedoms as much as past dangers from Nazi Germany and the Soviet Union. This new challenge comes from Japan. It takes the form of a drive toward global technological and economic mastery. Success in these areas is likely to bring de facto Japanese political dominance in its wake. The danger this time is very real, but in its subtle and pervasive nature it is more difficult to understand than the stark realities of military confrontation. This time there are no bombs at Hickham Field, no capsized *Arizona,* and no Day of Infamy speech. We can't say exactly when the new economic war began, but unlike our last conflict with Japan this one won't be over in forty-five months. Forty-five years is a more likely time frame, and we're less than halfway through it now.

Most Americans would deny that we are engaged in an economic hot war with the Japanese. And the Japanese never planned it this way. It is doubtful that, twenty-five years ago, they saw the possibilities of global technological and economic dominance. But the Japanese are winning this contest by default. Lack of response to their challenge, coupled with sheer indifference to our ever-increasing strategic technological and economic shortcomings, beckons them to press on.

In the past we categorized economic systems as either state-directed systems (communist) or free-market systems, but in the contest between the two the ball game is over and the free-market system wins hands down. There is a third alternative though. It is the Japanese economic system—the most powerful economic engine the world has ever known. The Japanese economic system is a capitalistic free-market system, but it is tempered by strategic considerations arrived at through consultation and bargaining between government and business. The outcome might be described as a state/market balance. Ezra Vogel terms it "guided free enterprise." Chalmers Johnson calls it "developmentalism." Under this system a global economic strategy is constantly subjected to the demanding rigors of the domestic and international marketplace.

Our reluctance to recognize the Japanese challenge, coupled with our failure to understand the operative method of Japan's spectacular technological and economic performance, is dooming the United States to economic decline. Industrial policy is the operative method of the Japanese miracle. Our continued blind faith in the free market, and our adamant refusal to see government as a strategic player in the economic sphere, make our markets and leading technologies easy targets for the Japanese. And with the imminent collapse of Communism we are more likely than ever to deify the efficacy of the market and condemn any strategic role for the state.

To put it simply, let us think of three, not two, economic alternatives: USSR–State, U.S.–Market, and Japan–State/Market. In a three-horse race, USSR–State has stumbled and is out of the race, but Japan–State/Market is well ahead and broadening its lead over U.S.–Market. Shaped by a state/market balance, the Japanese economic system is a demonstrably superior system. It can be countered effectively only by an economic system that is roughly equivalent. The alternative is economic decline.

Recent domestic developments give us little cause for optimism. The estimated cost of the savings and loan bailout has risen from $50 billion to more than $400 billion during the last three years. And the virus of junk bond failure that was a heavy contributor to the S&L debacle now appears to be headed through the banking system and on into the insurance industry. In 1990 any hopes for meaningful deficit reduction were dashed by the sorry spectacle of ten months of political deadlock in Washington. The American public was shocked, and rightly so, at the virtual paralysis of the federal government. As we shall see later in this book, these events do not surprise us when we see them in the context of a deeper understanding of the workings of our governmental machinery. The only real surprise would be a different outcome.

Any book that attempts to uncover the fundamental cause of American economic decline sets for itself a herculean task. A broad expanse of ground must be covered, and much of it quickly. In order to ensure that the reader, and perhaps also the author, does not wander too far from the main path, I summarize the argument here:

• America faces economic decline and the loss of world economic and political leadership.

- The proximate causes of American economic decline are serious and system-wide managerial, financial, and political shortcomings.

- Japan has undertaken a national effort to achieve global technological, economic, and perhaps even political dominance.

- Japan's success has been based on the comprehensive and system-wide use of industrial policy.

- Industrial policy is the state-induced willful shifting of the industrial structure toward high-technology, high-value-added industries.

- A strong central state and a top professional bureaucracy are essential preconditions for industrial policy.

- Japanese political institutions are European in origin and are replicated in most advanced industrial societies.

- America is totally lacking the statist traditions of Japan, Germany, and France. Our political development has been conditioned by an anti-statist tradition.

- American political institutions are utterly unique. The United States is the only advanced democratic society that lacks a strong central state and a top professional bureaucracy.

- The only way America can counter the Japanese challenge and regain world economic leadership is through the comprehensive use of industrial policy.

- Without a strong central state and a top professional bureaucracy—the two preconditions of industrial policy—America is doomed to economic decline.

- There is one way, and only one way, out of our current predicament: fundamental institutional change.

ACKNOWLEDGMENTS

This book would not have been possible without much help and support from a variety of sources. Erika King, Hillman Professor of Political Science at Chatham College, served as my research assistant throughout the project. Many of the source materials were located and placed in my hands by Erika. In particular, she made a major contribution to Chapter 8. Because my graduate school fields of concentration were theory and comparative politics, Erika's expertise and good judgment in the American field were indispensable—the organizing framework of Chapter 8 is essentially hers.

At the University of Pittsburgh, invaluable help was provided by Ellis Krauss, Guy Peters, and Fred Whelan. All three read the entire manuscript, and their input resulted in numerous improvements. In particular, Ellis Krauss's very close reading and rereading of the three chapters on Japan proved to be a godsend. The soundness of these chapters owes much to Ellis, while their shortcomings remain my responsibility.

During several pleasant and conversation-rich dinners, Janet and John Chapman heard the argument of this book (with heightened fervor and conviction as the hours and drinks accumulated) more than I'm sure they cared to. And WSK and DSW, who sat patiently—and sometimes not so patiently—through those dinners.

Without the faith, courage, and enthusiasm of Sanford G. Thatcher, director of Penn State Press, this book might not have seen the light of day. Kate Capps, Peggy Hoover, and the entire staff of the Press made the production of this book a memorable and enjoyable experience. Mario Ugoletti, working under a tight time schedule, provided critical updating of key economic data.

My devoted secretary of many years, Pauline Short, did her usual outstanding job, typing, checking, and generally keeping the project moving forward.

And last, my thanks to a man I never met: Richard Hofstadter (1916–1970), whose crystalline prose and deep understanding of this country led me a long way on his section of the trail. I would hope he'd be mildly tolerant of the results.

PART ONE

—

THE
AMERICAN
DILEMMA

THE U.S. ECONOMY IS IN DEEP TROUBLE. The nation's numerous short-comings are exacerbated and amplified by the fierce competitive thrust of Japan. Japanese triumphs in a string of strategic industries from steel to semiconductors are evidence that Japan is heading for world economic dominance, and possibly a lot more.

The evidence of American economic decline is varied and extensive: unacceptably high federal budget deficits, trade deficits, a ballooning foreign debt, and decades of overconsumption breeding undersaving and underinvestment. But the numbers tell only part of the story, as a look at the loss of U.S. leadership in four specific industries—steel, automobiles, consumer electronics, and semiconductors—will show. In each instance, when the Japanese penetrate the market with low-cost, high-quality commodity products, the stock U.S. response is to cede the low end of the line and retreat to making higher-margin and more technologically sophisticated products. But the Japanese don't stop with the lower end of the line; they advance upward until they achieve technological superiority and industry leadership. Finally, understanding (as Americans do not) that technological mastery leads to economic dominance, the Japanese have built dozens of technologically driven globally competitive corporations. Americans have been content to shuffle assets through leveraged buyouts and hostile takeovers.

As we seek an answer to the question of why the United States can't compete, one thing becomes quite clear. No single factor, or even a cluster of factors, offers an answer to that question. The many and varied facets of the competitive shortcomings of the United States can be put under three broad headings: management, finance, and politics. The reasons for these shortcomings are far more numerous than we might have imagined and are all closely interrelated. Grab ahold of one, and a number of others are likely to come along with it. There is simply no single explanation. The problems of the U.S. economy are system-wide, and their remedy will require a system-wide response. Our economic problems are not unsolvable—but they are close to it.

1

LOSING
THE ECONOMIC WAR
WITH JAPAN

Words ought to be a little wild for they are the
assault of thought on the unthinking.
　　　　　　　　　　　—John Maynard Keynes

The years ahead will not be good ones for the United States. After nearly two centuries of unparalleled success, America's destiny is no longer ours alone. We are now being inexorably and uncomfortably moved by what Alexander Solzhenitsyn called "the pitiless crowbar of events." A nation, of course, always lives with serious problems. Even at the height of the Pax Americana we faced the threat of nuclear war, an expanding sphere of Communist domination abroad, and racial and social injustice at home. There has been progress in some quarters, and ground lost in others, but at worst we held the line.

Americans now face a different type of threat, but nothing so dramatic as nuclear holocaust or legally enforced racial segregation. The challenge today is more subtle, more pervasive, and far more intractable. The

United States is threatened with loss of the technological and economic supremacy it has enjoyed throughout the twentieth century. Technology, productivity, and economic performance are the means by which we create national wealth and international power. We have long taken for granted America's preeminent economic strength and technological mastery. Arnold Toynbee once recalled:

> I remember watching the Diamond Jubilee Procession myself as a small boy. I remember the atmosphere. It was: here we are on top of the world and we have arrived at this peak to stay there forever. There is of course something called history, but history is something unpleasant that happens to other people. We are comfortably outside all of that.

History is now *happening to* the United States. The Japanese have confronted us with history. Japan has mounted a national effort to become the most technologically advanced and economically powerful nation in the world. As Americans have focused on the military cold war with the Soviets, the United States has been losing badly the economic hot war with Japan. Industry after critical industry in the United States has been devastated by the Japanese, as surely as if waves of bombers had come over to destroy our factories. In World War II our victories over Japan were Midway, Guadalcanal, Tarawa, Iwo Jima, and Okinawa. In the new economic war of the last third of the twentieth century, Japan's victories have been steel, automobiles, consumer electronics, machine tools, and semiconductors.

If Japan's economic machine is harnessed to the task of providing Japanese citizens with a decent standard of living and economic security, it can relax; it has clearly achieved these goals. But Japan is not relaxing, not slowing down. National commitment to the productive project is as vigorous today as it was during the bleak years of postwar recovery, or for that matter during the war years themselves. As surely as the United States was engaged with the Soviet Union in a political contest and a military arms race, so Americans are now engaged with Japan in a struggle for world technological and economic supremacy.

The stakes are overwhelming. Failure to respond adequately to the challenge will adversely affect every facet of American life. Today the United States is not responding. Worse yet, we are not convinced that we are even seriously challenged. While we stood armed and ready at the front door, vigilant against the Communist menace, the Japanese quietly and unobtrusively moved in through the back door and occupied much of the house. The economic destiny of the United States, and to some extent even its political future, is no longer in our own hands.

The extent of the American economic decline, registered in sharp losses to the Japanese challenge in industry after industry, is examined in the pages that follow. We shall also look at the strength and scope of the challenge and how it is driven by Japan's national industrial policy, which rests on a broad foundation of economic, political, and social factors that tap into the very fiber of the Japanese nation. But one factor weighs more heavily than any other in accounting for the extraordinary success the Japanese have achieved: the nature of Japan's political system. The political systems of Germany and France bear a striking resemblance to the Japanese political system, whereas the American system is altogether different. The extent to which the U.S. political system differs from the common state patterns found in Japan, Germany, and France has enormous consequences for our technological, economic, and even political prospects in the coming years. The United States has dug itself into a huge economic hole, and there is only one way out. But the solution will be difficult for Americans to accept.

The international competitive position of the United States began to deteriorate in the 1960s. From 1948 to 1973, the United States posted labor productivity gains of 2.5 percent per year, but since 1973 they have declined to a scant 0.4 percent. During the period from 1960 to 1988, average yearly U.S. labor productivity grew only 1.3 percent, compared with 3.1 percent in Germany and 5.3 percent in Japan. In addition, manufacturing productivity has also deteriorated; for example, the growth rate of manufacturing output per hour from 1960 to 1989 was the lowest among the Group of Five Countries, and Japan outpaced the United States by more than sixfold. With regard to capital investment, average growth rates for the period 1960 to 1988 (as a percentage of gross domestic product) in France and Germany has been 25 percent higher than in the United States, and in Japan it is 73 percent higher. Even more revealing is the fact that average capital investment in the United States is the lowest of all the OECD countries, and nondefense research and development spending as a percentage of GNP in Japan and Germany has been ahead of the United States for the last twenty years, and the gap has widened from 0.5 percent in 1977 to almost 1 percent in 1987. Real incomes, which had risen sharply in response to soaring productivity during the first two postwar decades, halted their long climb after 1965. During 1988, some 47 percent of all U.S. patents were issued to foreigners, with a high percentage going to Japanese companies. And by 1988 the value of stocks listed on the Tokyo Stock Exchange far exceeded the total value of New York Stock Exchange equities: 42 percent of the world's equity capitalization, as against 31 percent for the United States.[1]

The United States has littered its industrial landscape with failed or ailing companies and industries that were once symbolic of our economic might. The list of once-powerful U.S. industries that are now nearly extinct, mortally wounded, or currently under sharp attack is long—for example, steel, shipbuilding, cameras, watches, machine tools, motorcycles, automobiles, earth-moving machinery, office automation equipment, consumer electronics, robotics, optic fibers, lasers, computer peripherals, semiconductors, computers, and telecommunications equipment. And this list should not be confined to smokestack America; it extends also to industries at the very cutting edge of technology. In fact, as Japan pursues its vision of a twenty-first-century information society, the fire hose of Japanese industrial targeting has increasingly and steadily shifted from traditional manufacturing activities to industries that are driven by rapid technological advance.

Alongside the list of faltering American industries there are numerous macroeconomic indicators that are equally disturbing. Perhaps the best bottom-line indicators of our economic malaise are the staggering and unprecedented U.S. trade deficits. Our trade balance—positive from 1893—first turned negative in 1978 and has spiraled downward ever since. From $10 billion in 1980, the U.S. merchandise trade deficit deepened to $35 billion in 1982 and more than tripled to $135 billion in 1984. And despite a drastic reversal of the dollar-yen relationship, which saw the value of the dollar depreciate against the yen by 40 percent during the two-year period ending in December 1986, the 1986 trade deficit reached a record $156 billion. In the face of a further 10 percent drop in the value of the dollar during 1987, the seemingly insatiable appetite of Americans for imported goods propelled the 1987 deficit to a new record of $170 billion.[2] While some progress was made during the period

1988–90, the deficit appears to be stuck in a range of $110 billion to $125 billion.

If the numbers themselves are not alarming enough, America's trade with Japan (the largest source of our trade deficit) is equally illuminating with respect to the goods traded between the two countries. From the Japanese we buy transportation products, telecommunications equipment, machine tools, consumer electronics products, office automation equipment, and semiconductors. We sell Japan coal, lumber, and agricultural products and expend considerable energy to further open the Japanese market for our beef, oranges, and tobacco. We also sell them aircraft and computers, but the composition of U.S. trade patterns with Japan shows an increasingly stark contrast between the high-technology products Americans purchase and the raw materials we sell. In the past the purchase of manufactured goods and the selling of raw materials was the classic trading pattern of a colony with its mother country.

Persistent and large trade deficits, seemingly impervious to the assaults of a drastically shrunken dollar, are from a cumulative perspective an added threat. As early as the end of 1984 the United States assumed the position of the world's largest debtor nation; four years earlier it had been the world's largest creditor. Before 1914 the United States was a debtor nation, borrowing heavily to build capital stock in the form of mills, railroads, and other elements of an industrial infrastructure. In the 1980s we began to borrow again, but this time to consume and not to invest. The value of U.S. assets abroad, minus foreign assets in the United States, peaked at the end of 1981, with the United States showing a positive balance of $150 billion. In three years this accumulation of almost seventy years was wiped out.

At the end of 1987 the foreign debt of the United States exceeded $350 billion, nearly three times that of our nearest rival, Brazil. By 1990, the total was approaching $700 billion—a figure nearly equal to the foreign debt of all other net debtor nations combined. Well before 1995, our foreign debt will doubtless top $1 trillion.

At one time the widening U.S. merchandise trade deficit was largely offset by earnings on net investments abroad, but with a huge foreign debt this former plus has become a big minus. Sometime in the future the United States must register sizable merchandise trade surpluses simply to offset interest payments on our foreign debt. There is an old saw about the national debt (now over $3 trillion): "We owe it to ourselves." The same cannot be said about our foreign debt. It is a real debt owed to real people and real nations.

Our trade deficit, and its concomitant international debt, is only the centerpiece of a constellation of serious and growing economic problems.[3] Debt—whether national debt, corporate debt, or personal debt—stands at record levels. During the period from 1981 to 1990, national debt moved from 27 percent to 44 percent of our GNP. If 1987, for example, illustrated anything about the proper value of the U.S. dollar against foreign currencies, the answers were good for no more than a month or two. One month we sought vigorously to defend the dollar (while arm-twisting our trading partners to help), the next month a new wisdom thought it advisable to let the dollar float free. The best that can be said about the U.S. currency situation is that it is unstable.

Of all the world's developed nations, the United States has the lowest savings rate, and under current tax laws it is likely to remain so. Americans are undersaving, underinvesting, and overconsuming. We seem to be intent on consuming ourselves into economic oblivion. We are very much like the stereotypical cardiac case. Our economic failures put us in jeopardy no less than smoking, high cholesterol, excess weight, and lack of exercise cause heart disease. On Black Monday, October 19, 1987, we had a heart attack. Our economic medical staff in Washington told us it was nothing to worry about. In terms of its immediate effect on the economy, the Black Monday crash was relatively mild. But, like a heart attack, it was an unmistakable warning of difficult days ahead.

The national mood seems to be changing from one of instinctive optimism and confidence to a conviction that somehow things have gone wrong. Shortly before his death, Theodore White wrote an article entitled "The Danger from Japan." Reflecting back on the day he observed the Japanese surrender ceremonies aboard the battleship *Missouri*, he commented:

> It is difficult to recall now, after years of floundering and blunder, how very good we were in those days. As MacArthur intoned: "These proceedings are closed," we heard a drone and looked up. Four hundred B-29s had taken off from Guam and Saipan hours before to arrive over the Missouri at this precise minute of climax.[4]

Americans now automatically assume Japanese excellence in manufacturing, technology, finance, education, and many other economic and social dimensions. Our own worsening self-image has become the mirror image of Japanese success. After years of "floundering and blunder," we assume (even when it is not yet true) that most of the time Japan does it best. Consumers certainly know it; they vote with their dollars, in many instances paying substantial premiums for high-quality Japanese goods. After suffering a lengthy string of defeats by seemingly invincible Japanese competitors in industry after industry, many of America's business leaders actively acknowledge Japan's success by steadfastly refusing to engage the Japanese in many competitive arenas. Finally, in the fishbowl of international trade negotiations our political defeats are transparent. Outsmarted, outnegotiated, or simply outbluffed, the United States has time and time again given ground to the Japanese. We are rapidly developing a national inferiority complex.

During the last forty-five years there has been a vast increase in trade between nations, especially in manufactured goods. This trade volume has expanded at twice the rate of industrial production. Fostered by U.S. advocacy of the free-trade policies enshrined in the General Agreement on Tariffs and Trade (GATT), this remarkable trade growth has led to a real interdependence among the world's economies.[5]

The Organization of Petroleum Exporting Countries (OPEC) and the oil crisis helped educate Americans to the existence of a global economy. As of 1990, U.S. imports and exports each accounted for more than 12 percent of GNP, while in 1960 the comparable figures were 5 percent and 6 percent, respectively. Before 1965, foreign trade was not an important factor in the U.S. economy. Only a small percentage of American manufacturers traded internationally. We regarded our huge domestic market as a private preserve, our own global market. We were proud of our technological superiority and economic self-sufficiency. Other than some raw materials and a few shoddy goods that we thought beneath our dignity to manufacture (goods often marked "Made in Japan"), we felt comfortable going it alone.

Today, our exposure to foreign competition is quite broad. More than 90 percent of all goods produced in the United States are subject to competition from abroad. Given the emergence of a world economy, the on-going debate between free-market advocates and protectionists makes little sense. The obvious question before us today is whether we can successfully engage the new industrial competition of the global market-place or continue to attempt futilely to evade it. Tremendous additional pressures will be placed on the U.S. manufacturing sector in the years ahead.

In the first half of the twentieth century, the relative isolation and vast size of the U.S. market were two of the key elements contributing to America's industrial preeminence. But as the size of the Japanese market grew from 5 percent of the U.S. market to 50 percent in the second half of the century, the advantage the United States had as the first common market was lost. The European Economic Community (EEC) now exceeds the size of the U.S. market.

In years past, major U.S. corporations were able to build a huge market base within the United States before venturing abroad. Sheer market size, coupled with the obvious innovative and entrepreneurial strengths of American business, permitted the United States to pioneer a host of new industries, including jet aircraft, plastics, integrated circuits, and, most dramatic, computers.[6] Considering the relatively much smaller size of the U.S. home market today, and the fiercely competitive international environment, repetition of these past sweeping successes seems unlikely. It appears that America no longer has a God-given right to worldwide industrial dominance.

Theodore Levitt maintains that the existence of truly global markets demands a new type of corporation.[7] The "global corporation" has replaced the multinational corporation as the most effective international competitor. The multinational corporation conducts its business in various countries, adapting its products and practices to local conditions by customizing products for specific markets. In contrast, the global corporation avoids the high relative costs of the multinational corporation by offering universal standardized products for a homogeneous world market. The global corporation offering low-cost, high-quality goods helps create the international market while satisfying its growing imperative. Very much in the manner of Henry Ford ("They can have any color they want so long as it's black"), for the global corporation the customer is *not* king. Highly competitive products play a part in directing and shaping the market.

"Trouble increasingly stalks companies that lack clarified global focus and remain inattentive to the economics of simplicity and standardization. . . . Global competition spells the end of domestic territoriality."[8] For U.S. corporations faced with the new international competition, the lesson here is that Komatsu (not Caterpillar), Toyota (not General Motors), and Hitachi (not General Electric) most resemble the global corporation. In many industries, international competition now takes the form of a race for dominance in global markets, and once preeminence is lost it is exceedingly difficult to regain.

Rapid recovery in nations whose industrial plants were largely destroyed during World War II has created new international competitors for the United States. A technologically driven world economy of ever-increasing sophistication, coupled with other countries' widespread use of political instruments in creating and implementing national industrial policies, has intensified the impact of foreign competition. Americans have been slow even to recognize that things have changed, let alone to establish the national priorities and policies that would permit us to compete effectively in this harsh new world.

Any search for the broad outlines of the declining competitive posture of the United States quickly leads to the manufacturing sector, where the ailments and deficiencies of the economy as a whole exist in their most acute form. Clearly, the U.S. manufacturing base is shrinking dramatically. Since 1973, real hourly earnings of American manufacturing workers have fallen by an average of almost 0.5 percent each year, and from 1955 to 1980 the U.S. market share of world manufactured goods also declined greatly. Furthermore, between 1960 and 1988, U.S. manufacturing jobs as a percentage of total employment declined by 7.9 percent, compared with an increase in Japan of 2.9 percent and a decline in Germany of 2.5 percent.[9]

Perhaps the best measure of America's manufacturing decline is the broad and steep fall-off in productivity growth since 1970. Productivity growth rates in the United States have been just one-third those in Japan; since 1973, these rates have been the lowest for any major industrial country. Former Secretary of Commerce Peter Peterson has observed: "The U.S. economy suffers from a spreading paralysis of those activities that raise the standard of living. . . . Our standard of living has stopped growing precisely because our labor productivity has stagnated."[10] As scarce capital resources have increasingly been diverted into real estate and collectibles, low productivity growth rates have become so deeply embedded in the U.S. economy that major changes will be required before there is significant improvement.

Our manufacturing base not only is eroding but also, even more disturbing, shrinking in a wholly unmanaged fashion. We lurch from fits of protectionism at one extreme to misguided economic incentives at the other. The long-standing American protest over Japan's protection of many important markets now has little meaning. It has become apparent that we can scarcely compete in our own market on many products, let alone muster an effective export assault on Japan.

The reasons for the U.S. manufacturing decline are many and varied, but they generally sort themselves into macroeconomic and microeconomic factors. Most prominent among the macroeconomic explanations are the high cost of capital, a harsh regulatory environment, continued and severe overvaluation of the U.S. dollar, damaging credit cycles, tax policies favoring consumption and penalizing investment, the adverse effects of increasingly skillful special interest lobbyists, side effects of the foreign aid program, and international trade policies.[11] These explanations constitute a set of national economic policies that are generally insensitive to the well-being of the U.S. manufacturing sector.

Microeconomic factors have to do primarily with the failure of many U.S. companies and industries to execute competitive manufacturing strategies. Although serious strategic mistakes often bring a business to the brink of economic ruin (even with the hypothetical benefit of favorable national economic policies), more often than not these microeconomic blunders are played out against, and often in response to, a generally hostile macroeconomic environment.[12]

The plight of U.S. automakers illustrates the strategic mistakes that contributed to the decline of U.S. manufacturing. Until the mid-1970s the U.S. automotive industry (then our largest manufacturing industry) made little attempt to use manufacturing as a competitive weapon. It studiously avoided competition on the basis of price. Rather, styling changes, dealer networks, and aggressive advertising characterized the competitive arena.[13] Automotive producers—as well as many manufacturers of a full line of other products—consistently overpriced the low end of the line to support the higher overheads required for upscale prod-

ucts. When the Japanese penetrated the low-end market, the typical response was to retreat up the line rather than to defend lower-margined
products. This caused overhead burdens to be absorbed by fewer units,
thus setting the stage for the next Japanese thrust into the lower end of
the remaining product line. Demands for short-term financial performance precluded a vigorous defense of the entire line.

Since Daniel Bell coined the phrase "post-industrial society," it has
become fashionable to rationalize the obvious shortcomings and shrinkage of the U.S. manufacturing sector as a natural shift of all modern
economies from agriculture and mining (primary), to manufacturing
(secondary), and finally to services (tertiary).[14] Despite a devastating series of manufacturing setbacks and partial liquidation of important manufacturing industries since 1980, this easy rationalization of the decline
of our vital manufacturing sector dies hard. In fact, statements like the
following may make us wonder how many people still hold this view:
"The progression of an economy such as America's from agriculture to
manufacturing to services is a natural change" (from the Office of the
U.S. Trade Representative); "A strong manufacturing sector is not a req-
uisite for a prosperous economy" (from the New York Stock Exchange);
and "Strong modern economies do not seem to require a dominant manufacturing sector" (from Gary Becker, writing in *Business Week*).[15] Despite these disclaimers, the United States is beginning to understand that
manufacturing does matter.

Manufacturing is crucial to the future health of the U.S. economy in
two important respects. First, manufacturing is inextricably tied to technology. High technology does not exist in the isolation of a laboratory;
it is nurtured and developed on the factory floor. Second, there are service jobs and there are service jobs. Service jobs in eating and drinking
establishments, clerical jobs, and similar forms of employment have little
to do with our economic future, but *manufacturing support services*,
such as those in computer software, engineering, and financial services,
are high-paying, high-skilled service jobs. Send the factory abroad, and
it's not long before these critical support services also move to be near
the factory. Indeed, it is arguable whether these high-grade jobs should
be classified as service jobs or simply as the service component of our
manufacturing sector.

It is interesting to note, however, that in the case of agriculture the
United States did not move out of the primary sector at all. In fact, the

United States is producing more in that sector than ever before, but we have successfully applied technology, automated processes, and sharply reduced agricultural employment. By these means, we have created one of our few truly world-class competitive industries.[16]

A corollary to this argument maintains that there is a place in the future service economy for manufacturing, but only in high-technology industries: computers, yes; steel, no; automobiles, maybe. This vision of a high-tech future has a powerful appeal, but it raises more questions than it answers: Where is the cutoff point? Do we keep computers and abandon commodity semiconductors? Do we push robots and forget machine tools? Can we maintain dominance of the commercial aircraft market while sacrificing specialty steels and aluminum?

Unfortunately, to produce computers, robots, and airplanes, we need semiconductors, machine tools, and advanced materials. Most elements of the modern U.S. manufacturing complex are highly interrelated. Pull out enough bricks and the entire wall may come crashing down.

A simple lesson of classical economics teaches us that manufacturing consistently produces greater savings and investments than other sectors. More passive forms of investments, such as residential and commercial construction, are unlikely to produce comparable streams of reinvestment. A flourishing manufacturing sector, through its ability to seek out and harness a host of new technologies, opens up countless opportunities for above-average returns on new investment.[17]

Eventually, U.S. trade accounts must be balanced. If they are balanced by exports of high-technology, high-value-added products, Americans will enjoy a high standard of living. If we can achieve this balance only by exporting middle-technology products and certain raw materials, our standard of living will be drastically lower.

Manufacturing is important, but the composition of manufacturing is even more important. If the United States loses manufacturing mastery at a certain stage in the product-development cycle, it is difficult, perhaps impossible, to get it back. We lost leadership in the consumer electronics industry with color television; we then missed out entirely on video cassette recorders and compact disc players. We cannot manufacture high-tech products alone, because high technology permeates the manufacturing process across the entire range of products. Ultimately, the international standing of the United States will depend on our ability to apply technology to a broad spectrum of products, making them fully competitive globally.[18]

Many observers today are convinced that without a strong manufacturing base the United States faces economic decline and possible loss of political and military preeminence. Said Lester Thurow, "If American manufacturing goes down the tubes, most of the rest of us will go down with it." If current trends continue, the United States will find itself a diminishing supplier and ever-larger purchaser of the world's manufactured goods.

Statistics and trends tell only part of the story of American economic decline. To better appreciate how rapid our fall from economic hegemony has been, we shall examine actual case histories in the steel, auto, consumer electronics, and semiconductor industries. These specific examples exhibit a common and disturbing pattern. Japan challenges a seemingly invincible American industry in market dominance and technological superiority. Attempting to protect profitability above all else, the industry invariably retreats, ceding market share for short-term profit relief. The lack of an effective American response results in loss of market share, along with profitability and technological leadership.

There have been no happy endings in this stark description of American industrial decline, no cases where a battered and bloody industry slimmed down, fought back, and regained lost ground. American industrial supremacy ends with a whimper, not with a bang, to paraphrase T. S. Eliot. Steadily yielding market share, starved of necessary capital investments, abandoned by the federal government and its free-market apostles, and with a thoroughly demoralized work force, these companies are programmed for decline. They form joint ventures, sell out plants, divisions, or the entire company, and continue to retreat in the face of vigorous competition from new U.S.-based Japanese manufacturing facilities. Eventually, high-quality products come to be produced in state-of-the-art plants right here in the United States. The problem is that they're not *our* plants—they belong to the Japanese. We shall look at four industries, but there are many more.

The first industry we look at is the steel industry in the United States. During and after World War II, nothing symbolized American industrial might better than the domestic steel industry. At the outbreak of hostilities in 1941, the capacity of the U.S. steel industry was approximately ten times that of Japan. With skies blackened by day and red by night, the mills of Pittsburgh and other steel towns forged the tools and arms that won the war. Afterward the industry expanded to meet the needs of burgeoning postwar domestic markets and international reconstruction. Despite having the world's highest wage rates during the 1950s, the American steel industry stood unchallenged as the world's largest and most efficient. Its world dominance rested on reliable sources of low-cost raw materials, technological superiority, and decisive economies of scale. With a solid track record enthusiastically endorsed by the financial community, the industry moved quickly to expand. During a single decade, it added approximately 40 million tons of additional open-hearth steel-making capacity, raising the total from 100 million tons in 1950 to 148 million tons in 1959.[19]

Throughout the 1950s the U.S. steel industry was a net exporter. At the beginning of the period, it accounted for 47 percent of world production; despite considerable reconstruction abroad, the share stood at 26 percent.[20] The size of the average integrated U.S. steel plant was more than twice that of other major producing countries, and in none of those countries was the average producer even 20 percent as large as in the United States. In 1955 the eight largest U.S. steel producers all ranked among the fifty-five largest U.S. industrial corporations.[21]

The steel industry in the United States is once again symbolic of industrial conditions in America and today represents more graphically and more poignantly than any other industry the deteriorating competitive posture of industrial America. The 47 percent share of world steel production held by the United States in 1950 had by 1988 fallen to less than 14 percent. Only two of the eight largest steel concerns rank among the fifty-five largest industrial companies in America. In 1985, imports captured more than 25 percent of the domestic steel market. Caught between rapidly growing imports and numerous new mini-mill producers, the integrated industry's share of the market fell from 95 percent in 1960 to slightly above 50 percent in 1985, with a projected fall to 30 percent by the end of the century. The mini-mill sector has increased its market share from almost 14 percent in 1980 to 21 percent in 1985, with a projection of 40 percent by the year 2000.[22]

In 1982 the industry lost more than $3 billion, with cumulative losses for 1981–84 totaling $8 billion. McLouth and Wheeling Pittsburgh went into bankruptcy, while Youngstown Sheet and Tube and Republic temporarily were saved similar fates through a series of mergers culminating in the creation of debt-ridden LTV Steel. LTV, the parent company of LTV Steel, finally succumbed in 1986, at that time the largest U.S. corporation ever to file for bankruptcy.

By 1982 the average plant size of the U.S. integrated industry was 3.8 million tons, compared with 10.4 million tons in Japan.[23] Since 1980—using the most common measure of industry productivity, man-hours per ton (MHPT)—Japan's steel industry has been outproducing the United States in almost every major production process from blast furnaces to rolling mills.

The reasons for the appalling conditions of the U.S. steel industry are many and varied, but labor, management, and government share responsibility. The decline over the last thirty years has closely resembled a Greek tragedy. It is difficult to find a particular time or event where a reversal of fortunes might have been effected.

The United States became a net steel importer in 1959 and has remained so ever since. Faced with a competitive threat from abroad, as world trade in steel grew from 11 percent of total shipments in 1950 to almost 25 percent in 1990, the domestic industry proceeded vigorously to modernize existing capacity. Obsolete open-hearth furnaces were steadily if slowly replaced by more efficient oxygen-process steelmaking. And eleven advanced hot-strip mills, each capable of producing more than 4 million tons annually, were installed in rapid succession during the 1960s. These expenditures peaked in 1965.[24] As competition from imports and the newly emerging mini-mills intensified, it became evident that these capital projects would be unable to provide an adequate rate of return. With newer Japanese steel plants demonstrating the economies of huge blast furnaces and the advantages of continuous casting, the U.S. industry simply was unable to sustain sufficiently high rates of investments. In 1988, for example, the U.S. percentage of world steel exports was less than 1 percent, compared with 7 percent in 1970.

In the 1960s the United States ceased to be the world's low-cost steel producer. A vicious cycle soon ensued. Caught between the Scylla of low-cost imports and the Charybdis of a stronger and more aggressive unionized work force, the steel industry after 1959 bought twenty-seven years of labor peace at the high cost of overgenerous wage settlements. These wage contracts weakened its competitive position against foreign producers. Lower investments, coupled with steadily advancing employment costs, widened the cost gap and provided further inducements for foreign steel purchases. Having essentially no other choice, the industry turned from the economic solutions it had tried in the 1960s to the political and protectionist solutions of the 1970s and 1980s. During this period the stock market and institutional lenders made harsh pronouncements about the industry's prospects.

In the face of inadequate trade relief offered by the federal government, most steel companies sought salvation through nonsteel diversification. Whether moderately successful, as in the case of U.S. Steel's acquisition of Marathon Oil, or disastrous to the point of near-bankruptcy, as with Armco's headlong thrust into financial services, these moves further starved the industry's ever-voracious appetite for capital. Even worse, the industry also faced the continued shrinkage of substantial markets as many of its largest customers, most notably the automotive industry, lost market share to foreign competitors.

The U.S. steel industry probably hit bottom in 1985, the fourth year of billion-dollar-plus industry-wide losses. With a shrunken equity base (less than half that in 1981), debt ballooned and new investment slowed to a trickle. At least two of the five solvent remaining major producers appeared to be candidates for bankruptcy. Streamlining and improvement (rationalization) of the industry through closing additional facilities were partially forestalled by the extraordinary contingency costs associated with such shutdowns. Sheer survival dictated acceptance of continued losses as a more prudent course than huge write-offs triggering additional bankruptcy filings.

In 1990 the steel industry concluded its third year of solid profitability. While U.S. producers unquestionably benefited from herculean cost-cutting efforts, a major devaluation of the dollar and several years of voluntary export restraints on the part of foreign steel producers were perhaps more important. The unhappy ending to this story is that most U.S. producers are now often financed, strengthened by technological support, and in many cases owned by the Japanese. NKK has 90 percent of National Steel, and Armco's flat rolled division is now 50 percent owned by Kawasaki. Joint ventures have proliferated, with USX/Kobe, LTV/Sumitomo, Inland/Nippon, and Wheeling-Pittsburgh/Nisshin among the more prominent. Today the U.S. domestic industry increasingly takes on the appearance of a colonial outpost of the Japanese steel industry.

The automotive industry is America's third largest, exceeded in size only by the construction and electronics industries. For most of the twentieth century it has been at the heart of the U.S. economy; directly and indirectly it accounts for about one out of six jobs. It is a major consumer of other producers' output, including approximately 20 percent of the steel, 60 percent of the rubber, 11 percent of the aluminum, 30 percent of the ferrous castings, and 20 percent of the glass and machine tools. Not without significance is the industry's position as the largest nongovernment customer of the U.S. computer industry. Annually, through orders to more than 30,000 component suppliers, automotive manufacturers inject more than $40 billion into the economy. Automotive sales account for about 8 percent of the nation's GNP and more than 25 percent of its retail sales.[25] It may be possible to envision an American economy without a steel industry, but the notion that the automotive industry would be allowed to sink into similar oblivion is beyond belief.

No industrialist ever captured the imagination of the American public as Henry Ford did. With the advent of the moving assembly line and the Model T, which dominated the market for fifteen years, there was instituted an overall rationalization of manufacturing on a scale never before achieved. At the huge Highland Park plant a multitude of component production lines fed parts into a final assembly line that poured forth a torrent of low-cost and highly reliable products—literally creating a mass market where none had existed before.

Despite Ford's loss of automotive leadership in the late 1920s, General Motors, Chrysler, and many other companies built and perfected the fundamental mass-production principles pioneered by Henry Ford. In World War II, "Fordism" was the system that organized the industrial might (producing a remarkable 50,000 aircraft in a single year) that supported America's winning war effort. In the postwar period, it powered the engine that created the greatest era of sustained prosperity in our history.

For twenty-five years after World War II, Detroit dominated the U.S. market. Low-cost gasoline made the fuel-economical cars of foreign producers unattractive to most Americans. Cheap gasoline helped sharpen the focus of U.S. automakers on the rich returns reaped from satisfying America's unique demand for large cars. During this period Detroit was truly the center of the automotive universe, in fact as well as in name. In 1955 almost 80 percent of all new car registrations worldwide occurred in the United States; that year the Japanese automotive industry produced only 4,000 cars. In 1960 almost half the world's automotive production took place in the United States, while Japan provided just 3 percent. In a market essentially insulated from foreign competition, with a cost structure underwritten by significant productivity gains and frequent price increases, American autoworkers were among the highest-paid industrial workers in the nation. Walter Reuther, who headed the United Auto Workers in this period, blessed the process by calling for "full production, full employment, and full distribution." [26] Until about 1970, within the confines of the U.S. auto-industrial relationship, all parties were winners.

Dramatic changes took place in the next twelve years. Import penetration of the U.S. market doubled from 15 percent to 29 percent, and the U.S. share of the world market fell from 28 percent to 19 percent. For the first time, in 1980, Japan supplanted the United States as the world's leading manufacturer of motor vehicles by producing 11 million units to our 8 million. It appears unlikely that the United States will regain this lead in the foreseeable future. During the 1980–81 model year, U.S. producers had cumulative losses exceeding $6 billion. In 1979, with renewed demand for fuel-efficient small cars generated by the Iranian crisis, Japanese imports reached 1.77 million units. After considerable pressure, Japanese manufacturers instituted a voluntary restraint agreement capping the number in 1981 at 1.67 million units. In 1985, freed of formal restraints, the Japanese unilaterally raised their U.S. export levels to 2.4 million units.[27]

The twin oil shocks of 1973 and 1979 created an instantaneous demand for fuel-efficient small cars, which the domestic automotive industry was (through no fault of its own) unprepared to meet. Fortunately for the Japanese producers, and unfortunately for Detroit, this abrupt market change came at a time when the cost positions of the two industries were being reversed in the face of quantum productivity gains by Japanese manufacturers. In 1970 Detroit could deliver a car to the West Coast at a price that was less than half that of a comparable Japanese model. A decade later Japan enjoyed a cost advantage variously estimated at 20 percent to 40 percent.

But cost represents only part of the story. The J. D. Powers customer-satisfaction index shows Japanese cars, on average, ranking well above American products. If substantive quality differentials posed a genuine competitive threat to Detroit, these difficulties were exacerbated by even wider disparities in the realm of perceived quality. Within thirty years the stereotype that "Made in Japan" symbolized shoddy and inferior goods was completely reversed as American automakers and other manufacturers found themselves consistently on the defensive. General Motors, still in 1985 the world's largest manufacturing company, found itself facing three very disturbing facts: it captured only three of ten first-time American car buyers, the average age of the General Motors owner was forty-seven, and despite the Japanese cost advantage of approximately $2,000 per car, the Japanese automobile sold at about a $500 premium against the comparable GM offering.[28] Ford Motor Company chairman Donald Peterson was no more optimistic: "Ford is not going to pull out of the U.S. market, but, if policies in the United States prevent us from being a profitable manufacturer here, we will be forced to look abroad to obtain more components, and ultimately to produce the entire automobile."[29]

The latest assault of the unrelentingly ambitious Japanese automotive industry involves the rapid expansion of Japanese production in ultra-modern U.S. plants. Beginning with Honda in 1982, Nissan, Toyota, Mazda, Mitsubishi, Subaru, and Isuzu have all joined the stampede toward U.S. production. During the first quarter of 1990, these Japanese "transplant" facilities accounted for 22 percent of the cars built in America.[30] The eight facilities opened by the Japanese since 1982 are evenly matched by the shuttering of eight U.S. assembly plants.

In 1990 the global market shares of the Japanese and U.S. automotive industries (including significant GM and Ford production in Europe and elsewhere) stood at 28 percent for Japan and 35 percent for the United States. According to one industry analyst, another decade will probably see these positions reversed, with the Japanese holding a commanding 40 percent of the global automotive market and the United States having 28 percent.[31] It is likely that in the year 2000 the term "big three" will refer to Toyota, Nissan, and Honda, not GM, Ford, and Chrysler.

In the 1950s the monochrome (black-and-white) television market in the United States grew rapidly. Secured by a decisive technological and capital advantage, the domestic industry was able to satisfy this burgeoning demand fully. Faced with a small and closed market in Japan, domestic producers turned to Europe and surmounted the high tariff wall by establishing local production facilities. Tax laws at the time encouraged these investments in a reconstructing Europe. Hoping to glean some return from the growing Japanese market, U.S. companies adopted the expedient of licensing agreements; there was little concern about Japan as a future competitor. As a result, the technological gap between Japanese producers and the U.S. industry was quickly narrowed. The twin strategy of licensing agreements for the Japanese and local production in Europe had a far more detrimental consequence in locking U.S. producers into manufacturing only for our domestic market.[32]

Japan's Ministry of International Trade and Industry (MITI) took steps in the early 1960s to encourage development of the domestic consumer electronics sector as a strong international competitor. Substantive results were not long forthcoming as Japanese penetration of the U.S. market grew from less than 1 percent in 1961 to more than 11 percent in 1966. The Japanese assault in monochrome receivers was sufficiently threatening to invoke two responses from the domestic industry. First, much U.S. monochrome production was moved abroad to "export platforms" in Mexico, Taiwan, and elsewhere. Second, hoping to recoup the profits that were typical of the industry's cornucopia of the 1950s, money and energy were focused on the rapidly growing markets for color sets. Domestic monochrome receiver production dropped from 6.7 million units in 1967 to less than 1.7 million in 1976, and many of those units had a high percentage of foreign components.

After 1965, as the color-receiver market became the most hotly contested competitive arena, domestic producers found that their days of uncontested market dominance and high profits were ending. Whereas Japanese penetration of the monochrome market did not exceed 15 percent until fifteen years after the advent of mass production, the Japanese achieved comparable penetration of the color-receiver market after only five years of U.S. mass production. Although low labor costs were doubtless the principal contributor to low-cost Japanese monochrome production, technology was the leading factor in their penetration of the color market. More than 90 percent of their color production was converted to all solid-state technology a full three years before the same switch by U.S. producers.[33]

The American response to this new and more serious challenge followed the now familiar pattern. Production of completed sets and components was sent abroad while the industry vigorously sought protection in Washington. This lobbying effort spurred conclusion of an Orderly Marketing Agreement (OMA) in 1977. Limited to 1.75 million units, Japan's response was predictable and foreshadowed Japanese action in the automotive market. The Japanese maintained revenue and profit growth by "upscaling" their product mix, thereby attacking the industry at the higher-margined end of the line, where it hurt most.

The thirty-year record of Japanese challenge and American response saw a complete reversal of fortunes, and the Japanese today totally dominate the world market for consumer electronics. In 1977 the Japanese manufactured 42 percent of all the color receivers produced in the non-Communist world; they captured 37 percent of the U.S. market through direct imports and local U.S. production. By 1980 seven Japanese companies were producing more than 2 million units a year in the United States. In 1960 twenty-seven different U.S. companies produced television receivers, and by 1980 the number had been reduced to five, with only General Electric, RCA, and Zenith commanding significant volume. With the merger of General Electric and RCA followed by the 1987 spinoff of the company's combined consumer electronics operations to French interests, Zenith remains the last major domestic manufacturer of television receivers.

Pressured by Wall Street to improve its standing in the investment community by dumping its marginal television segment to concentrate on its highly successful line of laptop computers, Zenith surprised everyone in 1989 by selling its computer business. Today Zenith is a pygmy struggling against a half-dozen Japanese giants. Its survival, let alone resurgence, is highly problematic.

If these facts alone told the whole story, it would be sad enough. However, the results of the Japanese triumph in color television have broader consequences. Some of these are clear now, but the full significance of others will be recognized only in the future. Despite an early U.S. lead in developing the video cassette recorder, the U.S. consumer electronics industry, weakened and demoralized after its bruising and losing battle in the color television market, did not even enter this new competitive arena. Instead, the industry rushed to sign marketing agreements with various Japanese producers, reaping easy profits with little investment or risk. In 1990 some 10,200,000 VCRs were sold to distributors in the United States; less than 5 percent were produced by U.S. manufacturers.

Now a whole new generation of consumer electronic products, such as compact disc players and new high-definition television receivers, is coming on stage. There is little doubt that the Japanese will dominate these markets as completely as they have monopolized the VCR market. Once a nation gets off the moving train of technological product advance, it is difficult if not impossible to get back on.

But perhaps the most telling blow delivered by Japan to U.S. technological and economic preeminence as a result of its consumer electronics triumph is in the area of semiconductor production. It is significant that the six largest producers of Japanese consumer electronics—Hitachi, Matsushita, Mitsubishi, NEC, Sony, and Toshiba—all are among the largest producers of the central building block of the electronic age: integrated circuits.

If the steel and automotive industries signify America's past industrial glory, then it is the electronics industry that most represents hope for the future. The ubiquitous integrated circuit, or "chip," is the foundation on which computers, office automation products (such as copiers, fax machines, and word processors), consumer electronics, robots, telecommunications equipment, and many other technologically advanced industries are built.

Viewed from the narrow perspective of the semiconductor industry, all other electronics industries simply represent alternative configurations of different integrated circuits. Rapid technological advances within the computer field, from more powerful mainframes to the advent of minicomputers and micro-, or personal, computers, have occurred in lockstep with the commercial availability of increasingly powerful integrated circuits. Halt technological growth in the semiconductor field, and progress throughout the electronics universe would slow to a crawl. From 1977 to 1983 the worldwide value of electronic products doubled to $200 billion, and by 1989 it was over $650 billion. In the years ahead semiconductor technology will provide the keys to the electronics kingdom.

Since the invention of the transistor at Western Electric's Bell Laboratories in 1947, the United States dominated basic semiconductor technology until the mid-1980s. Through the work of Jack Kilby and Robert Noyce, the integrated circuit became a reality in 1959. In 1971 Ted Hoff at Intel produced the first microprocessor (a computer on a chip) and prompted the explosion of demand for small and powerful personal computers, such as the Apple II and the IBM-PC.

The U.S. and Japanese semiconductor industries developed in relative isolation from one another, until the middle 1970s. Up to that time, the Japanese lacked the technological prowess to mount a serious challenge to U.S. producers in America, and Japan's home market was completely closed to any penetration from the more powerful and more technologically advanced U.S. industry. However, as the 4K RAM (random access memory, the workhorse chip of computer memories) was replaced by the next generation of 16K RAM chips in 1978, Japanese producers mounted a powerful and timely export offensive for their high-quality 16K chips. By the end of 1979 they had captured 43 percent of the world market for 16K chips. Following the pattern demonstrated earlier in the case of automobiles and consumer electronics, they chose as their field of entry RAM chips—the high-volume, price-sensitive low end of the product line.

Several factors combined to make this stunning triumph a reality. First, battered by the 1975 recession, most U.S. merchant producers had sharply reduced their capital budgets, leaving them considerably short of capacity when demand for the 16K chip exploded in 1978. Second, IBM, whose production is captive for IBM products only, found itself short of capacity and entered the merchant market to secure chips for its new Series 4300 computer. Third, major purchases of U.S.-produced 16K chips were made by Japanese electronics concerns in lieu of local procurement, helping to enlarge the vacuum into which Japan's export drive was directed. Given the restricted nature of Japan's market, the giant Japanese electronics companies—at the same time the major producers and consumers of chips in Japan—doubtless reasoned that they could cut their imports of U.S. chips while continuing to expand their own export beachhead in the United States. A few years later, Japan dominated the world market for 64K chips and went on to command a 90 percent share of the rapidly growing market for 256K chips.

In 1984 Japan had captured more than 30 percent of the total U.S. market for semiconductors.[34] By 1987 the Japanese home market, with about half of the U.S. GNP, became the world's largest single market for semiconductors, and in 1988 Japan captured 52 percent of the world semiconductor market. Japan's overwhelming global dominance of consumer electronics helped fuel its insatiable appetite for these products. In the RAM market Japan's thrust was so powerful that many U.S. merchant producers became convinced that no money could be made producing standard RAM chips. Consequently, they turned to various niche markets that at least for the time being were free from Japanese competition.

To understand the difficulties U.S. semiconductor producers faced, it is necessary to be aware of how the semiconductor industries in Japan and the United States differ. In the United States, most semiconductor production has been done by independent "merchant producers" whose principal business has been the design, production, and marketing of a variety of semiconductor products to manufacturers of computers, consumer electronics, and other major chip users. The two largest U.S. producers—IBM and AT&T—are captive producers; their output is used exclusively for their own products.

Despite significant captive production, and backward integration into semiconductor production through the acquisition of some merchant producers by large manufacturing concerns (including the acquisition of fourteen independent houses by foreign producers), the dominant tone and dynamics of the semiconductor industry in the United States have been set by the merchant producers.[35] By contrast, the Japanese semiconductor market is served primarily by six giant integrated and broadbased electronics manufacturers: Fujitsu, Hitachi, Mitsubishi, Matsushita, NEC, and Toshiba.

In the forty years following the invention of the transistor, the breathtaking advances of the U.S. semiconductor industry were in large part introduced by the many and varied U.S. merchant producers. They were consistent favorites of venture capitalists. Once blessed with some success, the shares of these new companies consistently commanded high price-earnings multiples. But whereas the equity markets were innovative and supportive in start-up and growth phases, when many merchant producers became major corporations these same capital markets often worked to their disadvantage. After 1980, U.S. producers were constantly under severe competitive pressures from the Japanese and other domestic competitors in the race to capture a significant market share in new generations of chips.

Failure to satisfy the stock market's demands for steadily increasing quarterly earnings had dire consequences. Most often it provoked the displeasure of investors, resulting in a sharply lowered stock price and thus impairing the ability of these companies to raise the ever-larger sums of capital necessary to stay in the game. The six Japanese captives, fueled by the huge resources of their parent corporations and further backed by the tightly controlled Japanese banking system, received a steady flow of capital funds during both good times and bad. This enabled them to avoid the capital and investment constraints imposed on their American merchant competitors by the vicissitudes of the equity markets.

In the microprocessor market, and for many other semiconductor products outside the standard RAM memory chips, the United States still has a slim lead. But this lead is narrowing month by month. As merchant producers are denied the profits necessary to sustain the high rates of investment yielding the advanced products on which technological leadership depends, the U.S. semiconductor industry enters an era of extreme vulnerability. As the semiconductor industry advances toward relative maturity with ever-increasing capital intensity, competitive advantage will begin to shift from innovation and product development to manufacturing prowess resting on large and uninterrupted capital investments. The 35 percent Japanese penetration rate of the entire U.S. semiconductor market now exceeds total U.S. imports of either steel or automobiles. Today, by nearly every measurement of manufacturing proficiency, the Japanese producers outperform their American competitors.

Despite a recent and much heralded semiconductor trade agreement between the United States and Japan, the Japanese have since moved to increasing market domination in several product categories. The industry's perennially defensive posture, coupled with demands for government protection in the face of relentless market penetration by the Japanese, make the semiconductor story look more and more like a replay of the debacles in the automobile and consumer electronics industries. The most technologically advanced industries in the United States are now the ones most seriously threatened by the Japanese.

The 1990s will provide the final battleground for the capstone of the extended electronics industry—computers. The struggle is just beginning in earnest, but even at this early date we can discern the outlines of the Japanese strategy.

Computer hardware comes in four broad categories based on size, computing power, and order of development: mainframes, minicomputers, microcomputers (personal computers, or PCs), and laptop computers. The principal growth phase of each computer category may be assigned to a decade, with mainframes for the 1960s, minis for the 1970s, PCs for the 1980s, and laptops for the 1990s. Until the recent advent of laptops, the dominant/innovating companies of each computer product category were U.S. producers: IBM for mainframes, Digital Equipment for minicomputers, and Apple for personal computers. In the laptop segment, led by Toshiba and NEC, the Japanese are dominant. And Japan has not ignored mainframes. Fujitsu, Hitachi, and NEC have made an impressive showing in mainframes, and largely at the expense of IBM, their world market shares have grown steadily over the last ten years.

Unfortunately for IBM and the United States, and fortunately for the Japanese, a decisive shift in the allocation of data processing operations is now occurring. Mainframes and minicomputers are steadily losing ground to PCs and laptops. Furthermore, the Japanese have rapidly become the leading low-cost producers of many of the key components of personal computers, including displays, drives, keyboards, printers, and, most important, semiconductors.

Just when the center of the computer world is shifting to PCs and laptops, Japan is poised for explosive growth in these product categories. As PCs and laptops approach maturity, the third phase of a four-part product cycle—innovation, growth, maturity, decline—manufacturing prowess will become decisive. Leading PC producers in the United States, including IBM, Apple, and Compaq, are already purchasing a high percentage of their major components from the Japanese. Our past defeats in automobiles, consumer electronics, and semiconductors leave little doubt that once the Japanese are dominant in PCs they will move up through more complex product categories until they are triumphant in mainframes. They will accomplish this in less than ten years at the outside—probably sooner.

The story of U.S. failures in steel, automobiles, consumer electronics, and semiconductors is repeated in machine tools, office automation equipment, robotics, and other industries. In an increasing number of fields the United States is no longer internationally competitive, and in price, quality, and technological sophistication U.S. products do not measure up.

When thinking about American economic performance, we tend to focus on budget deficits, trade imbalances, and foreign debt—key economic indicators that capture the headlines. Those numbers represent the visible side of American economic decline, but they tell only one side of the story. In the laboratory, on the factory floor, in purchasing offices, and in retail outlets, there is the substantive but less visible side of the competitive contest. There one finds the tangible actions that create the discouraging economic reports. We must not forget that the competitive problems of the United States are not just quantitative—that is, economic figures. They are qualitative—products. Every technologically significant industry represents a competitive battlefield. How many more defeats will we suffer before we realize the severity of the problem?

A major theme of this book is the critical and decisive role of technology. In the past, industrial might and military power depended on land and natural resources, and technology played a supporting role, at best. Japan has demonstrated conclusively that a country doesn't need coal, iron ore, and oil to build a modern industrial infrastructure. Natural resources, agricultural products, and brand-name consumer goods are still economic pluses, but in a modern-day "wealth of nations"—in the ranking of world-class economies—they do not count for a lot. When several hundred million dollars of electronics components can be loaded aboard a Boeing 747, technology has leaped ahead of all other productive factors. Today technology can create a first-rank economy all by itself. In the period beyond 1990, technology will bring economic strength and ultimately political supremacy. Tokyo understands this, Washington does not.

Americans are too much inclined to associate high technology with science and research laboratories, not with its more rightful place, on the factory floor. Technological advance is seldom spawned by a single major breakthrough, but instead evolves through thousands of small yet steady process and product improvements. To speak of technology or "high tech" as somewhat separate from manufacturing is to lose sight of what technology is all about: as product and process improve, so does technology.

Technology benefits greatly from scientific breakthroughs, but in the long-term competitive struggle for market share in strategic industries, these major advances will seldom be decisive. To understand that manufacturing and not science is decisive for technological advance, one need only look at the very advanced state of science within the Soviet Union

and compare it with the pitiful condition of Soviet technology and manufactured products. Jumping from the scientific laboratory to the marketplace is like reading a hundred books on golf and then attempting to
swing a golf club for the first time. With technology, as with golf, you
learn by doing.

Because it multiplies the value of human labor, technology is critical to
economic growth and to national wealth. Look at a bushel of rice and a
bushel of integrated circuits, and you can learn much about Japan's awesome competitive strengths. While per capita GNP, trade surpluses, and
foreign credits provide the scoreboard on national economic performance, technological mastery of strategic industries—particularly the
extended electronics industry—represents the driving force behind economic and political power.

The pace of technological change is now so rapid that a failure to capture the next rung up on the ladder of technological development may
doom the loser to play a perennial game of catch-up. In consumer electronics, computer peripherals, telecommunications equipment, semiconductor fabrication equipment, and, most important, in semiconductors
themselves, we have lost the technological lead. The last quarter of the
twentieth century may be distinguished from earlier periods by the accel-
erating rate of technological change. In the past, technological change
was most often an adjunct to industrial development. It occurred intermittently and haphazardly, often as a result of tinkering on the factory
floor. Today technology is the main event. Industrial development may
best be understood as an adjunct of technology. Lavishly funded, it is
pursued by carefully linking applied research laboratories and product/
process engineering within manufacturing facilities.

Nowhere is the line of development more clearly shown than in successive generations of semiconductors. From 1978 to 1990 chip memory
capacity increased from 16,000 to 4,000,000 circuits—a 250-fold increase over twelve years and five product generations. Within fifteen
years we shall see chips with multibillions of circuits. The United States
lost the lead in commodity semiconductors to Japan at the 16K generation, and that lead has broadened each year. Similar technological ladders are replicated throughout the entire electronics field and in many
other industrial segments as well. While this kind of generation-
demarcated technological competition is really a phenomenon of the late
twentieth century, there has already been enough of it to indicate that

once you fall behind in the struggle for a particular product generation, you can't catch up.

In the twenty-first century, technology will grow in importance as an economic force. It will bring pressures to bear on every productive area, from agriculture to industries so advanced we can't even identify them today. In the twenty-first century the state of a nation's technological development will reveal its economic and political power. In the decades to come, technology will be the arbiter of global power as surely as conventional military strength and nuclear capability were in the past.

A powerful economy can be based only on the building block of the technologically driven global corporation. Japan is cultivating this kind of corporation, the United States is not. We are talking about such first-tier companies as Fujitsu, Hitachi, Mitsubishi Electric, NEC, Matsushita, Sony, and Toshiba. For Japan, these companies are national treasures, and when we include companies in the second and third tiers, the list runs to more than one hundred. With commanding positions in a variety of leading electronics industry segments—including computers, consumer electronics, integrated circuits, office automation equipment, and telecommunications equipment—these first-tier global giants are more and more without serious across-the-board challengers in the United States. Among U.S. corporations only IBM is of comparable stature, and its coverage of the extended electronics industry is much more limited.

One might ask, "How about General Electric?" By any standard, GE is a great international competitor with dozens of business units where it ranks globally either number one or two in size. But GE is not a serious contender in the critical electronics-based industries. At various periods in its history, GE elected to exit computers, integrated circuits, and consumer electronics. The GE/RCA merger provides a clue to GE strategy. RCA rested on three legs: NBC, defense, and consumer electronics. The first two businesses were immune to Japanese competition, while the consumer electronics segment was broadly and dangerously exposed to it. General Electric kept the first two businesses and disposed of the third, a strategy that can be seen as purely defensive: evade the Japanese, don't engage them. From GE's standpoint it was a well-executed strategy. The only loser was the long-term technological strength of the U.S. economy.

If you're not yet convinced of the downward spiral of the U.S. economic strength, from the intractable nature of our trade deficit (and since

1987 our high-technology trade deficit), our loss of world leadership in industry after industry, and our failure to develop great technologically driven global corporations, then read Daniel Burstein's *Yen!*, Stephen Cohen and John Zysman's *Manufacturing Matters,* Benjamin Friedman's *Day of Reckoning,* Clyde Prestowitz's *Trading Places,* or Steven Schloss-stein's *End of the American Century.* Missed all these? Don't worry. There will be a steady stream of similar books in the years ahead.

2

WHY AMERICA CAN'T COMPETE

*We are going to win and the industrial West is
going to lose out; there's not much you can do
about it, because the reasons for failure are
within yourselves.*
—*Konosuke Matsushita*

Why can't the United States compete? The answer to this question is
both simple and complex. The proximate causes of America's economic
decline are many and varied, and they are system-wide. Three principal
factors have contributed to our mounting economic problems: our management policies and methods, our financial system, and our political
system. But first we must look at the psychological and cultural backdrop against which these factors have played out their respective roles.

Imagine for a moment a business environment largely free of environmental controls and most government regulations. Such conditions existed in large part before 1929 and the advent of the New Deal in what
could be called a "golden age of production." No one captured the spirit
of the times better than Calvin Coolidge when he proclaimed in 1925,

"The business of America is business." And so it was from 1865 until 1945, even as a national consensus after 1932 demanded that the government pay considerably more attention to the economy than it had in the past.

Americans were long denied the fruits of their efforts by the vagaries of an economy they struggled to revive in the 1930s and again in the early 1940s through the self-denial of the war effort. In the postwar years they sought to harness their marvelous productive machine in the service of an ever-rising standard of living. When the productive job appeared to be complete, Americans embarked on a "golden age of consumption," during which the business of America was to be more than just business. This new age represented the payoff for an arduous century-long struggle to accumulate the capital necessary to forge the elements of a national industrial infrastructure. The quarter-century from 1945 to 1970 epitomized this age of consumption. While the great nations of the past sought a collective glory in conquests or culture, Americans seemed to take most pride in the bountifulness of their consumer goods and unparalleled individual liberties.

Consumption in its broad sense took many and varied forms extending well beyond appliances, automobiles, and new houses. Consumption also came to include more equitable income distribution, demands for a safe and clean environment, and, with impetus provided by Ralph Nader, a lengthy new list of consumer rights. Indeed, consumption pushed so far beyond material concerns that many facets of the productive project were deemed antithetical to an emerging life-style called "quality of life." The "quality-of-life society" has been described as "dedicated to increasing the satisfaction of its members not by increased production and mass use of material goods, but by greater harmony with self, others, and nature." [1]

The golden age of consumption was made possible because the U.S. economy emerged from World War II like a spinning top. Knocked off center on occasion, it automatically righted itself and continued to perform in a manner exceeding all reasonable expectations. Increasingly, however, the focused rationality of the "proindustrial, high-production coalition" was infringed on by a number of groups with markedly different priorities. Egalitarian demands from people who were not adequately participating in America's abundant prosperity, from the consumer movement, and from the environmentalists all had an impact.

Finally the so-called "counterculture" questioned not only the input—hard work—but also the output itself, material consumption.

Each of these groups sought to initiate and implement a consumption agenda that finally began to take a toll on America's productive capacities. The traditional call to work, save, and invest, though still a powerful appeal to many, was strongly challenged by reasoned arguments in favor of leisure, borrowing, and consumption. So strong was Lyndon Johnson's belief in the unlimited productive capacities of the nation that he authored simultaneously two commitments to consumption that were unprecedented in history: the war in Vietnam and the Great Society.

One small facet of the many Great Society social programs illustrates the fierce determination of the proponents of social justice to eradicate past wrongs quickly and decisively and gives witness to the blind faith in the unlimited productive resources of this country to accomplish the job. Forgotten along with the nation's poor and other disadvantaged groups were the physically handicapped. It was one thing to address their needs by eliminating certain major obstacles in their attempts to move about; it was quite another to spend billions modifying surface and underground transit systems to enable them to do everything the nonhandicapped could do. Demands that the handicapped be "mainstreamed" at any cost went hand in hand with the demands of extremists in the environmental movement, who refused to accept compelling financial constraints on the otherwise commendable drive for a clean environment.

Few today would take issue with the claim that the United States is now a far better place to live for the vast majority of Americans than in 1955. Much needed to be done, and much has been done. But some distinctly undesirable side effects have become apparent. For instance, according to sociologist Amitai Etzioni:

> The American society entered the 1980s with a weakened productive capacity, a tendency to underdevelop, a kind of industrialization in reverse. The rational mentality had lost vitality; the supportive power base had weakened; national bonds and the institutional framework were straining.[2]

Great Society programs, consumerism, and environmentalism did not cause American economic decline, and we are by no means in a zero-sum game. We can have a leading-edge industrial structure *and* an increasingly just and humane society. But when a singular concern with social issues obscures our strategic economic vision, we place our own productive capacities at risk. Americans often lack the binding sense of limits that has for centuries constrained an older and sometimes wiser Europe.

The serious and obvious shortcomings of American managerial policies and methods have contributed to America's decline. Although an industrial firm does not operate in an economic and political vacuum, it is at times difficult to separate a firm's problems from those of the political and financial system in which it functions.

The short-term management focus at most major American corporations is a frequent target of critics. Dependent on the public capital markets both for equity and for long-term debt, corporate management responds rationally to the short-term judgment of these markets by fixing sharply on quarterly and annual financial results. Such behavior is designed to guarantee adequate capital funds. The rise to prominence of professional money managers over the last twenty or more years has intensified the pressure for short-term performance as the careers and reputations of these new professionals have come to depend on their timely choice of stock market winners and losers. The vast sums of money under their control move more quickly than ever before in the face of disappointing financial performance. This forces on corporate management the implacable judgments of our transparent capital markets.

Increased emphasis on the near-term has accelerated the rise to prominence of the "mobile manager." Aiming at rapid advancement, the mobile manager seeks high visibility and an impressive résumé by making a decisive and measurable financial impact in a new work environment. This track record then paves the way for a more responsible job with a new employer. Managers anticipating a short tenure with an employer have little incentive to take the long view. And newcomers to a company often arrive with little or no firsthand knowledge of the company's products and manufacturing processes. This places a real obstacle in the path of long-term product development.

In contrast, Japan's sizable production gains have most often resulted from the introduction and implementation of more effective processes for producing old products, not in the creation of new products. Unfortunately, with U.S. financial markets demanding quick, tangible results, and with managers judged largely by this criterion, pressure mounts for constant introduction of new products. Often these new products are developed at the expense of more essential process and productivity improvements.

During the 1950s—in what we may now call the "great age of American abundance," when the United States dominated most of the world's major markets—leading U.S. industries were distinctly low technology, notably coal, steel, railroads, shipbuilding, and automobiles. In those halcyon days of American manufacturing, stable markets and manufacturing processes generally guaranteed high rates of return, and there was little need for product or process innovation. Indeed, such innovation served to destabilize and threaten a favorable status quo. Companies within these industries seemed to work hard to compete on any basis other than price.

Given the stable technology, favorable international environment, and handsome returns of the past, circumstances called more for the administrative minds of those with legal and financial backgrounds than for the technical minds of engineers and manufacturing experts. Today, however, almost half of America's key chief executive officers are likely to have backgrounds in law and finance, compared with only 13 percent in 1950, and relatively few business school graduates opt for careers in manufacturing. Beset by relentless demand for financial performance, many of America's top managers seem far better equipped to manage decline gracefully than to undertake the bold and risky steps necessary to alter their company's basic competitive posture.[3] New competitive forces, international in scope, threaten to overwhelm the companies and industries that have failed to maintain their competitive vitality and to adjust promptly to a troubling new set of realities.

A substantial portion of the blame for the current economic distress of the United States, particularly in the manufacturing sector, can be laid at the feet of America's managers and so-called "modern management principles," according to Robert Hayes and William Abernathy.[4] There are three broad elements of this new managerial orthodoxy: modern organization/control theory, financial portfolio management, and market-driven behavior.

Modern organization and control theory rests on three basic tenets:

decentralized profit centers, financially based managerial evaluation, and fast-track career paths. In response to rapid growth and expanding markets, major corporations adopted the profit center as a control device that functions as a business within a business. Profit centers offer flexibility by encouraging proliferation of product designs tailored to a variety of discrete markets. However, in the face of the global markets of the 1980s with specialized national-market products under attack from standardized global competition, the fragmentation and dilution of effort by the diversified corporation has been a distinct liability. Moreover, the profit center lends itself to the same near-term financial reporting that characterizes the corporation as a whole. Top managers far removed from the concrete realities of products and markets are forced to manage with a high degree of analytical detachment.

Managers are now evaluated almost exclusively on financial results. The most common yardstick for evaluating the performance of a profit center is return on invested capital (ROI). But corporate objectives requiring a specific rate of return often result in greater management efforts to reduce the denominator—invested capital—than in the growth of the numerator, profit. Over the long term, the profit component is critical, but quick results are all too often achieved by a reduction in invested capital. The day of reckoning comes long after the highly mobile manager has departed.

Fast-track career paths are becoming the rule rather than the exception. Traditional career paths to the top in major corporations wound their way slowly through large functional departments, resulting in a hands-on knowledge of the business. The new breed of "fast-track executive," well-equipped with the appropriate tools of financial analysis, is distinguished by the ability to effect the maximum change quickly and decisively within limited time constraints. Knowledge of procedures and systems is supplanting hands-on experience.[5]

Corporate portfolio management adopts methods similar to the methods used to balance risk within investment portfolios. It views the corporation's divisions and product lines as financial investments. Under these guidelines, the buy-hold-sell terminology of the money manager translates into a new kind of corporate management strategy: "buy" means to increase investments, "hold" calls for positioning the division as a cash cow to fund more attractive investments, "sell" dictates divestiture.

Corporate portfolio management adversely affects long-term performance in two ways. First, it suffuses throughout the corporation a philosophy of risk avoidance, which can result in many lost opportunities. Second, it tends at best to turn top management into administrators, and at worst to turn them into caretakers—rather than builders and creators. If it's broken, don't fix it. Sell it and replace it with a better business. A corollary of this "buy it, sell it" approach to business units is found in capital equipment acquisitions. In contrast to Japan and Germany, where a significant percentage of new manufacturing equipment is engineered and built in-house, U.S. companies tend to purchase turnkey installations, which do not give them any valuable lessons in product and process improvement.

Finally, market-driven behavior influences corporations through the well-intentioned dictate to become customer-oriented rather than process-oriented. This strategy worked well for General Motors in the late 1920s when it unseated Ford as the largest U.S. automotive manufacturer. GM's market-segmentation strategy offered automobiles appropriate for varying income levels, while Henry Ford stuck with the Model T and his famous saying that customers could have any color they wanted "so long as it was black."

But when consumer analysis and market surveys come to dominate all other considerations, the pendulum has swung too far and product and process innovation are critically impeded. Bold innovation is of course dangerous and unsettling, observed Joseph Schumpeter when he coined the term "creative destruction."[6] Major innovations may put large stocks of capital, both human and physical, at risk. And excessive reliance on market-driven strategies can easily result in imitative "me too" products, unintended product proliferation, inflated cost, and unfocused diversifications. All these short-term strategies manifest themselves in a declining commitment to the major long-term investments in new products and process technology that are so necessary for superior products and increased market share.

It has been more than ten years since Hayes and Abernathy fingered so precisely U.S. managerial deficiencies. The new financial weapons of the 1980s—junk bonds and hostile takeovers—were yet to come, and in their wake the short-term focus of U.S. managers has been heightened by an almost exclusive preoccupation with increasing shareholder value so as to avoid unfriendly takeover attempts. Many top managers readily acknowledge the problems that Hayes and Abernathy focus on. But to respond with the appropriate long-term vision often poses unacceptable risks to the independence of their companies and to their own job security.

So-called modern management methods have been called "paper entrepreneurialism" by political economist Robert Reich. Given the constraints imposed on new-product and process development by modern management theory, American managers have turned their innovational proclivities in new directions. These innovations are not technological or institutional; they are based on accounting, tax avoidance, financial management, mergers, acquisitions, and litigation. They have been innovations on paper. Gradually, over the last twenty years, America's professional managers have indeed become paper entrepreneurs.[7]

Rather than creating new wealth through technological advance and improved manufacturing skills, paper entrepreneurialism simply rearranges industrial assets in the quintessential zero-sum game where one company's gain becomes another's loss. The conglomerate and its many side effects are some of the more striking manifestations of paper entrepreneurship.

Conglomerates based almost exclusively on financial considerations seldom bring technical and/or hands-on experience to the disparate businesses under the corporate umbrella. Indeed, ranking high on everyone's list of great American businesses are nonconglomerates, such as IBM, John Deere, Hewlett-Packard, Caterpillar, Procter & Gamble, and Kodak, corporations built by managers who devoted themselves to the design and development of demonstrably superior products. These organizations succeeded because they spent decades mastering the subtleties and nuances of a particular line of business; they became learning organizations.

Newport News Shipbuilding Company, from the time of its founding by Colis P. Huntington, proudly displayed in front of its headquarters a bronze plaque that read: "We build good ships here. At a profit if we can, at a loss if we must, but always good ships." After its acquisition by the conglomerate Tenneco, the plaque was removed. Great American companies consistently made superior products that commanded a dominant market share; good profits followed as a matter of course. Growth by merger can be seen in one light as a form of nongrowth emphasizing selective downsizing and retrenchment in the service of risk avoidance.[8]

This is not to say that growth should not be pursued through diversification. It was Henry Ford's failure to broaden his product line that permitted GM to become the world's largest manufacturing company. On the other hand, Alfred Sloan, for many years chairman of General Motors, did not buy a motion picture studio or a tobacco company. Describing related diversifications, M.I.T. economist Lester Thurow observes:

> The key to successful Japanese diversification depends on discovering the linkage of the main business to any prospective new one and planning to employ fully the firm's accumulated capabilities. Empirical studies on diversifications indicate that related diversifications have produced better economic performance than unrelated ones.[9]

Related diversification has the advantage of combining the strategic view of those at the top with the specific information available to those at lower levels within the corporation.

Any study of U.S. management practices is incomplete without some examination of industrial relations and human resources policies. Here, in part, Americans are victims of historical circumstances.

For the quarter-century after 1945, U.S. companies competed primarily against one another, oblivious to competitive threats from abroad. Building on the traditions of British craft unions, the American labor movement at major industrial facilities sought the all-important objective of job security through the proliferation of work rules, job classifications, and elaborate seniority systems. When waves of low-cost, high-quality imported goods entered our once-insulated markets, the United States was at a distinct disadvantage. Lower wages, supported by unrestrictive work practices abroad, caused American manufacturers to reexamine their labor relations system. The credo of the American Federation of Labor (AFL), enunciated long ago by Samuel Gompers as "More, more, more," became inoperative in industry after industry as foreign competition forced price constraints on U.S. manufacturers. Lower selling prices in turn dictated wage restraints, and in many instances there was no more to give. The long-standing custom of adversarial "we/they" labor-management relations in the American and British labor movements was further buttressed by the adversarial nature of the Anglo-American common law judicial system, and it has become increasingly burdensome.

As American companies responded to the competitive thrust from abroad, many of them quite diligently, other facets of human resources management, particularly in Japan, were exposed. "Just in time" inventory practices, "total quality systems," and "quality circles" revealed themselves as critical elements of a new kind of manufacturing system.[10]

These new methods are best typified by the Toyota production system, where the painstaking management of people, material, and equipment translates into unequivocal manufacturing superiority. In what is now called the era of human capital, U.S. producers have discovered several deficiencies in human resources management. Training, particularly at the work force level, has been quite inadequate. Fast-track career paths have anointed a few while alienating many more. Japanese and American fringe-benefit practices present an instructive comparison. In Japan, company housing, recreational facilities, sports teams, and clubs further bond employees to the company. In the United States, sick leaves, coffee breaks, and vacations (in amounts far exceeding those in Japan) separate the worker physically and psychologically from the fate of the enterprise. The corporation is seen as embodied in the ownership of its stockholders; employees are of secondary concern. In Japan, by contrast, managers and employees are believed to constitute the core of the firm, while stockholders are seen as less important. Only belatedly have Americans realized that the competitive thrust from abroad is based on far more than cheap wages.

The many weaknesses (and occasional strengths) of the U.S. financial system have a major influence on the competitive posture of America's industrial concerns. Examining that system, we find ourselves midway between microeconomic American management principles and practices and the overarching macroeconomic role of U.S. political institutions. American managers must labor within the constraints imposed by the financial system and capital markets, but our financial structures themselves can be understood only within a much larger political framework.

The net U.S. savings rate for the period 1960–88 was the lowest of the Group of Five (France, Japan, United Kingdom, United States, and West Germany). The savings rate in West Germany was approximately twice the U.S. rate, and that of Japan was more than two and a half times as much.[11] The United States has gone further than most nations in promoting a higher standard of living through short-term consumer incentives, but that comes at the expense of long-term savings and investment. Before the 1981 tax reforms, punitive rates on interest and dividend income ran as high as 70 percent, as compared with 50 percent for earned income. Indeed, there is much evidence that U.S. policies subsidize consumption and penalize savings and capital formation.[12]

Of necessity, a low net savings rate translates into reduced rates of capital formation. The share of U.S. gross domestic product devoted to net investment between 1970 and 1980 was only 34 percent of the comparable share in Japan, and only 56 percent of that in West Germany. Our net investment in new plant and equipment showed successive declines from 4 percent (1966–70) to 3.1 percent (1971–75) and 2.8 percent (1976–80).[13] In light of our inordinately low rates of capital formation, it is not surprising that capital stock on a per capita basis (that is, the capital available to each U.S. worker) has declined steadily over the last twenty years. In the case of some basic industries, most notably the steel industry, negative capital formation has proceeded at an alarming rate.

The cost of capital here is approximately twice that in Japan.[14] In the United States there is a pronounced bias toward consumption, whereas in Japan the low cost of capital is borne by savers, taxpayers, and consumers. Because of the much larger role of equity markets in the United States, the risk factor shouldered by prospective lenders in arm's-length transactions is much greater, causing higher interest rates.

In Japan, however, more reliance on the administered banking system, and hence on the government, reduces the risk and the rates of the intermediate lenders, who are in effect both investors and shareholders. Thus, in times of financial trouble for a Japanese company, holders of debt and equities tend to speak with one voice in efforts to save it, while in America efforts at cross-purposes often assure bankruptcy. And because of the generally unified Japanese financial system, selected growth industries become the beneficiaries of targeted financing, which further reduces risks and rates. Finally, depreciation schedules in the United States have been inadequate generators of capital, especially in the face of double-digit inflation in the 1970s.

The American manufacturing sector has been the principal victim of the high cost of capital. When the financial markets act on their assessment of a company's meager prospects, the company is categorized as an increasingly marginal borrower. Higher capital costs then exacerbate its already subpar performance, and the financial market's original judgment becomes a self-fulfilling prophecy. Even for a company that receives the full approbation of the capital markets, high capital costs cause a myopic view of investment possibilities by establishing unreasonably high ROI thresholds for proposed capital projects.

Although there is great depth, variety, and resiliency in the U.S. financial system, its effectiveness is weakened by its fragmented, unfocused nature. In Japan the financial system is best seen as a means to an end, but in the United States it all too often becomes an end in itself. There are more than 12,000 banks in the United States, with the top ten commercial banks controlling only 21 percent of total commercial bank assets and only 6 percent of the assets of all financial intermediaries.[15]

The influence major banks have in the hugely diverse U.S. financial system is much less than the influence of their peer institutions abroad. Only recently, for instance, eight of the world's ten largest banks were Japanese, and only one U.S. bank, Citicorp, was in the top twenty.[16] Especially noteworthy is the vast power of the Japanese banking system in making economy-wide allocations of capital. This is tantamount more to quasi-organizational transactions than to the arm's-length transactions of the more unfettered U.S. capital markets.[17] The power marshaled in Japan, France, and Germany under the aegis of a centralized and powerful banking system is absent in the United States. Here, the world's largest equity markets are geared to provide more-expensive equity rather than less-expensive debt. Top corporate managers who in the past worked to further the long-term interests of the owners today all too often serve at the beck and call of a small cadre of money managers.

Nowhere is the pernicious effect our financial system has on America's economic performance seen more clearly than with the financial high jinks of recent years. What conglomerates were to the 1960s and 1970s, junk bonds, leveraged buyouts, and hostile takeovers were to the 1980s. High drama was offered up as the terms "white knight," "poison pill," and "greenmail" became part of the business vocabulary.

"Genius" is an uncommonly heavy word, most often reserved for the likes of Freud or Einstein, but it is an adjective that cannot be denied to Michael Milken, the most powerful financier since J. P. Morgan. Milken single-handedly invented the "manufactured" junk bond, thereby changing the ground rules of corporate finance. He created the financial instruments and markets leading to the deal mania of the roaring 1980s.

The junk-bond-fueled hostile takeover movement was not without some redeeming qualities. By exposing entrenched and uninspired management to the threat of raids, it pushed corporate America toward leaner management and greater concentration on creation of shareholder value. But the unintended side effects far offset the intended cure. When a company borrowed to the very limits of debt coverage, profits and taxes were virtually eliminated. In effect, Uncle Sam underwrote the economic buccaneering of a handful of takeover artists who became immensely wealthy in the process. Starved of necessary investment capital, and thus denied a long-term strategy, these companies were turned into financial machines whose sole purpose was to enrich their new owners.

But don't blame Carl Icahn, Henry Kravis, Carl Lindner, Ron Perelman, Saul Steinberg, and other dealmakers. They did exactly what the fragmented and overly deregulated U.S. financial system permitted them to do. The federal government preached the virtues of deregulation, but we need only look at the savings and loan mess to understand that we got a little more deregulation than we bargained for. The opportunity was there, and through an arresting blend of intellect and courage these corporate raiders exploited it. It's only a shame that this pool of talent (including Milken's awesome abilities) couldn't have been used for more productive ends. At the beginning of the new decade, more than $200 billion worth of junk bonds filled the coffers of mutual funds, insurance companies, pension funds, and savings banks. Milken has been convicted, Drexel Burnham is bankrupt, and the junk bond market is in turmoil. Throughout the 1990s, the U.S. economy will continue to pay the price of the junk bond binge.

Hostile takeovers and junk bonds did nothing to make the United States more internationally competitive. While the Japanese were building great technologically driven corporations like Fujitsu, Hitachi, Mitsubishi Electric, NEC, Matsushita, Sony, and Toshiba, Americans were shuffling assets, nothing more. A lucky few hit the jackpot, but our society as a whole was impoverished.

For better or for worse, the U.S. financial system is undergoing rapid change. Barriers that have sharply distinguished banks from other financial institutions are now disappearing. But the financial evolution is not toward European or Japanese investment banks and their producer-driven, long-term perspective. The demand-driven U.S. economy is moving the financial system slowly in the direction of financial supermarkets such as American Express, Citicorp, Merrill Lynch, and Sears.[18]

This, however, is not to discount the great strength of U.S. venture capital capability. The large pool of capital that stands ready to back a host of trailblazing enterprises is not replicated either in Europe or in Japan. Our financial system emphasizing venture capital and equity markets encourages innovation and the initiation of new industries, but it often fails to institutionalize and support them further down the line. Today's global economic contest is a marathon, not a sprint. The one signal strength of venture capital is hardly sufficient to overcome the many patent shortcomings of the existing U.S. financial structure.

The significant impact of the American consumption ethic, managerial practices, and financial system on the nation's ability to compete in the new global markets is easily comprehended, but the proposition that nothing affects our economic and social well-being so much as our political institutions is the heart of the argument of this book. The role of the state is crucial, not only because it has a direct impact on economic conditions, but also because it profoundly shapes and influences all other factors as well.

The slowing in productivity growth in the 1970s elicited a mounting chorus of conservatives, supply-siders, and monetarists—all speaking out in unison against the evils of big government and culminating in the landslide Reagan victory of 1980. The sharp economic setbacks of this period provided a convenient tinderbox for igniting ever-smoldering antigovernment sentiments. The conservative prescriptions of Arthur Laffer and Milton Friedman were simple and appealing: deregulate, cut taxes, and shrink the government, and good old Yankee ingenuity would do the rest. Provide the seeds, soil, and sunlight, and American industry was bound to flourish. In the words of George Lodge, "By the 1970s, the idea of the limited state had spawned in America a government whose authority and power was so fragmented that any kind of coherent definition of community need was difficult, if not impossible." And this very condition strengthened the hands of the free market champions as they pointed an accusing finger at the "bloated government" of the interventionist state.[19]

What is an interventionist state? A simple, four-part typology helps answer the question. Theoretically, there are four distinct state types: the limited state, the interventionist state, the developmental state, and the managerial state. A good way to distinguish among these types is to examine in each case the relationship between the state and the mechanism of the free market.

The limited state—the "night watchman" state of Adam Smith—gives free rein to the forces of the market. Although its proponents have been highly influential, particularly in the United States, this is the only one of the four types for which there is no concrete example. The siren call of the hypothetical limited state has significantly conditioned existing American political institutions.

The interventionist state today is best characterized by the United States. This state type has a long history in America, from the Progressives, to the New Deal, and through Lyndon Johnson's Great Society. Like the limited state, the interventionist state puts full faith in the economic and social benefits of the free market, but it advocates occasional intervention to ensure the market's optimum performance.

The developmental state—Japan being the best example—has great respect for the powerful workings of the market but trusts the market far less than the interventionist state does. Proponents of the developmental state maintain that a limited but critical number of endeavors are best removed from the free play of the market and gathered under the aegis of the state. They believe these activities are best conducted according to administrative principles rather than market rules.[20]

The managerial state, exemplified by the Soviet Union, puts total confidence in the administrative apparatus to operate a command economy. Advocates of the managerial state hold that administrative principles can completely supplant market rules. The abysmal performance—and under Gorbachev open admission of failure—of the Soviet Union and other Eastern Bloc economies is conclusive evidence of the inadequacies of the managerial state.

The realistic options, then, are the interventionist and the developmental models. From Thomas Jefferson's call for a government "which shall leave [people] . . . free to regulate their own pursuits," [21] to Ronald Reagan's demand to "get the government off our backs," the condemnation of state power both in theory and in practice has been a recurrent theme of American politics. Government is seen as a necessary evil. Neutrality is as close as most Americans get toward approval of their government, while criticism and condemnation of the federal government seemingly find no depths. Samuel Huntington summed it up well: "Because of the inherently antigovernment character of the American Creed, government that is strong is illegitimate, government that is legitimate is weak." [22] Most Americans believe a smaller, weaker, less-centralized government is far superior to a strong, purposive state, that because most state initiatives are harmful to the public welfare the state that acts least is best.

In continental Europe, where industrialization occurred later than in the United States, major businesses were either aided or in some cases created by the state. In America, demands for a somewhat stronger state, more like an interventionist state than a limited state, arose in response to the abuses of power by a new phenomenon, the giant industrial corporation. Thus, from 1890 a series of legislative, legal, financial, and personal clashes forced business and government in the United States into adversarial relations. Unfortunately, in over a century they have failed to break the antagonistic mold into which they were originally cast.

The short-term view that prevails in American management has its roots in the failure of the U.S. government to develop consistent and coherent economic policies. As the pace of economic change quickens and the influence of increased foreign trade is felt more acutely, our political institutions are unable to respond properly. We are not inclined philosophically to letting government take a more active role, but even if we were, our institutions are not equipped to implement the required measures.

In fact, our current institutional practices appear to lead us in the opposite direction. They promote rather than improve the long-standing adversarial relations among labor, management, and government. The cumulative effects of the policies of regulation and drift lessen the likelihood that the U.S. government will take purposive action. In the absence of such action, we tend to become more of a crisis-activated society than ever before.

A good example of our crisis-activated society is provided by the revolution in liability law since 1960. At that time, product liability was sharply limited; buyers and sellers tacitly agreed on the cost of accidents. Flagrant and willful violations of safety standards could and did trigger liability suits, but huge awards, class actions, and a flood of lawsuits were not part of the legal landscape. As an adjunct to Ralph Nader's consumer movement, a handful of legal scholars became convinced that the government was not protecting the individual consumer from the vast and sometimes abusive corporate power.[23]

The liability revolution was born out of the conviction that the courts and the new legal activists—not government regulating business in the traditional fashion—should determine the outer limits of liability. And how insane those outer limits became. In New York, a man attempted suicide by jumping in front of a subway train; claiming the driver was negligent by not stopping sooner, he cashed in for $650,000.[24] In Philadelphia, a psychic sued for the loss of her psychic powers after a CAT scan and was awarded $900,000.

But the real cost of the explosion in liability awards lies in the response of the corporations under attack. To avoid the possibility of devastating losses in a liability action, they reduce their rate of innovation and new product introduction. No situation better illustrates the extreme costs and perverse logic of the new liability law than drug companies' policies toward new vaccines. Various vaccines have all but eradicated polio, smallpox, diphtheria, and a long list of dread diseases; tens of millions of lives have been saved in the process. But with every vaccine there will be a small number of unexplainable, adverse reactions—some resulting in death. The introduction of a new whooping cough vaccine was greeted by a barrage of lawsuits demanding more than $2 billion in damages and amounting to nearly two hundred times the total annual sales of the product.[25] Under conditions such as these, insurance coverage either becomes prohibitively expensive or disappears altogether. How do drug companies respond? In all too many instances they don't sell new vaccines unless the government assumes responsibility for potential product liability.

The liability revolution is inherently antibusiness, anticompetitiveness, antistatist, and most decidedly anti-public-good. In a manner somewhat akin to the deal mania of the 1980s, in its effects if not in its intentions, it has created a sort of national lottery that enriches a few at the expense of millions. While manufacturing concerns are fighting a bitterly contested frontal economic war with the Japanese, they must at the same time contend with the guerrilla tactics of a small army of self-appointed legal reformers who openly question the legality and morality of private and public corporations, and at a more fundamental level the morality of any bureaucratically organized institution. The liability revolution is nothing less than a national disgrace.

Until thirty years ago the United States consistently produced reasonably coherent national policies. This was possible as long as the wellsprings of self-interest that drive all liberal democratic societies were channeled into major adversarial blocs by means of a vigorous party system. As social issues crowded the political agenda during the 1960s, however, the old coalitions began to fragment into smaller groups, including many of the so-called "single-issue" type. A flood of entitlement legislation raised expectations and caused single-issue groups to oppose any policy initiatives that didn't support their particular cause. At a time when more was asked of our government than ever before, the government's ability to respond was seriously impaired. Efforts to further democratize government and political parties at all levels created a multitude of vocal, dedicated, and often resourceful pockets of resistance, effectively granting veto power to everyone.

This democratic deadlock was frustrating to those who were charged with formulating and implementing national policy. David Stockman, former congressman and former director of the U.S. Office of Management and Budget, recalled the systemic failure of Congress:

> There is a breakdown in the Congressional machinery. There are 100 gantlets and 1,000 vetoes on Capitol Hill. You simply can't sustain any kind of policy through that process, whether it's the conduct of foreign affairs, the shaping of the budget or the management of the fiscal affairs of the nation, because there are 180 subcommittees with overlapping jurisdictions and huge staffs. All of these actors want to get in the process, and as a result, everybody has their hooks on everything.[26]

One year before Stockman began to grapple with the proliferation of veto groups, economist Lester Thurow aptly caught the sense and mood of this new world in the title of his book *The Zero-Sum Society*, which provides corroboration for Stockman's critique of an intransigent Congress. As Thurow saw it, we are faced with a static economy; if the lot of one specific group is to be improved, then the position of another group will have to be correspondingly lowered. In his book *The Hunting Hypothesis*, anthropologist Robert Ardrey tells us that an aggressor animal who wants to best a defender of the same species on his home territory must have twice the strength of the defender. Thurow provides theoretical corroboration for Ardrey's thesis when he finds that few majorities are capable of mustering twice the strength of an opposing minority.

In the past, political and economic power were distributed in such a fashion that the ruling majority was capable of imposing significant losses on certain segments of the population. The majority felt that the losses of any minority group were more than recouped by meaningful enhancements of the general interest. But today most groups judged as eligible for sacrifice in the name of a greater good are unwilling to accept their fate and powerful enough to thwart the majority in their own defense. Thurow sees the issue not as *us* versus *them*, resulting in a winner-loser/non-zero-sum game, but rather as "*us* versus *us* in a zero-sum game." [27] Given the strong antigovernment bias of so many Americans—reinforced by an instinctive and characteristically American distrust of political and social authority—it is unlikely that proponents of the national interest will be able to muster widespread support for their cause.

All too often, those seeking the causes of American economic decline focus on one set of factors in either management, finance, or politics, to the partial exclusion of the others. But the shortcomings of our economic performance are deeply rooted in all elements of the American system. Hayes and Abernathy are quite correct when they claim we are "managing our way to economic decline," but we must not forget that we managed our way to economic decline only within a given financial and political environment. Unless we change the environment we cannot manage our way *out* of economic decline. We can find numerous failures at the firm level, and we have examined industry-wide failures in steel, automobiles, consumer electronics, and semiconductors. But we can understand these problems only in the context of our financial system, which in turn is conditioned by our political system. The problems of the United States are *system-wide*. You can look in any window of our economic house and see them. We can better understand these problems by looking at the mirror image of American failure in Japan's success. The reasons for that success are system-wide too. In Japan all elements are important, but the political system is most important.

We have only touched on the failure of the policy outputs of the American political system. After exploring the reasons for the unprecedented economic performance of Japan and the critical role of Japan's political system in that success, we shall take a more detailed look at American political institutions. As political institutions are behind Japan's success, they also are the root cause of America's economic decline. There is a startling contrast between Japanese and American political institutions.

PART TWO

———

HOW THE
JAPANESE DO IT

HOW DO THE JAPANESE DO IT? The methods and means that have taken Japan to the threshold of technological and economic world leadership may best be termed "industrial policy." Little is gained toward understanding industrial policy by listening to the clangorous and confusing industrial policy debate that currently rages in the United States. The debate centers on isolated and sporadic industrial policy measures, not on the systematic and deep-seated commitment to economic growth found in Japan. Despite the confusion in the United States, two simple and straightforward definitions of industrial policy may be provided:

1. Industrial policy is the state-induced willful shifting of the industrial structure toward high-technology, high-value-added industries.
2. Industrial policy is what they do in Japan. The Japanese have invented, developed, and refined industrial policy.

Japan's industrial policy, and consequently industrial policy as it emerges elsewhere, has three levels, which are discussed in Chapter 3. At the uppermost level are hundreds of specific legislative and administrative measures designed to move Japan's industrial structure in the desired direction. At the next level is a theory of industrial policy that organizes and coordinates those specific measures into a comprehensive design. Indeed, the unwritten and unspoken adjective that invariably attaches itself to industrial policy is the word "comprehensive." Noncomprehensive industrial policy is a stereotypical oxymoron. At the third and deepest level is a bedrock foundation of economic, political, and social factors we have characterized as the Japanese system. The elements of the Japanese system are so deep-seated and pervasive that they affect every facet of Japanese society. The four nonpolitical elements of the system—culture, education, management, and finance—are the subject of Chapter 4.

The heart of the Japanese system, and thus the heart of that country's industrial policy, is the nature of Japanese political institutions, which we shall look at in Chapter 5. Japan's political architecture possesses two salient features that are critical to the conduct of industrial policy: a strong central state and a top professional bureaucracy. Only by means of the power of the central state can sufficient political force be mustered to establish and maintain a successful industrial policy.

The very nature of Japan's industrial policy and the political system that undergirds it has serious implications for would-be practitioners of industrial policy, including the United States. Japanese industrial policy cannot be grafted onto existing social structures by legislative means. It requires a national commitment and a decades-long process of organic growth within a nation's economic, political, and social systems. It is like nothing that has ever been remotely contemplated within the United States.

3

JAPANESE
INDUSTRIAL POLICY
AND THE
JAPANESE SYSTEM

*Our policy is to reduce the price, extend the
operations and improve the article. You will
notice that the reduction of the price comes first.
We have never considered any cost as fixed.*
—Henry Ford

The United States is confronted today by an entirely new competitive
environment, unquestionably created by Japan. Throughout East Asia,
several "little Japans"—including South Korea, Taiwan, Singapore, and
Hong Kong—have learned from and profited from Japan's pioneering
effort. And though the emerging pattern is not yet clear, there is little
doubt that the policies implemented by Japan's developmental state have
not been lost on the leaders of the People's Republic of China.

Two factors combine to make the United States the principal target
market of Japan. With the largest and most open market in the world,
the United States offers the best outlet for high-quality, low-cost mass-
produced Japanese goods. Furthermore, Japan's technologically ad-

vanced products have been quite well received in the world's most technologically sophisticated market.

Over the years, many reasons for America's loss of market share in industry after industry have been offered. In the late 1940s, Japanese imports were thought of primarily as something that might be found at the bottom of a Cracker Jack box, but the thinking was that such goods had a rightful place in the new economic order of the American century. Later, faced with a flood of high-quality, low-priced textile imports, Americans came to take the competition seriously but attributed the cost advantage solely to cheap labor. As Japan's exports advanced technologically, Americans came up with new reasons to blame for Japan's cost advantage: protectionism; a labor force of "human" robots; unusual managerial techniques; a mysterious amalgam of business, government, and national will known as "Japan Inc."; subsidized exports; and a grossly undervalued yen. Finally, as Japan approached technological parity in many industries, Americans sought consolation in an old adage: "They can copy, but they can't innovate."

There is an element of truth in all these statements, but at the same time Americans voiced concerns about fairness. If Japan played by the agreed-upon rules on a level playing field, the United States of America—Good Old Number One—would once again win the day. The fact is, however, that although many of the playing fields have become more level in recent years, Japan's cost advantage—and more recently its technological superiority—is now so overwhelming on an increasing number of products that even if we set aside all unfair advantages the United States still comes out second best.

The Japanese have organized for economic victory. Industrial policy provides the blueprint for this organization. Several theoretical concepts that help to define Japan's industrial policy—a fundamental commitment to GNP growth, a developmental strategy, portfolio management of prospective growth industries, a theory of dynamic comparative advantage, and the concept of managed internal competition—deserve closer examination.

Behind Japan's industrial policy is an explicit and unequivocal commitment to GNP growth that is reinforced by all the other elements of industrial policy. Since 1945 a single unified goal of equaling and surpassing the West has fueled the economic energies of Japan. This national effort has involved a full mix of microeconomic and macroeconomic policies. Growth industries and the "linkage" industries (such as steel and semiconductors, which serve as essential building blocks for future growth industries) have been the engines of economic progress. In Joseph Schumpeter's terms, they have provided the "gales of creative destruction" that affect industrial change.[1]

The export imperative is a salient feature of Japan's broad-based commitment to growth. Its twin aims are maximizing net exports and maximizing value added per worker. A small island nation vitally dependent on foreign trade for raw materials and markets feels the mandate of the export imperative acutely. Considering that Japan's foreign trade percentage of GNP is well below that of Great Britain and Germany, and only somewhat higher than that of the United States, Japan's striking export success in so many markets is all the more remarkable. What happens in the intensely competitive home market, which many consider the most hotly contested domestic market in the world, shapes the character of Japan's export drive. For example, newer companies and companies that rank third, fourth, or lower domestically find their local growth blocked by long-standing relationships in the dense thicket of Japan's distribution system. As a result, they are forced to seek expansion in foreign markets.

Manufacturing prowess and technological advantage are the hallmarks of the Japanese export drive. Manufacturing efficiency leads directly to cost leadership and to dominant market shares. In the single-minded drive to secure ever-increased market shares, profits are willingly sacrificed. Moreover, the Japanese have recognized more clearly than their global competitors that, despite an appalling lack of natural resources, they are not deficient in one resource, people. And that is today's most critical resource. The intelligence, skill, education, and dedication of the nation's work force inclines Japan strongly toward the production of goods with increasing technological sophistication. Studies by the OECD demonstrate that high-technology companies achieve 1.49 times the sales growth, 2.8 times the labor productivity gain, and 2.75 times the profitability growth of middle-technology companies.[2]

Japan's growth commitment and export drive is characterized by nervous anxiety and a pronounced sense of crisis, a national mood likened to a peacetime "psychological state of war."[3] Indeed, Japan has pursued economic objectives with much of the same passion that the United States once reserved for fighting communism: "From about 1941 to 1961 the Japanese economy remained on a war footing. The goal changed from military to economic victory, but the Japanese people could not have worked harder, saved more, or innovated more ruthlessly if they had actually been engaged in a war for national survival, as in fact they were."[4]

A developmental strategy may best be understood in opposition to a redistributional strategy. The former is tied to growth, productivity, and external competitiveness; the latter concerns itself with economic growth only peripherally. In fact, the political priorities of the two approaches are quite distinct. Developmentalism sets goals of substantive economic performance, and redistributionalism focuses on social equity.[5]

The trading system established by the United States in the postwar period was unable to accommodate a developmental strategy. The U.S. vision of free trade in a free world saw individual firms competing with one another while governments stood aside, providing only the rules of the game. Japan did not accept this vision. It moved early to challenge the free trade system. This challenge was spearheaded by well-managed export-oriented firms that were given vigorous support at every turn. Japanese government bureaucrats, industrialists, and influential citizens possessed a keen perception of this strategy.

Developmentalism aims at meeting ever-higher standards of international competition. Improvement proceeds on several fronts: single enterprises, enterprise environments, entire industries, and finally the industrial structure itself. Specific measures, covering both promotional and protectionist policies, include subsidies, import protection, export subsidies, antitrust restraints, government procurement, and tax incentives. Economy-wide rationalization and attendant specific policies are inextricably intertwined with the market. The Japanese clearly understand that the state needs the market and that the market needs the state. Nonmarket mechanisms are used to hasten the response of the market.

Developmental strategies in Japan are driven by the national interest, which must never be sacrificed to rules, procedures, or special interests. Peter Drucker is one who recommends the Japanese model—"under which both leaders and special interests derive their legitimacy from their stewardship of the national interest"—to other pluralist societies.[6] Skeptics argue, however, that the Japanese are guilty of bending the rules in pursuit of a policy of pure economic nationalism, an option not open to the United States because of its position of international leadership.

Developmentalism has deep roots in the history of modern Japan. An early slogan of the Meiji period—"Rich country and a strong defense"—was typical of an era when the keenest minds in Japan labored on behalf of trade and industry not as ends in themselves but toward the creation of the strategic foundations of the national interest.[7]

Before World War II, national interest and mercantilism became linked with militarism as Japan attempted to establish economic hegemony throughout Southeast Asia under the aegis of the Greater East Asia Co-Prosperity Sphere. Free of immediate external threats after 1945—its international security guaranteed by the United States—the national effort no longer had to serve the twin masters of military and economic nationalism. Somehow the dedication and discipline that characterized Japanese military forces during the war became sublimated in the service of a new economic nationalism.

Japanese developmentalism continues to have as its core an unrelenting emphasis on strategic, high-technology, high-value-added industries. Strategic direction is provided by MITI's "Long-Term Visions." The one issued in 1980 was called "The Industrial Structure of Japan in the 1980s—Future Outlook and Tasks."[8] This process has been called "engineering a societal cerebral cortex." In the fashion of a great head coach, MITI aids and encourages the development of strong single companies as individual players highly disciplined by the rigors of a demanding internal market. Afterward it welds them together as a team in the service of the national interest.

Through portfolio management of prospective growth industries, the Japanese have demonstrated that it is possible to upgrade a national industrial portfolio. Conscious management of the industrial structure has been a driving force behind the Japanese advance, but the process could be accomplished only with the enthusiastic backing of the state. The Japanese government is willing and able to create the institutions and policies that accelerate specific growth industries while cushioning the decline of less-promising ones.

Selectivity and concentration are two key principles of portfolio management. Japanese assaults on markets in the United States and elsewhere have come in narrow waves, with the resulting growth of market share occurring relatively quickly. The list of Japanese products that have achieved significant market penetration is not inordinately long, but it is growing. The nation's world-class competitors are inclined or encouraged to venture abroad only after they have been thoroughly tested in the white-hot crucible of the Japanese domestic market.

Competitive strength in Japan is divided quite unevenly. In agriculture and distribution, along with large segments of the service and manufacturing sectors, low productivity and poor competitive performance are very common. The picture of industrial Japan as an invincible monolith, popularized as "Japan Inc.," is far wide of the mark. But make no mistake. The hard truth is that when Japanese industries and companies are good, they are very good.

Textiles, steel, autos, semiconductors, computers—these industries (the first four signal Japanese victories, the last one an ominous challenge) spread themselves easily for the Japanese over a half-century technological spectrum. Each is the industry of a decade, beginning with textiles in the 1950s and culminating with computers for the 1990s. Portfolio management then becomes the strategic management of industries, each given its measure of importance and position on the economic agenda by virtue of its degree of technological sophistication. As these and other targeted industries entered their periods of greatest strategic significance, they were characterized by rapid growth, heightened technological development, and sharply declining costs. Indirectly, through discriminatory tax policies and government-induced bank-lending policies, the foreign exchange earnings of one dominant industry are used to fuel the budding prospects and cash needs of the next decade's champion.

The number of strategic industries on stage at any one time is limited. As new industries move to the center, less technologically sophisticated contenders are given diminished roles. Indeed, portfolio management concerns itself as much with well-played exits as with bold entrances. The production of low-technology, labor-intensive products is gradually moved to less-developed countries.

Exits in the case of textiles and shipbuilding were nearly industry-wide. With automobiles and consumer electronics, labor-intensive assembly and routine manufacturing are pushed offshore, while sophisticated manufacturing, design, and engineering are jealously safeguarded through restriction to the home islands. This division of labor applies not only to Japanese investments in the newly developing countries but also to their rapidly escalating stakes in the United States and Europe. We must not deceive ourselves. The current proliferation of Japanese automotive assembly plants in the United States will do little to advance American automotive engineering skills.

The Japanese government makes a continuous and concerted effort to enhance the technological capability of its economy through strategic knowledge-based production at home and low-cost, routine production abroad. Without doubt, technological development is the most important factor underlying Japan's phenomenal industrial growth. The knowledge-based industries, centering on the extended electronics industry—including computers, computer peripherals, consumer electronics, lasers, liquid-crystal displays (LCDs), office automation equipment, semiconductors, and telecommunications equipment—have been chosen by Japanese planners as the linchpin of economic development for resource-poor Japan. Information is now seen as the single productive factor capable of replacing land and energy.

As portfolio management establishes industrial priorities, within specific time frames, it relies on a theory of dynamic comparative advantage to shift industries according to a long-term strategic vision. The classical theory of comparative advantage was first articulated by David Ricardo in 1817. It argued that trade between England and Portugal in wine and cloth should be determined on the basis of the comparative advantage (relative to other products) of either country in the production of the two commodities. The product produced more competitively should be exported and the one produced least competitively should be imported. It was assumed that comparative advantage rested on static factors, such as land, climate, and natural resources.

In the early 1950s a static theory of comparative advantage would have dictated that Japan import steel from the United States while securing the required foreign exchange through U.S. purchases of Japanese textiles. With very little coking coal, no iron ore, limited capital in the face of the vast amounts required, and inadequate technology, the idea of the Japanese steel industry being a world leader was absurd. Within twenty-five years, however, Japan's steel industry was the most efficient in the world.

Real absolute disadvantages existing for Japan in 1950 were surmounted by policy-induced advantages that translated into absolute competitive advantages. Japan's steel industry was first protected against stiff competition from low-cost foreign competition, most notably the United States. Huge portside facilities permitted the purchase of low-cost raw materials on world markets. Coal and iron ore were hauled to Japan on large bulk carriers of Japanese design and construction. Finally, and most significant, immense sums of capital were continuously funneled into new plants of increasing sophistication. These efforts firmly established the Japanese steel industry as the world's undisputed technological leader. In Japan there is the saying "Steel is the rice of industry." Steel laid the necessary foundations for later Japanese triumphs in shipbuilding and automobiles. Steel's low-cost, high-quality products gave those industries a pronounced competitive advantage, but its embodiment of a theory of dynamic comparative advantage provided a model of far greater utility.

Dynamic comparative advantage has as its crucial assumption continuous investment in the targeted industry and in the physical infrastructure of related markets—suppliers and customers. As in the case of steel, investment is capable of improving "factor endowments," thereby creating competitive advantage for companies and industries and resulting in more favorable patterns of comparative advantage over time.[9]

A necessary corollary to dynamic comparative advantage is "product cycle theory," which assumes factor endowments are variable, not fixed. Therefore, investment and disinvestment decisions will be mandated at varying points in the product cycle. Improper timing of critical investment decisions will be counterproductive, creating competitive disadvantage. In contrast, properly timed investment decisions will create technological gains, thus establishing a company or industry as a low-cost producer. As there is nothing proprietary about the lessons of dynamic comparative advantage and product cycle theory, other nations may— and must—play by the same rules.

It is important to understand that selection through portfolio management of targeted markets is predicated on product cycle theory. A simple product cycle involves four phases: start-up, growth, maturity, and decline. As we have seen, the major source of Japan's competitive advantage has been manufacturing efficiencies, which have translated into cost leadership. During start-up and growth, product and marketing development are critical, but those phases have not been notable strengths for Japan. Japan's manufacturing prowess has its most telling effect during phase three, maturity. Capital-intensive, high-volume, price-sensitive products of standardized design characterize phase-three companies. Mature, low-margined products are most susceptible to Japanese competition. Japanese companies gain great strength through process innovation, product standardization, high quality, and steady incremental improvements.

Markets are carefully segmented, and penetration first occurs at the low-priced end of the product line because of the high volume, potential for product standardization, low margins, and great price sensitivity. Low-end products are most suitable for sale through mass merchandising outlets. The roots of this strategy can be found in the record of America's master of mass production, Henry Ford. In 1906 the Model T sold for $850; in 1915 it sold for $360. In 1907 some 6,400 Model T's were produced; in 1915 some 472,000. Ford's market share went from 15 percent in 1907 to 54 percent in 1913. Here was cost leadership with a vengeance.[10]

The usual response from industries threatened by foreign producers has in most cases worked to the advantage of the attacker. In mature markets, defending competitors are much more concerned with maintaining profit margins than with increasing volume, so managers are reluctant to invest large sums to reduce cost further. Low-margin products are generally seen as cash cows, not opportunities for further investment. Keenly aware of profitability and the fickle whims of the equity markets, the defender's most logical action is to seek trade protection for the low end of the line. Should this effort fail, the defender abandons the now-unprofitable product line and falls back on more-secure and more-limited higher-margin market niches. Having attained a satisfactory position, though one that in the early stages may yield little in the way of profit, the Japanese advance up the product line, minimizing profits and maximizing market share in quest of a long-term payoff.

In automobiles, consumer electronics, and semiconductors there are many concrete examples of Japan's effective use of the theory of dynamic comparative advantage. It is not difficult to imagine a similar scenario for personal computers. How might Apple, Compaq, and IBM fare against the kinds of pressures the Japanese have applied to other industries? Indeed, in the vitally important field of knowledge-processing, the Japanese will not soon frontally assault the mainframe producers, who for the time being are guarded by an all-but-impenetrable protective network of operating software. Instead, makers of components, peripherals, and personal computers will be the first to experience the intensity of Japan's drive to be number one in this field.

Without an abundance of available low-cost capital, this strategy would never leave the textbook. It would also not succeed unless it were skillfully executed. Europe and the United States are filled with examples of generously funded government-backed enterprises whose failures have been just as resounding as Japan's achievements. Japan's success is an arresting blend of financial and institutional underpinnings and the masterful execution of a strategy that is ever-sensitive to the demands of the global marketplace. That is what has made the Japanese challenge so effective.

An accurate description of Japan's attitude toward its marketplace might be captured in the phrase "managed internal competition." Unlike the prevalent thinking in the United States, the Japanese see nothing sacred about the free market. For them, competition is only one element of industrial policy, to be used in greater or lesser measure as the occasion warrants. In Japan the "free market" is just one means toward economic growth and international competitiveness, not the only means. It is not the sacred cow it is in the United States.

To understand managed internal competition, it is first necessary to recognize the central importance of the Japanese home market. Japanese foreign trade as a percentage of GNP (exports 14 percent, imports 12 percent, as of 1989) is only slightly more than that of the United States and well below the 20 percent of the European Economic Community. Many Japanese companies and industries have grown to positions of world cost leadership conditioned by the intensive competitive atmosphere of Japan's home market.

A strong argument can be made that Japan, not the United States, has the world's largest homogeneous market.[11] Indeed, Japan has the world's second largest GNP, great population density and compactness, ease of physical distribution, the most homogeneous population of any major nation, and the second-most egalitarian income distribution of the Group of Five. It offers larger markets for mass-produced goods than any other OECD nation except the United States.

Japan's home market is also the most sophisticated, demanding, quality-conscious consumer market in the world. It provides a living "consumer testing laboratory" that has more stringent requirements than those in other national markets. Japanese companies aim at two relentlessly moving targets: ever higher quality and ever lower prices. Because of intense price competition in the home market, Japan seldom enjoys the option of increasing prices to absorb higher costs. Instead, these costs must be offset by maximizing productivity gains.

The resource-poor, energy-deficient nature of Japan helps determine the type of products that succeed at home: small appliances, small motors, and small copiers. Small implies precision, and miniaturization is a recognizable leitmotif of Japanese manufacturing. The catch-phrase for many Japanese products is "kei-haku-tan-sho"—literally "light, thin, short, and small." [12]

Although overall capital availability within an industry may vary according to MITI's particular "vision," the success, failure, and ranking of companies within an industry is left to the market. It is important, however, to recognize that intense competition is not maximum competition. The scope of competition is influenced by the bureaucracy as it pressures certain companies to abandon marginal product lines to concentrate on what they do best. The remaining narrow product line, then, has supporting it much greater resources than before, and its prospects are enhanced:

> Japan's economic structure has clearly followed the strategic principle of "concentration of force," i.e., specialization, far more than that of any of the other large industrialized nations. Britain's relative lack of specialization in international trade, and by inference, the operation of much of its economy at suboptimal scale, has stood in particularly flagrant contrast. [13]

Japanese firms grow organically, most often through related technology, and not by acquisition. In the case of Yasukawa Electric, growth followed a sensible progression: from standard electric motors to miniature electric motors to computer disc drives and robots using large quantities of miniature electric motors. A similar pattern marked Matsushita: from light bulbs to appliances to televisions and finally to VCRs.[14]

Japan's management of the home market calls for efforts to channel and guide it but stops short of explicit contravention; competition must be coped with, not suppressed. The Japanese market is consciously conditioned by a number of organizational principles: the bureaucracy's administrative guidance of firms, the independent regulatory effects of industry-wide associations, and the large networks of affiliated supplier companies attaching themselves to major Japanese firms.

The notion of Japan's economy as export-driven has become so stereotyped that the seedbed of Japan's spectacular but narrowly based export thrusts, in the hotly competitive environment of the home market, is often overlooked. The Japanese government has provided a benign business environment that diffuses and cushions the bold risks that must be taken to ensure cost leadership. The giant global companies that have produced the flood of Japanese exports have been encouraged and aided by a business environment composed of government guidance and an intensely competitive home market.

A latter-day Calvin Coolidge might proclaim that today the business of Japan is business. And while there is a strong element of truth in this statement, it could not be further from the truth to assume that business success in Japan equates strictly to profitability. Consider the creed of Matsushita Electric: "As a member of an industrial organization. We try to improve people's social life. Home electric appliances as cheap and plentiful as 'water-supply.' "[15]

The mission of social betterment through superior industrial performance is supported in Japan by a number of principles: trust and confidence between the company and the consumer, profit justified through contribution to society, fair competition, mutual benefit between the corporation and the shareholders, and respect for people through management by participation.[16] By contrast, consider the bare-bones objectives of American business and labor: greater profits for the employer and higher wages for the employees.

In the United States national power is synonymous with military strength, but in Japan (which has self-imposed restraints on defense spending) economic might has become synonymous with national power. Japan's economic effort is in part sublimated into higher social purposes, the tangible manifestation of which is unabashed economic nationalism. The Japanese productive project is very much like a war effort. The call to labor in behalf of the twin objectives of a better society and a greater Japan represents a vital element that insulates Japanese industrial policy from the pressures of partisan politics.

Supported by a broad social mandate and strong institutional underpinnings, industrial policy is by no means a paper tiger. Through a quasi-administered financial system, it can make its will felt acutely at a number of pressure points throughout the economy. Nonetheless, Japan's industrial policy continues to have a healthy respect for the wisdom of the market.

An apt illustration of the type of balance struck between business and the bureaucracy is provided by MITI's experience with Japanese automakers. In the late 1960s, with Japanese auto production scattered among more than a dozen struggling competitors and with total output only a small fraction of U.S. production, MITI sought to restructure the industry. MITI believed that an internationally competitive Japanese automotive industry could be created by consolidating the numerous producers into as few as two concerns built around Toyota and Nissan. In this action, MITI registered a signal policy defeat and in a period of twelve years a fragmented industry of nine companies surged forward to become the largest and most efficient automotive industry in the world. In the process it sent the once-mighty U.S. industry reeling with losses.

Industrial policy critics have recounted ad nauseam MITI's automotive failure as conclusive evidence that industrial policy does not work, but nothing could be further from the truth. While the automotive consolidation policy was a defeat for MITI, it was a triumph for Japan's automotive industry and for the Japanese industrial policy process.

The real lesson to be learned from the struggle between MITI and the automotive industry is that guidance by the Japanese bureaucracy is always negotiated and not imposed by fiat. MITI does far more than jaw-bone; it has the tools to apply considerable pressure on recalcitrant companies and industries. In some cases, as with the auto producers, it may fail. In many other cases it succeeds.

The outcomes of the partnership between business and the bureaucracy in Japan are the products of constant negotiating. An all-powerful bureaucracy does not impose policy on a weak and compliant private sector. One of the least-understood elements of Japanese industrial policy is that it is heavily influenced by institutionalized consultation with business leaders. Business is willing to accept government policy, because business has a strong voice in policy formulation. The aim of industrial policy is to identify the fundamental problems of an industry and to suggest and encourage a most-likely course of development—all the while supporting the initiative, creativity, and resiliency of the private sector. Signals from the market are to be anticipated and accelerated, never thwarted. This may be termed a "market-conforming policy"—a middle course between state control and laissez-faire. Ira Magaziner and Thomas Hout suggest that there are "three fairly simple and obvious ideas. Individually, they are unremarkable; together they explain very effectively the dynamic of Japanese performance": "(1) Recognition of the country's need to develop a highly competitive manufacturing sector, (2) The deliberate restructuring of industry over time toward higher-value-added, higher-productivity industries, and (3) Aggressive domestic and international business strategies." [17]

In addition, certain important programs have contributed to Japan's economic growth—for instance, tax credits and special depreciation policies, research and development grants, assistance for declining industries, enhancements for smaller exporters, trial-and-error experimentation with high-value-added sectors, government procurement, proceeds from bicycle racing, VLSI (very large-scale integrated circuits) projects, special subsidies, infant-industry protection, overseas market development reserves, the Industrial Structure Council, and of course industrial targeting.[18] Such programs are often referred to as industrial policy, but taken separately, apart from a comprehensive industrial policy framework, they are likely to do more harm than good. Americans have tended to associate industrial policy with significant costs to the taxpayer in the form of assistance, grants, and subsidies, but despite a host of industrial policy initiatives in Japan, the cost of the sum of these programs has been quite modest. It is policy coherence, not money, that makes the difference.

We can best understand the striking success of Japan's industrial policy by recognizing that its separate policy components rest on a deep and double-layered foundation. Those components are the active ingredients in a policy framework comprising a fundamental commitment to growth, a developmental strategy, portfolio management, dynamic comparative advantage, and managed internal competition. This theoretical framework in turn rests on a subfoundation of seven economic, political, and social factors that we have termed the Japanese system.

4

NONPOLITICAL ELEMENTS
OF THE
JAPANESE SYSTEM

These proceedings are closed.
—Douglas MacArthur
(1945)

Japan as Number One.
—Ezra Vogel (1979)

The seven elements of the Japanese system are consensus and group solidarity deeply rooted in the nation's culture; an outstanding educational system; advanced management and industrial relations techniques; an administered financial system; the powerful Ministry of International Trade and Industry (MITI); a top professional bureaucracy; and the core central state. It is the last three political elements—MITI, the top professional bureaucracy, and the core central state—skillfully weaving together all the others, which tie the system together and drive the Japanese economic miracle. We now turn to the four nonpolitical components of the Japanese system: culture, education, management, and finance.

In assessing the influence of culture on Japan's economic performance, two contrasting theories must be considered. A minimal view maintains that Western influences soon will erase many of the dominant cultural strains that have long shaped Japanese society. It suggests that Western individualism will increasingly replace long-held beliefs, emphasizing group needs and a tolerance for authority. This vantage point gives cause for optimism on two counts. First, in this view, as the Japanese increasingly adopt Western cultural norms their rigorous work habits and institutional commitments will begin to flag, narrowing the economic gap between Japan and the West. Second, by downplaying cultural influence on Japan's economic growth, this view maintains that many of Japan's management techniques and institutional innovations can be successfully replicated in the West.

A maximal view sees in the Japanese experience a cultural core that is impervious to penetration by Western influence and methods. This view is generally pessimistic, as it traces several elements of the Japanese system to deep and strong cultural roots and suggests that success in applying Japanese methods to the economic problems of the United States is not likely.

The best choice probably lies somewhere in between. It is simply incorrect to minimize or ignore the role of culture in the Japanese experience. There is beyond question a vital and sustaining central core of experience that shapes many elements of the Japanese system. Conversely, most of Japan's institutional innovations are man-made creations heavily influenced by Western patterns. Although culture continues to shape the Japanese system in ways that are totally unique to Japan, human creativity and institutional engineering, more than the confining dictates of cultural determinism, account for much of what we see.

Any examination of Japanese culture must begin by contrasting its group-centered character to Western individualism. This characteristic, doubtless tracing its roots to cooperative rice-growing, created the group consciousness so clearly evident today. The lack of privacy in Japanese living quarters, and the open offices of most Japanese businesses, both draw on and reinforce group solidarity at the expense of individualism. The Japanese love group activities, from school or company field days, to association outings, to the ubiquitous foreign travel groups, and even to common graves for company employees. A Japanese proverb epitomizes this group-centered drive: "The nail that sticks out will be pounded down."

Underscoring Japanese group-centeredness, Chie Nakane has called

Japanese society a "frame" society. She defines "frame" by contrasting it with "attribute." If an individual says he is a professor, he is referring to an attribute; if the same professor tells us he teaches at Harvard, he is referring to a frame. In Japan, therefore, a Mitsui salesman will think of himself first as a Mitsui man and second as a salesman—thus emphasizing frame over attribute. Observes Nakane: "The group consciousness of the Japanese depends considerably on [the] immediate social context, frame."[1]

With increasing urbanization, jobs have replaced villages as the primary source of an individual's group identification. In Japan jobs are not simply contractual monetary agreements but "identification with a larger entity, . . . a satisfying sense of being part of something big and significant."[2] The Japanese employee is not merely a skilled individual but a permanent member of a prestigious business with a reputation that reflects favorably on all its members.

This group consciousness fostered by the employer renders social life beyond business almost nonexistent, so the business group becomes the basic building block for aggregating interests. In the United States the public company is seen as being owned by its shareholders; in Japan the feeling (legal technicalities aside) is that the company belongs to the employees. The impact of Japanese group consciousness is felt well beyond the business unit, which in turn is part of a host of other business associations. At its ultimate extension, group consciousness creates a final, all-encompassing group—the nation itself. All Japanese citizens have an acute understanding of precisely what it means to be Japanese.

Japanese society is pervaded by a strong sense of hierarchy, and it is by means of hierarchy that groups are progressively organized. One scholar has compared the organization of Japanese society to a formal seating arrangement. In a classic study, anthropologist Ruth Benedict stated: "Any attempt to understand the Japanese must begin with their version of what it means to 'take one's proper station.' . . . Japan's confidence in hierarchy is basic in her whole notion of man's relation to his fellow man and of man's relation to the state."[3] Men outrank women; the old get preference over the young; Nippon Steel ranks number one, NKK number two; the University of Tokyo stands preeminent over the University of Kyoto. These rankings, and many others of much more delicate distinction, are indelibly stamped in the minds of most Japanese.

The Greater East Asia Co-Prosperity Sphere, the political device by which Japan sought to organize conquered Southeast Asia during World War II, demonstrates the strong Japanese attachment to the principle of hierarchy. According to the view then prevailing in Japan, East Asia comprised lesser sovereign states that had not yet found their "proper place" in a regional hierarchy to be led by the Japanese Empire.

It may be argued, then, that Japan's principal war aim was to establish on a regional basis the same hierarchical order found at home. At first glance the Greater East Asia Co-Prosperity Sphere seems to have as little relevance to contemporary Japan as the British Empire has to today's England. However, the economic organizing principles that underlay this regional economic order may presage a future international hierarchy of national economies. A global co-prosperity sphere propagated by economic rather than military means may be the result of this economic drive.

Groups and organizations in the hierarchy are ranked, as are individuals within groups: senior, or *sempai;* junior, or *kohai.* Violations of these social norms present awkward situations. The Japanese word *narikin* describes a pawn rampaging around a chessboard in the absence of a hierarchical right to do so.[4]

Institutional affiliation, not social background, is the principal determinant of status within Japanese society. A person's hierarchical position in society is a combination of job level within a particular institution, seniority, and the ranking of the institution itself within its industry or field. Almost without exception the Japanese relate to one another as senior or junior. Seldom are attempts made to equalize interpersonal relations. Rather, these distinctions and accoutrements are emphasized in everyday life.

Understanding the twin building blocks of group consciousness and hierarchy, Chie Nakane identifies the "vertical principle" as the most characteristic feature of Japanese society. Under this principle, social stratification is established vertically through institutions and groups, rather than horizontally through classes or castes. Any tendency toward class stratification is halted by institutional hierarchy. Instead of workers versus owners, in Japan it is Company A versus Company B. Enterprise unions are a good example; unionism is generally an intracompany "household" affair.[5]

Given the importance of hierarchy and status in Japan, it would be easy to believe that Japanese culture tends to be inegalitarian. But that is not the case. Because there are so many fine gradations, any class lines soon blur into indistinction. Based on equality of income distribution, Japan stands alongside Sweden and Australia as one of the three industrialized democracies with the least income-spread between the rich and the poor.[6]

Upward mobility in hierarchical Japan is for the most part governed by rules of seniority. Advancement may be likened to travel on one of several escalators. Educational credentials and entrance examinations for government and business alike will determine whether a particular escalator reaches low, middle, or the highest positions in society. A meritocratic educational screening process determines which escalator is appropriate. Once the designation is made, advances in pay and status are determined by rules of seniority that most Japanese believe are more simple and more stable than a merit system. The seniority system "breeds less of the tensions and resentments that are caused in the West by differences in status":

> Those higher on the career escalator are seen as merely older persons who got on the escalator earlier, not as persons who have scrambled unfairly to the top. One's own time will come in due course. Or if they are on a superior career escalator than one's own, this is because of their superior achievements in education and examinations.[7]

In contrast to the United States, social status in Japan is linked far more to occupation than to wealth and income. As a result, status is much more easily accepted by those in less desirable positions. By the late 1980s, however, some of the rules of seniority advancement in Japan were being bent. With a rapidly aging population and continued economic pressures, a seniority system becomes more expensive to maintain; it is now being tempered by certain performance criteria.

Although the Japanese are not especially religious, there is a pronounced spiritual quality to their lives. In 1941, with paltry economic resources but secure in the conviction that spirit alone would win the day against personnel and material, Japan attacked the U.S. industrial colossus. Such fanaticism is long gone, but it is not difficult to find new fruits of the same spiritual strain in the "psychological state of war" typified by so many Japanese production workers and salaried-men.

Japan's educational system is an essential element of "the Japanese system." In 1871, only four years after the birth of the Meiji regime, the Ministry of Education was founded. Under its direction, and borrowing from Prussian and French models, a highly centralized and uniform educational structure was established.

The goal of near-universal literacy was reached quickly by emphasizing high-quality mass education for the majority and by establishing institutions of higher learning comparable to those in Europe. Tokyo University was and is the capstone of higher education in Japan. The educational effort remains primarily the direct responsibility of the Japanese government, or at least exists under de facto government control.

Today the Ministry of Education mandates nine years of schooling for all Japanese children. Course content is remarkably uniform throughout the nation, allowing for little regional variation in the quality of primary and secondary education.[8] The social character of the nearly homogeneous population receives powerful reinforcement from this standardized system, which emphasizes conformity to the smallest of details, including uniforms, book bags, and lunch boxes. A remark attributed to a prominent educator in the Third French Republic is appropriate also for the present Japanese educational system: he boasted that at a given hour in the day every French schoolchild of a particular age would be reading exactly the same page of the same book.

Any comparison of education in Japan and the United States quickly reveals a sharp difference in the simple matter of time spent in school. In Japan, with a school week of five and a half days and with the school year broken only briefly from late July to late August, students log almost one-third more time in the classroom than their American counterparts: 240 days a year, compared with 180. More than 90 percent of the Japanese complete high school, but less than 75 percent of Americans have high school diplomas, and 40 percent of Japanese males in their late twenties have college degrees, almost twice the number in the United States. Says Reischauer, "The Japanese probably absorb more formal learning on average than the people of any other nation."[9]

The Japanese education system thus has very distinctive characteristics: far longer hours in school; a rigid system of centrally enforced quality control; a respected, dedicated, and well-paid teaching corps; and intensity of application conditioned by willing acceptance of discipline and the awesome pressures of school and university entrance examinations. These all translate into a system that, in itself, plays a significant role in creating the model employees so indispensable to Japanese economic success.

Although Japan's primary and secondary education system has many advantages over the U.S. system, higher education in the United States is by almost every measure markedly superior to that in Japan. The excellent university systems and research facilities liberally sprinkled across the United States constitute one of our last significant competitive advantages in the economic contest with Japan.

Entrance examinations have played a crucial role both in the Japanese education system and in Japanese society. Indeed, acceptance into the recognized hierarchy of Japanese universities has been determined solely on entrance examination results. Letters of recommendation, extracurricular activities, and grades matter not at all.

Because attending the "right" secondary or primary school may enhance a student's chances of entering a prestigious national university, the fever-pitch intensity of examination preparation often cascades down the educational system, occasionally beginning with the "right" kindergarten. In addition, applicants for business and government positions must also take additional examinations after graduation from the university. All these examinations measure achievement more than intelligence and capacity to learn. Intelligence is a crucial factor, but disciplined effort over a protracted period of time also is viewed as essential to success. Thus, ambition and desire are measured as much as intellectual competence.

The principal objective of the Japanese educational system can be said to be to prepare students for entrance examinations rather than to provide the best education. The examination system has been widely criticized for measuring only one aspect of a student's potential capacity, for putting young children under too much pressure, sometimes resulting in suicides, and for emphasizing educational credentials over development of critical faculties. Still, there has been little or no movement in Japan toward any significant modification of the present system. Reflects scholar Ronald Dore:

> One suspects that Japan's more conservative leaders, though they are prepared to shake their heads over the examination system with those who deplore it, are secretly well satisfied. . . . As long as you can keep adolescents . . . glued to their textbooks from 7 in the morning to 11 at night, the society should manage to stave off for quite a long while yet that hedonism which . . . destroyed the Roman empire, knocked the stuffing out of Britain, and is currently spreading . . . through . . . the U.S.[10]

One of the system's virtues is that it welds together the efforts of students, family, and teachers in common purpose toward clearly defined goals. It provides two singular benefits: it gives the student a solid, high-quality (though unimaginative) education and it instills lifelong habits of hard work and intense commitment to the task at hand. The existence of a well-trained, curious, and teachable work force in Japan today is attributable in no small part to the examination system.

Education in Japan has a purpose far beyond its normal pedagogical function. The educational system has been used as a comprehensive social-selection process beginning in the preschool years and ending with university entrance examinations. In particular, the examination system is an integral part of a sorting-out process completed by age eighteen. It assigns each individual an economic and social role based on uniform, meritocratic educational selection.

In the United States the social-selection process may extend over a lifetime, allowing for several variables: "late bloomers," inheritance, class, family connections, the exercise of skill and cunning in lieu of formal education, and even a fair role for Lady Luck. In the much tighter Japanese social system, the importance of these factors is greatly diminished. The educational system, for better or for worse, carries the bulk of the burden of assigning each member of society a function and status, and thus his or her "proper place." Since the Meiji Restoration, the social-selection process has moved inexorably from an aristocratic ascriptive system based on birth and inheritance to a meritocratic system rooted in educational achievement.

Once educational credentials are established, the employee sets forth on a particular career "escalator," with advancement by seniority replacing meritocratic achievement. This mechanism of occupational allocation largely explains the dedication and commitment of the Japanese employee, from the lowest clerk or manual worker to the highest-ranking salaried employee. Each person carries out assigned duties to the best of his or her ability, secure in the knowledge as to how all workers—superiors and inferiors—were assigned their respective roles.

The educational system in Japan thus plays an indispensable role in granting credibility to the hierarchy of authority that exists throughout Japanese society. Even the political opposition has no fundamental quarrel with a hierarchy established through open competition in a meritocratic educational system. The distinction between managers and workers is seldom perceived as the difference between the middle class and the proletariat. Instead, superiors and subordinates alike share the common perception that personal ability, rather than an unfair society, creates the hierarchy. This minimizes many of the social tensions found in other societies, where social position is based on a bewildering multitude of factors, many of which may seem to lack legitimacy.

From any perspective, Japan's educational system is inextricably intertwined with the needs and interests of the state. One need only look at the establishing charter of Tokyo Imperial University, which proclaimed that learning was not to be pursued for learning's sake "but in accordance with the needs of the state." [11] These needs, from early Meiji Japan to the present, have involved the training of a self-conscious elite to staff the upper levels of the state bureaucracy. Social organization must be achieved not by happenstance, free of state control, but by means of an educational system that is controlled by the state and designed to achieve social objectives extending far beyond even a broad interpretation of the role of education. The whole matter of social organization in Japan is a central concern of the state.

No element of "the Japanese system" has received more attention from scholars, journalists, and business practitioners than Japanese management practices. The salient features of this complex and often misunderstood subject can be determined by looking at the organization of Japanese business, human resources management, and "just-in-time" manufacturing techniques. Three recurring themes are apparent: "Japanese management" most often refers to manufacturing concerns; it is conducted amid a constant tension between market and organizational principles; and its success rests in large measure on the intensive and imaginative management of people.

Any attempt to understand the organization of Japanese business requires thorough knowledge of business associations, the market sector concentration of Japanese firms, manufacturing expertise, trade-offs between market share and profits, superordinate goals, and Japanese chief executive officers (CEOs). Specialization and single-sector concentration enable Japanese companies to be organized into numerous business organizations, both formal and informal. At the pinnacle is Keidanren, an organization comprising the seven hundred or so largest concerns in Japan. Keidanren commands the active participation of its member CEOs and is supported by a large professional staff based in a fourteen-story building in Tokyo's financial district. The press often refers to Keidanren's chairman as the "prime minister" of Japanese business. He and his key associates have unimpeded access to the highest levels of the Japanese bureaucracy. The strength of Keidanren permits it to speak authoritatively for the collective interests of big business in Japan. While Keidanren sometimes is criticized for favoring big business at the expense of small business and the public, its immense influence principally reflects its ability to speak to the national interest. Peter Drucker observes:

> A substantial proportion of Japan's business leaders has for 100 years subscribed to the rule that the national interest comes first. . . . As a result, business management is respectfully listened to whenever it discusses economic and social policies.[12]

The superior organization, sources, and reputation of Keidanren enable it to propound the industrial viewpoint in a manner that scarcely can be imagined in the United States.

Most major industrial sectors are represented by industrial associations that negotiate with government bureaucratic divisions concerned with their particular industry. Cutting across these associations are groups of major corporations in disparate industries tied together by a minority of interlocking shareholdings (often below 10 percent) and normally centered on a large bank. These groups are known as *keiretsu*. Some, including such famous names as Mitsubishi, Mitsui, and Sumitomo, have their origins in the family-owned trust companies—the *zaibatsu* of the prewar period. Daiwa, Fuji, and other keiretsu are non-zaibatsu groups founded after the war. These industrial groups, through their diverse member firms, are especially well-qualified to undertake major projects abroad. The organization of the keiretsu helps to "socialize" risk by spreading it among the associated companies. When a member company encounters financial difficulty, it is often the keiretsu which organizes the rescue effort. This limits the need in Japan for government bailouts similar to the U.S. government's effort in the Chrysler and Lockheed cases.

The automotive industry is a good example of another form of Japanese business organization that provides an alternative to the integrated/nonintegrated character of U.S. manufacturers. General Motors, the most integrated of the "big three" U.S. automakers, produces most of its own components, while Chrysler buys a much higher percentage from independent manufacturers. In contrast, Toyota and other Japanese manufacturers may be termed quasi-integrated; the majority of their parts are produced by dozens and sometimes hundreds of partially owned subcontractors. These medium-sized firms, while usually independent, exist to supply the principal firm. The Toyota group alone comprises about 230 companies, which often are said to be kept alive, but not well, by Toyota. Approximately 60 percent of the manufacturing concerns in Japan are attached in this fashion to major corporations.[13]

Japanese industry is populated principally by single-product or dominant-product companies, along with businesses that have diversified into related products or technologies. The government and MITI both favor the traditional demarcation of tasks among major companies. This concentration is essential to the control they exert over the clearly defined industrial sectors. Specialization in a single sector lays bare the technological foundation on which a given company is based. MITI's assessment of the priority of a particular technology determines the degree of support it will provide.

Supplementing single-sector concentration is a policy of reduced vertical integration. It is generally argued in Japan that full-scale vertical integration tends to lessen the advantages of the division of labor found in firm specialization. At the same time, it is believed, full-scale integration thwarts the salutary effects of free-market competition. The Toyota Group form of quasi-vertical integration combines the advantages of integration and specialization. The Japanese take special care to integrate technologically advanced processes while ridding themselves of simple, routine operations.

All this is not to deny that diversification exists in Japan. But, like so much else there, this process is carefully and jointly managed by top executives and government bureaucrats. Because a company's labor and management are seen as indispensable resources, diversification is internally developed most often through the application of existing skills and technologies to products closely related to existing offerings.

This natural growth contrasts sharply with the more mechanical merger-and-acquisition strategy of major American corporations. Several impediments stand in the way of conglomerate-type growth in Japan. For one thing, to acquire by means of financial power what others have laboriously created is morally offensive to business and government alike. In the absence of legal and moral objections to growth by acquisition, the very character of the Japanese company argues against unrelated diversification. Japanese companies are seen as human communities infused with a "spirit of enterprise" rather than mere functional organizations. Finally, the keiretsu groups of loosely affiliated companies make conglomerates of the American type unnecessary and difficult to establish.[14] American-style hostile takeovers are almost impossible—just ask Boone Pickens.

In most instances, Japanese competitive assaults have been based not on financial or marketing prowess but on manufacturing and technological superiority. A common surprise for many visitors to Japan is the absence of the much-vaunted "factory of the future." Instead, visitors observe with keen interest the efficiently run "factory of the present." Constant attention to the minutest of details and an unflagging quest for incremental improvements have created this "factory of the present":

> "Pursuing the last grain of rice in the corner of the lunchbox" is a Japanese saying that describes, somewhat disparagingly, a person's tendency to be overscrupulous. But it conveys volumes about the Japanese character. As managers and as workers, the Japanese are smart and industrious—and never satisfied. They regard *all* problems as important.[15]

This incessant pursuit of both problems and solutions ultimately brings to Japanese manufacturing a discipline and consistency that are not often found in the United States.

During all stages of production, close links are forged between production and engineering. In contrast to U.S. manufacturers, the Japanese employ a higher ratio of engineers to production workers and build a far higher percentage of their manufacturing equipment in-house. The dividing line between strategic engineering and tactical production is intentionally blurred. Thus the vagaries of consumer demand lose importance to quality improvement and cost reduction, yielding a product so demonstrably superior that it alters consumer preferences.

Japanese managers work to produce low-cost, high-quality products while constantly striving for increased market share. There is a clear stratification of companies in Japan, and each company owes its relative ranking and prestige to the size of its market share. The sense of vulnerability that pervades resource-poor Japan as a whole is replicated by the single company as it fights with the tenacity of a cornered animal, fearing the loss of a single percentage point of market share may lead to ruin. Impetus to increase market share comes not only from the no-layoff policy of the lifetime employment system, but also from the intense competition of the home market. Market share either expands or contracts; it seldom remains static.

In Japan there is a ready willingness to maintain prudent trade-offs between lower profits and increased market share. Japanese managers are secure in their pursuit of these trade-offs because the banking system is committed to seeking growth through more loans to larger borrowers. This imperative of market share growth has helped to create the large-scale structure of Japanese business. When domestic growth is slowed or halted by frozen market shares, Japan's major corporations seek opportunities overseas. It is often the companies ranking third or lower in the domestic market that push hardest overseas. Sony rather than Matsushita, and Honda not Toyota, best represent this international strategy. Eventually the leaders follow, and market share is redefined to world market share. Toyota management now talks about G-12, or 12 percent of the global automotive market.

The quest for higher market share often is triggered by price cuts aimed at higher volume, thus requiring manufacturing managers to attain ever-lower costs through increased productivity. Low-cost producers gain market share, thus creating competitive strength for the company, for its industry, and finally for the nation itself. The global "market share" of Japan's key industries and of its entire economy is closely watched by business and government leaders alike.

Greater market share is not an end in itself. Japanese managers also effectively use what has been described as "superordinate goals" or "the significant meanings or guiding concepts that an organization imbues in its members." [16] These goals, imbedded into the organization by top management over many years, are deliberately vague and ill-defined, but they generally address the aim of the organization and the employee to serve society and "give" to a larger need, so that life has a higher purpose. A few lines of "The Hitachi Song" illustrate this: "We are Hitachi men, aroused and ready to promote the happiness of others. . . . With a sincerity that pierces steel, unflaggingly we strive. . . . Conscious of the honor of our race. Already we are world-famed Hitachi." [17]

The character and role of chief executive officers in Japan stem from the Japanese conception of the corporation. A sharp divorce of management from ownership left the predominantly inside board of directors in Japan with a reduced role, thereby elevating the CEO's concern about employees at the expense of shareholder concerns. The corporation is most often perceived as an association of employees.

Most Japanese CEOs blend into the background of their companies much more than their American counterparts. Often educated as engineers or social scientists, and seldom in law or finance, Japan's CEOs spend their entire careers with their companies and receive slow but steady promotion toward the top position, which is rarely attained before age fifty-five. The average pay of a Japanese CEO is only four or five times that of a blue-collar worker and no more than one-third that of U.S. chief executives. In addition, fringe benefits and perks are less than in the United States. The egalitarian symbolism of these relatively modest compensation packages is not lost on the unionized Japanese work force.[18] Very simply, Japanese CEOs do it not for the money but for the immense social prestige of the position. In a society that sets great store by the principle of hierarchy, respect for the business community, and the status and ranking of the executive's own corporation, give the CEO an emotional satisfaction and honor that money cannot provide.

Japanese chief executives spend an inordinate amount of time away from their own companies; they are expected to be actively involved in the many business organizations. Within the corporation, the CEO's role is best characterized as the administration of the "corporate employees' community."[19]

The unique way in which the employee community in Japan is managed lies at the heart of Japanese management. In Japan, labor is regarded as a much more critical resource than capital; in the United States the reverse is true. The perspectives of the two nations are illustrated by the prominence of the top personnel manager in Japan and the prominence of the chief financial officer in the United States. Because of the Japanese lifetime employment system, there is little labor mobility between companies, but far-greater mobility within a particular firm. In the United States, careers are developed within a given job category but across different companies; in Japan, a career path advances through different functions but within the confines of a single company. Frequent job rotations, coupled with intensive training, result in a highly internalized and efficient system of human capital development. As profits are occasionally sacrificed to increased market share, so too are they willingly forgone in the unceasing efforts to create and maintain a work force embodying an accumulation of technological knowledge. Japanese managers regard the work force as their single most important productive resource.

While in the United States considerable efforts are made to identify and promote the outstanding performer, in Japan much more effort is expended to create good teamwork. Employees are never treated as interchangeable factors of production; instead, their strengths and weaknesses are fitted into place alongside the corresponding traits of others, much in the manner of a jigsaw puzzle. This effort creates the work group, or section, which replaces the individual as the building block of Japanese organizations.

Japanese work groups are strengthened in several ways. The situation ethics of the Japanese lessen the influence of abstract notions of right and wrong. Individuals seek from their own group the moral guidance they do not get from abstract ideological principles. The work group emphasizes and apportions shared responsibility. Because most employees enter the corporation immediately after high school or college, work groups are further strengthened by the natural bonding of age cohorts.

The influence of the group is not confined to the work place; there is a good deal of spillover into after-work activities. Dormitory life for single workers, recreation leagues, company-organized hobbies, and vacations in company-owned resorts all reinforce the primacy of the work group. Building on the foundations provided by culture and the educational system, Japanese personnel management attempts to foster this group loyalty and thereby make the Japanese worker the "perfect" employee. In addition, endless hours of after-work drinking and socializing provide an important and somewhat notorious reinforcement for the primary work group.

A common saying in Japan maintains there are three treasures of the Japanese employment system: lifetime employment, the seniority promotion system, and enterprise unions. An examination of each shows that their common aim is to weld the individual to the enterprise by creating a strong sense of community within the organization.

From the time of Aristotle, political philosophy has distinguished between public realm and the private realm. Unique virtues and obligations have been attached to each, with the household and the workplace set in the private realm, and politics set in the public realm. In Japan many of the "public" qualities of virtue and obligation now attach to one's company:

> The main use of the "public"/"private" dichotomy in Japan was to warn . . . against the dangers of allowing "private" concerns to take precedence over "public" obligations. This is not to suggest that a loyal Hitachi man is as ready to disembowel himself for his company, . . . only that these are the moral categories to the lengthening shadows of which the employment relation is assimilated. In Hitachi the official term for an injury sustained at work is, even today, a "public injury"; an injury unconnected with work is a "private injury." [20]

The excesses of private concerns—which Alexis de Tocqueville discovered in Jacksonian America and called "individualism"—are in Japan partly mitigated by relinquishing a portion of one's private life to enjoy the emotional benefits of the public dimensions of the corporate community.

No aspect of the Japanese industrial relations system has received as much attention as the practice of lifetime employment. To understand the lifetime employment system, one must first be aware of its exceptions: it is used principally in major corporations; it applies to approximately one-third of the total work force; and retirement occurs between the ages of fifty and fifty-five. A dual economy is divided into segments characterized by major corporations that provide lifetime employment and by smaller companies that pay lower wages and offer limited job security. Temporary employees subject to lower pay scales and layoffs are often used by large concerns that maintain a primary core of permanent employees. Although the lifetime employment system has some antecedents that go back to the prewar era, it is primarily a product of the postwar period.

Loyalty to the employer and commitment to one's job are reinforced by the promise of lifetime employment. Applicants who secure positions as permanent employees with major corporations become part of an elite group, a new family. Japanese parents still hand a daughter over to her husband's family, just as families and schools hand over a son to his future employer. There is a strong belief in Japan that self-identity is best established in the workplace. Status within the work group depends on the strength of social contacts, which grow principally as time passes. Recruitment is handled on a centralized basis and with meticulous care in selecting the most highly qualified candidate.

When a major corporation goes to the labor market, it sees itself not as buying skills but as offering a lifetime job in exchange for a lifetime commitment. The abundant training a Japanese corporation provides employees is justified by the belief that the total commitment of employees will guarantee the employer a return on its investment. In the United States, by contrast, such training can be counterproductive because it often positions an employee to secure a better job elsewhere.

The wage and promotion system known as "nenko" is a seniority-based concept that fully complements lifetime employment. The dominant role that seniority and age play in the nenko system enables the wage curve to follow the rising income needs of the employee through marriage and raising a family. The insulation provided by the low intercompany mobility of lifetime employment permits the employer effectively to underpay younger workers and overpay older ones. Indeed, promotion policies generally are governed by seniority. Functional promotion is supplemented by a status-ranking system similar to that in the military, with such titles as assistant technician, technician, assistant engineer, and so on. In one sense, the seniority system may be seen as "promotion by merit within seniority." Individuals may be promoted by merit but will not be eligible for the promotion until their class's (by year of hiring) turn, which is determined by seniority.

The effect of this system is to build on the social-selection function of the Japanese educational system. This is accomplished through a highly articulated wage and promotion process that eliminates many of the tensions surrounding wage and salary policy in the United States. Blue-collar workers feel no less attached to the company than white-collar managers. The white-collar workers in Japanese unions include both technical and lower-ranking supervisory personnel, many of whom have university degrees, who later will assume high managerial positions. It is not unusual for Japanese CEOs to be former union presidents.

Most unionized employees in Japan belong to enterprise unions, which represent all blue-collar and most white-collar employees. Under pressure from American occupational authorities, union membership, which never exceeded 500,000 before the war, mushroomed to more than 7 million by 1949.[21] As neither craft nor industrial unions could have been organized this rapidly, enterprise unions were quickly established in existing industrial corporations. Enterprise unions, lifetime employment, and the nenko wage system all effectively grew from the same premise. Enterprise unions, along with the employment and wage systems, helped to preempt the demands of a vigorous labor movement.

Despite rather harmonious labor relations in Japan, it is a mistake to dismiss Japanese unions as weak. They are, for the most part, much better financed and managed than unions in either the United States or Great Britain.[22] They often rival the company in establishing important solidarity-creating social activities. Nevertheless, union members and leaders alike believe that their fortunes are tied to the success of the enterprise. Slogans such as "Protect the enterprise" and "Higher wages will bankrupt the firm" are tangible evidence of this congruency of goals. The enormous productivity increases achieved by Japanese industry have led to marked improvements in the living standards of the unionized work force in major corporations, supporting the claim that higher productivity produces higher wages.

The three treasures of Japanese industrial relations—the wage system, lifetime employment, and enterprise unions—join with almost every facet of human resources management to propagate a sense of community. In the United States and Great Britain, ownership both public and private assumes a tangible form, becoming a foreign object set apart from the work force. One cardinal achievement of Japanese management is that it has erased this distinction to the point that the employee and the company become one.

Japanese production management rests on two master principles: just-in-time production (JIT) and total quality control (TQC). Just-in-time production requires that goods be delivered to a production station, from either internal or external sources, only just before they are required. This principle goes far beyond a simple reduction in inventory; it requires a rethinking of every aspect of the production process. One of its salient benefits is its amplification properties: a single round of reduction in inventory buffer stocks forces better quality and greater machine reliability and in turn sets the stage for the next withdrawal of in-process inventories.

In the United States, production lot sizes are usually determined by economical order quantity (EOQ). The EOQ is the hypothetical middle point where lot sizes are neither large enough to impose excessive carrying costs nor small enough to require exorbitant setup time. The underlying assumption is that setup time is fixed within relatively narrow limits. In Japan, as we shall see, this principle was discarded, opening many new opportunities. For example, material handling costs are progressively reduced as inventories decline, and with far less inventory and material-handling equipment, storage areas are eliminated, aisles are cleared, and equipment can be placed closer together. Japanese plants are often one-third to one-half the size of comparable U.S. facilities.[23] Reduced lot size serves as the catalyst of JIT production, while large lot sizes serve to rationalize and hide errors in the production process.

Japanese production managers use just-in-time production and total quality control to wage war on what they call *muri, muda, mura*: excess, waste, and unevenness.[24] This struggle generates a great deal of stress, which one observer compares to the performance of an Indianapolis 500 pit crew.[25] With scarcely any inventory buffer stocks, the whole plant goes down if only one machine goes down. The Japanese take special pains to ensure that even one machine does not fail.

Total quality control is a principle based on the idea that quality can be built-in and thought-in, instead of inspected-in after the fact. The burden rests squarely on production workers and managers, not on an independent quality control department. A relentless lowering of the buffer stocks between operations exposes workers to immediate disruptions caused by defective parts. If a defective part is made and handed to the next worker, the production process is halted to uncover the error. But when there are ample buffer stocks, defective parts can be discarded, production can continue, and the defect is not uncovered. Excessive inventories both cover up defective operations and create a second, or hidden, factory for reworking faulty pieces.

Ultimately, total quality control comes to mean error-free production. In a Japanese factory ambivalence surrounds the discovery of a defective part. Remorse is registered, of course, in response to a failure of the system, but at the same time, the defect is much like the pearl in an oyster: it provides an opportunity to gain invaluable knowledge about how to improve the production process. An influential American business consultant argued persuasively that "quality is free."[26] The logical extension to Japanese TQC is that quality is better than free—it results in increased productivity.

The twin concepts of just-in-time production and total quality control are nowhere more evident than at Toyota City. As Henry Ford's giant River Rouge complex in the 1920s came to symbolize American productive efficiency, so Toyota's cluster of plants near Nagoya enjoys similar fame today. This complex, which totally assembles more cars than the Detroit plants of all automakers, best displays the prowess and excellence of Japanese manufacturing. The basic principles of Toyota's approach to manufacturing are known throughout the world as the "Toyota production system." Indeed, so powerful has the appeal of these manufacturing techniques become that General Motors' primary impetus to form its joint venture in California with Toyota came from a desire to gain firsthand knowledge of the famed Toyota production system. Toyota aims to produce the right items at the right time in the right quantity. With successive incremental refinements, the system produces high-quality, low-cost products and minimizes inventory, while simultaneously adjusting rapidly to shifting consumer demand.

Like so many advances in science and industry, the Toyota production system did not spring ready to use from the drawing board. It was born of necessity in the 1950s as Toyota sought to become a major automotive producer. Lack of capital and a limited home market prevented Toyota from adopting Detroit's philosophy of mass production; in America, a vast market permitted long runs supported by generous inventory levels. The mirror image of Fordism—short runs and low inventories—was the guiding principle for the Toyota production system, and that principle was maintained and improved on even as Japanese car production surpassed that of the United States.

Two elements of total quality control at Toyota are worthy of review. Because repeated production of defective parts is intolerable, a high percentage of machines are equipped with checking devices that halt production when a defective part is detected. This method of synchronous quality control is called "autonomation"—not to be confused with "automation." Small-group improvement activities, referred to as quality circles, commit employees to improving all facets of production and quality. In one year, for instance, Toyota production workers submitted more than 1.3 million suggestions, or an average of twenty-seven per employee.

At the very heart of the Toyota production system is a concept that is simple in theory yet painstakingly complex in its long development: "single minute exchange of die," or SMED, which refers to a complete change of die in less than ten minutes and was conceived by Shigeo Shingo, a former consultant to Toyota and a Japanese manufacturing folk hero of sorts. Die changes or machine setups in U.S. automotive stamping plants were usually a six- to eight-hour job. Because this was such a slow and expensive procedure, production runs were lengthened to achieve the maximum running time. In effect, the production system was built around the notion of fixed setup time. But when setup times were reduced from about seven hours to seven minutes, all the ground rules were irrevocably altered. Without the "SMED system," much of the Toyota production system would not have developed. Nevertheless, long after the memory of Shigeo Shingo is gone, the revolutionary advances of Eli Whitney's interchangeable parts and Henry Ford's moving assembly line will remain a clear vision. In fact, little in Japanese management can fairly be called revolutionary. The true genius of Japanese management is in the clever melding of theory and practice, spurred on by an unrelenting, inexhaustible quest for incremental improvements.

Effective management techniques alone—in the absence of the high investment rates necessary for ultramodern plants and equipment—would be insufficient to secure Japan a competitive edge in the global marketplace. Under firm but lessening government control, the Japanese financial system is designed to fuel economic growth in strategically important sectors by providing an abundant flow of low-cost capital. Varying estimates place capital cost in Japan at less than half that of comparable U.S. rates. During the 1980s the private savings rate in Japan averaged three times that in the United States.[27]

The principal advantages of the Japanese financial system are threefold. First, against a cultural and institutional backdrop that encourages savings, the government has initiated a variety of policies that promote savings and selectively penalize consumption. The result is one of the world's highest private savings rates. Second, through close control of financial intermediaries, the government ensures that this large savings pool is transmitted effectively into low-cost capital for deserving borrowers. Finally, financial incentives and disincentives are directed toward specific industries to channel economic growth in the most promising areas.

Numerous factors encourage a high savings rate in Japan. Relatively modest pension plans and social security programs give individuals a strong incentive to save for retirement years. In addition, the absence of scholarship programs at private universities dictates the early accumulation of funds. Similarly, mortgages typically require a much higher downpayment than in the United States, and astronomically high prices for land and housing dampen the enthusiasm of would-be homeowners. Last, the practice of paying approximately 20 percent of the yearly salary in the form of semiannual bonuses has made it easier to save, with budgets and living standards geared to the 80 percent of family income received monthly.[28]

The savings rate is quite high, but the rate of return to the Japanese saver is deliberately kept low. While it is true that a large pool of savings will usually translate into a lower rate of return, this tendency is further reinforced through certain government policies. In Japan, millions of small savers bargain with a few large banks and the government-controlled postal savings system, the latter alone accounting for more than 25 percent of household savings. The powerful government endorsement of the banking system (no bank in Japan has been permitted to fail since 1945) provides a nearly risk-free savings environment, further justifying lower rates. And the government has maintained strict control over the rates paid to depositors. The principal lenders to Japanese business are approximately twenty-three banks, including twelve city banks, trust banks, and long-term credit banks. Japan's central bank, the Bank of Japan, will lend only to major banks.[29]

The role of the Japanese banking system is quite large for a variety of reasons, among them the fact that debt plays a much greater role in the capital structure of Japanese companies than it does in the United States. Total debt-to-equity ratios of 3 and 4 to 1 are common, compared with the average 1 to 1, or 1.5 to 1, in the United States. Short-term debt levels in Japan are twice as high as in any other G-5 nation. High debt-to-equity ratios, coupled with thin equity markets typified by nonassertive shareholders, leave the banks in a commanding position.[30]

Large banks often are investors in companies with whom they have a lending relationship, and they may hold up to 5 percent of a company's equity. The industrial groups, or *keiretsu,* are held together financially in two ways. A city bank will usually be the principal lender to the group and in that capacity will hold an equity stake in most of the member firms.

The group itself also is linked through interlocking, minority owner-ship shareholdings with group members. The influence of the dominant city bank will thus be strengthened by its indirect, as well as its direct, ownership in its large borrowers. Finally, a limited number of large lend-ers provide borrowers with fewer alternatives and incline them to estab-lish close relationships with their principal bank. Altogether, the dense web of relationships among major borrowers, lenders, and the govern-ment might be seen as an administrative system—a "banking industrial complex"—rather than a market system.

A beneficial by-product of the strength of the Japanese banking system and the weakness of the equity markets is the dearth of hostile acquisi-tions and merger mania that currently roils the U.S. business community. In Japan the employee, not the shareholder, gets first consideration.

The paramount position of the banking system in Japan should not be equated with self-sufficient independence and excessive power. What is seen as the power and influence of the major banks is in effect the re-flected power of the government, and particularly of the Ministry of Finance:

> Large enterprises obtain their capital through loans from the city banks, which are in turn overloaned and therefore utterly dependent on the guarantees of the Bank of Japan, which is itself—after a fierce struggle in the 1950's that the bank lost—essentially an operating arm of the Ministry of Finance.[31]

Government regulations limit the twelve city banks, roughly equal in size, to prescribed geographical and service areas, but with sufficient overlap to create a hotly contested market for available loans. This man-aged competition, as illustrated earlier in the case of industrial enter-prises, ensures that banks will pass the low-interest advantage of their low-cost deposit base on, minimizing transaction costs and providing Japanese industry with abundant low-cost capital. Regulatory control of the banking system offers a stark contrast to that of the United States, where the Federal Reserve, the Federal Deposit Insurance Corporation, the comptroller of the currency, and various state departments of banking each regulate a portion of the system with much overlap and great duplication of effort. In Japan there is but one regulator: the Ministry of Finance.

The strengths of the Japanese financial system go well beyond providing low-cost capital. Given the overborrowed position of industrial companies and the overloaned condition of the city banks, the government, as the lender of last resort, is able to direct investment toward areas that will yield maximum benefits to the economy. Discriminatory tax policies reinforce these targeting efforts. Wide variances in depreciation schedules are so finely divided that they have created specific categories for a single type of industrial machinery. Although allowing for the judgment of the competitive marketplace, the Japanese financial system is so structured and operated that it is a powerful and effective instrument of state policy.

Today the Japanese financial system is undergoing rapid change. As the world's financial markets become more international, Japan is evolving into a major exporter of capital to other parts of the world. The strengthening of equity markets has prompted a change in the capital structure of Japanese companies toward more equity and less debt. Credit allocation in Japan is likely to become more subject to market pressures and less dependent on administrative guidance. Despite these important changes, it is probable that for some time the Japanese financial system will remain unified, concentrated, and far more subject to government influence than that of the United States.

Industrial policy in Japan and elsewhere is complex, pervasive, and utterly dependent on deep-seated and interrelated economic, political, and social factors. As defined by the Japanese, industrial policy is not trade policy or tax policy, but a strategic plan that affects every facet of the nation's economic system. As we have seen, Japanese industrial policy has three levels. Policy initiatives rest on a theoretical base and draw sustenance from the seven-element Japanese system: culture, education, management, finance, MITI, the higher bureaucracy, and the central state. Industrial policy didn't just happen in Japan; it didn't spring from the mutation and natural selection of a free-market mechanism. Instead, it is the result of a decades-long process of conscious, purposive, and highly adaptive policy-making.

In George Orwell's anti-Communist satire, *Animal Farm,* one of the pigs proclaims, "All animals are equal but some animals are more equal than others." [32] Similarly, all the elements of the Japanese system are necessary and important, but some are more important than others. Without a strong central state and a higher professional bureaucracy, the Japanese could not do it. The state is the prime mover of Japanese industrial policy. It is the center of the nation's economic system. Its political power holds in place other system elements, which in turn shape lesser factors. Through legislative and administrative initiatives, the state directly affects industrial policy, and it indirectly conditions industrial policy by influencing culture, education, management, and finance. And don't forget: no strong central state, no higher bureaucracy, no industrial policy. It's as simple as that.

5

THE CRITICAL ROLE
OF THE
JAPANESE STATE

*All realistic study of government has to do with
an understanding of bureaucracy . . . because no
government can function without it.*
—*Carl J. Friedrich*

The central state with the higher bureaucracy at its core constitutes the
political dimension of the Japanese system. Through its higher bureaucracy, the Japanese state is the prime mover of the Japanese economic
miracle. In fact, the existence of a central state in this classic European
sense is based on the careful nurturing of a competent, respected, and
powerful bureaucracy.

Japan's Ministry of International Trade and Industry (MITI) and the
central state play a critical role in Japan's industrial policy, the salient
features of which include a fundamental commitment to growth, developmentalism, portfolio management, dynamic comparative advantage,
and managed internal competition. Far less obvious but perhaps even

more important than these MITI-induced and state-endorsed industrial policies is the pervasive influence of the state in developing the nonpolitical building blocks of the Japanese system: culture, education, management, and finance. While there can be no mistaking the heavy influence of the state in both education and finance, policy initiatives that have an impact on Japanese culture and management must not be overlooked. Job and company have replaced the agricultural village as the locus of Japanese group-centered social existence. The developmental orientation of the Japanese state gives a depth of meaning to the workplace seldom found in the West. A sense of hierarchy and the importance of vertical relationships in Japan clearly extends to the state, and in the person of the emperor finds an ultimate though highly symbolic reference point. The often-demonstrated willingness of Japanese business leaders to speak for and act on the primacy of the national interest reciprocates comfortably with the probusiness stance of the government.

The crown jewel of Japanese industrial development, MITI, can best be understood with reference to the higher bureaucracy and within the setting of the entire Japanese political system. Therefore we shall first look at the Japanese state, then the higher bureaucracy, and finally MITI, noting from many perspectives the pervasive influence of a strong central state and a powerful higher bureaucracy. Locked in a symbiotic relationship, they could not exist without each other.

No nation has burst the bonds of feudalism and rushed to join the fraternity of modern industrial societies as quickly and with as much success as Japan. Following the collapse of the Tokugawa Shogunate and the restoration of the emperor Meiji in 1868, Japan was guided toward political and economic modernity by a handful of skillful statesmen. Foremost among them was Ito Hirobumi, future prime minister and an astute student of Western political institutions. As a result of his work as head of the group formed to draft a new constitution, Ito is fully deserving of the title "Father of the Meiji Constitution."

In 1870 Ito Hirobumi journeyed to Washington, D.C., and met with Secretary of State Hamilton Fish, who provided him with several state documents and a copy of the Federalist Papers. The impact of this trip on Ito's desires for Japan's political future was mainly negative. The vast power of the U.S. Congress and the sweeping force of public opinion reinforced Ito's already strong convictions about the pitfalls of popular democracy.

An eighteen-month trip to Europe beginning in 1882 found Ito heading to the capital city most likely to provide the concrete examples he thought best suited to Japan's political needs, Berlin. There he conferred with Bismarck and studied constitutional theory with Lorenz von Stein and Rudolph von Gneist. In von Stein's conception of a "social monarchy" transcendent over both European class struggles and the unfettered individualism of America, Ito found a political theory much to his liking. He reasoned that a central state strong enough to arbitrate decisively among the competing interests of differing groups while preventing the exploitation of the weak by the strong would be capable of maintaining the social harmony he believed so essential to Japan's future wellbeing. Reflecting on these ideas, Ito remarked that "the onslaught of extremely democratic ideas" must be resisted, because "in such a country as ours, it was evident that it would be necessary to compensate for its smallness of size and population by a compact solidity of social organization."[1]

Of a more practical note, given the emperor's 1881 promise of a parliament, was Ito's appreciation of Bismarck's shrewd melding of the imperial prerogatives of a divinely anointed monarchy with a parliamentary vehicle capable of both ventilating and at the same time containing the social demands of an aspiring democracy. The Meiji Constitution promulgated in 1889 clearly displays the influence of the Prussian and German models. The Japanese scholar Tomio Nakano has shown that forty-six of the seventy-one articles are directly traceable to the Prussian constitution, and eighteen articles can be traced to constitutions of various other German monarchies.[2]

The influential role of the higher bureaucracy in Meiji Japan has its roots in the gradual bureaucratization of the Samurai class during the Tokugawa period (1600–1868). The relative smoothness of the dramatic changes brought about by the Meiji Restoration must be attributed largely to the continuity of administrative efficiency this governing elite provided. The wave of reform that swept Japan in the decade prior to the 1890 enactment of the Meiji Constitution did not leave the bureaucracy untouched. The most energetic spirit of this reform was Ito Hirobumi. In 1886 Ito issued his "Five Chapters on Governmental Reorganization," which addressed administrative economy, definitions of official responsibility, and discipline. Its centerpiece was the introduction of the examination method of recruitment and promotion. The "Civil Official's Examination and Internship System" adopted in 1888 closely resembled the Prussian model. It provided different sets of examinations for various official ranks.

With the advent of a meritocratic system based on examinations, the prerequisite of high social status gradually but steadily gave way to educational achievements. An expression of the time, "Birth is much but education is more," was evidence of a widened social base for the recruitment of top bureaucrats.[3] Families with sufficient means to enroll their children in one of the nation's eight higher schools (years 12 through 14, roughly equivalent to the German "gymnasium" and French "lycée") might reasonably expect to have them enter the Imperial University of Tokyo and thus be assured a high-level position. During the Meiji era, four out of five high-level civil servants were graduates of the University of Tokyo.

No single Western university had such an overwhelming impact on the training of a government elite. The Imperial Ordinance of 1886 redefined the role of Tokyo Imperial University from teaching "advanced academic knowledge" to teaching academic knowledge and arts that meet "the needs of the state."[4] Prime Minister Ito voiced his approval of this shift in focus by proclaiming, "Now there is a Military Academy for the Army and a Naval Academy for the Navy . . . , but there seems to be no place to educate public administrators; therefore, the Imperial University should take this responsibility."[5]

The unchallenged status of the higher civil service was objectively certified by a long and arduous educational path, further endorsed by successful completion of rigorous examinations and finally capped by the ultimate imprimatur of imperial appointment or approval.

During the early years of the American Occupation (September 1945 to April 1952) the power and status of the Japanese bureaucracy was seriously threatened. At a time when the Pax Americana held out to the rest of the world the shining example of an open democratic society that showed little need for a centralized state directed by an influential bureaucracy, the presence of a powerful and elitist Japanese bureaucracy provided a target of the highest priority for the reform-minded Occupation. But despite American unease, one of the most telling outcomes was that the Japanese bureaucracy survived in form and function little altered from the Meiji period.

The "power elite" that C. Wright Mills searched for in postwar America—industrialists, politicians, and military leaders—existed in full flower in prewar Japan. The triumvirate that ruled Japan before and during the war consisted of *zaibatsu* (the giant family-based industrial combines) such as Mitsui and Sumitomo, the higher bureaucracy, and the military clique that finally dominated the other two during the war years. With military defeat and the prompt action of SCAP (Supreme Commander Allied Powers) to break up the monopolistic zaibatsu, the higher bureaucracy soon found itself the lone survivor of the three. In the absence of experienced politicians due to the long dominance of the military and the Occupation's purge of many prewar political leaders, the bureaucracy was increasingly called on by SCAP to run the country. In particular, the economic ministries—MITI and the Ministry of Finance (MOF)—exercised undreamed-of power as they struggled to revive the moribund economy of 1945.

Beginning in 1948, with U.S. concerns shifting from the goal of making over much of Japan in the image of American democracy to the role of Japan as a powerful and valuable ally in the cold war struggle with the Soviet Union, what was called the "reverse course" was instituted. This was the direct result of vigorous efforts to establish an economically revived Japan as the bulwark of democracy and anticommunism in the Far East. When clearly defined choices between additional reforms and economic recovery presented themselves, the economic imperative not only thwarted new reform prospects but even undid some earlier measures. The influence of the Japanese bureaucracy throughout the recovery period and for some time after continued to grow. Commenting twenty years after the end of the Occupation on the fate of the Japanese bureaucracy in the hands of General Douglas MacArthur, the Japan *Times* observed:

> Japan's bureaucratic structure was one aspect of Japanese life which General Douglas MacArthur failed to reform. Instead of chopping away at the base of the bureaucratic pyramid, he simply chopped off the apex, by purging key wartime Govern-

ment officials. In due course, the pyramid grew a new apex, much like a starfish renewing a dismembered limb, and the bureaucracy continued unchanged from the prewar days.[6]

By far the most important legacy of the Occupation is the SCAP, or MacArthur, Constitution, promulgated on May 3, 1947. The origins of this remarkable and thus far enduring document were distinctly inauspicious. On February 3, 1947, MacArthur directed the head of the Government Section, Major General Courtney Whitney, to produce a constitutional draft the Japanese government would use as a "guide" in its own efforts at constitutional revision. Whitney's work, known as the GHQ draft, was completed in the astounding time of six days. It was submitted to the Japanese cabinet on February 13 and approved in principle, with scant alterations, by the cabinet on February 22, 1947.

Left to their own devices, Japanese constitutional architects undoubtedly would have crafted a more centralized state, distinctly less democratic in tone and temper than the product of the MacArthur Constitution. But caught between the Scylla of a heavy dose of democracy and the Charybdis of unthinkable proposals emanating from Soviet participation (through the Far Eastern Commission), the ever-pragmatic Japanese made the best of what they regarded as a bad situation.

Despite some broad similarities between the architecture of the Meiji and MacArthur constitutions, the preamble of the 1947 document unequivocally shifts the locus of authority from the emperor to the people: "We, the Japanese people, acting through our duly elected representatives in the National Diet, . . . do proclaim that sovereign power resides with the people."[7] A panoply of structural and procedural safeguards designed to ensure the responsiveness of the government to the people at all times was elaborately built into the constitution at several levels. Civil rights, no longer a handful of concessions magnanimously conferred by a sovereign emperor, were indelibly stamped as universal and inalienable possessions not legitimately subject to infringement by human authority. Moreover, the guarantee of civil liberties by the MacArthur Constitution goes far beyond the guarantees provided by the U.S. Bill of Rights. It specifically addresses the rights of academic freedom, collective bargaining, and employment.

With a life span of more than forty years, the MacArthur Constitution now seems remarkably well suited to the political needs of the Japanese. Because it was designed to make amendment extremely difficult, the constitution has gained in authority with longevity and immutability. It is ironic that, despite the markedly conservative cast of Japanese policies and institutions, the most strident demands for revision have come from the right and not from the left. Far more significant than the right's unsuccessful attempts at constitutional revision has been its more frequent and successful employment of what might be called administrative interpretations. It was largely by means of such interpretations that many of SCAP's stronger doses of local democracy and decentralized administrative control in the fields of education, law enforcement, and finance have been quietly but decisively returned to the font of central government.

The principal burden of bureaucratic government in Japan is carried out by the twelve ministries represented in the cabinet. The three most important are the Ministry of Finance, the Ministry of International Trade and Industry, and the Ministry of Foreign Affairs. At the top of most ministries are only two nonbureaucratic posts: the minister and a parliamentary vice-minister.[8] The senior career official within a ministry is the administrative vice-minister, through whom virtually all a minister's contact with a ministry is channeled. With a term of office seldom stretching beyond a year, the minister is absolutely dependent on the information and direction provided by the ministry's top professional, the vice-minister. Because political penetration into the ministry is limited, it maintains itself under the watchful eye of the administrative vice-minister as a quasi-insulated corporate unity. This helps make the centralized ministries in Japan worlds apart in power from their amorphous counterparts in the United States.

It is one thing for the Japanese political system to create the appropriate arena for sufficient exercise of bureaucratic prerogatives, and quite another to have available a corps of competent and dedicated higher civil servants to carry it out. This fortuitous combination of institutional hardware and a meritocratic elite provides the Japanese with a governing class of extraordinary quality.

Today's bureaucracy springs from broad-based social origins. In the early Meiji period, bureaucratic social origins were heavily weighted toward the samurai from the southwestern domains most active in the anti-

Tokugawa movement. Once examinations became mandatory after 1890, social origins became much more diverse because family status no longer either guaranteed or prevented one from entering the civil service. In fact, it is more appropriate to say that a position in the higher bureaucracy now actually gives a person higher status. The number of promising young civil servants who marry into more socially prominent families serves as an indication of a substantial degree of upward mobility.[9]

Given the few differences among the Japanese in such attributes as ethnic origin, language, religion, and regionalism, the role of education when it comes to values and attitudes is greatly magnified. The importance of education in the bureaucratic selection process is further reinforced by a highly stratified and centralized educational system. While there is truth to the boast that the higher civil service is "open to the talents," there is for all practical purposes one major door—and that is through the Imperial University of Tokyo. Excepting only the French *grandes écoles*, Tokyo University graduates dominate the top posts of the higher bureaucracy in a manner that other Western elite universities cannot even approach.[10]

Almost like a club within a club, the Law Faculty of Tokyo University is chosen by those aspiring to top bureaucratic positions. Unlike law schools in the United States, the Law Faculty at Tokyo does not offer specialized legal training. Instead, it aims at producing generalists by providing a course of study somewhat akin to a combination of political science, public administration, and law. Because Tokyo attracts the most brilliant students throughout Japan—without regard to social and regional origins—and then funnels them through a common course of study, their intellectual quality, homogeneity, and common perceptions bind them together throughout their careers. This attitude is registered in the expression "Tokyo University *gakubatsu* [academic clique]." In the words of Reischauer:

> The higher civil service is a truly elite corps, which is the cream of the Japanese educational system, drawn from the most prestigious universities, especially Tokyo University, by a selection process of rigorous examinations. Professionally very competent and enjoying security in their positions, these higher civil servants are very self-confident in their dealings with politi-

cians, in a way that would rarely be found in the United States.[11]

The haughtiness and arrogance attaching to the prewar bureaucracy have been effaced by the universal postwar acceptance of democratic attitudes. Nonetheless, the present-day recruitment process, culminating in the Examination for Senior Public Servants, launches the public careers of a governing elite with a self-confidence that is second to none in the Western world. Today's senior examinations are built on a tradition of rigorous selection and exceptional performance dating back nearly a century. To understand just how rigorous the screening process is, we should note that in a typical year only 1,300 out of 50,000 aspirants who took the higher civil service examinations passed. The best students in Japan are educated at the University of Tokyo, where the ablest students enter the Law Faculty, and each year less than fifty of the top graduates of the Law Faculty enter the Ministries of Finance, International Trade and Industry, or Foreign Affairs.

At this juncture we must quantify the term "higher civil servants." The total Japanese bureaucracy, both national and local and including the military, numbers approximately 5 million, of which just under 40 percent belong to the national bureaucracy. Out of eight total grades in the national bureaucracy of 2 million, grades one, two, and three account for 15,886, broken down as follows: 1,070 first grade, 4,277 second grade, and 10,539 third grade. According to Robert E. Ward, about 7,000 positions out of the first three grades are truly important, and that is the number we should keep in mind when we think about higher civil servants in Japan. Americans tend to equate bureaucratic strength with numbers, but in Japan, Germany, and France this is not the case; higher civil servants for the three countries vary from 4,000 to 7,000 in number. These bureaucracies are truly powerful in part because their numbers are strictly limited.

While ample recognition is given to the abilities of the 500 or so elite-track Japanese bureaucrats within a ministry, promotion patterns are governed by rigid rules of seniority based on the year of entrance to the ministry. There are no "boy wonders" among the top Japanese bureaucracy; bureaucrats must patiently wait their turn. Careers average between twenty and twenty-five years for those retiring directly from a ministry. When a new administrative vice-minister is chosen for a two-year term, all members of the class of the incoming vice-minister (who will be slightly over the age of fifty) will resign to allow the new incumbent absolute seniority.

Young bureaucrats, upon entering a ministry, are given meaningful line responsibilities, and thus vital experience, virtually from the inception of their careers. Senior officials are fond of proclaiming that it is the job of the young to be innovative, energetic, and on occasion irreverent, while the task of their elders is to temper their work with judgment and experience. Early career paths involve rapid job rotation through a succession of lower-level posts to prepare for greater responsibilities in the future. Careers are normally confined to a particular ministry; intra-ministerial mobility is high, while interministerial mobility is quite low. The average age of Japanese top civil servants is at least ten years younger than their American counterparts; early retirement and the practical cap enforced by the accession of a new administrative vice-minister account for this difference.

Promotion policy with respect to top bureaucrats involves few surprises. After the initial training period, the most promising of the elite are selected to fill certain key slots and are therefore likely candidates to fill the limited number of positions as bureau chiefs from which the future vice-minister is to be selected. The career paths of each yearly entering class of higher civil servants pass upward through a graded series of bureaucratic positions that function like increasingly fine sieves. Most bureaucrats will be made section chiefs, a lesser number will become division heads, only a handful will be bureau chiefs, and just one becomes administrative vice-minister. This process triggers a massive outflow of top bureaucrats into early retirement.

Exiting the higher reaches of Japan's civil service must be thought of not as career termination but as the beginning of the postministerial, or second, phase of a single career. Indeed, for some, the ministerial phase of their career is a time of preparation for the far greater responsibilities of the postministerial phase. Retirement for most top bureaucrats means launching new careers in business, politics, and semigovernmental agencies or auxiliary units of the government.

About 30 percent of retiring bureaucrats are given positions in the so-called "semigovernmental agencies," which include direct governmental enterprises such as Japanese Railways and Japan Monopoly Corporation (for tobacco and salt), and special legal entities like Japan Public Highway Corporation and National Space Development Agency. Some have charged that the proliferation of such "public policy companies" was prompted by the need to find retirement slots for former bureaucrats.[12]

The private sector of the economy attracts an equal number of former bureaucrats, and it is the business community's reemployment of these officials that has attracted the greatest public attention and criticism. The practice of retired bureaucrats securing positions at the highest levels of various private corporations is known in Japan as *amakudari,* "descent from heaven." The reemergence of high-level officials of the Ministry of Finance and MITI, most specifically the retiring vice-ministers, is watched by the Japanese public and press with keen interest.[13] Amakudari is principally a postwar phenomenon that gained increasing momentum as an ad hoc response to the real needs of business and the bureaucracy. The extensive licensing and approval authority of the Japanese government places a premium on the ability of private firms to maneuver successfully through the regulatory jungle.

Amakudari provides more than ample lubrication for the meshing of public and private objectives. The attitude of Japanese society toward amakudari is at best one of toleration rather than endorsement. While specific instances of abuse have not been widespread, it is commonly acknowledged that the demand for postretirement positions in private industry has the potential to weaken the overall independence of Japan's civil service. But as Chalmers Johnson, a leading U.S. Japanese scholar, observes, "From the point of view of the government, it seems clear, although it is impossible to prove, that placement of *amakudari* officials has been motivated not only by a desire to secure post-retirement employment for them but also as a matter of positive policy to enhance the effectiveness of administrative guidance."[14]

Although fewer in numbers, the postretirement political careers of former bureaucrats may hold the greatest significance for a proper understanding of Japanese politics. About one out of four Liberal Democratic party (LDP) House members are former bureaucrats, and a still higher percentage are found among those with cabinet experience, including a considerable number of the postwar prime ministers. A former bureaucrat standing for election to the Diet under the LDP label has an immediate leg up on rivals. While Japan is certainly not the only country where the power of the bureaucracy looms large relative to that of political parties, the numerical strength and decisive influence of former bureaucrats in higher party councils in Japan is equaled only in France.

A student of Japanese politics seeking the single most appropriate term to describe the higher Japanese bureaucracy would most likely choose the word "powerful." The strong degree of consensus between the Liberal Democratic party and the higher bureaucracy helps create a bulwark capable of tempering and modifying the demands of most interest groups. The bureaucracy's frequent role as a neutral arbiter among competing interest groups serves to enhance its stature and influence. Because of the control it exercises over so many segments of Japanese society, the bureaucracy can gather together and mobilize diverse interest groups to ensure that no one group gets a disproportionate share of society's goods. But, in the words of Chalmers Johnson, "for the bureaucracy to have mobilized resources and committed them to a heavy industrial structure as it did in postwar Japan, the claims of interest groups and individual citizens had to be held in check." [15] The power of the bureaucracy permits management of the economy to be markedly less partisan than in Great Britain or the United States. In many instances the bureaucratic viewpoint prevailed when set against the demands of important social or economic groups. [16]

The power of the bureaucracy, compared with the power of the Japanese Diet, lies mostly with its initiation and drafting of most of the LDP-backed legislation. The bureaucratic control of the legislative process extends beyond initial drafting to include a degree of "bill management" within the Diet itself. This capability is in turn based on the superior information resources at the disposal of the bureaucracy. The Diet itself has no independent research staff akin to the U.S. Congressional Budget Office. It must rely on bureaucrats for specialized information. Japanese officials quote a saying: "The original draft is in a 70 percent position of strength." [17] With the technical complexities of modern legislation, the specialized expertise of bureaucracy wins the day against more broad and vague political initiatives more often than not. Occasionally some bureaucrats will deliberately bypass the cabinet and the Diet to establish a direct dialogue with key LDP figures, who in turn welcome a direct pipeline to the bureaucracy.

Finally, the bureaucracy is powerful because it has survived. It has functioned effectively under the Meiji oligarchy, under the activist parties of the 1920s and 1930s, under the militarists, and under the Occupation, and it continues to thrive under the MacArthur Constitution and LDP hegemony. As Reinhard Bendix has observed, a bureaucracy tends to be powerful and independent of the other organs of the state to the extent that it exists as a homogeneous group with a common perspective on bureaucratic authority and responsibility. Despite hotly contested inter-ministerial battles over jurisdiction and policy, everything in the education, recruitment, and career paths of top Japanese bureaucrats serves to foster a common mind-set. And if all this is not enough, the bureaucracy, lacking much of the arrogance of its Meiji predecessors, mounts an extensive public relations effort backed by a press club in every ministry. The ministries work assiduously with Japan's formidable print and electronic media to present the bureaucracy to the public in the best light.

With the possible exception of France, no other advanced industrial society accords its bureaucrats the exceptional status they enjoy in Japan. The public is keenly aware of why the higher civil servants occupy the positions they do: the exacting educational requirements, the stringent examinations, and most important, the arduous efforts and Spartan regimen required to clear these hurdles. Salaries, fringe benefits, and working conditions for Japanese bureaucrats are less generous than in Meiji times and quite modest in comparison to private industry. Hours are long even by Japanese standards; work often continues well into the night and, during periods of intense activity, cots are provided for overnight stays; Saturday work is not uncommon. All these factors combine to give top bureaucrats a well-deserved reputation for diligence, sacrifice, and impartiality, causing most Japanese to regard them as the rightful guardians of the public interest. In the public mind, the good reputations of top bureaucrats contrast sharply with the popular perception of venality and self-serving motives so often attributed to politicians.

The high status of top civil servants in Japan relates in part to the degree of independence they enjoy. As technicians operating in specialized fields, they have wide latitude in administering and interpreting existing law. Their relatively limited numbers have encouraged a group consciousness and cohesiveness that set them apart from the mass of state employees. They have skillfully avoided temptations to enlarge their numbers rapidly, and the more fatal sin of substituting direct management of the economy for more subtle and indirect administrative guidance. Ultimately, the independence and status of Japan's top civil servants tend to rest largely on the quality of advice they have offered and the results of their use of administrative leverage. Their reputation has become closely linked with the nation's social and economic performance.

The status of Japan's high civil servants is made clear by the exceeding deference that top businessmen, often many years their seniors, pay them. A favorite pastime of many business leaders is entertaining government officials in pursuit of "favorable policies." Japanese scholar Albert Craig recorded the recollections of one young bureaucrat who had received the flattering attentions of certain Japanese businessmen. He was treated "with such a combination of respect and deference (English does not do justice to the expressions used) that for the first time in his life he felt the 'indescribable pleasure' of embodying in himself 'the power of the state.' "[18]

All this notwithstanding, the media devote considerable time and energy to attacking the bureaucracy for inefficiency, red tape, formalism, legalism, and, despite its well-deserved reputation for honesty, corruption. And for advocates of more participative forms of democracy the present system does yield keen disappointment. The Japanese bureaucratic government restricts a great number of decisions to the realm of administration, leaving to the democratic arena only the most fundamental and far-reaching social and political issues.

The top bureaucracy is the heart of the Japanese political system, but while bureaucratic government is central to the system it is by no means all of it. In the last fifteen years the balance of political power in Japan has gradually shifted in favor of the Liberal Democratic party and interest groups, at the expense of the bureaucracy. Japanese bureaucrats of today and tomorrow may look back to the twenty-year period from 1950 to 1970 as the golden age of the Japanese bureaucracy. As we noted, Japanese bureaucrats moved boldly into the power vacuum left by the defeat of the military and the breakup of the zaibatsu. During this period, when democratic politics and institutions were untested, and in some circles untrusted, there was no realistic alternative to bureaucratic hegemony.

With the revival of Japanese industry and later its spectacular flowering, economic interests began to bargain with the bureaucracy on a more equal footing. And as democratic politics became a comfortable habit, an increasingly powerful and resourceful LDP provided counterbureaucratic pressure from another quarter. What we see here is not so much a line of development as a redress of past bureaucratic-political imbalance. But we need not fear for the staying power of the bureaucracy. Today the Japanese bureaucracy is still vital and healthy—no less powerful than in France and more powerful than in Germany. The appropriate bureaucratic-political balance in Japan is now as well maintained as in Germany and France. Later, as we look at the United States, we shall find a marked imbalance in favor of the political.

It is not unfair to apply the label "conservative" to the political leanings of the top bureaucracy in Japan, and the more private the conversation is, the more pronounced and emphatic these predispositions become. But the factors underlying the success and its political leanings notwithstanding, Japan's top bureaucracy must be judged as the world's most successful. It has stimulated and guided the Japanese economy from near total destruction in 1945 to the world's second largest economy only forty-five years later; it has achieved this economic performance with the second most egalitarian income distribution among the Group of Five; and by a host of measures in health care, education, and other social services, Japan has delicately balanced the growth imperative with the need for social justice.

The instrumental role of the Ministry of International Trade and Industry in the formulation and conduct of Japanese economic policy can be understood only within the context of the Japanese political system. MITI has been able to carry out its mission of imparting strategic direction to Japanese economic growth and development only because it can draw on the powerful institutional resources provided by the Japanese state. Therefore, the notion that the achievements of MITI might be replicated in the United States merely by grafting a surrogate MITI onto existing U.S. political institutions is unrealistic.

Today's MITI is the culmination of more than one hundred years of trial-and-error involvement by the state in the economic destinies of the nation. MITI's earliest predecessor, the Ministry of Agriculture and Commerce (MAC), was established in 1881. One of the first lines of demarcation drawn between the polar conditions of a state-dominated command economy and a market-driven laissez-faire economy came early on, with the sale of a variety of state enterprises. This was more a matter of fiscal necessity than conscious decision. The purchasers of these large businesses were primarily private merchant houses, such as Mitsui, Mitsubishi, and Sumitomo—the forerunners of the zaibatsu. In 1925 MAC was split into the Ministry of Agriculture and a new Ministry of Commerce and Industry (MCI). The modern history of MITI extends from this time. Historical continuity is quite strong, as most of the top MITI officials who established the high-growth policies of the postwar years were already doing meaningful work at MCI during this period. According to Chalmers Johnson,

> The theme of historical continuity draws attention to the fact that industrial policy is rooted in Japanese political rationality and conscious institutional innovation, and not primarily or exclusively in Japanese culture, vestiges of feudalism, insularity, frugality, the primacy of the social group over the individual, or any other special characteristic of Japanese society.[19]

The worldwide economic upheavals of the 1930s ushered in an era of increased activity at the Ministry of Commerce and Industry. Deflationary pressures and cutthroat competition threatened chaos within an uncontrolled free market. As before, the Japanese sought to learn from abroad. In 1930 an MCI official and future postwar prime minister, Kishi Nobusuke, spent seven months in Germany studying the widely heralded industrial rationalization movement. The lessons learned in Germany helped establish the fundamental principles of the posture of the Japanese state with respect to the operation of market forces that have conditioned MCI/MITI policies down to the present day. The vice-minister of MCI at the time, Shinji Yoshino, observed:

> Holding to absolute freedom will not rescue the industrial world from its present disturbances. Industry needs a plan of comprehensive development and a measure of control. Concerning the idea of control, there are many complex explana-

tions of it in terms of logical principles, but all one really needs to understand it is common sense.[20]

Henceforth, competition was to be melded with government-enforced cooperation through mergers and the creation of industrial cartels. Large enterprises, acting in concert with MCI's strategic objectives, were encouraged and forced to become stronger international competitors. Their success was to be measured not by profits alone but by their ability to produce large volumes of high-quality, technologically sophisticated products.

Given the entrenched position of the zaibatsu, coupled with increasing influence of the militarists, the results of these policies under the aegis of what Chalmers Johnson calls the developmental state did not see full flowering until the 1950s. After the war, the old triangular power structure of the militarists, the zaibatsu, and the bureaucracy was destroyed. Military defeat in 1945 eliminated the militarists, and SCAP insistence on industrial decentralization broke up the zaibatsu, leaving only one side of this prewar triangle: the bureaucracy, specifically MCI or, after 1949, MITI. With the bureaucratic structure still intact, political influence lessened by purges of prominent politicians, and dire economic conditions calling out for action, the experienced bureaucrats of MITI were given free rein to develop an industrial strategy building on the valuable practical experience of the last twenty years.

The smallest of the economic ministries, MITI has approximately 14,000 employees, 3,500 of whom are in Tokyo; of these, 20 percent (about 700) have passed the highest-level examinations. MITI's objectives are broad, long-term, and ambitious, and the tools at its disposal are many and varied. Economic nationalism underlies all MITI does. It seeks to advance the well-being of the Japanese people through rapid economic growth, which provides the wherewithal for so much else.

MITI's operative method is to change the industrial structure by placing it in accordance with world markets and competitive forces driven by advancing technology. To do this it maintains an exhaustive information-gathering apparatus and performs numerous "think tank" functions, establishing "long-term visions" of various industrial structures of the future. It is organized with vertical bureaus, demarcated by industry, and capable of implementing industrial policy at the microeconomic level. It indirectly influences the allocation of capital at crucial pressure points throughout the economy, resulting in differential growth rates yielding altered structures in concert with strategic goals. Means are found to reward cooperative companies and punish the uncooperative. While keeping in mind the need to adjust to changing market conditions, MITI shapes and alters market forces and accepts the market's judgments of the success or failure of such initiatives. Finally, MITI's visions are not born in bureaucratic isolation, but rather reflect endless discussions with industrialists, financial leaders, journalists, academics, and of course politicians.

The success of MITI does not depend solely on its significant statutory authority. In large measure its power rests on its track record too. Major firms, combines, and financial institutions cooperate with MITI because its long-term objectives and visions have been proven correct through ratification in the international marketplace. Much in the manner of a head coach, MITI fields a team of great Japanese corporations capable of winning individually and jointly on the global playing field. Underlining the important role of state institutions in creating the Japanese "economic miracle," Chalmers Johnson comments: "The most important 'improved institutional arrangement' of them all was MITI. It has no precise counterpart in any other advanced industrial democracy to play its role as 'pilot agency' or 'economic general staff.' "[21]

It is often said that institutions are only as good as the people in them. The extraordinary self-esteem and self-confidence of the seven hundred or so top bureaucrats at MITI, and the continuing approbation of the economic community and the public at large, justify rating MITI "very good" as an institution. One prominent Japanese journalist has called MITI "without doubt the greatest concentration of brain power in Japan."[22] In a lighter vein, the visceral concern of MITI's officials for the economic well-being of particular firms and industries has given them the nickname "kyoiku mama," or overanxious mothers hovering over their children's education and future.[23]

MITI has been able to function as the crown jewel of Japanese industrial policy only because of the elaborate institutional setting within which it rests. The Japanese political system, although democratic by any reasonable standards, insulates top economic decision-makers from an excess of sharp and disruptive thrusts by special interests. It allows them the freedom necessary to take the initiative and operate effectively in the best interests of the nation as a whole.

At every point in our examination of Japan's political system, we confront the power of the Japanese state. No pluralist input/output theory denigrates the role of the state; the state is seen everywhere as an independent force whose purpose is to ensure the well-being of the entire nation. Most Japanese believe strongly that the state has a moral duty to oversee the economy in support of the public interest.

Japan's political system, taken at its most fundamental level, centers on the idea of the state. The state requires little theoretical justification, as its roots lie deep within the national psyche. In Japan there is no analogue to France's Rights of Man or to English social contract theory seeking both to define and to limit the state. In terms of prewar Japanese political theory, the defining characteristic of the state and nation was summed up in the term *kokutai,* or national polity. The idea of the national polity, as well as the idea of the state, was given expression in the preamble of the Meiji Constitution, which proudly proclaimed that Japan had been "reigned over and governed by a line of Emperors unbroken for ages eternal." [24] Of course, as we have seen, the 1947 constitution irrevocably changed the basis of sovereignty from the emperor to the people, and *kokutai* is a prewar concept seldom used in contemporary Japan. Nonetheless, popular support for state institutions has remained quite strong, resting on both theoretical justification and demonstrated practical utility.

A number of factors incline the Japanese toward a centralized political system. Being racially, ethnically, and linguistically homogeneous, Japan has experienced no demands for any degree of regional autonomy. Japan is a small country, especially considering the nonmountainous 20 percent of the land that supports the population, but further impetus toward centralization is provided by the dense, narrow belt of population along the east coast of Honshu—the so-called Tokyo-Osaka corridor. Historically, Japan's de facto poverty of natural resources, coupled with its perceived military vulnerability, has caused it to seek solutions through state mobilization of resources. Japan has been called the first of the neo-mercantilist states. If it is true that the world today is in the age of the administrative state, then Japan must certainly be accounted as having deliberately and consistently persevered in this direction longer than most.

Despite cultural predispositions and other factors favoring a strong state, the Japanese have proven themselves, at critical periods in their history, skillful institution-builders. They willingly borrowed from abroad, gleaning a rich understanding of the effective use of state power from Bismarck's Germany and, after 1945, acquiring a taste for democratic institutions from MacArthur's America. But foreign influences notwithstanding, the real political genius of the Japanese becomes more obvious when we note that the original lessons learned about bureaucratic government and state power were not abandoned after 1945, but rather adroitly and adeptly harnessed to the new political and social goals of a democratic society. As Harvard sociologist Ezra Vogel puts it, "No country is more experienced in evaluating the effectiveness of existing institutions and in creating or reshaping institutions by rational planning." [25]

Strong government in Japan is not the same as big government with a large sprawling bureaucracy. The Japanese government employs only about 9 percent of the labor force and spends about 22 percent of the nation's gross national product; comparable figures for the remaining Group of Five countries would be 14 to 20 percent of the labor force and 31 to 50 percent of the GNP. The defining feature of government in Japan centers on a small, inexpensive top bureaucracy managing a limited but effective public sector.

We have observed more than once the crucial and decisive role played by the Japanese higher bureaucracy, and the term "bureaucratic" government seems appropriate. By means of administrative guidance, through corporatist interest-group mediation, the Japanese government has orchestrated national goals free of the congressional immobilism of the United States and the parliamentary U-turns that are so devastating to the British economy. The Japanese bureaucracy has both successfully managed the affairs of the developmental state and authored and propagated a value system that supports the idea of developmental nationalism. While the Japanese state does not stand out amid the group-centered thicket of Japanese society, as the French state does against the backdrop of atomistic and intransigent French individualism, it clearly serves as the preeminent example of the constructive use of state power in the late twentieth century.

Although the force and scope of Japanese industrial policy are original and until recently unique, Japan's political institutions are anything but unique. We have seen the very direct lessons Prussian state-building provided for the Meiji founders, but, direct influences aside and the heavy democratic infusion through the MacArthur Constitution notwithstanding, the essentials of the Japanese political institutions are largely congruent with those of France and Germany. The Japanese political system is not the product of an alien culture; it is firmly rooted within the political philosophy, political tradition, and historical development of Western Europe. Taken together, the Japanese, German, and French political systems fit comfortably into what we may call a "pattern European state," from which, as we shall see, the American political system is utterly distinct.[26]

Hegel set the foundations of the modern state on a delicate balance between the authoritative institutions of the central state and the autonomy, freedom, and vitality of civil society. He felt no more comfortable with the excess of civil society and the lack of a central state in America than he did with the absolutist state of eighteenth-century France. Today the political institutions of Japan, Germany, and France fit comfortably together in conformance with Hegel's theory of the modern state. The political systems and institutional architecture of Japan, Germany, and France display striking congruities and scant differences. The common thread connecting these political systems, and indeed those of most advanced industrial societies today, is the existence of a strong central state and a top professional bureaucracy.

The three pattern European states have numerous common political elements. Bureaucratic development and state-building traditions date back more than three hundred years. The central administrative apparatus is directed almost exclusively by a top professional bureaucracy with only one or two posts occupied by elected officials.[27] Top bureaucrats number between 4,000 and 7,000. Similar state-directed educational systems channel a high percentage of the most able students into the ranks of the top bureaucracy. The common social origins, training, and outlook shared by top bureaucrats, and a sense of cohesiveness and widespread respect throughout society, make top bureaucracies powerful directing forces in their respective countries. Finally, bureaucratic influence is not confined to administration; it has a direct impact on the legislative bodies in these three countries. A significant number of bureaucrats and former bureaucrats become elected officials and are influential far beyond their numbers.[28]

Sharing common bonds of democracy and capitalism with Japan, Germany, and France, the United States is invariably associated with them as a liberal democracy. But close examination of U.S. political institutions, when compared with those of the so-called pattern European states, quickly reveals sharp differences. The lack of a strong central state and a top professional bureaucracy distinguishes the United States from those pattern states as much as the Soviet Union has been set apart by its managed economy and oppressive statism.

When we refer to the political systems of Germany and France, we are talking about institutional architecture and nothing else. Relative economic performance and the development (or lack of development) of industrial policy in those states extend beyond the scope of the present discussion. Comparisons between the pattern states of Japan, Germany, and France, on the one hand, and the United States, on the other hand, point to only one major conclusion: The pattern states have the institutional capacity and political prerequisites to conduct industrial policy. The United States does not.

But even though Germany and France have political institutions similar to Japan's, it does not mean that either individually or severally they are capable of challenging the Japanese economic juggernaut. Given the critical role of leading-edge technology, the game for global economic dominance is probably lost to the EEC (1992 notwithstanding) as well as to the United States. What is significant about the fact that Germany and France have political institutions characterized by a strong central state and a top professional bureaucracy is that they will be better able to maintain their economic integrity and defend themselves against the Japanese.[29] The United States, however, lacks not only the means to challenge the Japanese but also the simple economic tools of self-defense.

For the reader who wants more detail, Appendixes A and B contain brief examinations of the German and French political systems. But if you are inclined to accept the fact that the political systems of Japan, Germany, and France contain many similarities, continue now to Part Three for a look at the American political tradition and the unique political institutions it has spawned.

PART THREE

THE
POLITICAL ROOTS
OF
AMERICAN ECONOMIC
DECLINE

WHAT ARE THE POLITICAL ROOTS of American economic decline? They are unique political institutions shaped by a centuries-long American political tradition. In a different age our political institutions appeared to work well for us, but in the face of a Japanese economic challenge of exceptional intensity they now work against us. They have condemned the United States to economic decline.

If we were to seek a one-word description of the American political tradition, which is the focus of Chapter 6, the word "anti-statist" would be most appropriate. In a great many respects the anti-statist tradition represents the mirror image of the European state-building tradition. We shall identify a total of ten physical, cultural, psychological, and institutional elements of the anti-statist tradition.

The world's first large-scale democracy arose out of the anti-statist tradition in America. For democracy to endure and prevail, it had to be stable; experiments with democracy in ancient Greece had met with failure. The founders were obsessed with stability, and at every turn this concern guided their crafting of America's institutional architecture. They succeeded beyond their wildest dreams. By dividing power between the states and the federal government, between the three branches of the federal government, and within the legislative branch itself, they induced great stability. But the price paid for that stability through the side effects of political and institutional immobility would not be realized for 175 years or more.

Chapter 7 traces the enduring strength of the anti-statist tradition in

America through the words and actions of our leading statesmen. Thomas Jefferson is the philosopher and, more important, the living embodiment of the anti-statist tradition. His work and teachings had a more profound effect on the political development of the United States than those of any other statesman, and by a very wide margin. Jefferson did not create the anti-statist tradition, but we can best understand it by understanding Jefferson.

Only one other figure in U.S. political thought rises to challenge Jefferson: Alexander Hamilton. But despite awesome intellect and abilities, the physical, cultural, psychological, and institutional elements of the anti-statist tradition stacked the deck against Hamilton. His political defeat and ignominious end in a duel with Aaron Burr tell us as much about our political tradition as Jefferson's triumph does. Andrew Jackson, Abraham Lincoln, William Jennings Bryan, and Theodore Roosevelt ratified and reinforced the anti-statist tradition in the United States.

The institutional fruits of the anti-statist tradition are explored in Chapter 8. The upper levels of the federal bureaucracy in the United States bear little resemblance to the top professional bureaucracies in Japan, Germany, and France. Certain elements that serve to define top bureaucrats in the pattern European states are lacking in American federal bureaucrats: a bureaucratic tradition, distinction as a social and intellectual elite, common background and perceptions, and, most significant, substantive political and administrative power. An unholy alliance between a weak and demoralized bureaucracy, voracious private interest groups, and an ever-expanding sphere of congressional influence provide the ground rules for the aberrant bureaucratic behavior in the United States, and consequently for much of U.S. public-policy-making. All this, coupled with the 2,000 or so short-term political appointees—which effectively constitute the administrative elite—virtually precludes the adoption of a coherent American economic policy, let alone the full-scale industrial policy necessary to counter Japan. The president of the United States labors in vain to implement economic policy on the shifting sands of short-term political appointees and a generally intransigent Congress filled with long-term incumbents, each with an agenda of his or her own.

When we look closely at the policy-making machinery in the United States, it's no surprise that we haven't done better in the competitive struggle with Japan. The big surprise is that we haven't done worse.

6

THE ANTI-STATIST
TRADITION IN AMERICA

When the Americans moved . . . to the contrac-
tual idea of organizing the state, they were not
conscious of having already done anything to
fortify the state, but were conscious only that
they were about to limit it. One side of Locke
became virtually the whole of him.
                                    —Louis Hartz

Before we examine American political institutions and their profound implications for our economic future, we must understand the unique political tradition of the United States. In Japan, Germany, and France, strong statist traditions lie at the heart of political development, but for the United States it is altogether different. The American political tradition may best be described as anti-statist. Distrust and dislike of political and institutional authority are as American as apple pie. Americans revel in their fragmented political authority and the hyperindividualism that comes in its wake. The anti-statist tradition has fully conditioned our political thought for more than three hundred years.

As good Americans, "individualism" is the word we admire most; "statism," along with the related words "bureaucracy," "government," and "state," is the word we like least. Essentially, the two concepts—

individualism (personal liberty) and statism (central state authority)—
stand inversely related to one another; the one can advance only as the
other retreats. America has been preeminently the land of individualism.
Under the American system, individuals have been granted a maximum
of personal autonomy to pursue their own private ends freely. Our minds
are constantly bombarded by a host of ideas and images that reinforce
the idea of the primacy of the individual in America: rugged individualism, self-help, Yankee ingenuity, the cowboy, the entrepreneur, the pioneer. Charles Lindbergh—in the popular imagination perhaps the last
authentic American hero—we remember as "The Lone Eagle," and in a
luminous but unduly harsh hyperbole, D. H. Lawrence tells us that the
essential American soul is "hard, isolate, stoic, and a killer." [1] Lawrence's
characterization is overdone, of course, but we isolate and stoic Americans have certainly killed one thing—the desire for a strong central state.

As Americans and as individualists, we feel strongly that our particular
points of view, even our personalities, would be crippled by any move
toward the centralization of political power. In politics we admire the
amateur and scorn the professional. We distrust our professional politicians as well as our professional bureaucrats, although our feelings are
registered most strongly against the bureaucrats because they are absolutely professional, while the politician may lay some claim to amateur
status. Our model public figure is the Cincinnatus-like leader who lays
down his plow and reluctantly answers the call of his country. Political
success or failure, and party affiliation aside, we might ask ourselves
whether we have been more "comfortable" with the amateurs (Dwight
Eisenhower, Jimmy Carter, Ronald Reagan) or with the professionals
(Lyndon Johnson and Richard Nixon). To ask the question is to answer it.

Our fear of central state power goes far beyond the question of political preference or even political philosophy. At a more fundamental level
it rests on a dominant strain in our national character: distrust of institutional authority. Alexis de Tocqueville, finding in America political institutions of relatively modest strength and the absence of an aristocratic
tradition, discovered the source of American social cohesion and authority in the force of public opinion and went as far as to speak of the "tyranny of public opinion." How does our acceptance of authority stem-
ming from public opinion square with our fundamental bias against
authority? Americans tend to accept authority based on public opinion
because its source is diffuse and widespread; in one sense it belongs to

ourselves. But when we locate it specifically within individuals, groups, or institutions, our antiauthoritarian prejudices are soon activated.

Above all, Americans prefer individual initiative and enterprise. Should this favored mode of action be unequal to the task at hand, we join together in a private group of sufficient size and strength to get the job done. Failing in this, we reluctantly seek assistance from the government—preferably at the local level, reluctantly from our state government, and only as a last resort and with a heavy heart do we go to the federal government.

In order to understand the strength and vitality of the anti-statist tradition in the United States, we begin with a look at the causes of the proindividualist anti-statist mind-set of Americans. Despite the perennial popularity of Frederick Jackson Turner's frontier thesis, we shall see that a monocausal explanation of the exceptional American political persuasion is not possible. Instead, we choose from a multitude of factors a total of ten that seem to provide the best explanation. Two are physical: America's insular position and lack of hostile neighbors; and America's abundant natural resources, including a virtually inexhaustible supply of free land. Three are cultural: lack of a feudal past and hence the absence of the scarring effects of a democratic social revolution; the English liberal tradition given most prominent theoretical support in the writings of John Locke; and religion in the form of Protestantism, Puritanism, and the Dissenting tradition. Three are psychological: a pronounced tendency of the American mind toward anti-intellectualism; the psychological profile of those who uprooted themselves to come to America; and an optimistic cast of mind. Last, two are institutional: the structure of the national government as established by the U.S. Constitution; and the federal nature of our political system, mandated by the prior existence of the thirteen independent colonies.

The physical and psychological factors are relatively straightforward, so the bulk of the discussion here traces the cultural roots of American individualism and the governmental forms the founders established as the institutional embodiment of the physical, cultural, and psychological elements of the anti-statist tradition.

Because hostile neighbors, wars, standing armies, and strong central states are closely related, it is not difficult to understand why America in its formative period did not feel the need for a central state. Separated by

3,000 miles of water from the powerful warring centers of European factionalism, and sharing the continent with weak and friendly neighbors, Americans lacked one of the principal reasons for having a strong central state. Early on, Americans had been free to pursue their own private ends with little concern about foreign entanglement or reasons of state.

Several other geographical factors played a part in cultivating American individualism. Sparsely populated, with free land available for the asking, the country enjoyed a mild climate and good soil that gave the land enhanced value. And with the dawning of the industrial age, all the coal, iron ore, copper, oil, and other mineral wealth Americans needed was available in overgenerous quantities. From the beginning we have operated on the premise of abundance; we have been, in David Potter's words, a "people of plenty." Until the late nineteenth century, about the time Frederick Jackson Turner presented his famous essay "The Significance of the Frontier in American History," the lives of Americans were shaped in the vast interior of a nearly empty continent for more than two hundred years.

Turner's influential frontier thesis successfully links the facts of abundance and free land with the wholehearted acceptance of individualism and distrust of central government. In the ever-expanding frontier, Turner saw the broad features of what was literally an open society with an irresistible promise of growth. The West oriented the American mind toward space and expansion, away from the confining strictures of history. In Europe the basic dimension of imagination has always been temporal; in America it has been spatial. For Europeans the term "frontier" meant a border, a limitation sharply fixing the spatial dimensions of a nation; for Americans the frontier symbolized opportunity. In the settled eastern United States limitations and restrictions similar to those in Europe were prevalent as well, and people moved west in search of new land and a better life. Thus America expanded by means of a natural outmigration—an unconscious unfolding—rather than consciously being pushed out from the center through a process of European-like nation-building.

The frontier, as Turner explained it, provided an ever-present option of movement and a second chance. It served as a "safety valve" for limiting any threatening political tensions. Americans did not have to petition the government or organize or revolt; they could simply move. And perhaps more important, if they elected to stay where they were they knew the option of moving was always available. The demands of pioneering on the American frontier formed habits of self-direction, independence, and egalitarianism. In Turner's mind, abundant land and democracy were inextricably linked: "Democracy born of free land [is] strong in selfishness and individualism."[2] This selfishness and individualism revitalized American democracy at the local level and made it resistant and even antagonistic to higher governmental authority. Turner tells us: "Not the constitution but free land and an abundance of natural resources . . . made the democratic type of society in America."[3]

The American farmer owned his own land. In a strictly American context, that statement is so commonplace as to be trite. But set against seventeenth- and eighteenth-century European patterns of landholding, which were characterized by extensive tenancy, primogeniture, and entail, the notion of the self-sufficient cultivator and small landowner was of revolutionary significance. Because only one's own backbreaking efforts cleared the untamed land, plots were broken up and limited to the extent of individual energies. As the magnetic appeal of new land drew Americans west, land was bought and sold, often with great rapidity. The American farmer was a social type worlds removed from the peasants and serfs of Europe.

To describe American farmers as simply farmers or landowners is to give them much less than their due. Compared with the European nobility, their holdings were quite small, but incomparably greater than those of the peasant. While farmers lived on their land, they shared the bourgeois outlook of the petty capitalists of the European towns. In American terms, they were small country businessmen who moved frequently, worked hard, and all too often paid more attention to rising land values than to their crops. De Tocqueville caught the hybrid quality of this new American type when he observed, "The Americans carry their businesslike qualities into agriculture, and their trading passions are displayed in that as in their other pursuits."[4] In America the peasant thus becomes a capitalist landowner and the proletarian becomes an incipient entrepreneur. A remarkable fluidity of capital in America utterly effaced the class distinctions that constituted the reference points of the European social structure.

The social mobility created by America's postfeudal or nonfeudal social conditions is of signal importance in understanding the anti-statist
tradition in the United States. "The great advantage of the Americans,"
proclaimed de Tocqueville, "is that they arrived at a state of democracy
without having to endure a democratic revolution; and that they are
born equal, instead of becoming so."[5] Abroad, the destruction of the
aristocratic social order and the ensuing social democratic transformation have been accompanied either by bloody revolutions or by cata-
strophic military defeat. The American Revolution was fundamentally
political and legalistic. No social upheaval was necessary to establish
democratic social conditions; those conditions were with us from the
beginning. In lieu of a social revolution, we witnessed the providential
unfolding of a pristine democratic condition.

European and Asian aristocracies, on the decline for hundreds of years
and slowly corroded by capitalism and liberalism, never gave up ground
easily. The final dates of their death knells are a tribute to their stubborn
endurance: France 1789, Russia 1917, Germany 1918, and Japan 1945.
But in all those countries the gradual erosion and final destruction of the
aristocratic social order entailed more than the inexorable advance of
liberalism and capitalism. From an institutional perspective, the demise
of aristocratic power required the creation of a strong central state. That
demise came about largely with the transfer of the aristocracies' useful
economic and political functions into the hands of a bureaucratically administered state. And after a social revolution a strong state was required
to stand guard over a society's newfound democratic prerogatives and to
secure them from any harm, real or imagined, by the reactionary right.

America, lacking a landed aristocracy, a feudal system, and a social
revolutionary tradition, was destined also to lack a strong central state.
Indeed, at the moment of the American Revolution our instinctive distaste for the idea of sovereignty was heightened by outrage against the
perception of centralized power in England—whether the symbolic sovereignty of the Crown or the de facto sovereignty of Parliament. The
question in 1776 was one of political independence, not a new social
structure. Louis Hartz observed:

The action of England inspired the American colonists with a
hatred of centralized authority; but had that action been a

transplanted American feudalism, rich in the chaos of ages, then they would surely have had to dream of centralizing authority themselves.[6]

As a corollary to our benign social state, to being "born equal," we inherited a unique political tradition. Because the preformed democratic social state made it unnecessary to ask the kinds of fundamental questions pursued in European political dialogue, the political spectrum is notably foreshortened for Americans. Having no aristocracy, America had no reactionists, monarchists, or restorationists, and having thus experienced no social revolution to overthrow a nonexistent aristocracy, there was no need for proletarian revolutionaries, Marxists, or even democratic socialists. The entire political range for Americans, then, covers only the center panel of the European political triptych; our counterparts to their panels of the reactionary right and revolutionary left are missing. American political extremities reach only to the borders of the European liberal center. What sometimes seem to us stark political alternatives—Reagan's right and the democratic left—blur into indistinction when viewed from the broader European perspective. Historians Daniel Boorstin, Louis Hartz, and Richard Hofstadter have all noted that ours is a liberal society, and comfortably so, and that our fundamental premises are seldom questioned.

Chief among those premises is the role of the limited state. John Locke, whose philosophy is the soul of liberalism, defined it best. The Lockean notion of the limited state is easily understood once we are familiar with the social assumptions on which it rests. These assumptions are essentially those of the liberal society conceived by Locke, and they are very much those of the United States today. The best one-word definition of liberalism is perhaps "individualism." The single reference point of liberal society is the individual. The multiple reference points of feudal society were groups and associations of class, guilds, church, and place. Feudal man was defined by his membership in a variety of corporate bodies that prescribed detailed codes of social conduct and ordered relationships that left the scope of private life severely constricted. As feudal and aristocratic barriers to private action were steadily reduced, the individual's sphere of activity under modern liberalism came to cover nearly the whole of society. The emerging liberal man was largely self-defining.

To present liberal man as an autonomous individual interacting with fellow human beings in a social arena cleared of the corporate under-brush of feudalism, Locke employed the idea of "the state of nature." For Locke, as well as for Hobbes, Rousseau, and other political theorists, the state of nature was not a historically verifiable condition, but rather an imaginative social reconstruction. Unlike Thomas Hobbes's state of na-ture—a warring place that forces people to join together to create an all-powerful sovereign government—Locke's state of nature is pleasant, almost idyllic, and marred only by certain "inconveniences." One incon-venience of the state of nature, according to Locke, is its lack of a civil government. That corporate body was erased with other collective enti-ties when Locke wiped the slate clean to create his state of nature. Civil government, then, is established as individuals join together of their own volition to create a government whose sole purpose is to preserve the natural freedom with which they are blessed in the Lockean state of nature.

In order for individuals to be autonomous, self-defining, energetic, and creative in the pursuit of their private ends, they need, above all else, freedom. Locke is the first of the great political theorists to posit freedom as the supreme end of government. In Lockean terms, freedom goes far beyond the right to do what the law permits or freedom to obey God's commands. As the centerpiece of Locke's philosophy, it becomes an end in itself. Hitherto, government had been in theory and in practice har-nessed to supposedly more noble ends, such as salvation, moral perfec-tion, or national greatness. These goals all transcend individual rights; they make state and society more, and the individual less. Under a liberal society it is incumbent on people to make the best of their own lives according to their own definitions. The proper role of government is to help people secure the goods that they have chosen—not to supply them with goods, but to make it possible for them to acquire them by their own efforts. In Lockean liberalism the role of government is not only limited but also conditional. It rests solely on the consent of the governed and may be modified by reform or replaced by "right of revolution."

Liberalism, a powerful force in the philosophy and politics of Europe, found its most fertile field in America, where within the future confines of the continental United States there were more than 3 million square miles of nearly empty space. Here, in fact, was something very much like the missing "historically verifiable condition." "Thus in the beginning," Locke wrote in connection with the state of nature, "all the world was America." [7] In America there was no feudal remnant, no tough knots of resisting corporate bodies; liberalism could sweep across the continent unimpeded in a single tide. In a subtle and all-pervasive manner, Locke dominates the political thinking of America as surely as Lenin once dominated that of the Soviet Union. The utter dominion of Lockean liberalism explains much about America. It provides the philosophical premises of our liberal and stateless society. [8]

In what has aptly been described as our "unrepentant individualism" and thoroughgoing distrust of institutional power, the United States is very much a Protestant nation. Regardless of particular religious persuasions, or even in their absence, the American mind is very much a Protestant mind—the mind of a dissenter. Edmund Burke fingered precisely this side of the American character when he declared: "All Protestantism, even the most cold and passive, is a sort of dissent. But [in America there] is a refinement of the principles of resistance; it is the dissidence of dissent, and the Protestantism of the Protestant religion." He also noted, "The dissenting interests [in America] have sprung up in direct opposition to all the ordinary powers of the world." [9] The absence of a state church in the United States has made the American form of Protestantism unique in the Protestant world. Of all the roots of the anti-statist tradition, none runs deeper than the anti-authoritarian mind-set of our Protestant founders.

In Puritanism we find the confluence of Lockean liberalism and Protestantism that created the mainstream of American political thought. The word "Puritan" was given to English Protestants who during the period from 1550 to 1650 attempted to "purify" the Anglican church created by the "Elizabethan settlement" of 1559. These "Puritans" sought to extirpate from the church all the superfluous elements not granted specific biblical warrant, including the prayer book, ritual, the episcopal hierarchy, and most important, royal headship of the church.

A Puritan "Congregational" minority sought to supplant the national church organization, holding that each church was particular and quasi-autonomous in that it was created by the individual voluntary "covenant" of each of its members. Absent any compelling governing hierarchies, whether of bishop or synod, the covenanted churches were to be autonomous and self-governing. From this Congregational mode of church governance, it was a short but radical step to deny any allegiance to the Anglican church, and sects that did so were called Separatists and Independents. Among them, of course, were the Pilgrims of Plymouth Plantation.

As the perceptive Perry Miller has noted, the Puritans brought with them the vital political and legal traditions that had been theirs from birth. But what they did not bring is equally significant. The idea of sovereign state power, whether emanating from Parliament or from the Crown, was effectively left behind. These conditions alone—without the influence of Puritan theology—would have provided fertile ground for liberalism and emerging democracy, but coupled with Puritanism they produced an irresistible drive toward American liberalism and limited government.

In looking at the political implications of Puritanism, the concept of covenant within the Congregational church order is important. Those who joined the Congregational order "covenanted" of their own free will to bind themselves to accept church doctrine. Among the Congregational Puritans, then, a "covenant" was not so much a mutual agreement creating government as it was an agreement between ruler and ruled. The idea of covenant is therefore a double-bitted ax: on the one side is the theocratic and constricting church authority over the covenanter, and on the other side is a clear conception of freely given consent. Note the words of archconservative John Cotton, the supposed "chief of the theocracy." His subject was political and religious obedience, but in a more secular context the message was decidedly liberal. Said Cotton:

> There is a strain in a man's heart that will sometime or other run out to excess. . . . It is necessary, therefore, that all power that is on earth be limited. . . . If there be power given to speak great things, then look for great blasphemies, look for a licentious abuse of it.[10]

These words would fit easily in the writings of John Adams. The first part of the idea of covenant, the doctrine of consent, became a cardinal political principle of the Puritans, while the less appealing second part, the binding commitment to authority, was quietly forgotten.

Because of our Puritan heritage, no region of the nation has stamped itself more indelibly on the American mind than New England. "New England civilization," declared de Tocqueville, "has been like beacons on mountain peaks whose warmth is first felt close by but whose light shines to the farthest limits of the horizon." [11] The suggestive contribution of Puritanism to American liberalism and to the acceptance of the Lockean state was twofold. As we have seen, the Congregational "covenant" contained within it the seeds of popular government, but somewhat more indirectly the virtuous Puritan was subtly transformed into the virtuous citizen.

The Lockean state presupposed a certain inner discipline in its citizens—what de Tocqueville called "gentleness of mores" and modern writers term "civic culture." The Lockean limited state was decidedly not the disciplinary holy commonwealth of Calvin's Geneva, nor was it the fearsome Leviathan state of Thomas Hobbes. It had about it a benign quality; it believed in and rested on the restraint and good behavior of its citizens. We are reminded of John Milton's famous eulogy of Cromwell: "A commander first over himself." There can be little doubt that Puritanism made an essential contribution to forging the conscience and self-discipline required by Lockean liberalism. The existence of a virtuous and well-behaved citizenry helped relieve American political institutions of many of the more onerous burdens of governing that were shouldered as a matter of course by European states.

To understand fully the strength of the anti-statist tradition in the United States, we must not fail to recognize the influence of certain psychological factors, and in particular the fact of self-selective immigration. It was, of course, not bishops and dukes who sought opportunities in the New World, but people from the middle and lower orders of society who felt oppressed. Beyond this, it was particularly people with the determination to do something about it. America may have received proportionately more than its share of rebellious, questioning, challenging, and intractable types, who were quick to lash out at religious, social, and governmental authority of whatever stripe.

There is in America a pronounced anti-intellectual tradition that reinforces at many points the rejection of state authority. Recalling the psychological type who repudiated the aristocratic social structure of Europe, one finds that this rejection denies the intellectual authority monopolized by the European aristocracy and church. Instead, we turn toward an American Arcadia where the common sense and practical knowledge of the many outweighed the intellectual achievements of the few. European intellectual achievement was all too often tied to a European social structure tainted at best by privilege and heredity and at worst by corruption and exploitation.

Anti-intellectualism in American life is seen nowhere more clearly than in the political sphere. American liberalism and democracy put great confidence in the moral and intellectual capacities of the individual. Of necessity, this unbounded confidence translated into distrust of permanent forms of organization, which included experts and bureaucratic hierarchy. But it is expert, specialized knowledge on which bureaucracies rest. The populistic predispositions of Americans have always put unbridled faith in the competence of the common man, a faith that makes the putative intellectual capacities of the expert suspect. Because intellectual attainments are clearly hierarchal, they must in one sense be anti-democratic—and thus, in the birthplace of modern democracy, un-American.

Last, Americans are an optimistic people. As things steadily improved for America, optimism became an increasingly self-fulfilling prophecy. Except for the national sin of slavery and the bloody civil war that saw its liquidation, Americans have been spared revolution and domestic turmoil and had less than their share of wars and economic disruptions. All this has inclined Americans to stick with what they had: a liberal society and a limited state. Because we have been by circumstance a chosen people, we have not felt any need for a national purpose and a state to implement it. We have had something much better: providential success. "When one talks to an American of his national purpose," remarked H. G. Wells, "he seems a little at a loss; if one speaks of his national destiny, he responds with alacrity." [12]

In the summer of 1787, when the founders hammered out that masterpiece of practical statecraft that became the United States Constitution, the overwhelming weight of the physical, cultural, and psychological factors we have discussed was keenly felt. Given the difficult task of uniting the thirteen largely independent states, and considering the strong tradition of popular government long established in the colonies, the institutional outcome of the Constitutional Convention in the form of a federal republic is hardly surprising.

Without doubt, the founders merit the perennial approbation conferred by the word "genius," but not on the basis of their contribution to political philosophy. Democracy—or popular government, as it was commonly called—was not created by the U.S. Constitution. And despite the claims of such historians as Charles Beard and Vernon Parrington, the democratic intent of the Declaration of Independence was not somehow subverted by the founding fathers in a kind of Thermidorean reaction resulting in an antidemocratic constitution. Rather, the inspired and workman-like construction of a *durable* constitutional architecture earned them the accolades conferred by the term "genius of the founders." We now turn to the stark conception of human nature that firmly undergirded the constitution-making of the nation's founders: the instinctive and unwavering commitment to popular government, the overriding concern with institutional stability, and finally, some of the devices they employed to achieve their objectives.

The delegates to the 1787 Constitutional Convention did not represent a socioeconomic cross section of America. The distinctions that did exist were primarily between various forms of wealth. Merchants, planters, lawyers, and businessmen had different interests, but they were united in that they were all men of property and affairs. They were also generally ambitious, self-made men who were firm in their belief that many years of experience had given them a full and rich understanding of human nature. On balance, their collective view of human nature was realistic, stark, and even pessimistic; they thought it best to prepare for the worst possible conditions.

These instinctive beliefs of the founders received ample corroboration from the leading intellects among them. Alexander Hamilton, reflecting on the political philosophy of David Hume, wrote:

> Political writers . . . have established it as a maxim, that, in contriving any system of government, and fixing the several checks

and controls of the constitution, *every man* ought to be supposed a *knave;* and to have no other end, in all his actions, but *private interest.*[13]

And John Adams, reflecting on Machiavelli, stated:

Those who have written on civil government lay it down as a first principle, and all historians demonstrate the same, that whoever would found a state and make proper laws for the government of it must presume that all men are bad by nature: that they will not fail to show that natural depravity of heart whenever they have a fair opportunity.[14]

A somewhat more melioristic view of human nature was set forth by James Madison: "As there is a degree of depravity in mankind which requires a certain degree of circumspection and distrust, so there are other qualities in human nature which justify a certain portion of esteem and confidence." [15]

At the Constitutional Convention, intelligence and practical experience were firmly united in rejection of the belief of classical politics—that virtue was the animating principle of democracy. One of the supreme ironies of American history must be that full faith in the good judgment and common sense of ordinary people, and hence belief and unbounded confidence in democracy itself, grew out of the stable and moderately democratic political structure conceived by the founders to guard against human weakness and democratic excess. Because they saw human nature as fixed and immutable—not to be improved on by even the most ingenious of institutional contrivances—the founders sought to create a constitution that was capable of withstanding the batterings and abuses it was sure to incur.

The terms people of the late eighteenth century most commonly used to express democratic political conditions were "popular" or "republican" government. The word "democracy" still had certain pejorative connotations from the more unhappy aspects of the ancients' experiments with direct democracy. James Madison, generally regarded as the philosopher of the Constitution, defined a republic as "government which derives all its powers directly or indirectly from the great body of the people, and is administered by persons holding their offices during pleasure for a limited period."[16]

Several factors combined to ensure that republican or popular government emerged from the labors of the Constitutional Convention. Since this was the prevalent form of government in each state represented at the convention, there was an easy acceptance of popular government active in the minds of the attending delegates. The English liberal tradition provided a strong example of the notion of limiting the power of the executive, but American political thinking went far beyond the idea of limited monarchy. The American Revolution not only settled the question of American independence but also pronounced decisively on the question of executive power and arbitrary rule. "Wholly popular" government mandated that the executive and judicial functions of government be subject to popular control, along with its traditional base in the legislature.

There was still some fifty years difference between the founders' restrained views on voting qualifications and the adoption of universal male suffrage. Modest property qualifications, prompted by a strong belief in a "stake in society theory," testified to fears of the tyrannical depredations of the propertyless masses. This specter was raised not by social conditions in America but by conditions in Europe. Nonetheless, it prompted the founders to exercise extreme caution as they struggled with the problem of the orderly release of popular demands and ultimately channeled them through an intricate institutional labyrinth.

The near obsession of the founders with property, property rights, and freedom can be better understood when the word "democracy" is properly placed in its eighteenth-century context. The direct democracy of ancient Greece, particularly that of Athens, carried with it the notion of a degenerative political condition characterized by turbulence, violence, and mob passions directed against the concentrated power and wealth of the rich. The depths of these fears of democratically inspired instability were expressed well by John Adams:

Nowhere does human nature show itself so completely depraved, so nearly approaching brutality and devilism, as in the last stages of democracy. It has only one saving grace. It never lasts long, "It soon wastes, exhausts, and murders itself. There never was a democracy yet that did not commit suicide."[17]

The cumulative effects of the physical, cultural, and psychological factors undergirding the anti-statist tradition in America made the realization of Adams's fears remote. Nevertheless, the founders were acutely aware that their efforts to establish "wholly popular" government on a large scale were breaking new ground in the annals of constitution-making. Accordingly, they proceeded with great caution, taking little for granted.

The delegates to the Constitutional Convention in Philadelphia gathered principally to remedy certain deficiencies in the Articles of Confederation. The excessive autonomy of the loosely and recently united colonies lay at the roots of the many inadequacies of the Articles. A stronger institutional structure, in the form of a more energetic government, was clearly called for. Having found the former sovereignty of Parliament altogether too energetic for their liking, the founders searched out middle ground between the weakness and ineptitude of the Articles and the potential tyrannies of monarchial or parliamentary sovereignty. An energetic government capable of getting the job done might degenerate into tyranny, and popular government demanded by the American political tradition might lapse into a condition of anarchy. The novel and delicate task was to balance artfully the requirements of energy and republicanism within an institutional structure intended to have considerable longevity. They succeeded beyond even their most optimistic expectations.

Popular government was already with them. History was rife with examples of effective and energetic government. How then to combine the two and avoid the cardinal sin of political instability that would bring in its wake first anarchy and finally tyranny? On this front, the founders were breaking entirely new ground. Energy was to be achieved not by the national government recommending to the states but through direct coercive action on individuals. "What is the meaning of government?" asked Madison. "An institution to make people do their duty. A government leaving it to a man to do his duty or not, as he pleases, would be a new species of government, or rather no government at all."[18] Anarchy and tyranny were to be avoided not through good behavior and self-restraint or through the constitutional ordering of human affairs, but by the delicate balancing of the various sources of human ambitions. The genius of the founders is in large measure embodied in their architectonic conception of the Constitution as a dynamic rather than a static system. Instead of piling up a constitutional bulwark of restraints against a flood of emotions, they thought it best to let those passions work against one another.

The constitution the founders constructed avoided any concentration of political power by dividing it in several ways. The federal system allocated certain enumerated powers to the national government while leaving the remainder in the hands of the various states. By providing for the classic separation of powers between the executive, legislative, and judicial branches of the national government, the founders hoped to thwart aggrandizement by any one branch. And to make "assurance doubly sure," they created a bicameral legislative branch to divide further the legislative power it thought most likely to be the aggressor. The intricate design of the constitutional architecture slowed down and refined popular impulses, but it was in no way at fundamental odds with the sacred principle of republican government. The states and the three branches of the national government were legitimately republican institutions deserving of the title "wholly popular."

The limits of power contained in the Constitution rest not on any formal limitation of power but in the workings of the constitutional model itself. "Ambition must be made to counteract ambition," declared Madison. "The interest of the man must be connected with the constitutional rights of the place." [19] Better to repose trust in the wellsprings of an immutable human nature they understood, thought the founders, than to rely on less permanent rules written on parchment.

The world's first experiment with republican government on a broad scale required new approaches to the perennial question of political sovereignty. It was James Madison's belief that in the past sovereignty was indivisible, to be found either in national government or in a league of governments, but never in both. [20] The institutional fruits of the Constitutional Convention of 1787 were neither completely national nor federal, but a combination of both. Sovereignty hitherto indivisible now appeared in a new divisible form, with each of the states transferring a portion of its sovereignty to the national government while still retaining a significant amount. Madison emphatically rejected Blackstone's theory of absolute, inalienable, and indivisible sovereignty. He saw the actions of the Constitutional Convention in the light of a social compact, creating government where none existed before. Each participant (or state) was to give over to the government (or national government) a portion of its sovereign powers. The federal character of the Constitution, as well as its doctrine of the separation of powers, has its roots in Madison's philosophical conception of divided sovereignty.

Madison defined the "genius of republican liberty" as demanding "dependence on the people, . . . short duration of their appointments, . . . [and] trust . . . placed not in a few, but a number of hands." [21] The House of Representatives alone among the bodies constituting the federal government seems to meet these exacting requirements of republican government. The Senate, the President, and the federal judiciary, despite their republican roots, seem designed to deflect or diffuse any swelling of democratic passions arising from the "more democratical house."

John Adams also saw the lower house as the most democratic branch and the sine qua non of freedom. Like Madison, he sought political stability through a balance of power, although he approached it from a different angle. Simple government, whether of the one, the few, or the many, invariably leads to tyranny, he claimed. Adams believed that republican freedom will be maintained only by a balance between the one, in the person of the President; the few, represented by the Senate; and the many, in the House. Political conflict in all ages, he argued, is triggered by differences in wealth. When all political power rests within a single assembly, it soon comes to be dominated and ultimately tyrannized over by the masterful few. Adams's solution was to "ostracize" those domineering individuals into an upper body composed of their peers—the U.S. Senate. It is the task of the executive to mediate the differences that will emanate from the aristocratic bias of the Senate and the democratic temperament of the House. Adams asked, "What is the ingredient which in England has preserved the democratical authority?" and answered, "The balance, and that only." [22] According to Adams, the balanced government created by the Constitution is desirable because it is grounded in the natural disparities in human abilities.

The institutional architecture of the U.S. Constitution was designed to anticipate the worst conditions. Instead of attempting to bottle up human passions, the founders designed an intricate and complicated system permitting the free exercise of people's ambitions. No movement very far in a straight line was possible. A written constitution, a separation of powers, a presidential veto, judicial review, representation, staggered elections, and the delaying machinery of Congress all added up to a political model of Newtonian mechanics. For every action there would be an equal and opposite reaction.

Here then was the perfect capstone to the anti-statist tradition: a state designed to reign but not to rule, a state established to preside over the providential unfolding of the world's greatest democracy. Louis Hartz described the founders' work as "a scheme to deal with conflict that could only survive in a land of solidarity."[23] The doubts and fears of the founders, and their concern with the "novelty of the undertaking," were soon forgotten. As America succeeded politically and economically beyond our wildest dreams, we began to forget most of the physical, cultural, and psychological factors of the anti-statist tradition. We now focus on and venerate the one element of this tradition which stood as a genuine human contrivance: the United States Constitution, the world's first modern democratic constitution.

7

THOMAS JEFFERSON, PATRON SAINT OF THE ANTI-STATIST TRADITION

> *I am convinced that those societies (as the Indians) which live without government enjoy in their general mass an infinitely greater degree of happiness than those who live under European governments. . . . I do not exaggerate.*
> —*Thomas Jefferson*

America has not produced a single major political thinker to rank among the foremost Europeans, largely because of the all-encompassing sway of our Lockean liberal center. Americans lack the stark alternatives that define the depth and breadth of European political philosophy. We are quite comfortable and secure under the unanimity of our liberal anti-statist tradition. In lieu of major thinkers representing the compass points of political dialogue, America has offered up a pantheon of great leaders who through their words and deeds have created and symbolized the American political tradition.

Thomas Jefferson gives precedence only to Abraham Lincoln and George Washington in any rank ordering of America's political greats. But as a figure of influence Jefferson stands in a class by himself as the symbol of American democracy. One can grasp the essence of the political thought of Adams, Hamilton, and Madison a good deal more easily than one can come to grips with Jefferson. Historian Vernon Parrington—a Jeffersonian if ever there was one—calls him "elusive." The protean Jefferson is more difficult to pin down and hence more malleable and adaptable. Alone among the founders, Jefferson is as relevant today—one might add more relevant—than he was two hundred years ago.

The hypothetical political polarities represented by the nationalism and statism of Alexander Hamilton and the joyous individualism of Thomas Jefferson are just that: hypothetical. The United States is entirely under the dominion of Jeffersonian individualism. Jefferson is very much the conscious symbol under which Americans live. And as we shall see, eighty years of history from Andrew Jackson to Theodore Roosevelt are evidence of just how much this is Jefferson's America.

The founder and apostle of a statist tradition in anti-statist America would undoubtedly have been Alexander Hamilton. Legend has it that Talleyrand proclaimed Napoleon, Pitt, and Hamilton to be the three greatest men of his age. "If I had to choose," he declared, "I would without hesitation give the first place to Hamilton." [1] We can easily discern in Hamilton's writings and work the outlines of a statist tradition and a concern with national purpose. But today this tradition stands merely as a vestigial remnant, submerged under the universal acceptance of Jefferson and the anti-statist tradition.

In the political thought of Jefferson and Hamilton are the polarities of American political reflection on the role of the state. Since the founding of the republic their political philosophies as well as their reputations have remained on a perennial teeter-totter—raise the one, and the other is lowered. But the notion of balance or reputational highs and lows tells only a small part of the story, because for the better part of two hundred years the awesome reputation of Jefferson has remained high while that of Hamilton has seldom gotten off the ground. We will devote more time to Jefferson than to Hamilton, for it is Jefferson's America in which we live today. But to understand fully the dominant role of Jefferson in American political thought, some knowledge of Hamilton's political principles is essential. One cannot really be understood without the other.

Of all prominent American political figures, Alexander Hamilton had the most trust and confidence in government. Among all the qualities of government, Hamilton admired none more than what he termed "energy." The manifest inadequacies of the Articles of Confederation prompted Hamilton to seek an "energetic national government," and he was always equating the union with energy and purpose. Like Jefferson, he was concerned with the abuse of executive authority, but unlike Jefferson he believed that the guiding hand of a strong government was an essential weapon in the struggle to preserve liberty and stability. "In a government framed for durable liberty," Hamilton asserted, "not less regard must be paid to . . . authority . . . than to guarding against encroachments upon the rights of the community. As too much power leads to despotism, too little leads to anarchy, and both eventually to the ruin of the people." [2]

Hamilton fully absorbed the principles of political economy contained in Adam Smith's *Wealth of Nations,* but he did not accept Smith's advocacy of strict "laissez-faire." Hamilton understood that economic well-being must be joined to the powerful motor of private interests, but he wanted to join Smith's invisible hand of the market with the guiding hand of an economically sympathetic and enthusiastic government. How well Hamilton would have understood Ezra Vogel's description of the Japanese economy as "guided free enterprise"! Were a latter-day Hamilton to weigh the facts surrounding the current debate over American competitiveness, he would certainly be an enthusiastic supporter of industrial policy. He would have little difficulty understanding and appreciating the complexities and subtleties of "the Japanese system."

Hamilton had a premonition of great things to come for America—a vision of empire. In the words of Richard B. Morris: "he anticipated America." While the great project of 1787 was the creation of the world's first large-scale democracy, Hamilton wanted more. His image of the good society differed from the images Adams and Jefferson had. Like Adams, Hamilton believed stability was essential, but he insisted that it be animated and progressive, that it "bubble and hustle." And like Jefferson he enthusiastically supported personal liberty and the pursuit of happiness, but while he believed these conditions were necessary, they alone were not sufficient. He was convinced that the personal interests of the individual were bound up in and dependent on the well-being of the entire community. Hamilton's "good society" had markedly less than the maximum room for the untrammeled individualism of Jeffersonian democracy. Hamilton sought to rein in the unleashed energies of liberalism and capitalism, but not in the name of Jeffersonian egalitarianism. Rather, he wanted to harness private interests and initiative toward reinforcing the cause of national greatness. He envisioned a symbiotic relationship between the greatness of society and the well-being of the individual. The Japanese are today fervent believers in these Hamiltonian principles, but in the mind of Thomas Jefferson they were mutually exclusive conditions. For Jefferson, the individual becomes less as the state becomes more.

Energy in government, strength of the union, and national greatness represent deep-seated Hamiltonian convictions that find repeated expression in the term "public good":

On unchecked democracy: "Can a democratic assembly, who annually resolve in the mass of the people, be supposed steadily to pursue the public good?"

On funding for the national government: "How is it possible that a government half supplied and always necessitous can . . . undertake or execute any liberal or enlarged plans of the public good?"

To George Washington on presidential etiquette: "The public good requires as a primary object, that the dignity of the office should be supported." [3]

Hamilton's statist leanings, and his convictions that the community must be more than the sum of its parts, helped breathe life into the words of the Constitution and into the new nation itself. But perhaps his hard-headed realism and state activism were needed far less than he ever imagined in a nation smiled on by providential destiny.

Writing in 1791 to President Washington in the Opinion on the Constitutionality of the Bank of the United States, Hamilton proclaimed: "The powers contained in a constitution of government, especially those which concern the general administration of the affairs of a country, . . . ought to be construed liberally in advancement of the public good." [4]

Hamilton's political thought had a dominant conservative strain, but we must add the qualifying adjective "progressive." The progressive/conservative Hamilton saw in the Constitution an anchor against democratic excess, but in his doctrine of liberal construction he found the engine of deliberate and conscious progress. In his eager anticipation of national greatness on a continental scale, Hamilton envisioned a government endowed with the creative powers and constitutional capacity to meet and surmount the challenges of the future. In Hamilton's view, the national government had to be sufficiently vigorous to withstand the buffeting winds of democracy, while at the same time progressively promoting the public interest against entrenched local monopolies and their regressive tendencies.

The Hamiltonian-Jeffersonian dialogue on liberal construction and expanded power, versus strict construction and limited power, has been with us now for nearly two hundred years. We must be careful to frame this dialogue on constitutional construction in its appropriate Hamiltonian-statist, Jeffersonian–anti-statist reference points, and not on the more familiar right/left political spectrum. It is ironic that the Hamiltonian state (or what little we have of it) has been used primarily for Jeffersonian individualistic ends, and not for the Hamiltonian statist goals of maximizing the public interest.

Hamilton's reputation and America's tolerance for a strong central state might be slightly improved if Hamilton had not compounded bad luck with bad judgment. He achieved great fame and success at an early age; his most creative period as Secretary of the Treasury came during his mid-thirties. Clinton Rossiter observes, "Hamilton's influence was persuasive [sic] when the Constitution was anticipated, prominent when it was written and ratified, commanding when it was put to work, and decisive when it was put on trial." [5] There can be no doubt about Hamilton's genius, impetuosity, impatience, and undue concern for fame and reputation. Personal indiscretions (dishonesty not among them), a desire for certain luxuries, and the unfortunate habit of speaking out when silence was best advised (as in the case of his bizarre claim to have written all numbers of the Federalist Papers) combined to make Hamilton "less noble than Washington, less kindly than Franklin, less virtuous than Adams, and less hopeful than Jefferson." [6]

Something of a Napoleonic quality to Hamilton's life made him more acceptable as a hero to Europeans than to Americans. The substance was there, but the appropriate style was lacking. Abraham Lincoln seldom if ever mentioned his name; eminent historian Henry Adams dismissed him with "I dislike Hamilton"; and Woodrow Wilson did him undeniable harm when he called him "a great man but not a great American." But Hamilton was not without defenders. Theodore Roosevelt declared: "I have never hesitated to criticize Jefferson; he was infinitely below Hamilton."[7] On the academic battlefield, however, Hamilton has at best mustered a corporal's guard against an army of Jeffersonians. Vernon Parrington, one of the more fervent of a long line of Jefferson champions, dispatched Hamilton with the charge "He was frankly a monarchist," and offers as evidence two of Hamilton's less-than-judicious references to the public will: "I am not much attached to the *majesty of the multitude*" and the infamous "The people!—the people is a great beast!"[8]

In the final analysis it was not so much Hamilton's lingering doubts about democracy, or even his arrogance, pushiness, or willingness to accept the hero's mantle, that cost him his reputation. Hamilton's monumental achievements notwithstanding, his fatal liability was his statism and his advocacy of an energetic national government. The Jeffersonian tradition earned and deserved the ardent support of the Democratic party; Hamilton's reputation needed the Whigs and later the Republicans. But because the state has been anathema to the American free-market right, Hamilton was denied this necessary constituency. America has been a nation steeped in the anti-statist tradition, a country that simply didn't need Hamilton's way of doing things.

The inscription on Jefferson's tombstone memorializes him as "author of the Declaration of American Independence, the Statute of Virginia for religious freedom, and Father of the University of Virginia." Had Jefferson not written the Declaration of Independence, his intrinsic greatness would have been little diminished. But his fortuitous association with that sacred document forever aligned his name with democracy and causes him to stand alone as the symbol of American democracy and American greatness.

The first sentence of the second paragraph of the Declaration summarizes the political philosophy of the United States in only 111 words. It is a liberal democratic philosophy, and the Declaration marks the first attempt to found a nation on these principles:

> We hold these truths to be self-evident: that all men are created equal; that they are endowed by their Creator with certain inalienable rights; that among these are life, liberty, and the pursuit of happiness; that to secure these rights, governments are instituted among men, deriving their just powers from the consent of the governed; that whenever any form of government becomes destructive of these ends, it is the right of the people to alter or to abolish it, and to institute new government, laying its foundation on such principles, and organizing its powers in such form, as to them shall seem most likely to effect their safety and happiness.

The liberal part of it, without doubt, came from Locke, for Lockean ideas were in the air. "Where Jefferson got his ideas," observed Carl Becker, "is hardly so much a question as where he could have got away from them." [9] In Great Britain it was a long way from Locke to the advent of democracy late into the nineteenth century, but in America it was only a short step, given the absence of the heavy hand of an aristocracy.

As the Declaration of Independence represented the full flowering of Lockean liberalism and an auspicious beginning for democracy, it marked the starting point—year zero—for the not yet constituted United States of America. As America became rich and powerful, succeeding well beyond the founders' expectations, the Declaration took on a more solemn significance than either Adams or Jefferson had thought possible.

The Declaration of Independence called forth a revolution. Although more political and legal than social, it was the beginning of what historian R. R. Palmer called "the Age of Democratic Revolution." Because the Declaration bound together liberalism, democracy, democratic revolution, and America itself, Jefferson's name was inextricably intertwined with all those forces. As America succeeded, so did Jefferson. In the popular imagination he became very much the author of the "Declaration of Democracy."

Jefferson was fortunate to be called on to author the Declaration, and he was in another sense fortunate to be in Europe and absent during the deliberations of the 1787 Constitutional Convention. The task of that convention was a good deal more difficult and complex than the job of 1776. There were hard-bargained trade-offs and tough decisions, resulting in compromises that gave critics of all persuasions something to dislike. In 1787 the democratic precepts embodied in the world's first democratic republic seemed a bold experiment. A century later, as we came to take democracy's success in America for granted, the Constitution became an immovable roadblock in the minds of many ardent democrats, who favored a more egalitarian society. The democratic left saw the Constitution as thwarting the nation's fullest expression of their desired democratic impulse. These antidemocratic charges against the Constitution emanated from numerous quarters. The best example is Charles Beard's famous 1913 work, *An Economic Interpretation of the Constitution.*

Because Jefferson was in France during the Constitutional Convention, he escaped responsibility for any supposed democratic shortcomings of the Constitution. In fact, Jefferson was in the main favorably inclined toward the document, recommending only a bill of rights and expressing reservations about the ability of the president to succeed himself. But he did sharply attack what he regarded as the Hamiltonian-Federalist perversion of the Constitution's democratic intent. So Jefferson had it best on both counts: he was present in 1776 to sound democracy's clarion call and absent for the uncertain trumpet of 1787.

Confident that America was moving in the direction he thought best, Jefferson proudly announced in his first inaugural: "We are all republicans—we are all federalists." [10] What was it then that yielded unity after the sharp clashes of the Federalist period? Jefferson said:

> A wise and frugal government, which shall restrain men from injuring one another, which shall leave them otherwise free to regulate their own pursuits of industry and improvement, and shall not take from the mouth of labor the bread it has earned. [11]

That is pure Locke, with the individual sanctified and the state limited and little needed. There is no vision of empire here; no call for sacrifices in favor of the public interest; no room for the public good, aside from the private interests and well-being of the individual. Hamilton's brief attempt to get America outside itself, to use uncommon means in pursuit of uncommon ends, was doomed to failure. Hamiltonian means, when they were used at all, were now employed in the service of Jeffersonian ends.

While Jefferson is remembered best as the quintessential American democrat, his democracy was always liberal democracy. At the hard-fixed core of his thought, he was a liberal first and a democrat second. Egalitarianism was desirable, but not at the cost of restricting individual freedom. His unqualified and "unrepentant individualism" has given his reputation resilience and durability. He has been the champion of all parties. William Jennings Bryan and Mark Hanna, as well as Huey Long and Franklin Roosevelt, could all lay claim to the Jeffersonian mantle.

The social base on which Jefferson erected his liberal democratic political philosophy was explicitly agrarian. "Those who labour in the earth are the chosen people of God, if ever he had a chosen people," he declared. "Corruption of morals in the mass of cultivators is a phenomenon of which no age nor nation has furnished an example."[12] Through one quality above all others, the American farmer appealed to Jefferson as the model democratic citizen: his independence. From this single axiom flowed a host of corollaries upon which he established his political beliefs. The simple fact of landownership gave the farmer security unknown to the propertyless wage earner. With subsistence agriculture of greater importance than commercial agriculture, at least in Jefferson's eyes, self-sufficiency was added to security. As cultivation of the land exacted an unrelenting demand for hard work and self-discipline, it shaped the character of the agrarian into forms that were conducive to democratic society. Finally, with the extent of a person's domains and wealth directly proportional to the sum of his or her own efforts, most citizens were destined toward middling prosperity, eliminating extremes of wealth and poverty.

Much of what Jefferson idealized about the moral primacy of the yeoman farmer was based on fact, but ominous storm clouds were on the horizon in the form of the dawning of the industrial age. In one sense Jefferson discovered more about the virtues of agrarian America in Europe than in his native land. In Europe, Jefferson was exposed to a complex, commercial, urban, and newly industrializing society, and he did not like what he saw: manufacturing, urban classes, cities, and, hovering over all else, the authority of a strong state. There was no relief from this bleak picture when he turned to the land, where he saw remnants of the feudal chain of dependence still submerging personal identity in the service of a suffocating social system.

Jefferson lived long enough to see that his hopes for an agrarian-based democracy of small landholders in America no longer squared with the widespread growth of manufacturing. In 1816 he wrote, "We must now place the manufacturer by the side of the agriculturist." [13] But if Jefferson erred initially by underestimating the importance of manufacturing as against Hamilton's more prophetic pronouncements on America's industrial future, his conception of the moral primacy of the yeoman farmer forms one of the central myths of our society. America's independent farmers became a permanent fixture in the American imagination. Even today we still speak of "grass-roots democracy."

Much of Jefferson's antipathy to the authority of the state stems from his conception of human nature, which is in stark contrast to the somber judgments of the other founders and thus to the philosophy of the Constitution itself. Jefferson puts everyone in one of two groups: those who trust the people and those who fear the people. "I cannot act as if all men were unfaithful," he argued, "because some are so; nor believe all will betray me, because some do. I had rather be the victim of occasional infidelities." [14] Rather than following the founders in preparing for the worst, Jefferson keenly anticipated the most favorable circumstances. While the founders were apprehensive, Jefferson was optimistic.

Jefferson believed that, given the favorable environment of the New World, the people could do little wrong. He felt preservation of order was less important than ample opportunity for self-expression and self-realization. Jefferson's faith in human nature extended to a deep-seated confidence in the sanctity of the will of the majority—and his writings are devoid of references to any fear of the majority. It followed, then, that where the people are governed by their own integrity and good sense, political authority can be reduced to a minimum.

Jeffersonian democracy, as Jefferson conceived it and later generations reflected on it, was local and populistic. Having grown up in what was at that time the West, Jefferson thought of democracy in the frontier sense, involving local citizens dealing with and solving local problems. His love of direct local democracy goes a long way toward explaining his preference for the locality over the state and his ardent defense of states' rights against the national authority of the federal government. National banks, the federal judiciary, and all other newly created federal apparatus, in Jefferson's mind, sapped the vitality and independence of the locality and the individual. Hamilton, the Federalists, and the modest governing apparatus they helped establish earned Jefferson's unyielding opposition. He frequently hurled against them the damning and damaging charge of being "undemocratic."

Jefferson's unbounded faith in the inherent goodness of the people, and his emphasis on direct local democracy, led him to share with Pericles the belief that government was everybody's business. Because the people were capable and the issues were simple and straightforward, government did not at any level require professional politicians or bureaucratic functionaries. The citizen-volunteer who reluctantly shoulders the burdens of public responsibility and then eagerly returns to the greater joys of private life stands as the Jeffersonian model of the non-professional public servant.

Europe, however, saw society's competence as emanating from a central administrative core peopled by an intellectually certifiable elite. As the Old World coercive state was absent in America, so were its professional administrators and experts. In America, with its more socially homogeneous population, its agrarian economy, and its pervasive decentralization, there was no need for an intellectual elite to cut the Gordian knot of social complexity. Sufficient wisdom could be generated from the public themselves, and the role of government was to be largely eliminated by its absorption into society.[15] "This preference for the wisdom of the common man," observed Richard Hofstadter, "flowered, in the most extreme statements of the democratic creed, into a kind of militant popular anti-intellectualism."[16] The tradition of Jeffersonian democracy then builds on and reinforces an anti-intellectual tradition in America, both finding in the central state their most vulnerable target.

As a further guarantee that political power remained close to the people, Jefferson marshaled arguments in support of the right of revolution. The philosophy of the Declaration of Independence affirmed the right of the people both to establish a new government and to overthrow an existing one. When fears about threatened political instability ran high during Shays's Rebellion (1786–87), Jefferson wrote to Madison: "I hold it that a little rebellion now and then is a good thing, and as necessary in the political world as storms in the physical. . . . It is a medicine necessary for the sound health of government."[17] In a nation where political stability had put down deep roots, Jefferson believed that opposition to government—and even, on occasion, rebellion—could do little if any harm, and more likely much good.

Jefferson's idea of the social contract was clearly at odds with Burke's notion of a contract between "the dead, living, and yet unborn." Jefferson believed a generational span of twenty years was a reasonable life for a constitution. "The earth belongs in usufruct to the living," he proclaimed. "The dead have neither powers nor rights over it."[18] The practical difficulties implicit in his defense of the sovereign constitution-making rights of each generation seemed of little concern to Jefferson.

A necessary corollary to Jefferson's doctrine of the right of revolution was his staunch support of states' rights against actual or purported encroachments by the national government. Within the American political tradition, Jefferson stands second only to John Calhoun as a defender of states' rights. Jefferson saw the principle of states' rights as deriving from the more fundamental doctrines of individual liberty and self-government. It was a means by which to move government toward the ideal condition of direct local democracy. The vehemence of Jefferson's arguments in the Kentucky Resolutions of 1798 made him a hero of the nullifiers and did some damage to his otherwise invincible reputation in the aftermath of the Civil War.

Jefferson was very much a child of the Enlightenment, and as a result his thinking was thoroughly suffused with a high degree of optimism. He was convinced that the dreams of the Enlightenment thinkers were destined to be fulfilled not in Europe but in America. For Jefferson the past was not the repository of the wisdom of the ages it was for Burke, but rather a voluminous catalog of ignorance and miseries. Because America was new, it was not burdened with sins of history. As democracy and America marched forward hand in hand, one strengthening the other, Jeffersonian optimism became a self-fulfilling prophecy. "Through all Jefferson's work," Hofstadter tells us, "there runs like a fresh underground stream the deep conviction that all will turn out well, that life will somehow assert itself."[19]

Henry Adams remarked that Jefferson could not be portrayed with "a few broad strokes of the brush, . . . only touch by touch with a fine pencil." [20] There is little doubt about the positions of John Adams, Hamilton, and Madison within the American political tradition, but because Jefferson is a larger and more protean figure than any of the other founders, his reputation avoids the damaging charges leveled at many of the more specific doctrines of his contemporaries. While we continue to associate John Adams with balanced government, Alexander Hamilton with energetic government, and James Madison with the "extended sphere" and the Constitution itself, it was through Jefferson's foresight, courage, and good fortune that the unbreakable bonds between Jefferson's name and the magic word "democracy" were forged. In an unkind but not altogether inaccurate description of Jefferson's sensitivity to the judgment of posterity, Hamilton said: "He is as likely as any man I know to temporize—to calculate what will be likely to promote his own reputation and advantage." [21]

About Jefferson there are few negatives—not the narrow-mindedness of Adams, not the tendency toward megalomania of Hamilton. His reputation is richly earned: philosopher, scientist, inventor, statesman, educator, patriot, humanist, and above all, democrat. If it may be said that his association with democracy catapulted his reputation into the stratosphere, then let it be said also that he struck great blows on democracy's behalf. His commitment to democracy was ardent when that of others was lukewarm.

One of the principal factors underlying the strength and durability of Jefferson's reputation is its open-ended quality. At the very least, Jeffersonian democracy has about it a distinctly egalitarian cast; it speaks on behalf of the common man. But when we refer to an egalitarian Jefferson, we must be careful to use the words "cast" or "flavor" instead of "doctrine." Jefferson's egalitarian persuasion had an indeterminate condition about it. When we turn to Jefferson as the champion of liberty, the defender of individualism, and the opponent of the state, however, we may comfortably refer to absolute conditions—to doctrine. The dominant liberal side of the Jeffersonian heritage is summed up well by Hofstadter: "It was not, after all, a system of economics or politics that he was leaving, not even a political party, but an imperishable faith expressed in imperishable rhetoric." [22]

The amazing strength of Jefferson's reputation rests on its ability to cut both ways. While the decades of rapid industrialization that followed the Civil War sounded the death knell of the yeoman democracy he helped idealize, Jefferson not only prevailed but triumphed by riding easily in the two opposing camps. His agrarian, populist, and egalitarian side endeared him to William Jennings Bryan and the Populists; his unqualified support of liberty, individualism, a laissez-faire economy, and a minimal state placed him in sympathy with Herbert Spencer's social Darwinism; and industrialists Andrew Carnegie and John D. Rockefeller easily claimed Jefferson as a defender of free enterprise and an opponent of government intervention.

Amid nearly universal acclaim for Jefferson, there were some critics. Henry Randall, author of the then definitive *Life of Jefferson* (1858), writing to the great Whig advocate Lord Macaulay, received a disappointing response. Macaulay was long remembered for asserting, "Your Constitution is all sail and no anchor." He attributed America's rapid and unquestioned political and economic progress not to Jeffersonian liberal-democratic principles or to the limited state but to the country's vast land and abundant natural resources. Macaulay argued that the true test of Jeffersonian individualism as against Hamiltonian statism would come only at some distant date—when America's resources were pinched, requiring her to stand against other nations on an equal footing. They are prophetic words today.

It is difficult to overstate Jefferson's apotheosis of the individual in a liberal democratic society and his great disdain for the state and its energetic efforts aimed at the public good. However, an admiring biographer of Alexander Hamilton, F. S. Oliver, comes close when he tells us:

> [Jefferson] would have rejoiced to see the state a dismasted hulk, so confident was he that by the action of beneficent and eternal currents, she would drift for ever upon a smiling sea, within bow-shot of the delectable islands, without the aid of sails or rudder.[23]

Whether Jefferson might have pleaded for some qualification of Oliver's charge is of little consequence. What is important is that an army of Jeffersonian standard-bearers have been fervent believers in this image of America as a stateless society. Time and again, Jefferson placed personal liberty as his highest value without exception; he posited a visceral dislike of government as an oppressive tool of the rich, the powerful, and the well-born. At times his hatred of European statism drove him close to a position of philosophical anarchism. In a letter to Edward Carrington, he wrote:

> I am convinced that those societies (as the Indians) which live without government enjoy in their general mass an infinitely greater degree of happiness than those who live under European governments. Among the former, public opinion is in the place of law, and restrains morals as powerfully as laws ever did any where. Among the latter, under pretence of governing they have divided their nations into two classes, wolves and sheep. I do not exaggerate. This is a true picture of Europe.[24]

Had Thomas Jefferson never lived, there would still today be an extraordinary powerful anti-statist tradition in the United States. But here was one of our greatest leaders, who believed with all his might—even when doubt was in the air—that America and democracy had a providential destiny. America didn't need a strong state to make it go; it would go almost by itself. America, democracy, and the anti-statist tradition were fused together, and Jefferson became the standard-bearer of all three.

The Jeffersonian tradition of liberal democracy was notably reinforced by Andrew Jackson. To the popular imagination, the rough-hewn Jackson—a one-generation aristocrat—provided the ideal vehicle for giving flesh-and-blood meaning to the intellectualized egalitarianism of Jefferson. But more significantly like Jefferson, Jackson presents an individualist-liberal face as well as a democratic-egalitarian face. The latter is best remembered, but the former is most important. The threat to democracy—real or perceived—of the unholy Hamiltonian alliance of wealth and government was as real for Jackson as it was for Jefferson. Jackson—frontiersman, military hero, and self-made man, with limited educational attainments—provided the perfect symbol for the newly enfranchised voters added through gradual elimination of property qualifications. Under Jackson, Jefferson's democratic philosophy became a party movement spurred by the desire to increase both freedom and equality.

With the approach of universal suffrage and its accompanying egalitarian passions, Jackson found the rewards of appointive office a useful device for building party support. Jackson did not consider appointive positions as necessary links in an administrative chain, but rather favors to be sprinkled judiciously among the party faithful. As a result the Hamiltonian idea of expert administration was soon forgotten. Rotation of offices and the use of patronage for partisan purposes rested squarely on the assumption that the duties of public administration could be performed by any person of reasonable intelligence. In his first annual message to Congress, Jackson declared: "In a country where offices are created solely for the benefit of the people no one man has any more intrinsic right to official station than another." [25] He firmly believed that administrative offices should be made fully as responsive to the popular will as elective offices.

If all this struck a positive blow on behalf of democracy, it had a pernicious effect in the denigration of the quality and reputation of public administration in the United States. With the requirements of office made simple, qualifications modest, salaries low, turnover high, and reputation questionable, public administration in America moved 180 degrees away from the traditions of European administrative excellence. Stringent qualifications, lifelong tenure, administrative specialization, and high prestige were all deeply distrusted and resented by most Americans, precisely because they had been and still were so often the administrative tools of European statism in the service of aristocracy, monarchy, and despotism. Easy access to office was seen as one of the most effective democratic safeguards against the emergence of an undemocratic ruling class. When Jackson declared the rotation of offices "a leading principle in the Republican Creed," he did much to foster the enduring divorce of intellect and training from political power.

The most notable struggle of Andrew Jackson's presidency involved his successful attempt to destroy the monopoly power of the United States Bank. Behind the clashing figures of Jackson and bank director Nicholas Biddle stood the familiar images of Jefferson and Hamilton. Decentralization, easy credit, and agrarian forces on the one side were set against centralization, wealth, hard money, and industry on the other side. The bank loomed before the public imagination as a vast, complex, and secret structure beyond the people's control or understanding—much in the manner of the professional administration Jackson did so much to uproot. Despite the bank's private though quasi-public status, the issue was not the question of private versus public control. Andrew Jackson would have been no happier with a central bank under his direct control than with a permanent and professional bureaucracy. The critical question was centralization versus decentralization—and at a more fundamental level, statism versus liberalism. Thus Jackson's war against a centralized banking system, public or private, was cut out of the same cloth as his attack on a professional, expert public administration. Like Jefferson, from whom he drew so much inspiration, Jackson was at heart a Lockean liberal first and a democrat and egalitarian second. These deeply felt liberal sentiments were well expressed at the end of the bank recharter veto message when Jackson proclaimed: "Distinctions in society will always exist under every just government. Equality of talents, of education, or of wealth cannot be produced by human institutions."[26]

Abraham Lincoln presided over the greatest expansion of the federal government prior to Franklin D. Roosevelt's New Deal. While Lincoln's often-stated aim was to save the Union, at a more fundamental level the preservation of the Union and the defeat of the Confederacy were subordinate to Lincoln's sacred principle of free labor and the legacy of Jeffersonian liberal democracy.

Lincoln is the stuff of legends. An essential element of the Lincoln legend, of which Lincoln himself was part author, was his rise from humble origins. His ambition, which his law partner, William Herndon, described as "a little engine that knew no rest," propelled him forward throughout his career and provides the key to his political thought. Lincoln grew up in an open and intensely competitive society. His rise to power in the political sphere was as much a dramatization of the possibilities inherent in Lockean liberalism as was Andrew Carnegie's triumph in industry. In a public address, Lincoln proudly stated:

> Twenty-five years ago I was a hired laborer. The hired laborer
> of yesterday labors on his own account today, and will hire oth-

ers to labor for him tomorrow. Advancement—improvement in condition—is the order of things in a society of equals.[27]

Here Lincoln is speaking for the millions who came before him and the tens of millions afterward who begin life as farmhands, clerks, and mechanics and later become landowners, merchants, and manufacturers. This fervent belief in opportunity for the self-made man became the core of Lincoln's case against slavery.

Lincoln was no abolitionist. In fact, it was only in 1854, at the age of forty-five, that he first spoke out against slavery.[28] With the passage of the Kansas-Nebraska Act and its repeal of the Missouri Compromise, and the possibility that slavery would spread to new states, Lincoln's acute political sensitivity fastened on slavery as the critical issue of his time. He reached the White House because he gained the support of the two opposing Northern political blocs: the Abolitionists and the much larger although far less vocal group who opposed them. These Northerners who opposed the Abolitionists feared that a flood of cheap free-black labor might threaten their own value in the labor market and thus their very economic livelihood. The fear of emancipation made this majority Negrophobes. The further the institution of slavery spread, the more threatening the final day of reckoning became.

Lincoln's answer to the problem may best be summed up in the word "containment." Satisfying the Abolitionists, he denounced slavery as the worst of evils and charged that slavery must not be allowed to advance further. Then, catering to the larger number concerned about living alongside free blacks, he proposed to halt slavery's spread into the North by confining the people and the institution to the southern states. Indeed, when war finally came it was Lincoln's clearly stated objective to bring the South back into the Union "with slavery intact." As Lincoln sought to rally the Union in the cause of a long and difficult struggle, his war aims fastened on slavery and the Confederacy as a threat to the idea of free labor within an open society, "a war upon the rights of all working people."[29] He saw the South attacking the sacred principles of the Declaration of Independence.

Lincoln found the source of much of his political inspiration in Jefferson. He declared Jefferson to be "the most distinguished politician of our history. The principles of Jefferson are the definitions and axioms of free society." [30] Lincoln saw Jefferson's Declaration as the greatest creative myth of American society. Immediately, the preservation of the Union was at stake, but at a more fundamental level the Civil War in Lincoln's mind was fought for the preservation of the "principle of liberty for all." He never wavered from the principles of Jeffersonian individualism. State and constitution are but a backdrop for the autonomous individual. Lincoln beautifully imaged these convictions—his idea of America—by taking a line from the twenty-fifth chapter of Proverbs: "A word fitly spoken is like apples of gold in pictures of silver." [31] He proclaimed:

> The assertion of that *principle* [liberty], *at that time* [1776] was *the* word, "fitly spoken" which has proved an "apple of gold" to us. The *Union,* and the *Constitution,* are the *picture* of *silver,* subsequently framed around it. The picture was made, not to *conceal,* or *destroy* the apple; but to *adorn,* and *preserve* it. The picture was made *for* the apple—*not* the apple for the picture. [32]

Lincoln exercised more power than any of his predecessors, and circumstances dictated his actions. But there is within Lincoln no lesson for state-building. After Lincoln, there is no Southern minority position, no alternative. The slate is wiped clean, and the unrepentant individualism, implicit in America from the very beginning, is left free to flower.

William Jennings Bryan, the Great Commoner, was three times the Democratic party's nominee for president. From the time he thundered on the national scene with his "Cross of Gold" speech in 1896, until his pathetic performance as the leader of the anti-evolutionists at the Scopes trial, evangelism and popular democracy were intertwined in his mind as a single faith. According to Bryan's "populistic faith," the common man is fully capable of understanding and deciding the problems of government as easily as he can understand the word of God:

> The people of the United States . . . have sufficient patriotism and sufficient intelligence to sit in judgment on every question which has arisen or which will arise, no matter how long our government will endure. The great political questions are in their final analysis great moral questions. [33]

Bryan's crusade against evolution at Dayton, Tennessee, thus goes far beyond a fundamentalist reaction to modernity. In Bryan's mind, evolution, science, and, most important, intellect not only threatened religion but also called into question the capabilities of the common mind. As a result they posed a real danger to the viability of democracy as Bryan understood it. A virulent anti-intellectualism striking out against organized authority in government, business, or religion was an essential part of Bryan's makeup.

Bryan rose to national prominence on the populistic phase of the great tide of reform that culminated in the New Deal. Drastically reduced farm income during the last third of the nineteenth century, coupled with a political center of gravity shifting from agrarian to industrial dominance, galvanized the beleaguered agrarian interests to action. Their political response took a variety of forms, but easy credit based on the free coinage of silver provided Bryan with his single greatest cause. The Populists, although unleashing the flow of protest that led to the substantive reforms of progressivism, did not look forward. They looked back to the lost agrarian Eden they associated with Jeffersonian democracy.

Bryan was forever the defender of Jeffersonian principles. In words reminiscent of Jackson's bank veto message, he proclaimed:

> Property is and will remain the stimulus to endeavor and the compensation for toil. We believe, as asserted in the Declaration of Independence, that all men are created equal; but that does not mean that all men are or can be equal in possessions, in ability, or in merit; it simply means that all shall stand equal before the law.[34]

Bryan did not seek to improve the lot of the common man through the medium of a strong central state sympathetic to their plight. Insofar as he sought to use the national political institutions, it was to restore the conditions of a less complex and more just agrarian past.

In an agrarian age Jefferson's prescriptions at least looked reasonable, but a similar approach in the hands of Bryan seemed naive and pathetic. Bryan is an easy target. We all too clearly remember the saddened figure, weeks away from death at Dayton, attacked by Clarence Darrow and subjected to withering ridicule by H. L. Mencken. Bryan was called a socialist and an anarchist, but the boy orator, who first captured the

Democratic presidential nomination at the age of thirty-six, was so rewarded only because he tapped deeply into the wellsprings of the dominant liberal tradition in America.

In Theodore Roosevelt we encounter the first major figure of the progressive era. Progressivism is the centerpiece of the reform movement stretching from populism to the New Deal. Progressivism grew out of populism and shared many of its concerns with the restoration of equal opportunity and fair competition for the average person threatened by huge economic enterprise. However, progressivism differed from populism in several important respects. Unlike populism it came to grips with the indisputable fact that America was becoming an urban and industrial society. Progressivism was forward-looking, not a reaction to a vanishing past. Because it addressed the concerns of America's industrial future, its approach was national, leaving behind the sectional orientation of populism. The federal government, rather than the states, was to be the principal lever of change. And in the person of Theodore Roosevelt the heartbeat of the movement centered on the presidency and not on Congress.

At its most fundamental level, progressivism was a reaction against and a forthright attempt to deal with the problem of the age of organization ushered in through huge combinations of industrial capital. It is ironic that the giant trusts many reformers believed to be economic Frankensteins did not grow out of the visible and purposive hand of Hamiltonian statism, but instead burst forth from the fertile soil of Jeffersonian liberalism under the benign neglect of the limited state. As the Jeffersonian ends of individual opportunity and political democracy were threatened by the economic monopoly of the trusts and the political monopoly of party bosses, remedy was sought in the power of the national government.

The well-born Theodore Roosevelt shared the disdain of his class for the pecuniary ambitions of what he termed "the commercial classes," but as much as he despised the attitudes and habits of the new rich, he harbored an instinctive fear of the mob. He desired above all else to steer a neutral course, avoiding abuse by the rich and confiscation by the poor, and no platform was better suited to this evenhanded use of power than the presidency. In 1902 his successful arbitration of the bitter anthracite strike and vigorous prosecution of the Northern Securities Company set the tone for his vision of a neutral and activist presidency. He sought to redress imbalances created by monopoly labor as well as by capital. Favored by times free of war or major economic disruptions, the sheer enjoyment of the presidency for Roosevelt far overshadowed its burdens. Age, temperament, and circumstances inclined Roosevelt to extend the limits of presidential power. He was uncomfortable with the individualism implicit in the Sherman Act, which aimed at the restoration of atomistic economic competition. He favored regulation over dissolution and argued with considerable historical insight that "to bolster up an individualism already proved to be both futile and mischievous; to remedy by more individualism the concentration that was the inevitable result of the already existing individualism . . . was a hopeless effort."[35]

But we cannot say that Theodore Roosevelt applied Hamiltonian means to achieve Jeffersonian ends. The progressive reform movement's main line of development took a decidedly Jeffersonian turn. William Howard Taft's vigorous application of the Sherman Act renounced Roosevelt's policy of regulating the trusts in favor of dissolution aimed at restoring an earlier era of free and unrestricted competition. Taft's efforts were later ratified by the decidedly procompetition doctrines of Woodrow Wilson's New Freedom. And the final death knell to any guiding hand of Hamiltonian statecraft was sounded by a barrage of progressive direct-democracy legislation, including referendums, direct election of senators, primaries, and recall. Thus, the essence of progressive reform sees the national government not as countervailing power or even as a "bully pulpit," but as a smooth-flowing transmission, directing the democratic will on resisting knots of economic and political privilege. Despite a brief flirtation with Hamilton, the favored solution of progressivism was Jeffersonian means yielding Jeffersonian ends.

While we most easily remember Jackson as a democrat and an egalitarian, Lincoln as the great emancipator and preserver of the Union, Bryan as a radical and a populist, and Theodore Roosevelt as a nationalist and presidential activist, their inner philosophical predispositions have to a man made these great Americans Lockean liberals, individualists, and loyal adherents to the anti-statist tradition. We could continue our survey for another eighty years, looking at Woodrow Wilson, Franklin Roosevelt, Dwight Eisenhower, and Ronald Reagan; it would be more of the same. We need only compare the sentiments of Jefferson and Reagan on the evils of central government, the dangers of bureaucratic control, the positive effects of local government, and the absolute sanctity of individual rights. The Jeffersonian anti-statist tradition has not simply endured—it has prevailed.

In the more than eighty years since Theodore Roosevelt, two world wars, the depression, the demands of a global defense establishment, and the complexities of a global economy have totally transformed the U.S. government. By any conceivable measure, the sprawling federal apparatus is today larger, more costly, and infinitely more complex. It has altered the lives of all Americans in countless ways that could not have been imagined during the twentieth century's first decade. We shall outline several of these changes in Chapter 8. But bigger government doesn't imply better government, and by no means does it lead to stronger or more effective government. If the huge increase in the size of our federal establishment, and its more active presence in our daily lives, have done anything to change our feelings about government, it has certainly served to heighten the dislike and distrust of most Americans toward the federal government.

8

POLITICS AND BUREAUCRACY
IN AMERICA

Government is not the solution to our problem.
Government is the problem.
—*Ronald Reagan*

On the surface, broad similarities exist between the pattern European states—Japan, Germany, France—and the United States. They are all advanced industrial societies firmly committed to individual freedoms, capitalism, and democratic political institutions. In terms of living standards, social welfare, income distribution, and other important policy outputs, the overarching common patterns outweigh certain differences—especially when set against Communist-bloc or developing nations. But in the architecture of their political institutions and their implications for economic performance in the technologically driven global markets of the future, there are stunning differences. Twenty-five years ago, in the absence of global markets and the new industrial competition, America's idiosyncratic political institutions appeared to have little bear-

ing on the economic performance of the United States. Today the implications of our institutional aberrations are deep and profound.

The institutional architectures of the pattern European states show a
high degree of congruency and few fundamental differences. Through
the parliamentary systems of Japan and Germany, and in the mixed-
presidential system of France, the authority of the state is registered with
a degree of force that can scarcely be imagined in the United States. At
the font of state authority in these nations is a top professional bureaucracy that is commonly educated, socialized, and trained. In addition to
the statist traditions in these three countries there are long and venerable
bureaucratic traditions; the administrative system long predates present
and most prior constitutional arrangements. The power of the state and
the power of the bureaucracy are inextricably joined; one could not exist
without the other. As servants of the state and as guardians of the statist
tradition, top bureaucrats are accorded a high degree of respect by politicians and the public alike. Governments in Japan, Germany, and France
all rely on careful compromise between political and bureaucratic viewpoints—between political and bureaucratic power.

The United States does not have a top professional bureaucracy in the
sense that we have defined top professional bureaucracies in Japan, Germany, and France. It is not a matter of ours being different, somehow
Americanized. We simply don't have one—period.[1] In the United States
political appointees fill the important positions that senior bureaucrats
in other major Western democracies have.

Because top-ranking American political officials fear and distrust the
bureaucracy, they appoint large numbers of people from outside the civil
service to formulate major policies and to serve as managers of the federal departments and agencies. Senior careerists are commonly separated
from the pinnacle of power by several layers of political appointees.
More frequently than not, these appointees are strangers to the political-
administrative scene in the nation's capital when they arrive, and remain
a part of it only fleetingly. Aptly termed "birds of passage," they are a
very different species from the ranks of professional bureaucrats who
serve as top policymakers in the pattern European states.[2]

Politicians are not the only Americans who are hostile to the bureaucracy. Society at large is contemptuous of bureaucratic institutions and
personnel. No administrative system predates the Constitution of the
United States, and only passing reference to administration is contained

in that document. Many Americans view today's large-scale bureaucracy as a major threat to our constitutional government. The democratic left reviles the national security bureaucracy, while conservatives resent bureaucratic intrusions in the social welfare and economic domain.[3] The "imperial bureaucracy" is a favorite target of politicians across the ideological spectrum, and the unelected, uncaring bureaucrat receives constant negative attention in the mass media. As one prominent scholar says, "There is a certain aura of illegitimacy about bureaucracy—a suspicion that its presence and activities in the governmental structure are not altogether in accord with the American constitutional order."[4] So it should come as no surprise that top-ranking college and university graduates are less enthusiastic about civil service careers than about careers within the private sector. And those who do choose the civil service and rise to its highest positions must be content to remain far removed from real decision-making.

Given America's antibureaucratic leanings, we need to look at the characteristics and unique historical development of our atypical bureaucracy and, in particular, its lack of a top professional bureaucracy. America's founders had a great fear of unbridled government power. Their solution was to build into the Constitution an elaborate system that incorporated representative government, federalism, and a tripartite structure of formally distinct branches so constructed as to check and balance one another through a system of overlapping powers. In the words of Richard Neustadt, the Constitution created "a government of separated institutions *sharing* powers."[5] The result was a governmental mix of powers and restraints—and of deliberate fragmentation.

The federal administrative system reflects this general constitutional pattern. As Peter Woll notes, "The effect of the Constitution is to fragment the bureaucracy. Lines of control are blurred, organizational patterns are diverse, and in general unity is absent."[6] Article II of the Constitution vests extensive power in the president and mandates that he execute the laws. The president is constitutionally authorized to appoint senior administrative officials in the executive branch and to "require the opinion, in writing, of the principal officer in each of the executive departments, upon any subject relating to the duties of their respective offices." But by no means is the president firmly in charge of the federal administration, for the Constitution grants Congress far-reaching powers over the structure and lines of control of the federal bureaucracy.

Congress is constitutionally assigned the power to determine the organization and jurisdiction of executive agencies and departments. The legislature creates, destroys, and decides on the formal lines of accountability of executive agencies. It determines what an agency may and may not do. If it so desires, Congress may grant administrative agencies independence from presidential control. Congress also holds the power of the purse; it appropriates the funds the executive branch needs to function. And although the president has the exclusive power to nominate top executive branch officials, the "advice and consent" of the Senate is necessary for their appointment.

As we shall see, Congress benefits not only from a fragmented bureaucracy but also from a bureaucracy that has no powerful central corps of permanent, top civil servants. Modern presidents have themselves become deeply hostile to a cohesive bureaucracy and a powerful higher civil service. They have done everything possible to ensure that senior careerists are excluded from top managerial and policy-making roles.

In the years after the Civil War the complexities of governing a rapidly industrializing society gave rise to the demand for civil service reform. The debate over reform pitted a powerful majority that believed in patronage rewards, rotation of office, and universal competency against a determined minority calling for competition, efficiency, and economy. The reformers did not lack for suggestive models, as both France and Prussia presented clear examples of highly developed bureaucratic administration. However, it was British civil service reform (signaled by the publication of the Northcote-Trevelyan report in 1854) that stimulated American thinking about the usefulness of educational requirements and examinations as the primary means of improving the quality of public administration.

The British believed that a class-based, elite education was a prerequisite for high administrative office. Americans against reform seized on this as a convenient reason to condemn the whole idea of narrowing the channels of recruitment through education and examination.[7] Attacking an 1868 early reform bill, Representative John Logan of Illinois declared,

"This bill is the opening wedge to an aristocracy in this country. . . . Schools will monopolize all avenues of approach to the Government." And a few years later, Senator Matthew Carpenter of Wisconsin proclaimed: "And now, when our maimed soldiers have returned, and apply for a Federal office, the duties of which they are perfectly competent to discharge, they are to be rejected to give place to those who were cramming themselves with facts and principles from the books." Tammany stalwarts and other political insiders delighted in referring to the movement as "snivel service reform." [8]

These and a host of similar charges were by no means the products of an extremist fringe. They represented the mainstream of American opinion, which quickly labeled a meritocratic bureaucracy based on educational qualifications and competitive examinations as blatantly "antidemocratic." As a result, the Pendleton Act establishing a civil service was not passed until 1883, and then only in the wake of national sympathy following the assassination of President James Garfield by a disappointed office-seeker. The unrelenting opponents of a meritocratic civil service, who delayed for so many years its arrival and who worked to limit its scope and power afterward, tapped deeply into the smoldering sentiments of an anti-intellectual tradition that is still with us today.[9]

The Pendleton Act created the Civil Service Commission and established a merit system that mandated employment on the basis of competent performance on a written examination, attainment of job tenure after a specified period, and removal only through specified procedures. Almost a century after the creation of the republic, a civil service system had finally been added. Unfortunately, however, civil service reformers were reluctant to blur the line between politics and administration, so no serious attention was given to defining the political functions of upper-level careerists.[10]

In the closing decades of the nineteenth century, America was a nation in the throes of massive and unprecedented change. A national government consciously designed to be limited and fragmented was being called on to perform in ways never dreamed of by the founders. Demands for the national government to play a more active role in regulating an increasingly complex society thrust on the Congress a host of new responsibilities it was unequipped to meet. Congress responded by creating a federal administrative apparatus to which it delegated responsibility for limited government intervention.[11]

Having the constitutional power to create executive agencies, Congress began in the 1880s to establish a new type of administrative agency—the regulatory commission—to cope with the problem of economic monopolies and other big-business abuse of a tolerant laissez-faire environment. The Interstate Commerce Commission (ICC), the first of these new executive bodies, was established in 1887 to regulate the powerful railroad industry and curb its more questionable practices. Granted far-reaching legislative powers to set railroad rate charges and to issue rules governing railroad services (and soon given adjudicative power as well), the ICC was also granted independence from presidential as well as congressional control. In so doing, Congress began to accept the notion that a nonpartisan and relatively permanent body of experts was the best means of ensuring implementation of a consistent regulatory policy.[12] It also dashed any hopes for strengthening the existing bureaucracy and the newly minted civil service.

The Interstate Commerce Commission set the pattern for dozens of independent regulatory agencies and government corporations to follow. The Federal Reserve System, the Federal Trade Commission, and the Federal Power Commission were all modeled after the ICC. In the pattern European states the functions these bodies perform are placed under the appropriate jurisdiction of the national bureaucracy. The existence of these agencies within the current U.S. governmental structure confounds attempts to formulate coherent policy and further weakens a fragmented and demoralized executive branch.

"I am prepared," declared Franklin Roosevelt in his 1933 inaugural address, "under my constitutional duty to recommend the measures that a stricken Nation in the midst of a stricken world may require."[13] True to his word, he plunged ahead with a series of emergency measures designed to stimulate the economy. Congress immediately acceded to his proposals to create a number of agencies to administer the programs of the New Deal.

Because there were now so many agency executives reporting directly to the president, it became increasingly apparent that the president would need a support staff to coordinate and control this administrative jungle. The President's Committee on Administrative Management, chaired by Louis Brownlow, issued a report the following year.

The Brownlow committee declared that the president's effectiveness at that time was "limited and restricted, in spite of the clear intent of the Constitution to the contrary." A fundamental imbalance between presidential responsibilities and powers needed to be redressed. The committee recommended a series of modernization and reorganization schemes, including consolidation of existing agencies into a few large departments directly responsible to the chief executive, incorporation of independent agencies into those departments, reorganization of the fiscal and civil service systems as managerial arms of the chief executive, and, because "the president needs help," expansion of the president's personal staff to help him supervise the administrative functions of planning, budgeting, and personnel.[14]

In his statement accompanying the report as submitted to Congress, Roosevelt underscored the report's constitutional interpretation of presidential control of the administration:

> The plain fact is that the present organization and equipment of the executive branch of the Government defeats the constitutional intent that there be a single responsible Chief Executive to coordinate and manage the departments and activities in accordance with the laws enacted by Congress. Under these conditions the Government cannot be thoroughly effective in working, under popular control, for the common good.[15]

The administrative reform bill, coming in the wake of the 1937 "court-packing scheme," was promptly labeled the "Dictator Bill." Over 300,000 opposing telegrams poured into Washington, causing Roosevelt—never at a loss for words or wit—to issue an extraordinary statement: "A. I have no inclination to be a dictator. B. I have none of the qualifications that would make me a successful dictator."[16] Although Congress emphatically rejected the sweeping—and necessary—interpretation of presidential power contained in the administrative reform bill, it did pass the Executive Reorganization Act of 1939, granting the president authority to reorganize the executive branch. This act authorized the creation of the Executive Office of the President (EOP).

How then was the president to manage the vast federal bureaucracy?

In the absence of substantive reform, Roosevelt's administrative heritage was to promote the belief that a sufficiently skilled and determined politician could control the huge federal apparatus in an unorthodox, ad hoc, and personalized fashion. He played administrators off against one another and, whenever and wherever necessary, created (with congressional approval) new administrative agencies that were more responsive to his command.[17] Roosevelt deliberately bypassed senior careerists in the Cabinet departments, believing they were too slow and set in their ways to fit his needs, and instead brought in outsiders to serve as his politically faithful administrators and policymakers. A large "counter-bureaucracy" was beginning to take root in the Executive Office; the modern president's distaste for the permanent bureaucracy was making its first appearance. The message was clear: a top professional bureaucracy was not going to be part of the political system of modern America.

After Franklin Roosevelt, federal policies and bureaucratic units proliferated, and as the permanent bureaucracy expanded in scope, so also did the staff agencies of the Executive Office of the President. The presidents after Roosevelt were not inclined to look on the permanent administration with favor. In fact, just the opposite occurred, and this trend toward greater distrust of the federal bureaucracy presently shows no signs of abating. More and more political appointees have been brought in to oversee the permanent bureaucracy. Those operating out of the Executive Office have also been increasingly called on to operate government programs as well as to facilitate the president's management of them. The result has been a uniquely American two-track system of administrative management: one track composed of careerists, and another, superimposed on it, composed of transient appointees.[18]

What are the characteristics of this dual structure, the tensions within it, and the grave problems that have resulted from it? America's federal bureaucracy consists of approximately 2.9 million civilian employees scattered throughout a variety of organizations, ranging from the fourteen federal executive departments, to some sixty independent agencies, regulatory agencies, and corporations, to hundreds of advisory boards and commissions. They vary in size from the giant Department of Defense, which has close to a million employees, to boards consisting of only a handful of personnel.

The complexity of the U.S. federal bureaucracy extends to the personnel system as well. Although the vast majority of federal bureaucrats are covered by civil service merit rules, no single civil service system applies to everyone. The General Schedule (GS) covers the bulk of civilian employees, but important agencies, including the State Department, the Federal Bureau of Investigation, the Central Intelligence Agency, and the Postal Service, maintain separate, self-contained personnel systems. Civil servants under the General Schedule are classified into eighteen grades. At the apex of this personnel scale are the so-called "supergrades" (GS-16 through GS-18), which are the career executive positions of the higher civil service. The 6,300 or so supergrade career executives are the technical and managerial elite of the American civil service, but they have only a faint shadow of the responsibility, authority, and prestige of top bureaucrats in Japan, Germany, and France.

Who are these senior careerists, by what paths have they attained their current positions, and what roles do they play in American government? Like the top bureaucrats in the pattern European states, senior American civil servants are quite well educated. In the mid-1970s more than two-thirds had at least a master's degree, and nearly one-quarter had a doctorate.[19] But senior American careerists do not constitute an educational elite in the Japanese or European sense. They are highly educated professionals, but they are far from the cream of the crop of university and professional school graduates. Nor do higher-level civil servants constitute a social elite. America's best and brightest young minds invariably prefer to enter the private sector.

Senior American civil servants are not educated to be administrative generalists, as is the case in Japan, Germany, and France. Nor do they usually plan while still in college to join the civil service. They enter the bureaucracy in their twenties or thirties as well-educated specialists trained in a particular discipline; knowledge about management and public affairs tends to be acquired only haphazardly as they move through their careers. And their careers are quite circumscribed.[20] Most senior careerists have achieved their current positions through promotion from within a single agency. About two-thirds of supergrade officials have worked for the same agency since they achieved the rank of GS-13 or its equivalent. Only a small percentage have been promoted directly from another government agency, and almost none come from outside government. They are thus lifetime government employees in what is virtually a closed career system.[21]

The career paths of senior civil servants reflect the fragmented and compartmentalized nature of the American federal bureaucracy. There is no such thing as a collective bureaucratic entity in Washington. Socialized within a single agency and brought up through its ranks, senior bureaucrats have little feeling of common identity or personal contact with those of comparable grade and background in other agencies. Even within a particular agency or department, career ladders are usually narrowly confined. It is therefore not surprising that these senior career bureaucrats tend to be parochial and particularistic in their outlook. Their attitudes reflect the needs and concerns of their own specific and self-contained bureaucratic unit rather than those of the bureaucracy as a whole.

Lacking a government-wide career structure, civil service executives display little loyalty to the collective civil service.[22] As bureaucrats they identify with their unit; as professionals they identify with their peers who have been trained in the same field of expertise. In the telling words of a retired senior civil servant:

> I've never thought of myself as a career civil servant. . . . Ask a civil servant who he is and you'll probably find he'll say he is an economist who works for the Treasury Department, a manager for the Housing Department and so on. What he's *not* likely to say first is that he's a civil servant.[23]

How different are the sentiments of top bureaucrats abroad.

Longevity of tenure coupled with interagency and even intraagency job immobility has affected career executives in some important ways. First, because they have acquired detailed and specialized knowledge about the workings of their own bureaucratic unit, they have become experts with long institutional memories—and tunnel vision. Second, they have a deep commitment to their bureau's programs which extends far longer than any president's term in office, so they hesitate to become overly identified with a particular presidential administration and its political appointees and identify instead with their bureau and its responsibilities. They adopt a long-range perspective on policy and are reluctant to make the rapid policy shifts and "quick fixes" so often promoted by an incoming administration. Careerists believe real change comes about gradually and incrementally.[24]

Such a perspective hardly endears senior careerists to a president and his political lieutenants. Politicians have a short time perspective and need to move with dispatch. They want to make their political mark, and rapidly. But to upper-level bureaucrats, the president and his appointees are "transient interlopers" in their world of long-standing traditions and relationships.[25] Remember, by the time bureaucrats reach senior ranks they have usually seen several presidents come and go.

While the interaction between senior bureaucrats and their political bosses in the executive branch may be short-lived, their relationships with Congress are of a far different nature. Congress, not the federal executive, has the final power of life and death over federal agencies, and Congress keeps an ever-watchful eye on its administrative wards. A major component of the career executive's ongoing world is the growing network of congressional committees and subcommittees that are in charge of agency authorizations, appropriations, and oversight.

The constitutional reality of congressional control of the bureaucracy has a dramatic impact on the nature of the federal bureaucracy and the behavior of top careerists. We have already noted that the specialized professional backgrounds and narrow career paths of senior bureaucrats militate against a cohesive civil service elite. The close ties bureaucrats must maintain with a very dispersed and decentralized Congress constitute yet another reason for bureaucratic fragmentation and compartmentalization. They help explain America's failure to develop a unified corps of senior civil servants.

The contemporary Congress operates on the basis of a committee and subcommittee system that disperses power into almost three hundred semiautonomous fiefdoms. This fragmentation of power is well suited to an institution whose members aspire to long-term careers; lengthy tenure demands a satisfied constituency. As a result, Congress has organized itself so that every member has the opportunity to serve on a committee that has jurisdiction over a federal agency relevant to his or her home district. In words reminiscent of Huey Long we can say: In today's Congress every member *is* a king.

Congressional committees are themselves divided into subcommittees, each of which maintains control over a small portion of the federal bureaucracy. The giant cabinet-level departments and agencies are divided into a myriad of separate bureaus and offices, each responsible for implementing different bits of public policy. And because congressional sub-committees oversee the bureaucracy at the bureau level, each department or agency falls under the jurisdictional turf of a number of small congressional bodies.

Because of this highly specialized committee and subcommittee system, members of Congress have the opportunity (far less readily available to their European and Japanese counterparts) to become specialists in particular policy areas.[26] Their ability to achieve expertise in even the technical aspects of policy-making is greatly magnified by the recent explosion in congressional staffs. It is now estimated that more than 31,000 people are employed as professional congressional staffers, more than ten times the number of legislative staff in Germany and France. The administrative budget of the U.S. Congress currently exceeds $2 billion. A large, entrenched, and specialized congressional bureaucracy—with a stake in maintaining the power and jurisdiction of the executive bureaus Congress oversees—exacerbates the complex network of symbiotic relationships that exist between subunits of Congress and the bureaucracy.[27]

Relationships between Congress and the bureaucracy are generally cooperative. Members of Congress reap benefits for their districts and states, and hence for their own reelection chances, from federal bureaus anxious to please the legislators who hold the purse strings. The arsenal of instruments with which Congress can punish or reward federal bureaus extends well beyond enabling legislation and appropriation. Congress may repeal its authorization of an agency; it may transfer a bureau's powers to a different agency; it may reduce funds available for a particular program; it may conduct investigations and hearings. In his study of federal bureau chiefs, Herbert Kaufman notes that Congress's powers "can be used with the discrimination of a stiletto or the explosive power of a bomb," and continues, "All of the chiefs I watched were alert to the moods of Congress, sensitive to the attitudes of their committees, and careful not to give offense even when demands could not be fully met."[28] One extensive analysis of bureaucratic decisions about water and sewer grants, model cities grants, and military base locations found that bureaucrats allocated benefits significantly more frequently to the districts of members who sat on committees and subcommittees that had jurisdiction over these programs. There was something for everyone: the legislators got increased federal spending for their districts, and the bureaucrats secured important goals of budgetary security and growth for their programs.[29]

The bureaus are not without their own resources vis-à-vis Congress. Federal bureaus operate the various programs of the executive departments and thus make important decisions about the physical locations of their projects, many of which legislators want to secure for their respective districts. Bureaus also provide services to constituents. Constituency casework has become an increasingly important component of congressional activity and reelection. Many cases take the form of requests that a member intercede with a particular bureau on the constituent's behalf. The bureaus thus possess some significant leverage over congressional actions.

Interest groups that have a stake in certain bits of public policy find it easy to penetrate the congressional committees and subcommittees responsible for particular federal bureaus. Along with subcommittee members and their staffs and relevant bureaucrats, these client groups form "cozy little triangles," or subgovernments, that control much of American public policy in an uncomfortably self-serving manner. Subgovernment relationships are enduring. As we have seen, civil servants tend to remain in their respective bureaus for more than two decades. Members of Congress from safe districts also have a comparable average tenure in office and retain seats on the committees and subcommittees that are of most electoral relevance to them. The result is a mutually rewarding system of exchange and reciprocity which operates on the basis of *decentralized* congressional stewardship of a *decentralized* bureaucracy.[30]

Congress could, if it so desired, exert coordinated control over the bureaucracy. But it has no desire to do so because dispersion of control best fits members' electoral needs. Scholar Morris Fiorina states the situation best:

> When we see a public agency spending inordinate amounts of public funds to pave over certain congressional districts, we are not observing an out of control agency. We are observing an agency that is paying off the members of Congress who nurture it. . . . Part of the agency may be genuinely out of control, but *Congress wants it that way.* It is a necessary cost of maintaining a bureaucracy that is sufficiently . . . permeable to congressional influence.[31]

The effect of such a system on the behavior of senior careerists in the bureaucracy is obvious: their myopic loyalties to specific programs and bureaus are enhanced. Because their training, career paths, and interactions with congressional committees all operate to constrict their perspectives, there is little incentive for top bureaucrats to look at the broader picture. Higher civil servants who choose to ignore the specialized needs of congressional committee members can be denied funding, have their decisions overturned, and ultimately even witness the termination of their unit. Thus, parochialism provides its own reward. By identifying one's career with a given program and bureau, bureaucratic promotional opportunities are enhanced through ever-present political influence.[32]

The American bureaucracy is also subject to far greater judicial scrutiny and challenge than its Japanese and European counterparts. Ours is an adversarial political culture in which the defense and expansion of personal rights are of paramount importance. Since the 1960s, judicial review of administrative activity has expanded dramatically. An explosion in the number of lawyers, public-interest law firms, and activist judges willing to expand the scope of judicial oversight are all part of a changing legal landscape.

Judicial activism vis-à-vis the bureaucracy has some prominent and outspoken advocates. In 1976 David Bazelon, chief justice of the Court of Appeals for the District of Columbia Circuit, asserted: "As the Constitutional right to due process of law expands more and more, administrators will find themselves locked into involuntary partnerships with courts."[33] Supreme Court Justice William O. Douglas bluntly condemned America's powerful and indifferent bureaucracy as he called for judicial protection of individual rights. In a 1971 opinion he claimed: "The bureaucracy of modern government is not only slow, lumbering and oppressive; it is omnipresent." In a similar vein he stated in a 1974 opinion that "today's mounting bureaucracy promises to be suffocating and repressive unless it is put into the harness of procedural due process."[34]

In the areas of public employment, receipt of public benefits, involuntary institutionalization, and civil suits, the courts are playing an increasingly active role in defense of the individual. As a consequence a flood of court litigation challenging government actions has restricted the scope of agency discretion. It delays bureaucratic procedures, slows down action, and reduces policy outputs. Societal litigiousness also exacerbates the tendency of bureaucratic agencies and their senior personnel to be cautious. They are inclined to shy away from bold new initiatives. The result is a less efficient and less productive bureaucracy.[35]

In Japan, Germany, and France top professional bureaucrats reap the benefits of working closely with political leaders. They are rewarded for constraining bureaucratic attitudes and for adopting a government-wide perspective. The American system, in dramatic contrast, imposes considerable risks and penalties on senior careerists who fail to abide by the parochial rules of the triangular relationship between bureaucrats, congressional committees, and interest groups. Those who adopt the broader perspective of the president may immediately put their civil service careers in jeopardy. A similar fate awaits bureaucrats who contravene the interests of the permanent congressional subgovernment that has jurisdiction over a particular agency. The alternative is to accept a post as a political appointee, but this means giving up the job security of civil service status. And when the inevitable change in presidents occurs, a top-ranking former bureaucrat who is too closely identified with the outgoing administration is likely to be in trouble with its successor.

Even in the wake of recent civil service reforms, the pitfalls of an intimate relationship between senior bureaucrats and the federal executive remain. By the 1950s, academics, bureaucrats, and politicians had concluded that a mobile corps of senior careerist administrators should be established to enhance the president's managerial capability. Congress belatedly and halfheartedly acceded to these proposals in 1978 by passing the first civil service reform legislation in nearly a century. The 1978 Civil Service Reform Act created a Senior Executive Service (SES), a new category of top administrators formed primarily from supergrade officials in grades GS-16 through GS-18.

The Senior Executive Service is supposed to give the president's politically appointed officials greater managerial ability and flexibility by putting at their disposal a highly trained, knowledgeable, and experienced cadre of senior careerists. Members of the SES are to be mobile rather than agency-bound and to be easily shifted from one post to another as top officials in the executive branch deem necessary. Some 8,500 SES slots were created, 90 percent to be filled by professional bureaucrats, 10 percent by political appointees. Careerists must temporarily relinquish their civil service protection, but in return they are promised more important decision-making and managerial positions along with greater financial rewards.

From its inception, however, the Senior Executive Service has run into serious trouble. Senior-level bureaucrats remain hesitant to abandon the security of their agency niches and do not believe that the merit pay increases and performance bonuses of the SES, which have been significantly reduced by Congress, adequately compensate for loss of job security. They also fear political reprisals from the White House. Members of the SES may be transferred at will across agencies and even exiled to a bureaucratic outpost anywhere in the nation, a matter of particular concern to Washington-based careerists. Nor have the president and his appointees grown any more inclined to believe that SES bureaucrats are truly responsive to the administration's policy goals. Like the bureaucracy in general, SES careerists remain a target of presidential hostility and contempt. Presidents invariably turn to political appointees to serve as their senior managers and policymakers.

As a result, more than 1,000 careerist slots in the Senior Executive Service have gone begging, and morale among the uppermost ranks of the bureaucracy is at a very low point. Shortly after the creation of the SES, the exodus of top careerists from government service increased dramatically. In 1978 only 18 percent of those eligible for voluntary retirement after thirty years of service were leaving the bureaucracy, but by 1981 the figure was a whopping 95 percent.[36]

Senior careerists normally serve more than twenty years. But although they are experienced experts who collectively comprise the institutional memory of our government, their knowledge and expertise are valued little by contemporary presidents, who are looking primarily for political loyalty from subordinates. The ethic of impersonal duty to the state, which is so important among higher bureaucrats in the European statist models—Japan, Germany, and France—carries little weight with an American president. Ideological attachment to a president's policies and/

or a history of personal support for presidential aspirations (as demonstrated by campaign service) are what count most.

In the United States, presidents invariably turn to their political appointees to serve as their top policymakers and administrators. Appointees are selected on the basis of their political and programmatic allegiance to the president. And quite unlike the situation abroad, political appointments are not confined to the highest administrative levels, but are extending further and further down into the bureaucratic hierarchy. Of the approximately 8,000 positions open to presidential appointment, about 1,600 constitute the higher political executive posts.

At the top of the hierarchy of appointees stand the fourteen cabinet secretaries, who report directly to the president. Most have had distinguished private careers as lawyers, corporate executives, and academics, and they usually have some previous federal government experience, though not as agency careerists. They are "in-and-outers" who shuttle back and forth between the public and private sectors. Like George Shultz and Caspar Weinberger, they have frequently served as top presidential aides, in other cabinet posts, or in subcabinet positions. They tend to be generalists and are usually well qualified for their managerial and policy-making roles.[37] Similar characteristics also apply to the directors of the major independent executive agencies, such as the CIA and NASA.

These top appointees are undoubtedly capable, but their tenure in any given administration is brief. At either the president's or their own initiative, they soon choose to resign. The median time in office for cabinet members since World War II is just over two years. Why the quick exodus? The explanation lies in the nature of their relationship to the president and to their departments. As department heads they are legally obligated to execute the laws falling within their department's jurisdiction. They are answerable to Congress and to the courts as well as the president. And if three masters are not enough, they must be responsive as well to their department's senior civil servants and relevant clientele groups. The White House views such responsiveness with apprehension, believing that it indicates an erosion of loyalty to the president.[38]

Cabinet secretaries and major agency heads are thus "birds of passage," and this is often the case for cabinet ministers in the other major Western democracies. But in countries like Japan, Germany, and France these transient officials turn to seasoned bureaucrats for assistance and advice. The career positions begin just below the minister. A permanent corps of top bureaucrats thus act as the senior managers and policymakers in the ministries. With a few notable exceptions (such as the Foreign Service and the FBI), this is not the case in the United States, where top-level appointees are advised and aided not by careerists but by several layers of transient political appointees. Career positions begin distinctly further down in the government hierarchy, and American bureaucrats are far less likely than those in Japan and Europe to have contact with their department heads.[39]

In the United States the multiple layers of political executives appointed by an incoming administration have grown greatly in recent decades, and they continue to increase. Each cabinet department has an appointed chain of command. Reporting to each cabinet-level department secretary is usually a deputy secretary, to whom a number of undersecretaries report. The subcabinet posts of undersecretary and their subordinates (deputy undersecretary and assistant secretary) are all filled by appointees. Below these are the sub-subcabinet positions, which carry the titles of deputy assistant secretary, bureau chief, deputy bureau chief, and regional director. Some deputy assistant secretaries, bureau chiefs, regional directors, and their deputies are careerists drawn from the ranks of the Senior Executive Service, but most of these positions are held by appointees. A comparable chain of command with numerous levels of political appointees exists in each independent agency as well. Layers of political appointees also are proliferating in the agencies of the Executive Office of the President. There are now directors, deputy directors, assistant deputy directors, and so on.[40]

Loyalty to presidential policies is a key factor in the determination of who will be appointed to subcabinet and sub-subcabinet positions. Candidates are often recommended by economic and professional groups concerned about particular programs. Many of those chosen are members of interest groups, think tanks, law firms, consulting firms, and congressional staffs that share the policy orientations of the president. Appointees are as well educated as senior careerists, but more likely to be liberal arts generalists coming from better universities, and their socioeconomic background is normally a cut above those of top-level bureaucrats. They may be knowledgeable about public policy, but they tend to lack prior federal government experience. Most have had less than two years of experience in the federal government. As a group, political appointees lack managerial experience, yet they are expected to run bureaucratic units that may have thousands of employees.[41]

Like cabinet members and heads of major agencies, these second- and third-tier political appointees do not remain long in office. Effectively there is a revolving political door: more than half of the undersecretaries and assistant secretaries tend to leave office after less than two years, and a fifth left after less than one year. What are the effects of this rapid turnover of personnel? Hugh Heclo aptly describes "a government of strangers" composed of people who are not known to one another before their appointment and who will have "only a fleeting chance to learn how to work together."[42] There is simply no time to build relationships of confidence and trust among political appointees, or between appointees and careerists within a single agency.

The president selects political executives because of their loyalty to him and to his programs, but there is no guarantee that appointees will remain loyal members of the president's team. Drawn from interest groups, think tanks, and so on, such appointees are likely to have their own constituencies and their own agendas. They are prone to remain staunch advocates for certain policies even if the president shifts his position once in office. And these advocate appointees operate under a very short time frame. They want to get their agenda across, and quickly. They may be quite unwilling to implement executive directives if presidential initiatives change course.

We must not neglect another important component of the political appointee system: political executives in the Executive Office of the President. The EOP has grown steadily in size, function, and complexity since Franklin Roosevelt's presidency. Some offices, such as the Council of Economic Advisors and the National Security Council, have been added by Congress; others have been established by presidential submission of a reorganization plan to Congress or by executive order. Today there are nine EOP offices, the most important of which are the White House Office, the Office of Management and Budget (as the Bureau of the Budget was renamed in 1970), the Council of Economic Advisors (CEA), and the National Security Council (NSC). Out of a total EOP work force of 1,500, almost 1,000 people work in the White House Office and Office of Management and Budget (OMB) alone. Today's EOP is actively in-volved in policy-making and policy implementation as well as executive branch coordination. As a result of its wide-ranging influence over eco-nomic, national security, domestic, and science and technology policy, its work overlaps, second-guesses, and often conflicts with that of the de-partments and agencies.[43]

The White House Office has become, in the words of scholar John Hart, "the directing force" and most powerful division within the Exec-utive Office of the President. The higher reaches of the White House staff are filled by more than fifty noncareer, highly partisan political execu-tives. These are "the president's men," the people the president most trusts to do his bidding. Light years removed from the anonymous exec-utive assistants envisioned by Brownlow, these senior aides quickly be-come prominent figures who make important policy decisions. They are interposed more often than not between the president and his cabinet secretaries and agency heads.[44] Their function is to manage and coordi-nate the policy-formulation process and to strengthen the hand of the president. Unfortunately this ideal is rarely achieved. The White House Office, with some five hundred employees, has itself become an unwieldy, politicized, and often unruly and divided bureaucracy. Political scientist James Fesler has concluded that the White House contribution "becomes not the comprehensive, long-range view of policy and honest brokering of conflicting departmental advocacy positions, but often a poorly coor-dinated battle for the president's mind among his own assistants."[45]

Even more than other political appointees, White House appointees are selected on the basis of personal loyalty to the president, campaign service in his behalf, and congruence with his policy views.[46] They share with all appointees a very short time frame. But they are more likely than departmental appointees to be strangers to the Washington political scene and to bring with them a great contempt for the permanent bu-reaucracy. This particular group of "strangers" is inclined to be hostile and arrogant; their antipathy frequently extends to top-ranking appoin-tees in the cabinet departments as well as to careerists.

As presidential distrust of the permanent bureaucracy has increased, so has presidential use of White House appointees to bypass both senior careerists and top-ranking cabinet appointees. We have noted Franklin Roosevelt's distaste for a slow-moving and unresponsive federal bureaucracy. All modern presidents have shared his views. Harry Truman reportedly complained, "I thought I was the president, but when it comes to bureaucrats, I can't do a damn thing." In a similar vein, John F. Kennedy is reported to have said to a caller, "I agree with you, but I don't know if the government will." And Jimmy Carter said in a 1980 press conference, "Before I became president, I realized and was warned that dealing with the federal bureaucracy would be one of the worst problems I would have to face. It has been worse than I had anticipated." In a 1969 television address Richard Nixon declared: "A third of a century of centralizing power and responsibility in Washington has produced a bureaucratic monstrosity, cumbersome, unresponsive, ineffective." In one of the Watergate transcripts Nixon complained to close adviser John Ehrlichman: "We have no discipline in this bureaucracy. We never fire anybody. We never reprimand anybody. We never demote anybody. We always promote the sons-of-bitches that kick us in the ass." Ehrlichman himself remarked at a press briefing that, once cabinet officials were appointed, "We only see them at the annual White House Christmas party; they go off and marry the natives." [47]

Contemporary presidents use White House appointees to formulate policies that in Japan and Europe would be the prerogative of ministers and their top bureaucrats. The White House is not even willing to give department heads carte blanche to select their own political subordinates. Cabinet secretaries and agency heads must persuade the White House to appoint second- and third-tier appointees whom they support. Sometimes this process is cooperative, but when the White House has reason to question the loyalty of a department head, the process becomes antagonistic and presidential loyalists are implacably pushed on an unwilling secretary. [48]

Presidential distaste for senior careerists is so pervasive that even the careerists located in the Executive Office of the President are viewed with suspicion. Top EOP bureaucrats, like their counterparts in the cabinet departments, are increasingly insulated from top decision-making and managerial roles by several layers of political appointees. The Office of Management and Budget provides an excellent illustration of the replacement of top-level careerists by political appointees. When the OMB's predecessor, the Bureau of the Budget, became part of the Executive Office of the President in 1939 it was staffed by quite competent careerists who reported to a single presidential appointee. Beginning in the 1960s, however, several presidential appointees were inserted between the director and staff careerists.

This trend continued. Nine of the top ten officials Jimmy Carter initially appointed to Office of Management and Budget had no previous experience in the executive branch. By 1980 the top ten staff members were all political appointees. One observer noted: "Successive presidents have increasingly devalued the expert knowledge of their own career budget staff in the Executive Office of the President, even though there is no one but the President to whom the staff could be loyal." [49] The Reagan administration used the OMB to exercise unprecedented budget authority over other agencies. It made certain that OMB appointees were thoroughly in agreement with the Reagan budget-cutting agenda. Reagan appointees viewed OMB careerists with great suspicion and effectively removed them from decision-making positions.

The dual administrative structure in the U.S. government means that the nation's federal executive branch is increasingly directed by short-term amateurs. These relative strangers to the Washington scene arrive with limited previous knowledge of the federal administration and yet must immediately begin to function as senior managers and policymakers. More than half of all presidential appointees come from outside government, almost half come from outside Washington, fewer than half have spent even five years of their working lives in the federal government, and more than one-fourth have no prior federal government experience.[50]

The vast majority of appointees are intelligent, industrious, and capable, and many are quite knowledgeable about issues and policies, but any new arrival to a job, no matter how bright, well-informed, and motivated, needs time to learn about it. Managing vast bureaucratic organizations and their many units is an extraordinarily complex task. Said former Secretary of Commerce Maurice Stans, "A business executive needs at least two years to become effective in government, to understand the intricacies of his programs, and to make beneficial changes." [51] Yet time is one luxury appointees simply do not have. One-third may remain for eighteen months or less, and fewer than one-third stay as long as three years.[52] Just as they are beginning to acquire the experience necessary to do their jobs properly, they leave, often never to return. The casualties are consistent public policy and effective public management.

Government by transients and amateurs tends to be inept government. Under severe time constraints, an incoming administration is pressured to push its policy agenda while still under the glow of the presidential "honeymoon" with the public, Congress, and the media. The first six months in office provide the greatest opportunity for presidential policy initiatives, but the new team is seldom prepared. Numerous appointee slots at the subcabinet and sub-subcabinet levels remain unfilled. An inexperienced campaign staff and transitional advisers are forced to fashion early legislative proposals.

Thus the policy formulation process is at its weakest precisely at the time when potential legislative support is greatest. A valuable opportunity is lost and never regained, for at no other time in a president's term will the political environment be so receptive to the presidential legislative agenda. A change in administration does far more than behead each department; several layers of appointees are displaced. The top 50 to 175 officials of a cabinet-level department will usually be replaced, including the secretary, the deputy and undersecretaries, assistant and deputy assistant secretaries, bureau chiefs, and regional directors. For instance, 93 high-level officials can be displaced in the Department of Commerce, and 65 in the Agriculture Department.[53]

With more and more people being hired as appointees, it is becoming extremely difficult to recruit well-qualified candidates, especially at lower levels. New administrations lack personnel information resources, because personnel files do not pass from one administration to another. New personnel officers themselves tend to lack Washington experience. And as selections have become increasingly political and ideological, so has the probability of ending up with incompetent officials. A report by the National Academy of Public Administration notes:

> No modern administration has yet fully succeeded in developing a set of initial staffing procedures that are comprehensive, timely, or adequately related to the new president's immediate policy objectives. . . . No corporation or other private enterprise could long endure a recruitment process like the one used by the federal government to fill its senior executive positions.[54]

Some candidates for appointment are put off by the slow, hostile, and heavily politicized Senate confirmation process. Pay scales are also a problem, as they lag well behind those in the private sector. But most appointees are willing to put up with these aggravations. Far more detrimental to policy formulation and departmental management are the growing delays in confirmation. The whole process is bogging down. Over the most recent decades, the average length of time to complete the appointment process has increased significantly. In the Lyndon Johnson administration the average time from the final candidate selection to confirmation was seven weeks, but with each succeeding administration this figure has risen. Under Reagan it stood at fourteen weeks.[55]

Particularly damaging to administration and the policy process is the rapid turnover of personnel at the top of the executive branch. Appointees have barely shaken off their status as inexperienced amateurs when they decide to leave. New recruits must take their places, and once again the cycle begins. Their replacements must learn anew to master the intricacies of policy-making and management. Because there is little institutional memory at the top, mistakes are repeated. Valuable time is lost, and heightened inefficiency results.

Effectively isolated from the president and the offices of the cabinet secretaries, most top careerists retreat to the relative safety of their subgovernments. They concentrate on collaborating with congressional subcommittees and clientele groups to produce mutually rewarding pieces of public policy. Rejected as important decision-makers and managers by presidents and their appointees, there remains little incentive for most upper-level civil servants to develop a government-wide perspective. They seek as much bureau autonomy as possible, a goal that normally receives warm approval from Congress.

Senior American careerists are capable of performing in an important policy-making and managerial capacity. They have the expertise and depth of experience that appointees lack, and with appropriate incentives and training they could overcome their myopic, subgovernmental perspectives. Congress, as we have seen, has little reason to elevate the horizons of senior careerists because these bureaucrats are such an important component of the triangular relationship between interest groups, bureaucrats, and the Congress. But although the president and top-level appointees do have a stake in the formulation and implementation of coherent and cohesive public policies, they too consistently refuse to make use of the most capable and most readily available personnel.

Senior bureaucrats are at best ignored by the president and his aides; at worst they become a target of presidential attacks on the Washington establishment. Neglected and unappreciated by key political officials in the executive branch, senior careerists languish demoralized and frustrated in the backwaters of numerous subgovernments. Even in the State Department, an agency in which senior careerists have traditionally held high positions, the recent influx of political appointees has lowered morale among high-ranking foreign service officers who now face reduced promotional opportunities often followed by forced early retirement. Political scientist Nelson Polsby contends that the emergence of a "presidential branch" of government separate and apart from the executive branch is "perhaps the most interesting development in the postwar period":

> It is the presidential branch that sits *across* the table from the executive branch at budgetary hearings, and that imperfectly attempts to coordinate both the executive and legislative branches in its own behalf. Against this development—this growing estrangement if not outright hostility of the presidential branch—the executive branch has been helpless, and that is the root cause of the decline in the caliber of the career bureaucracies.[56]

Senior careerists in the executive branch do not have a monopoly on low morale and frustration. These sentiments are not uncommon among senior departmental in-and-outers who feel caught between careerists who find them too political and/or too inexperienced, and White House staffers who accuse them of not being sufficiently loyal to the president. The general environment in the executive branch has become one of pervasive distrust and hostility: careerists, White House appointees, and departmental appointees are increasingly suspicious of one another. As a former assistant treasury secretary observed:

> The operating agencies and departments feel that White House aides unwisely isolate the President and influence his decisions

without considering the technical advice that others have provided. White House assistants retort that Cabinet officials are
immersed in operating details and become captives of institutional goals rather than concentrating on the needs of the President. Political appointees are placed in a no win situation: the
career employees responsible for their programs resent pressures they believe are politically motivated and White House
officers argue that the appointed officials should be better team
players.[57]

These adversarial relationships within and across executive agencies and
the Executive Office of the President do little to promote cohesive and
coordinated public policy and effective management.

A fragmented and distrustful executive branch is ill-suited to confront
the policy demands of the awesome competitive challenges now facing
the United States. As new issues crowd into the arena, the policy agenda
has become congested. The federal government is not just doing more
things, it is doing more things that affect one another. Any particular
government program—even one seemingly narrow in scope—cascades
across a host of traditional policy and organizational boundaries. Public
policy is growing technically more sophisticated, and the task of managing the federal executive branch is becoming more politically and administratively complex.[58] In such an environment, the influence of a continuing body of managerial and policy-making experts would be of
enormous help. But this is precisely the solution that all modern presidents have rejected.

Contemporary public administration scholars warn of the loss of valuable experience and expertise in a system that relegates senior career
executives to a subordinate status. They lament the lack of attention devoted to the recruitment, training, and development of new generations
of career managers, and they are nearly unanimous in their call for a
reduction in the number of transient political appointees and a concomitant elevation of a well-trained corps of senior civil servants to top managerial and policy-making positions.

But there is overwhelmingly formidable opposition to the creation of
a Japanese-style or European-style top professional bureaucracy in the
United States. Like the earlier civil service reformers, who believed that
administration and politics should remain clearly divided, many contem-

porary observers and public officials—including the president and his top advisers and many members of think tanks, interest groups, Congress, and the media—believe that only the elected president and his political appointees should be in charge of policy-making. A select group of top bureaucrats with substantive policy-making functions, so the argument goes, would violate the tenets of our constitutional design and our democratic heritage.

What we see here is an underlying distrust of the state, a bedrock conviction that a powerful central state apparatus is destructive of democracy. In an age that cries out for a geopolitical economic grand strategy solidly backed by bureaucratically administered comprehensive industrial policy, our anti-statist tradition and our idiosyncratic political institutions leave us ill-prepared to face the increasingly ominous Japanese challenge.

PART FOUR

ECONOMIC POLICY
AND
THE INDUSTRIAL POLICY
DEBATE
IN AMERICA

ECONOMIC POLICY-MAKING IN THE UNITED STATES follows closely the path predicted by our anti-statist political tradition, our fragmented political institutions, and our disjointed policy-making apparatus. The fiscal and monetary policy of the United States today reflects the nature of our limited state and our noninterventionist economic policies, as we shall see in Chapter 9. Neutrality is a key factor in U.S. fiscal and monetary policy. Because the Federal Reserve System, our central bank, is regarded as politically independent, the monetary policy it produces is seen by Americans as greatly preferable to fiscal policy emanating from a more politically sensitive federal government. For instance, tax policies in general and depreciation schedules in particular have the power to channel industrial growth in certain directions, which is precisely what happens in Japan. In the United States, however, we have generally resisted the temptation to use fiscal policy as an economic directing force.

Not only do Americans believe in government neutrality and the unconstrained free market on the domestic scene, but we also expect foreign governments to be neutral in the realm of international trade. The United States has maintained a free-trade policy that has provided the most open market in the world, for a long time and at great cost to our competitive posture. American protectionism—a growing trend despite our unabashed free-market rhetoric—has been intermittent, uncoordinated, and generally unproductive.

Spontaneity and "ad-hocracy" have also been hallmarks of the few industrial policy initiatives the federal government has undertaken.

What the Federal Reserve System has done in the case of monetarism to relieve the federal government of its unwanted and supposedly unneeded fiscal interventionism, the courts have undertaken in the area of antitrust policy—for instance, the successful and unsuccessful attempts to break up AT&T and IBM, respectively. Finally, the Chrysler bailout prompted a highly politicized struggle waged in the Congress. Politics, not economics, and certainly not industrial strategy, was the driving force throughout.

It is ironic that, at a time when the possibility of comprehensive Japanese-style industrial policy is as remote as ever, something called "the industrial policy debate" over how to improve our declining competitive posture is raging in the United States. In Chapter 10 we look at the recommendations from the political right and the political left. The right has no time for industrial policy because even industrial policy initiatives of limited scope threaten to violate the sanctity of the free market. So industrial policy is primarily the child of the Democratic party and the political left.

Unfortunately, the industrial policy debate in the United States has generated far more heat than light, in large measure because social justice and redistributional issues have become intertwined with economic policy recommendations. The spectrum of industrial policy proposals running from the moderate to the radical left moves progressively from economic issues to political issues. Republicans and the political right—no friend of industrial policy in the first place—fear industrial policy proposals because of their market-encroaching, interventionist character and their tendency to have an egalitarian, redistributionalist thrust. They have come to see industrial policy as a Trojan horse for a democratic, antibusiness policy agenda. No matter how severe American economic decline becomes, and no matter how ominous the threat from Japan, full-blown industrial policy doesn't stand a chance in the United States without friends on both the right and the left, among Republicans and Democrats.

9

FAILURES OF U.S. ECONOMIC POLICY-MAKING

He's no use to us if Detroit is his idea of a small town.
—*F. Scott Fitzgerald* (The Great Gatsby)

The economic fortunes of the United States can be reversed only if the nation adopts a comprehensive industrial policy akin to that in Japan. Our working definition of industrial policy in this book—*industrial policy is the state-induced willful shifting of the industrial structure toward high-technology, high-value-added industries*—defines in a nutshell the Japanese experience described in Part Two. The success of individual American firms, industries, and the entire industrial structure must be ratified in the domestic and international marketplace. This market-sensitive shifting of the industrial structure will maximize high-technology exports and direct necessary imports toward raw materials and low-technology products. Successful industrial policy will result in high per capita GNP, international dominance of strategic high-technology industries, and favorable international trade and foreign account balances.

Recent economic policy-making in the United States is worlds removed from industrial policy as we have defined it above. In Chapter 10 we shall discover that the so-called debate over industrial policy in America is really a debate between the free-market right and the social-justice left about government intervention, and that neither side favors Japanese-style industrial policy.

Real industrial policy advocates in the United States are virtually nonexistent. When even watered-down industrial policy is discussed in this country, there are usually two stock responses. The most frequent dismissals of industrial policy charge that American economic policy failures and abortive government initiatives are solid evidence of the uselessness of industrial policy in the United States. And most of the small number of industrial policy advocates tell us that our singular political and social institutions make it impossible for an industrial policy to be adopted here.

These industrial policy critics are in a limited sense correct on both counts. The ad hoc and uncoordinated industrial policy initiatives in the United States have been failures, and a comprehensive Japanese-style industrial policy is impossible within the context of the current political environment. But the fundamental mistake is the framing of the industrial policy debate in terms of the domestic economic and political environment in the United States.

Any meaningful discussion of industrial policy must be cast in an *international* dimension. Industrial policy was invented and perfected abroad. Its successes and failures must be measured by the relative economic performance of its consummate Japanese practitioners. By these standards, as we have seen, it must be judged a thumping success.

There is, and has been for some time, a new game of international competitiveness. The Japanese have invented the game and written the rulebook. South Korea, Taiwan, and many other newly industrializing nations, along with most other advanced industrial societies, are beginning to play by the new rules of economic nationalism and industrial policy. Much like past revolutionary advances in military technology—from gunpowder to the tank to aircraft—Japan's invention and perfection of industrial policy and its attendant economic nationalism has recast the rules of economic performance and competitiveness. Unfortunately for the United States, a nation that doesn't have an industrial policy can't get into the game.

The free-trade system implemented by the United States during the immediate post–World War II period was made possible only through the nation's overwhelming economic strength in a war-devastated world. Early on the Japanese challenged the prevailing U.S.-sponsored free-trade/state-neutral economic philosophy with economic nationalism. The U.S. bulldog was for many years little concerned that the Japanese kitten was pawing around in a new game called "economic nationalism backed by industrial policy." Americans were amused and occasionally annoyed, but that was about all. Now, however, the kitten has grown into a tiger and we have been put on the defensive.

And what does the Japanese tiger feed on? Technology. In the waning years of the twentieth century, technology is indisputably the key to economic, political, and military dominance. Technology is the ballgame. We may and probably will sooner or later balance the budget, erase our trade deficit, and reduce our mountain of foreign debt. But if we do it by exporting raw materials along with low- and middle-technology products, if we do it without technological preeminence, we will lose world leadership in all dimensions.

Americans face a simple and very fundamental choice. We can continue to play the game by our long-cherished rules of state-neutral free markets and free trade, or we can elect to engage the Japanese through the use of industrial policy. The first option keeps us on the current road to economic decline; the second option points the way toward economic revival.

An understanding of our idiosyncratic political institutions and the anti-statist tradition out of which they were born prepares us to examine the crazy-quilt pattern of recent U.S. economic policy-making. The economic policy of the United States stands in stark contrast to the strategic vision and adept tactical execution inherent in Japan's industrial policy and its underlying foundation, the Japanese system. The fragmented nature of American political institutions and the American political process results in ad hoc, inconsistent, and incoherent economic policy. And American economic policy is not only uncoordinated but also purposely kept that way. Americans don't want a strategic plan and a set of priorities designed to move the economy toward a preconceived future. Strong in the belief that the best American firms are competitive international champions fully capable of beating foreign challengers, we don't think it's necessary to train or coach. We send our players onto the field and cheer loudly for free enterprise, free markets, and neutral states. But we are losing the game, and it's not even close.

Let's take a quick look at where the United States is today with respect to economic policy. From 1945 until the early 1970s, fiscal and monetary policy in the United States was concerned very little with economic events abroad. Americans were wrapped securely within the cocoon of a largely self-sufficient national economy, our attention focused squarely on creating and stimulating demand sufficient to absorb the cornucopia of goods pouring out from our unparalleled productive capabilities. With the production problem solved, tax policies were directly linked to consumption and to questions of demand management. As a result of the highly successful Kennedy tax cut of 1963, tax policy became a viable means for applying broad aggregate demand stimulus to the economy. With reduced taxes, consumers would have more to spend, which in turn would raise corporate sales and profits and eventually return even more to the government's coffers.

Unfortunately, demand stimulus tended to channel spending toward increased consumption and less investment. Mortgage interest deductibility, coupled with the high inflation rates of the 1970s, pushed huge amounts of money into residential housing. The cost of capital for residential construction remained low relative to that for new plant and equipment. During this period the widespread use of tax shelters resulted in extraordinary energies and inventiveness employed in directing investments toward tax avoidance first and investment merits second. Not only were tax reductions made on an across-the-board basis, resulting in most tax savings going into consumption rather than productive investment, but even worse, in the few instances where exceptions to tax uniformity were made, concessions were most often given to sunset industries already severely damaged by competitive pressures. Generally it was a matter of too little too late.

Tax policy aimed at stimulating specific investments with a developmental component is called "targeting." In Japan, as we have seen, industrial targeting has helped create one world-class industry after another.

In the United States, differential tax rates and depreciation schedules designed to nudge industrial development into more desirable channels are in the vast majority of cases dismissed out of hand. The common and pejorative expression for targeting, particularly among its opponents, is "picking the winners and losers." This approach is universally regarded as unworkable and, beyond that, unfair.

In 1979 a new role for monetary policy was signaled by President Carter's appointment of Paul Volcker as head of the Federal Reserve Board. By the end of the Carter administration, rampant inflation had been declared public enemy number one. Volcker attacked and defeated it by tight monetary policies so severe that they induced the worst recession of the postwar period. The most pernicious consequence of the Volcker-Reagan war on inflation was the devastating effect it had on the already weakened manufacturing sector. Extraordinarily high interest rates created an overvalued dollar, which crippled U.S. export efforts while opening the door for a flood of artificially cheap imports. Here blame should be laid not so much on the Reagan administration for its dose of painful but necessary corrective action as on the economic policies of previous Democratic and Republican administrations that created the problem in the first place.

Reagan's triumph over inflation, coupled with the sharp rebound of the economy (after unemployment had reached a high-water mark of 11 percent), ushered in a new era. It provided an appropriate and reassuring backdrop for the marriage of the free-market monetarism of Milton Friedman and the minimalist noninterventionist state of Ronald Reagan. As economist Andrew Shonfield described this approach, "The call for the limitation of public power, through the political elevation of the central bank or some other independent agency to impose discipline on the politicians, is part of a more general anti-government pro-market polemic."[1] Monetarism's alluring appeal to those on the right who feared and loathed the welfare state, an obtrusive meddling government, and weakened individual initiative was its apolitical, antiseptic quality.

Monetarism struck a responsive chord among the noninterventionists as a one-time fix, an economic prime mover, because it took many economic decisions out of the hands of a federal government that was at best bumbling and incompetent and at worst the prisoner of selfish special interests. Basking in the glow of the economic recovery of 1983, the monetarists—desiring more than half a loaf—pushed ahead. Like a host of busy Lilliputians desiring to secure fast the federal Gulliver, they sought a constitutional amendment mandating a balanced budget.[2]

As concern about the competitive posture of the United States became more widespread after 1980, few proposals failed to take into account the need for increased levels of investment. The Reagan administration, convinced that high marginal tax rates sapped the incentive to save and invest, moved quickly on tax reduction aimed at stimulating investment. Under the 1981 tax act, increased use of the investment tax credit (ITC), combined with drastic revision of depreciation schedules (reducing by almost 50 percent the depreciable lives of buildings and equipment), proclaimed a proinvestment, pro-capital-formation economic policy with a pronounced industrial viewpoint.

Unfortunately, tax reform was again high on the administration's agenda early in 1985, but this time the investment tax credit and liberalized depreciation schedules were destined to fall victim in 1986 to simplified and reduced personal rates that shifted more of the tax burden from individuals to business. Rate reduction and simplification, coupled with elimination of a host of tax shelter abuses, unquestionably produced a fairer tax code. However, the dismantling of the proinvestment, accelerated depreciation schedules and the ITC components of the 1981 bill yielded a proconsumption anti-investment bias that is likely to be with Americans for some time. This consumption-investment-consumption U-turn is reminiscent of conservative/labor economic policy shifts in Great Britain. We even accomplished it without having to change parties.

Most of the framers and supporters of these new laws believed that the liberalized depreciation and ITC components of the 1981 act skewed investment toward heavy industry and smokestack America and away from the promised bright future of sunrise enterprises in the high-technology and service fields. The proponents of the new tax bill were firmly in the American grain. By reducing the tax benefits provided by the investment tax credit and liberalized depreciation, they nipped in the bud any incipient move toward industrial targeting and industrial policy. Investment decisions, they believed, should be allocated solely by means of the competitive market.

It was hoped that the new act would bring about better investments, resulting in heightened productivity growth and yielding increased capital formation. All this assumed a growth in the personal savings rate sufficient to offset the decline in business savings. We do need both good investments and more of them, but the siren of consumption proved too strong for the average American, and the personal savings rate worked its way down to an all-time low by the end of the 1980s. With additional personal disposable income going to consumption rather than savings, less net savings reduced investment. Lowered investment reduces productivity growth, showing up in less GNP growth and finally diminished savings rates—a vicious cycle of the worst kind. On balance, the 1986 bill must be regarded as fundamentally anti-capital-formation and anti-investment, during a period in which we have obviously been overconsuming and underinvesting.

Private sector savings is, of course, only one side of the coin. Regardless of the tax structure, total savings is dependent on private sector savings coupled with public savings or dissavings through budget surpluses or deficits. Economic recovery has been achieved only in the face of the most massive and persistent budget deficits in U.S. history. Unfortunately, contrary to the Keynesian orthodoxy that deficits will be eliminated as recovery occurs and unemployment is reduced, Americans now face the new and frightening phenomenon of full-employment deficits— a perverted one-eyed Keynesianism. In a society where the personal savings rate has not been sufficient to fuel enough new investment, growing budget deficits pose a continuing threat to the maintenance of our standard of living.

The free-trade philosophy of the United States was securely enshrined at the 1944 Bretton Woods monetary conference. With the United States as the world's primary creditor nation, the dollar displaced the British pound as the international reserve currency. As the world's undisputed economic and political power, the United States sought international economic recovery and the worldwide growth of democratic governments through a system of free trade. Americans had much to gain and little to fear from this new economic order.

Trade expansion and the reduction of existing tariff barriers were given further impetus and more specific direction through the establishment in 1948 of the General Agreement on Tariffs and Trade (GATT). This international organization was mandated to expand world trade through successive rounds of multilateral tariff reduction. Because the threat of international communism was acute from 1945 on, whereas serious economic challenge on a broad front was only dimly perceived until the mid-1970s, U.S. trade policy was and remains conditioned by overarching foreign policy and national security goals. The Commerce Department—no MITI—is never a match for the State Department or the Defense Department. When economic and foreign policy goals conflict, the tentative and hesitant policies of the former are inevitably sacrificed to the grand strategies of the latter.

The same free-market limited-state philosophy that has permeated every aspect of U.S. domestic monetary and fiscal policy has consistently carried over into the international sphere. Tariffs, quotas, aid to domestic firms injured by foreign competition, and export promotion policies are all regarded as alien to basic American political and economic beliefs. Americans abhor the bureaucratic meddling and interference that is necessary to design and implement these policies at home, and they oppose and condemn those actions when they are adopted by governments abroad.

We implement some of these policies ourselves, but intermittently, halfheartedly, and reluctantly because they require state action and bureaucratic design. We do this because irresistible political pressure erupts in the Congress and forces us to—kicking and screaming all the way. Whether we implement such policies on an ad hoc basis here at home or find them used as consistent elements in a far-reaching industrial policy by our competitors abroad, they are distasteful to us. Americans do not like state action; they see it as un-American. Until quite recently, free-trade rhetoric asked only that we play on a level playing field, and one that is not completely level at that. The United States has been so confident of its ability to compete that it willingly conceded its opponents some margin of advantage.

Despite the firm and enduring philosophical commitment of Americans to the principle of free trade, the United States has inadvertently and very much in a reactive mode become more protectionist. In the United States, protectionism has a uniquely American flavor; it originates within specific industries and is promoted by a political constituency intent on instant relief from painful economic injury. No administration has ever espoused or adopted strategic protectionist policies designed to facilitate domestic market adjustment for declining sectors or to promote exports for more promising industries. Without explicit strategies for adjustment and promotion, protection will at best freeze an industry in place and at worst tend to accelerate its already declining fortunes.

Antidumping charges seeking injury findings by the U.S. International Trade Commission are difficult and time-consuming to investigate, nearly impossible to prove, and over the long term almost guaranteed to do the injured party more harm than good. Perhaps therein lie the unwritten rules of American trade policies. Because Americans have committed themselves philosophically and politically to free trade and encourage similar attitudes among their international trading partners, they are intellectually and emotionally unsympathetic to firms and industries that do not measure up to the standards of international competitiveness. As these injured industries come crawling to Washington pleading vigorously but reluctantly for federal intervention, the federal government contrives, as if by design, a half-baked program—enough to buy off their powerful supporters in Congress but not enough to reverse their declining fortunes. Forced to act against its instincts and better judgment, the executive branch manages to botch the job, turning the fate of the manufacturing sector over to the vicissitudes of so-called "unrestricted" free trade. According to one observer:

There is no public evidence that the government has considered the question of how *far* it would let any sector die out before it determined to stop or reverse the situation. That is, there seems to be no policy position that the United States ought to have a given amount of steel production, or of textiles, autos, or any industry within its borders.[3]

On balance an administration will agree to certain protectionist measures only in support of broader economic and political objectives that require the votes of the protectionist coalition. In the early 1960s the Kennedy administration, trying to "get the country moving again" in the face of stiff legislative head winds, bowed to Southern congressional demands for assistance to a beleaguered textile industry. The decision in this case had little to do with the strategic concerns of the textile industry; it was endorsed to marshal support in the South for New Frontier social programs.

In Japan and elsewhere abroad, tariff protection has been a systematic part of a coherent strategy designed to boost the international competitiveness of a particular industry. Although tariffs and other protectionist devices have been used in Japan for declining industries—agriculture being the most blatant example—their primary role has been support of newly emerging industries. In the United States, as international trade authority Charles Kindleberger observes, "Most tariffs are not to shield an infant [industry] in youthful and adolescent years, but to defend an adult one approaching senescence."[4] More often than not, import relief has been granted or withheld at random, devoid of commitments to renovation or adjustment.

A two-pronged approach calling for protection and readjustment on the one hand and export promotion on the other hand has never been part of U.S. trade policy. Throwing up last-ditch protectionist defenses around beleaguered industries in the terminal stages of decline while letting more healthy industries fend for themselves has seemed a much more acceptable solution. Over the past few years, many of the actions of the federal government seemed to suggest that major industries, such as steel and autos, might be allowed to disappear. According to this line of thinking, if the market pronounces decisively against these industries, we need not be unduly concerned, since the same process of economic natural selection will spawn a new crop of more vigorous sunrise industries.

The "old protection" of tariffs and quotas has gradually given way to a "new protection" of voluntary export restraints (VERs) and orderly marketing agreements (OMAs). By 1971 the dollar value of imported goods subject to restraint agreements exceeded the value of goods governed by tariffs and quotas.[5] Voluntary export restraints and orderly marketing agreements are distinguished by several features. They are bargained accords negotiated between the importing and exporting nations fixing imports at levels that are less than unrestricted competition would dictate. VERs and OMAs, the new language of protectionism, are both selective and quantitative. They apply only to certain goods, and they limit shipments based on the number of units, not on the total value.

This is simply protectionism by another name. The word "voluntary" has an especially hollow ring; "coercive" would be much closer to the mark. Until the late 1960s cotton textiles remained the primary products governed by restraint agreements, but after 1968 similar agreements were drafted to cover color television receivers, steel, automobiles, and other manufactured goods.

Deficiencies inherent in the new protection provided by voluntary export restraints and orderly marketing agreements abound. Perhaps the most serious side effect of restraint agreements is the ability of restricted exporters to sidestep the agreement by upgrading their products. A good illustration is provided early on with the Long-Term Agreement Regarding International Trade in Cotton Textiles, negotiated by the Kennedy administration in 1962. This agreement, which effectively restricted cotton textile imports, had the unintended consequence of shifting the import thrust of Asian products from cottons to synthetics. It was in synthetic fibers that the United States at that time enjoyed some technological superiority. But in short order, pressured by the necessity of earning foreign exchange, Japan and its Asian neighbors spurred their efforts to mount an effective assault on this segment of the market.

Of less strategic importance, but further illustrative of the dramatic shifts in targeted products, is the case of the footwear industry. Orderly marketing agreements negotiated in the late 1970s with several Far East nations provided for significant limitations only on non-rubber-soled footwear. Lacking the political clout of the textile industry, the footwear industry in the United States found itself rained on by a barrage of imported rubber footwear, plus rubber-sole replacement for traditional nonrubber materials.

Similar scenarios were played out in the steel and automobile industries as the Japanese in particular proved themselves adept at moving into high-value products. In steel, low-cost reinforcing bars and small merchant shapes quickly gave way to sophisticated high-value flat-rolled and oil-country tubulars. With Japan's auto imports capped at 1.67 million units in 1981, option-laden models commanding much higher sticker prices came to supplant earlier bottom-of-the-line offerings. This kept the total dollar value of automobile shipments moving steadily upward. In particular, the 1981 voluntary export restraints created the perception that Japan's automotive products were in tight supply, keeping prices well above the normal price in the absence of restraints. The restraints effectively increased automobile prices to the American consumer by an estimated $1,000. Auto manufacturers in the United States, driven as always by short-term profit goals, compounded their problems by raising prices instead of attempting to regain market share.

Invariably, when voluntary export restraints and orderly market agreements seemed imminent, a surge of the products in question poured into U.S. ports, causing greater present injury while relief was still far in the future. An effective alliance was forged between U.S. purchasers who were denied the savings of low-cost imports, and foreign producers facing the loss of valuable markets. Buyer and seller then jointly worked out numerous devices both to evade and to cheat on the new restraint agreements.

The twenty-five-year experience with restraint agreements in a number of industries has been disappointing. It is difficult to find any industry working with VERs and OMAs that did not become weaker and fall even more behind Japan technologically. These agreements did not work for two reasons. First, the United States was simply outnegotiated. The top trade officials of MITI and their counterparts in other countries were seasoned and skilled professionals whose thinking was cast in a strategic developmental mode. Despite a high level of competence and dedication, U.S. political appointees—in office for a year or two at most—were seldom a match for the more seasoned Asians. It was a case of amateurs against professionals. Second, we were not successful because deep in our hearts we were not convinced that these agreements were in either country's best interests. The United States negotiated because political pressure had built to the point where something had to be done. We did what we felt compelled to do, and no more.

The elements of American industrial policy that do exist are scattered about the economy in a crazy-quilt pattern of intermittent interventions. If Japan's industrial policy is best termed comprehensive, then America's economic policy is most appropriately described as ad hoc and noncomprehensive. In the United States, any attempt to link separate policy initiatives into a more coherent pattern is quickly shot down as tantamount to sub rosa efforts to institute national economic planning. Makeshift policies that avoid long-term commitments and vision are invariably the choice.

From a host of separate measures—for instance, accelerated depreciation, investment tax credits, tax cuts, loan guarantees, industrial revenue
bonds, and safe-harbor leasing—the United States has patched together
ad hoc programs, such as the Chrysler and Lockheed bailouts, the farm
and merchant marine programs, and housing subsidies. Because the
guiding assumption is that in variety and self-containment there is weakness, these measures and programs are not likely to coalesce into an administrative doctrine that threatens free-market noninterventionist
orthodoxy.

The closest we have come to a strategic consideration of sector priorities is the vague notion, shared by most Americans, that somehow our
industrial future is bound up with high-technology industries. For those
who doubt exactly how vague this vision of our high-technology future
is, we need only consider the way our semiconductor industry has been
battered and nearly beaten to death by the Japanese in the period since
1980. By the mid-1980s many U.S. merchant producers were forced to
seek financial alliances abroad—most often with the Japanese. Ample
evidence of how weak and demoralized the American semiconductor industry had become by 1986 is the fact that Japan's largest computer
company, Fujitsu, attempted to purchase an 80 percent stake in the Fair-
child semiconductor company, at that time the nation's second largest
merchant producer.[6] The sale was finally blocked by pressure from the
Defense Department. For once the U.S. government said "Enough is
enough."

Industrial policy initiatives have come from many quarters, not the least
of which has been the federal judiciary. Two landmark antitrust cases
illustrate the pitfalls of formulating industrial policy within the federal
courts.

On the last day of the Johnson administration, Attorney General Ram-
sey Clark filed an antitrust action against IBM. The case droned on for
thirteen years until 1982. With legal costs of several hundred million dollars, a thousand witnesses, 104,000 transcript pages, and more than
seven hundred trial days, the case was a monumental undertaking made
even more difficult by the ever-changing battery of Justice Department
lawyers. One participant in the case, John Diebold, observed, "Eight
years into the IBM case, for example, the government tried to subpoena

IBM documents that would have taken 62,000 man-years to produce—
at a cost of $1 billion!"[7] Throughout this period, IBM's share of the
domestic computer market was shrinking in the face of explosive growth
in minicomputers, personal computers, IBM plug compatibles, software
engineering, and, most significant, from foreign competition.

If any one aspect of the trial could best epitomize the ineptitude and
futility of this exercise, it was the Justice Department's contention, supported by Presiding Judge David Edelstein, that foreign competitors—
most notably, of course, the rapidly emerging Japanese—should not be
considered a competitive factor within the domestic computer industry.
Obviously, in the event of a Justice Department victory the splintered
remnants of the breakup would lack the staying power of the old IBM in
the impending struggle for dominance of global computer markets. But
the Japanese were quite offended that the competitive punch of their entire computer industry was given such a backhanded dismissal. All the
time the Japanese were striving desperately to create world-class computer companies, Americans were laboring to dismantle their own great
world champion. Mercifully, the government quietly dropped the case in
1982, ending one of the more inglorious chapters in U.S. antitrust history.

On January 8, 1982, the same day the government dropped its case
against IBM, it won by consent decree an eight-year quest to break up
American Telephone and Telegraph. Within the first decade of the commercial computer business, it became apparent that the distinction between telephone data transmission and computer data-processing was
fuzzy at best. Nonetheless, in 1956, through a consent decree, the Justice
Department permitted the Bell System to maintain its regulated monopoly over telephone service in the United States in return for forfeiting any
attempt to enter the computer business. By the mid-1970s, however,
AT&T's regulated monopoly was under attack from a number of quarters. Western Electric's control of home and business telephone equipment was threatened by such interconnect companies as Rolm and a host
of competitors. More significant, with direct challenges offered to
AT&T's highly profitable long lines division by MCI, and others providing microwave-based low-cost long distance transmission, the 1956 ruling began to look even more unrealistic.

Everybody got into the act: the Federal Communications Commission,
the Justice Department, Congress, and the federal judiciary. But Federal

Judge Harold Green was unquestionably the ringmaster of this long-running show. Few would argue that it was not good to allow the vast technological resources of AT&T to have free play in the expanding computer market. And given the initial lackluster commercial performance demonstrated by the new AT&T, it seemed to pose little threat to IBM or its smaller competitors. Whether the twenty-two Bell operating companies had to be sundered from the parent and reorganized into larger regional entities is open to serious question.

What is quite obvious is that Judge Green, despite his earnestness and judicial competence, was called on by the process he orchestrated to make decisions that required far greater technical competence and intimate knowledge of the telecommunications business than either he or any other federal judge might have been reasonably expected to command. An incisive study of the AT&T case notes: "The crucial decisions were driven by opportunism, short-term politics, ego, desperation, miscalculation, happenstance, greed, conflicting ideologies and personalities and finally a perceived necessity." [8] The case of Japan makes it clear that, to be successful, industrial policy must be not only politically sensitive but also politically insulated. Because the AT&T case was politically driven at every stage, it was destined to yield a half-baked economic policy at best.

Perhaps the single most dramatic instance of ad hoc industrial policy was the Chrysler Loan Guarantee Act of 1979. The so-called "Chrysler bailout" was politically charged throughout. The bill was opposed publicly by General Motors Chairman Thomas Murphy and former Commerce Secretary Peter Peterson. Testifying before Senator William Proxmire's banking committee, Peterson expressed his concern about the dangerous precedent of a federal rescue. Even more vocal was Citicorp's head, Walter Wriston: "There is no avoiding the fact that it is an attempt by the government to move economic resources to places where they would not otherwise go." [9] Statements of strong opposition came from the National Association of Manufacturers and the blue-ribbon Business Round Table. The chorus of nay-sayers was joined by such unlikely bedfellows as the *Wall Street Journal* and Ralph Nader's Congress Watch.

A massive lobbying effort spearheaded by skilled professionals, thousands of Chrysler dealers, and, most important, the political muscle of the United Auto Workers and its articulate and forceful leader, Douglas Fraser, finally carried the day. Threatened with the loss of as many as

500,000 jobs throughout the Chrysler supplier-dealer chain, the political pressure was irresistible. About his own personal lobbying efforts, Lee Iacocca said:

> I had better luck with the Italian caucus in the House. . . . All but one voted for us. Some were Republicans, some were Democrats, but in this case they voted the straight Italian ticket. We were desperate, and we had to play every angle. It was democracy in action.[10]

The Chrysler bailout was not at all concerned with whether Chrysler's impending failure was symptomatic of a deeper malaise afflicting the entire U.S. auto industry or the manufacturing sector as a whole. Chrysler had a problem. In one sense the solutions of its friends and enemies alike were cut from the same cloth. Its opponents said, "Keep away and let it fail." Its supporters recommended a one-time surgical fix: "Get it done and then stay away."

Examples of the failures of ad hoc industrial policy abound, from the disastrous sinkhole of the maritime aid program to the high-minded but ineffectual idealism of the Foreign Corrupt Practices Act. Indeed, a great deal of the regulatory policy the United States freely substitutes for industrial policy is based on the now erroneous assumption that the competitive posture of America is unassailable.

The abortive attempts over successive administrations to address the energy problem are another clear example of the need for consistent policy. From Richard Nixon's Project Independence after the first oil crisis in 1973, to the fall of the Shah in 1979 and Carter's call for response to the new energy crisis of "the moral equivalent of war," little of a constructive nature was done. The unfortunate tragedy at Three Mile Island sounded the death knell to any further expansion of the U.S. nuclear power industry, which was already under heavy and unrelenting siege from litigious environmentalists and consumer advocates. Spurred by talk of $50-a-barrel oil, drilling activity intensified from 1979 to 1981 and then plummeted from 1982 onward, throwing the oil patch into a depression far deeper than the automotive industry had experienced a few years earlier. As domestic discovery goes down, Americans face greater reliance on oil imports, but we adamantly refuse, in the face of all good reason, to allow a sizable federal tax on gasoline. The United

States is the only major industrial country to stubbornly avoid this very modest act of self-discipline.

The threads of the intricate workings of the industrial policy process in Japan can be traced back to their point of origin: the upper reaches of the state bureaucracy. Any understanding of Japan's industrial policy must include recognition of the primacy of government initiatives within a coherent economic strategy. In the case of the United States, however, even the most casual observer can see that there is no mechanism with which to formulate an explicit industrial policy. Instead, there are myriad potential participants in the vital information-processing sector within the federal government—for example, the Pentagon, the Justice Department, the Commerce Department, the U.S. trade representative, the science adviser to the president, the National Bureau of Standards, the National Science Foundation, NASA, the Federal Communications Commission, and Congress.[11]

Any discussion of U.S. industrial policy brings to mind faceless bureaucrats conspiring with self-serving industrial oligarchs in the now infamous process of "picking the winners and losers." Negative images of state action constantly bombard the public, so it is no surprise that Americans are instinctively distrustful of Washington. According to Lester Thurow: "In the end all of the critics of American industrial policies come back to [one] comment. American government is incompetent and exercises bad judgment. Therefore even if industrial policies work abroad they cannot work here."[12] Any call for interventionist action on the part of the state to improve America's competitive posture brings back painful memories of the more egregious failures of the past.

The one exception to the blanket rejection of state power in the United States involves matters of national security. In this light many (in Congress too) are arguing that industrial policy should be an element of our national security policy. These proponents of a defense-based industrial policy suggest that industrial policy should be subsumed under national security policy. They contend that through the Defense Advanced Research Projects Agency (DARPA) the Pentagon is actually carrying out an industrial policy. They argue that DARPA is the best agency to assume more responsibility for promoting American technological competitiveness.

The best that can be said about these recommendations is that they have not gotten very far off the ground. A defense-led industrial policy would be counterproductive. Competitiveness involves commercializing products for the nondefense marketplace. Furthermore, the drain of money and scarce technological expertise into the defense area has already weakened our ability to compete with the Japanese. The concept of national security has been too narrowly defined as military defense; it should be broadened to include economic and technological competitiveness. Americans are currently a long way from judging their very obvious economic failures as seriously as they judge any perceived military weaknesses.

While it was quite difficult to formulate any coherent economic policy before Watergate, it was twice as difficult afterward. The meager resources of presidential authority were funneled off to an increasingly powerful Congress. To achieve meaningful success the architects of industrial policy must be sufficiently independent to exercise discretion and judgment. But U.S. economic policy makers are required to labor under the crippling condition of a fragmented political system that is designed to reflect, largely unimpeded and undistilled, the public will.

With a weakened executive branch incapable of shaping appropriate economic initiatives, Congress of necessity assumes the leading role. If industrial policies, of whatever sort, are to be in the future for the United States, they will either be initiated by Congress or Congress will transform administrative proposals so dramatically that they will be much more the child of Congress than of the president. Industrial policy must be made by people, not by laws, and a continuous series of midcourse adjustments to changing economic circumstances will be necessary. Congress might authorize an agency empowered to conduct policy in such a manner, but that is unlikely.

It is more likely that the fruits of congressional concern with the competitive well-being of the United States will be a host of specific fixes designed to address single problems adequately while keeping administrative discretion to an absolute minimum. In the absence of executive leadership, Congress is now attempting to formulate specific policies for superconductivity and high-definition television, but without a comprehensive strategy we cannot be optimistic about the results. Trying to conduct industrial policy through a series of congressional initiatives is much like trying to repair a Swiss watch while wearing boxing gloves. With the recent wildfire growth of political action committees (PACs), individual congressmen are under more pressure than ever to support the special interests that provide their economic wherewithal. The full flowering of PACs has heightened the natural adversarialism and contentiousness of the congressional arena.

For more than two hundred years the American system of checks and balances has kept the nation's political traditions close to the middle, banishing the extreme right and left to well-deserved political obscurity. "The checks and balances," says George Will, are "designed to channel and manipulate self-interestedness into a social equilibrium."[13] But today, with respect to the competitive posture of the United States, equilibrium is not sufficient, for the current trend line points down, not up. What was once interest-group pluralism, a political "process" characterized by interest-group mediation, now becomes the politics of special interests. Today each of these special interests has sufficient political power to block legislation that threatens its particular sphere of influence.

In today's "broker state," special interests bargain among themselves to secure benefits; they join together only in the face of threats from legislation advancing the common interest. Industrial policies most assuredly represent such an "advance of the common interest." Special interests are quite willing to sacrifice long-term industrial policy and the common interest to defend their narrow, real, and near-term needs. But a nation that fills its veins with the cholesterol of special interests is likely to suffer economic decline.[14] When we total up the score, it seems that today—more often than not—sector and parochial interests predominate over the national and the universal.

10

AMERICAN INDUSTRIAL POLICY—
NO INDUSTRIAL POLICY

*We have an industrial policy in this country. The
policy is that we don't want an industrial policy.*
—Frank A. Weil
Former Undersecretary of Commerce

The current debate over industrial policy in America concerns only a
handful of specific industrial policy initiatives, and nothing like the full-
blown system operating in Japan. Few proposals for industrial policy
emanate from the political right, but that end of the political spectrum
has answers and programs for restructuring the competitive posture of
the United States that are quite close to existing policies and to the mainstream of public opinion. In fact, looking for industrial policy proposals
from the right is like asking the National Rifle Association to present a
gun control plan.

The most interesting and imaginative proposals have usually come
from the political left, both the left-center and the radical left. For the
radical left, industrial policy theory takes on much added ideological

baggage, and it is 180 degrees from the Japanese position. Those who are basically opposed to industrial policy include virtually all of the political right and a portion of the left.

One of the most convenient ways of dismissing the advocates of industrial policy is to deny that there is a competitiveness problem. Robert Lawrence, senior fellow of the Brookings Institution, makes precisely this argument in his book *Can America Compete?* His position parallels former Budget Director and CEA Chairman Charles Schultze's vigorous attack on the idea that America has a competitiveness problem. The crux of Lawrence's argument is that the greatly overvalued dollar was the dominant reason for the problems facing U.S. manufacturing. A falling dollar, he says, increases our international competitiveness by making U.S. goods less costly for foreign purchasers, but a falling dollar also lowers our standard of living by making us competitive, not so much on the basis of high productivity but on the basis of low wages.[1] Can America compete? Everyone can compete, even Bangladesh. The more appropriate question is: Can America compete while maintaining high wages based on rapid productivity growth? Can America compete while maintaining a standard of living that is among the highest in the world? The answer today is at best maybe, but evidence to the contrary is accumulating daily.

Less intellectually taxing, and of much wider appeal than the Lawrence thesis, is the argument offered by the executive editor of *Forbes* magazine in the 1982 article entitled "The Molting of America." Textiles, steel, machine tools, and automobiles have been virtually wiped out by low-priced foreign products—but not to worry. Like a reptile shedding its old skin for a new one, we will expeditiously drop the armor plate of smokestack America for the new lightweight, up-to-date protective covering offered by America's high-tech future. When high technology comes under attack, we will deftly move into specialty niches and service sectors that are immune from overseas assault. As the niches get tighter and the playing field becomes more restrictive, our Japanese competitors may well be paraphrasing boxer Joe Louis: "The United States can run but it can't hide."

Those on the right who find industrial policy anathema cling to the free market like the Holy Grail. One need only look at the Eastern Bloc countries, and other nations with considerable state ownership and allocation of productive factors by the central government, to know that the market and not the government best allocates labor, capital, and other resources. But according to the free-market orthodoxy, a government that successfully limits inflation, that reduces unemployment, and that avoids excessive industrial concentration has done all it can reasonably be expected to do.

Free market, free trade, and free country—it all fits together nicely. If we are forced, for the moment, to watch our once proud industries topple like tenpins under the onslaught of the new industrial competition, we need only stay the course—so the argument goes. And before long the same market forces that destroyed these industries will, through what Joseph Schumpeter called "gales of creative destruction," establish new ones in their stead. Unfortunately, we have been misled by the black-or-white either/or nature of American ideology into an endless and meaningless debate over what Robert Reich calls "the relative merits of two highly artificial concepts: the 'free market' and 'national planning.' " According to Reich, the choice America really faces "is rather between evading the new global context or engaging it. . . . Either way, government will be actively involved." [2]

The market is good and the government is bad. These views are as American as apple pie. And to those who have the temerity to question these tenets of faith, defenders proclaim that the very same policies made the United States the most economically and militarily powerful nation on earth.

A corollary to the free market orthodoxy of the opponents of industrial policy is a pronounced antigovernment bias. The first oil shock triggering Nixon's experimental wage and price controls in the early 1970s signaled the postwar high-water mark of the proplanning interventionists in the United States. In a wider context, Andrew Shonfield observes:

> The reaction against the earlier pretension of omnicompetence of certain governments is understandable, and the particular rejection of "fine tuning" of the economy by Keynesian methods of demand management is fully sustained by the post-war evidence of failure. But it has been followed by a movement,

which seems likely to prove just as untenable, to the other extreme.[3]

When he campaigned against Nixon's imperial presidency and talked about returning the "government to the people," Jimmy Carter did much to pave the way for the Reagan Revolution of the 1980s. The promarket, antigovernment right found its ideal standard-bearer and strongest candidate in Ronald Reagan, who appeared to have nearly as much disdain and distrust for his own government as he did for the "evil empire" of the Soviet Union.

In his 1981 inaugural address, Reagan declared: "Government is not the solution to our problem. Government is the problem." When asked how he selected key members of his new administration, he said: "My basic rule is that I want people who don't want a job in government."[4] Outmoded and ineffective social programs that delivered one dollar of benefits for two dollars of costs, and unnecessary regulations that impaired the ability of key U.S. industries to compete effectively, were all to be scrapped—their destinies to be sorted out and judged by a fair and impartial market mechanism. Of course, some social programs were clearly failures, and some business regulations were blatantly counterproductive. Much validity, then, was given to a broad-front effort to roll back big government and return tax dollars and decision-making powers to individuals and private businesses.

Specific corrective proposals from the right show the degree to which they are influenced by this promarket, antigovernment ideology. That ideology is by no means a proprietary product of the right. Ronald Reagan didn't invent it; he simply became its most eloquent and persuasive spokesman. While its strongest supporters are on the right, the same ideology also informs much of the thinking on the left, even the radical left. As we have seen, this antigovernment bias is an essential part of a centuries-long anti-statist tradition.

Supply-side economics was to provide the theoretical foundation for the Reagan administration's efforts to rekindle productivity growth and to correct past fiscal excesses. The symbol of supply-side economics, known as the Laffer curve, was provided by a young conservative economist, Arthur Laffer. In a Washington restaurant, Laffer sketched on a cocktail napkin a simple curve demonstrating that at a certain point on the curve further tax increases would actually lower tax receipts, as people lose the incentive to produce in the face of confiscatory taxes. Nobody took issue with the basic truth behind the Laffer curve. At some point, confiscatory tax rates do kill incentives and ultimately do reduce total tax receipts—no question about that. Serious argument, however, centered on the assertions of Jack Kemp, David Stockman, and others, supported by Laffer's own calculations, that we had already passed the point of maximum revenues on the curve. These supply-siders argued that a tax cut would free up funds for much-needed investment without draining tax revenues from the federal government. The logic was compelling—a real win-win situation. The Laffer curve may have been bad economics, but it was brilliant politics.

Despite the something-for-nothing hype surrounding its introduction, supply-side economics unquestionably represented a step in the right direction. In its rejection of the fine-tuning of Keynesian demand management, supply-side economics focused attention on U.S. investment rates and productive capacities. For a nation that had long been underinvesting and overconsuming, supply-side economics at least presented a promising new alternative. Improved international competitiveness had to begin with a broad-based supply-side policy at home.

Among a number of supply-side recommendations, four stand out: personal tax cuts, increased depreciation allowances, reduction of government expenditures, and elimination of excessive business regulation. However, the centerpiece of the supply-side program was tax reduction; rate reductions were skewed to favor higher income earners. Supply-side theory assumed this was the group most likely to save its additional income, which would result in increased investments, new and more productive equipment, and renewed economic growth. The results of the 1981 tax cuts were a keen disappointment to enthusiastic supply-siders. Private savings rates fell instead of increasing, an indication that at least for the moment Americans at all income levels are more ardent spenders than savers.[5] The liberalized depreciation component of the 1981 act appeared to be more successful, but this was largely reversed in the 1986 act, once again to permit further reductions in personal rates.

A relatively small number of industrial policy proposals have emanated from the political right. As we have observed, Japanese industrial policy, the real thing, is unqualifiedly a policy of the right. It is formulated and implemented by top bureaucrats within the government and top businessmen outside the government, both groups linked by a deep commitment to an industrial viewpoint. In the United States, government intervention from progressivism through the New Deal down to the present has had a distinctly adversarial antibusiness bias.

A moderate Republican, Kevin Phillips, has attempted to stake out an industrial policy position that would be acceptable to the mainstream of the Republican party. His book entitled *Staying on Top: The Business Case for a National Industrial Strategy* demonstrates just how difficult a job this is. Phillips begins by saying that Americans need to take industrial competition with Japan as seriously as military competition with the Soviet Union. So far so good. With only a few remarkable exceptions (Thorton Bradshaw, former RCA chairman; and J. Irwin Miller, former chairman of Cummings Engine), government intervention is anathema to the business community. Industrial policies are so closely identified—and rightly so—with state intervention that Phillips cloaks his modest proposals under the name national industrial "strategy," not industrial policy.

In an admirable and straightforward attempt to orient the thinking of the business community toward greater realism and relevance, Phillips tells Republicans:

> The laissez-faire conservative's view of the role of government is simply inadequate in today's global economy. To have any real impact on the debate about competitiveness, conservatives are going to have to do two things: first, look to the conservative activism in Western Europe and Japan; and second, draw on the example of business-government partnership in the early days of our own republic.[6]

Phillips proposes a five-point program calling for reform of federal trade organization, policy, and law; lobbying; taxes; labor-management relations; and education. The focal point of this program is his call for a new Department of International Trade and Industry, or DITI. (Does that name sound familiar?) DITI would combine the trade policy functions that are now divided between the Commerce Department and the Office of the U.S. Trade Representative. Phillips knows the problem is serious and believes something significant must be done, but then he tries, with limited success, to walk a narrow line between quick one-time fixes that may be acceptable to the free-market, antigovernment right and the substantive remedies that can be applied only by decisive long-term government intervention. Some of his recommendations show just how narrow is the line he attempts to walk:

> Tax policy also needs an overhaul. A special commission is the best solution. . . . I make a case for a national crash program in education, scientific research and technology. . . . The formulation of U.S. tax strategy must take into account the need to stay competitive globally. And probably the best way to develop new tax approaches is for the President to appoint a blue-ribbon commission. . . . [7]

The problem is that Japan doesn't make industrial policy with blue-ribbon commissions and crash programs. Japanese industrial policy is made by a competent, dedicated bureaucracy backed by a strong central state.

A program akin at least in intent to Japan's "portfolio management of prospective growth industries" is detailed by Julian Gresser, a practicing attorney living in Hawaii and Tokyo, in his *Partners in Prosperity: Strategic Industries for the United States and Japan*. Gresser calls for an industrial strategy based on promoting a limited number of critical strategic industries. Strategic industries are defined as industries that act as the levers and catalysts of economic growth at a given place and time. Examples would be cotton at the time of the industrial revolution in England, railroads in nineteenth-century America, steel and autos in postwar Japan, and semiconductors and computers in the late twentieth century.

Gresser recommends the creation of a new White House office, the Office of Strategic Industries (OSI), modeled along the lines of the Office of the U.S. Trade Representative. Upon consultation with a broad spectrum of interests, the OSI would evaluate and recommend a list of strategic industries ranked according to the strength of their leverage. The heart of Gresser's program involves voluntary bargaining between firms within a designated strategic industry along with government agencies, congressional committees, labor, consumer groups, environmentalists, minority interests, and apparently anyone else who wants to participate. This multilateral negotiation process would be what Gresser defines as a "negotiated industrial investment strategy" (NIIS). The result would be a "public contract" having a "hybrid status in law." According to Gresser, "it is like a private contract in that it is an agreement on specific terms and conditions."[8]

Gresser's ideas have much to recommend them. This procedure would at least focus national attention on the fortunes of firms and industries that are vitally important to the economic well-being of the nation, which would be a vast improvement over the current policy of every firm and industry for itself. This procedure could be implemented within the framework of our existing political institutions and is not at odds with the American political tradition. It is voluntary and ad hoc. Agreements might be general or specific, depending on the circumstances.

But two seemingly insurmountable obstacles soon present themselves. Could the negotiated industrial investment strategy forge an agreement? If in the face of a national energy crisis, Congress could not produce even a watered-down energy program—or, more recently, a fiscal tax package in a reasonable period of time—what could be expected from the less institutionalized and more amorphous NIIS? Assuming for the moment that this hurdle is passed and there is a "public contract," would it be enforceable? Tough decisions must be made, and certain interest groups will have to absorb unacceptable costs. It is doubtful that the United States has the institutional hardware to do the job. As Wendy's once asked: "Where's the beef?"

If the proposals of Phillips and Gresser sound like watered-down versions of industrial policy dressed up in free-market regalia to pass muster at the Reagan reviewing stand, let's look briefly at one unadulterated message of the right. In *Business Plan for America: An Entrepreneur's Manifesto,* venture capitalist Don Gevirtz sounds the call for America's economic renaissance: "Liberate the entrepreneurs!"

There is no confusing the good guys and the bad guys in this book. "Managerial aristocracy, corporate titans, and giantism" are starkly juxtaposed against "non-conformers, outsiders, and unconventionality." DuPont's Irving Shapiro, AT&T's Charles Brown, and Lazard Freres'

Felix Rohatyn are on one side of the street returning the steely-eyed stares of the likes of Jim Ling, Howard Hughes, and William Randolph Hearst. Big is bad and small is beautiful.

Despite an overexuberant presentation of a simple solution to a complex set of problems, Gevirtz makes some good points. American entrepreneurialism, resulting in the creation of millions of new businesses and tens of millions of new jobs, is one of the great strengths of this country. We do it, hands down, better than anyone else in the world. Favorable tax treatment of capital gains, and a stronger political voice for small business, can enhance entrepreneurialism's important role in the country's economic growth. But small businesses cannot do it alone. We must have a solid core of world-competitive major corporations, a stable of national champions.[9]

In 1980 Atsuyoshi Ouchi, senior vice-president of Nippon Electric, declared: "Boutique-style integrated circuit producers have no place in the highly competitive marketplace, whether their plants are in Silicon Valley, Silicon Island [Kyushu], or anywhere else where they are produced. Too many U.S. producers are too small." Citing examples such as Advanced Micro-Devices and National Semiconductor, Gevirtz argues that these producers "have mounted a massive counterattack on the Japanese monolith."[10] It turned out to be a counterattack that fizzled. Several of these U.S. companies, as of this writing, have shown large consecutive quarterly losses and are rapidly retreating into specialized niches or seeking accommodation with the Japanese.

One company that rejected the niche strategy and decided to meet the Japanese head-on was Micron Technology in Boise, Idaho. Reasoning correctly that the battle for commodity memory chips would be won or lost on the manufacturing floor and not in the design laboratory, Micron chose the low land and labor costs of Idaho and carefully positioned itself to be a low-cost producer. In 1984 it turned in a spectacular performance, earning $29 million on total revenues of $84 million. So striking was the success of Micron against the Japanese behemoths—almost like an electronic Clint Eastwood out there on the high plains—that it served as the centerpiece of a book by the most eloquent of the neoconservative economists, George Gilder. Micron, Gilder wrote, "shows once again that the crucial capital of industry is not money or machinery, but mind and spirit, and that America—in these crucial domains of enterprise—remains Number One." [11] By 1986, however, Micron had been flattened by the Japanese steamroller. It was fortunate to survive.

The left side of the political spectrum is much more favorably disposed toward the use of industrial policy than the political right. Several strands of thought unite the industrial policy recommendations emanating from the various different political viewpoints on the left. These businessmen, economists, and political scientists are all convinced that the threat of economic decline is very real and that something must be done because staying the course is no longer a reasonable alternative.

Advocates of an American industrial policy believe that macroeconomic policy and aggregate capital formation will not be enough. They propose the use of government initiatives to guide the market at specific points to achieve concrete objectives, which would require more generous use of social organization. Many advocates of industrial policy seek a voice as counsel to the policymakers of the Democratic party. And the industrial policy advocates in the Democratic party have a political agenda as well as an economic agenda. They want the United States to expand the dimensions of social justice at the same time it is taking steps to regain its economic strength and competitive edge.

From the moderate to the radical left we hear the cause of social justice and economic redistribution spoken in sotto voce by Felix Rohatyn and more plainly by Lester Thurow and Robert Reich, until finally it reaches a crescendo on the far left. Felix Rohatyn, a senior partner of the investment banking firm of Lazard Freres, gained national political prominence in 1975 when as chairman of the Municipal Assistance Corporation (MAC) he steered New York City back from the brink of bankruptcy. Based in part on his hands-on experience at MAC, Rohatyn has made the use of a modern-day Reconstruction Finance Corporation (RFC) the keystone of his industrial policy proposals.

He begins by recommending creation of a tripartite board appointed by the president and consisting of representatives of business, labor, and government. The new Reconstruction Finance Corporation would be the financing agency of the tripartite board. Authorized by Congress, with

$5 billion in capital provided by the U.S. Treasury, it would issue $25 billion (five times its capital) in bonds and finance up to 50 percent of any project, public or private. So structured, this agency would have the capacity to generate up to $60 billion in targeted new investments.[12] Candidates for RFC financing might include the now resolved Chrysler and Lockheed cases, along with municipal needs such as the New York Metropolitan Transit Authority.

Rohatyn's closeness to the political right becomes clear when he tells us: "The RFC need not stay in existence more than seven to ten years, after which it could be liquidated, with its assets taken over by the Treasury."[13] He doesn't mind tampering with the market, but he does not want to do it for an extended period of time. He knows that by itself the RFC would not constitute an adequate industrial policy. It would have to be supplemented by tax changes, adjustment of trade regulations, and other competitiveness-enhancing measures. Specifically, the tripartite board would bargain with prospective borrowers much in the manner of the Chrysler Loan Guarantee Board. Through the bargaining process RFC funding would be magnified several-fold by means of sacrifices on the part of management, labor, and suppliers, along with states and municipalities benefiting from the economic revival of a particular firm or industry. To critics on his left, who charge economic concentration and undemocratic decision-making within a new bureaucracy, Rohatyn responds, "To cries of elitism or the fear of creating a new 'establishment,' I say that where we are going otherwise is infinitely worse."[14]

Two major roadblocks stand in the way of success for Rohatyn's recommendations. First, the present political environment probably could not marshal sufficient support for the program, and second, a modern-day RFC would be likely to succumb quickly to partisan pressure to pursue politically appealing projects instead of economically sound ones.

Lester Thurow's widely acclaimed books, *The Zero-Sum Society* and *The Zero-Sum Solution,* have catapulted this M.I.T. economist to the forefront of the intellectual brain trust of the Democratic party. While not all the Democratic party's economists—most notable among them Charles Schultze—are convinced that the United States has a chronic competitiveness problem, Thurow stands at the head of a growing body of opinion that sees industrial decline as the nation's number one problem:

"America is now in a competitive fight for its economic life. . . . The rest of the world is organizing itself to make America a loser."[15] Thurow attacks the Republican party's rejection of industrial policy by noting that it implicitly assumes the United States will automatically win any competitiveness contest in a free and open market. Twenty and more years ago this assumption was generally valid, but today we lose more often than we win. The knee-jerk reaction is to cry foul—if we don't win, then it must be that the game is fixed. With productivity barely growing, real wage rates have ceased to grow. The economic recovery that began in 1983 has been largely a borrowed prosperity financed through foreign purchases of U.S. government securities.

Thurow advocates the use of investment or merchant banks in the United States. Such firms as Morgan Stanley and Goldman Sachs are called investment banks, but in reality they are only brokers matching borrowers and savers. The huge Japanese and German banks provide the best examples of the types of institutions Thurow has in mind. They provide both equity and debt financing for their major customers, and by so doing they can maintain large, continuous flows of funds through good times and bad. When a firm encounters serious difficulties, these investment banks are unlikely to pull the plug because their own equity in the firm is at risk. If managerial changes are called for, they are in a position to initiate the necessary changes while providing the funding required to restore the firm to financial health.

Industrial America was built in large part by merchant banks, the house of Morgan preeminent among them, but the Glass-Steagall Act of 1933, in reaction to the market crash, outlawed merchant banks, finding them principal culprits in the speculative excesses of the hitherto unregulated financial markets. One need only look at today's frenzied merger activity, corporate raiders, junk bond financing, and insider trading scandals to realize that the strength of investment banks in Japan and Germany precludes such nonsense. The closest thing the United States has to genuine investment banking is venture capital. But while venture capital will handle a $5 million electronic start-up, it is not up to the job of mainstream private financing of large projects.

With the exception of prohibitions against market-sharing cartels and predatory pricing, Thurow recommends abolition of U.S. antitrust laws.[16] With strong foreign competition, domestic market concentration is not nearly the problem it was twenty-five years ago. The United States can no longer afford the luxury of several firms developing the same technologically sophisticated product. Today those firms will face fierce competition from a limited number of Japanese competitors who have developed their technology jointly through MITI-sponsored research efforts. Nowhere has this been proven more decisively than in the case of the U.S. semiconductor industry. The costs of current antitrust policies clearly outweigh the benefits.

In Thurow's opinion, "industrial policies are to a nation what strategic planning is to a firm." [17] These policies are designed to speed up, not slow down, market-driven changes. Thurow favors engineering a comparative advantage by means of policies emanating from institutions that have real political clout.[18] And there is no mistake about what Thurow means by "institutions with real political clout": he means the federal government. The government must act much like a head coach by encouraging, training, and strategizing the activities of the most critical American industries. It would not own the firms or dictate the details of policy, but it must have sufficient power to reward and punish in order to make itself felt. Today the United States has only ad hoc, incoherent, implicit industrial policies. Thurow wants to make them explicit and coherent. Only the power of the federal government can do the job.

Thurow is keenly sensitive to the problems of declining, or sunset, American industries, for which appropriate disinvestment policies are more difficult to formulate than investment plans for sunrise industries. Instead of speeding up the process of capital transfer from low-growth to high-growth industries, it is impeded by means of protection and subsidies. These policies are ultimately more costly than providing an economic safety net for those cut loose by the coordinated abandonment of obsolescent plants and firms.

In The Zero-Sum Society, Thurow argues that we must, among other things, increase our investment, and in order to do this we must cut someone's consumption. But there are no volunteers. Thurow correctly points out that decreased consumption must not be shouldered by those already economically disadvantaged. He recommends a more equitable distribution of incomes among Americans through various forms of progressive taxation, and he suggests that the minimum economic floor to be placed under the needy should be no less than half as large as the income of the average American.

Somewhat more controversial is Thurow's proposal for a national income distribution with a spread no greater than that which presently exists for white males—that is, 5 to 1. The present ratio between the top and bottom quintiles of the U.S. population as a whole is 27 to 1.[19] To regain economic competitiveness, Americans certainly do not have to take a step in the direction of greater income *inequality*—we can easily concede Thurow that much. But whether we can simultaneously establish and meet the twin goals of greater industrial strength and a much fuller measure of social justice is highly questionable.

When Thurow introduces the subject of equity goals as a major component of his plan to revitalize the competitive posture of the United States, he further politicizes a subject that requires less of politics and more of administration. Nonetheless, Thurow demonstrates a keen understanding of just how complex America's competitiveness problem is when he tells us, "You can't build a high-quality economy out of low-quality parts, so you need a lot of things other than industrial policies: a well-trained work force, a high level of savings and investments, a constant supply of new engineers, and so on."[20]

Robert Reich also argues persuasively for America's use of industrial policy. He is convinced that the competitiveness problem of the United States is quite severe and that only a conscious national effort will bring about a remedy. However, meaningful debate over the question of industrial policy has become increasingly difficult because both advocates and opponents tend to stake out ideological rather than pragmatic positions. Any discussion of industrial policy tends to polarize between notions of the free market and notions of central planning.

Japanese industrial policies are marked by their pragmatic and administrative character. Reich, along with Thurow and Rohatyn, has a visceral understanding of the need for a pragmatic approach, but unlike them, he rejects their strong bureaucratic bias of economic interventions, whether in Japan, Germany, or France. He finds this kind of intervention unacceptable because he sees it as elitist, centralist, and undemocratic. He summarily dismisses the use of foreign institutional models by attributing Japanese and German "consensus about structural policy" largely to "their recently feudal (and more recently totalitarian) histories than [to] institutional design."[21]

Reich clearly understands the fundamentals of an effective industrial policy. Industrial policy pays less attention to supply-siders' unswerving emphasis on aggregate capital formation, a necessary but not sufficient condition, than to capital allocation. Industrial policy is closer to a strategic-planning model than to traditional macroeconomics. The government will use industrial policies to guide, channel, and reinforce the market at intermittent and critical points without contravening or subverting its more fundamental signals. While promising growth sectors must be supported, significant effort should be marshaled behind declining industries to ease the burdens on communities and employees. Reich recognizes that a host of de facto industrial policies have characterized our ad hoc, quick-fix approach to economic and industrial problems. Not only do we reluctantly initiate these policies, but also, when we do, we take pains to disguise them as mandated by national security—defense—concerns. The National *Defense* Highway Act of 1956, which created the interstate highway system, and the National *Defense* Education Act are good examples.

Reich's pronounced distaste for the elitist bureaucratic style of foreign industrial policies is evident in his vision of America's industrial future, where standardized mass production is replaced with what he terms "flexible-system production." Flexible production systems are best seen as the mirror image of yesterday's high-volume, capital-intensive standardized production systems—Fordism. America's mass-production industries, such as textiles, steel, and automobiles, typified the old industrial structure. Because these industries depend on large capacity, competitively priced labor, and raw materials for their success, we are likely to lose market share in these industries to newly industrializing countries that have the required low-cost factor endowments. Noting that the United States has lagged behind Japan and Germany in converting to technologically based flexible systems, Reich provides the examples of specialty steel, synthetic fibers, and precision-engineered automobiles as typical of foreign successes. Among the most notable features of flexible production systems, he finds, are flat organizations with fewer hierarchal management levels, no great distinction between those who plan the work and those who execute it, a sharing and diffusion of information through all levels of the organization, a lack of advanced planning, and finally an atmosphere of instability. Because one reason for America's industrial decline has been a failure to adopt flexible production systems rapidly and successfully, the best examples are found abroad.

Reich cites Japan as the leader in the development of these flexible systems. This is surprising, however, because the strength of the Japanese export drive has rested squarely on their ability to marshal low-cost factor endowments into mass-produced, low-cost goods. These Japanese goods have successfully gained market share at the low end of the American product line, driving U.S. producers back into the specialty niches that should more appropriately be the home of flexible production systems. In fact, what the Japanese have done is graft certain elements of flexible systems, such as shop-floor engineering and rapid tool change, onto mass production systems. This approach yields flexible output of diverse products with little sacrifice of product cost or quality.

But this is not what Reich is talking about. He tells us in no uncertain terms:

> Flexible-system processes cannot be simply grafted onto business organizations that are highly specialized for producing long runs of standardized goods. The premises of high-volume, standardized production—the once-potent formula of scientific management—are simply inapplicable to flexible-system production.[22]

In fact, when Reich talks about flexible systems it is politics, not production, that he has uppermost in his mind. While he is hopeful that new forms of industrial organization will help restore our economic vitality, he believes their political fallout is most important. Reich's own words best illustrate the radical social transformation he envisions:

> Standardized production will to a great extent be replaced by flexible-system production, in which integrated teams of workers identify and solve problems. This new organization of work necessarily will be more collaborative, participatory, and egalitarian. . . . The firm's employees collectively will run these company-wide human capital programs. They will elect representatives who will select the combination of benefits and choose the providers. Through labor-management councils

also comprised of worker representatives, workers will participate in company decisions about physical capital, helping
choose the direction and magnitude of new investment in research, plant, and machinery. . . . Business enterprises, therefore, will largely replace geographic jurisdictions as conduits of
government support for economic and human development.
Companies, rather than state and local governments, will be
the agents and intermediaries through which such assistance is
provided.[23]

However laudable or nonsensical all this may be, it is not what happens
in Japan, it does not have much to do with America's competitiveness
problem, and it is most assuredly not industrial policy.

Much of what Reich has to say about America's competitiveness problem makes good sense. He understands the seriousness of the situation
and believes that macroeconomic policies alone are not sufficient to restore our industrial vitality. He knows that the two essential elements of
industrial policy are economic restructuring toward higher technological
plateaus and enhancement of competitive capability. He does not advocate either the tripartism of Rohatyn or the specific recommendations of
Thurow, such as investment banks and relaxation of antitrust laws.[24] His
most specific and consistent recommendation is for a "visible and centralized forum" through which industrial policy-making can be made
explicit and public.

Rather than insulate industrial policies from the vicissitudes of the political arena, Reich would place them directly within what he terms "a
highly contentious political system in which disorder, opportunism, and
ad hoc arrangements abound."[25] Attempting to politicize industrial policy, which some regard as already overpoliticized, he comes to share
much common ground with the radical left. The far left is adamant in its
belief that America's industrial and social ills must be corrected by the
same radical surgery.

The recommendations that come from the radical left serve their most
useful function by influencing and informing, as a Weberian ideal type,
the policy recommendations of Reich, Thurow, and others, not by providing specific proposals for reversing American industrial decline. If

Japan's industrial policy is administrative, suffused with a growth imperative, market sensitive, nonideological, and bureaucratic, then 180 degrees from these value orientations would be the mainstream of the thought of the radical left.

By and large, the radical left deems economic growth desirable, if carefully balanced against certain other economic, political, and social goals that it believes are of far greater importance. The left does not accept the economic imperative that has the United States moving relentlessly up the technological ladder; being number one technologically or economically is not believed to be all that important. Instead, the radical left assumes that questions of equity, community, and democratic control are much more fundamental than productivity and competitiveness. A rising standard of living more equitably shared is its primary goal, and if this cannot be achieved, then a lower standard of living more equitably shared is a reasonable alternative. The left's favored measure of economic performance is full employment, which is seen also as a measure of social justice. Public works projects and low-wage nonproductive employment are believed to be preferable to high-growth policies that intermittently or continuously create demographic or geographic pockets of unemployment. Perhaps the most extreme item on the radical left's agenda is Tom Hayden's suggestion in *The American Future* that we simply stop beating around the bush and abandon growth for fellowship, replacing competition with cooperation.[26]

The best one-word description of the program of the radical left is "antibureaucratic." The left regards the private, autonomous, bureaucratic control of major U.S. corporations as an unwarranted, socially unredeeming, greed-generated usurpation of public powers that should be democratically controlled. This lack of corporate accountability through private control is seen as distinctly antidemocratic. Social and investment decisions should take human values into consideration. Blind obedience to a profit motive, which tends to keep Americans materialistic, self-absorbed, and apathetic, is to be avoided. It will be necessary, as economists Barry Bluestone and Bennett Harrison put it,

to radically *transform the nature of active popular participation in the day-to-day running of the basic institutions of the economy and the society.* This principle of "economic democracy" must be applied at every level of the system, from the factory (or office) through the neighborhood, the municipality, the statehouse, regional organizations, and ultimately to the national government itself.[27]

Politics then, not economics, is the principal concern of the anti-bureaucratic participatory-democratic left. Bureaucratic, hierarchal decision-making, insulated from public view and direct public participation, whether in business, in nonprofit organizations, or in various levels of governmental authority, must everywhere be recognized, exposed, and permeated by democratic participatory decision-making. This is a tall order. Save for a few brief years of Mao's Cultural Revolution, when the Red Guards pushed this program on millions of doubting and reluctant Chinese, it has never been a political reality and a viable option—not in the Soviet Union, not in Yugoslavia, not even in Cuba. In America it flared up as a possibility briefly during the late 1960s, with the blossoming of a counterculture and the hopeful pronouncements of Charles Reich's *The Greening of America*. But as the flower children of the 1960s grew up to become the yuppies of the 1970s and 1980s, these well-intentioned dreams were quietly put away like forgotten toys in the attic.

The radical left has a love/hate relationship with the national government and with the idea of the state. On balance, it welcomes federal intervention, with which it seeks to bludgeon private capital and private power into more malleable and tractable entities. The radical left seeks to suffuse them with democratic control. But when the state is used to democratize private power, there is a real risk that the very same centralizing bureaucratic power the left attacks in the rest of society will be strengthened. If the democratizing job is botched, the radical left might create a greater monster—in the form of a state-directed, bureaucratized society—than the smaller ones it attempted to slay.

In the mind of the radical left, the interventionist state can do a great deal of good. It can socialize private wealth and power, it can place a safety net under the most disadvantaged citizens, it can promote effective full-employment policies, and it can more equitably distribute the goods and services provided by the economic system. But those objectives require a strong central bureaucracy, which in turn requires experts that can make crucial value-laden decisions for the nonexpert apathetic many. The radical left adamantly rejects that approach, one which is quite acceptable to most mainstream Democrats. The left firmly believes that democratic ends are inseparable from the democratic means of carrying them out, that the democracy of the radical left must be decentralized, pervasive, and participatory, or it is not democracy.

An eloquent description of the political state envisioned by the radical left is provided by political philosopher Michael Walzer:

[It must] be held tightly to its own limits, drained of whatever superfluous moral content and unnecessary political power it has usurped, reduced so far as possible to a transparent administrative shell (overarching, protective, enabling) within which smaller groups can grow and prosper. The state is not going to wither away; it must be hollowed out.[28]

The program of the radical left was never a viable option although twenty or twenty-five years ago, at the height of U.S. global economic supremacy, it was more of a possibility. During the heady days of the Pax Americana and the Great Society, when we regarded the production problem as solved, we eagerly sought new worlds to conquer. Now Americans are seriously challenged on grounds they once regarded as indisputably theirs. With the house now on fire, there is little time or energy to entertain suggestions about how the furnishings might be rearranged or improved.

Although the political and economic proposals of the radical left are in almost every aspect diametrically opposed to Japanese industrial policy, they share a common element that separates them from the American right. The Japanese and the American radical left both deny the unfettered supremacy of the free market; they believe in the fundamental dominance of politics over economics. Classical liberalism is at every turn market-supporting.

Japan's political structure actively supports the market in favor of the economic growth imperative, dominating only at the point where private consumption and enrichment become subordinate to national economic power and to pride in the Japanese nation. The radical left in America desires to rein in the unrestricted market and to intertwine political economic decision-making at every stage. It argues that a democratic society cannot be truly democratic unless democratic control is economic as well as political.

The industrial policies of the radical left may be seen, fairly or unfairly, as a kind of political Trojan horse. Utilizing the interventionist state to improve economic performance opens the door to a more far-reaching political agenda. Once the back is off the watch and minor economic repairs are effected, the radical left, or occasionally the moderate left, is sorely tempted to use the opportunity to introduce other elements of its far-reaching political program. A modest understanding of this political agenda helps us appreciate more fully the political right's deep distrust of any industrial policies proposed by the left and implemented by the interventionist state. Since the time of the New Deal, the business community believes there have been ten negative programs for every positive one. As a result, cooperation between business and government—Japanese-style—is utterly unfathomable within the terms of the politics American business has experienced.

Even though the United States is as far or even further away from the use of industrial policies as it was more than a decade ago, the body of literature recommending industrial policies of various types continues to grow. A partial list of industrial policy advocates includes James Abegglen, James Alic, Gar Alperovitz, Fred Bergsten, Barry Bluestone, David Calleo, Pat Choate, John Diebold, William Diebold, Otto Eckstein, Amitai Etzioni, Julian Gresser, Eleanor Hadley, Bennett Harrison, Thomas Hout, Chalmers Johnson, Paul Krugman, George Lodge, Ira Magaziner, Ronald Müller, Clyde Prestowitz Jr., Robert Reich, Felix Rohatyn, Steve Schlossstein, Bruce Scott, Irving Shapiro, Andrew Shonfield, Lester Thurow, Ezra Vogel, and Frank Weil. There are undoubtedly some uneasy bedfellows there, and perhaps some who would disclaim outright any industrial policy advocacy. Nonetheless, it is possible to stake out three broad areas of consensus that tie together much of the literature on American industrial policy.

The United States has a competitiveness problem, and the indexes of the severity of the problem, whether measured by merchandise trade deficits, foreign accounts balance, foreign debt, high-tech trade balance, or any of many other measures, all seem to be pointing in the wrong direction. The problem stems less and less from any one single factor, such as Japanese protectionism or a deliberately undervalued yen, and more from a lengthening list of highly complex and interrelated factors. The problem can no longer be viewed simply as a problem with Japan, although Japan is and will continue to be the focal point of American concerns about the new industrial competition. Japanese successes have created models for industrial policy and institutional support that have been replicated throughout Southeast Asia, and the prospects for their universal application are increasingly favorable.

Consensus seems to be developing around the idea that the United States must implement a series of more-or-less comprehensive microeconomic policies (industrial policies) to reverse the present ominous trend. Macroeconomic policies alone—Reaganomics, supply-side economics, fair trade policies, unleashing the entrepreneurs, and other noninterventionist market-driven solutions—are seen as not capable of doing the job. Additional weight in support of the industrial policy side, as against the free-market/noninterventionist camp, is the fact that the debate has moved well beyond the scope of academic controversy.

The eight years of the Reagan presidency in large measure provided a living laboratory for evaluating the noninterventionist, anti-industrial-policy viewpoint. If Ronald Reagan didn't get all he wanted from Congress, he got a great deal more than any of his predecessors in recent memory—so much so that we commonly speak of the Reagan Revolution. There is no denying that the Reagan administration stopped inflation dead in its tracks, but as far as reversing America's declining industrial fortunes goes, the record is for the most part devoid of substantive achievements. Thus, the suggestion that we try something else appears to have considerable merit.

Why then are we not farther down the road toward taking industrial policies seriously? Here again there is widespread agreement among industrial policy advocates that the difficulties faced in designing and implementing industrial policies are well nigh insurmountable. "The success of Japanese industrial policy," Chalmers Johnson reminds us, "has been its depoliticization to the greatest degree consistent with a democratic government" (for "depoliticization" read "bureaucratically administered").[29] A quick comparison of Japanese and American political institutions demonstrates that the United States lacks the two essential prerequisites of Japanese-style comprehensive industrial policies: a strong central state and a top professional bureaucracy.

Before we go further, let it be said emphatically that most of the industrial policy supporters in the United States do not want Japan's industrial policies for the United States. From James Alic to Frank Weil, there is a broad range of options, but the weight of opinion, while calling for much more than we have now, would fall considerably short of the economic machine created by the Japanese. But oddly enough, opinion among those favoring the more modest proposals is no more sanguine than that of those who prescribe much stronger medicine. The fragmented and contentious American political system would react immediately, effectively, and with determination against any attempt to rein in special interests in the uncertain cause of a more remote and less appealing national interest. How strong is the feeling in the United States against any fundamental change in our economic system? Listen to this exchange between Herbert Stein, former chairman of the Council of Economic Advisors under President Nixon, and Lester Thurow:

DR. THUROW: What makes you sure that the United States at the moment isn't Great Britain circa 1900? The rest of the world is breathing at our heels and they aren't going to slow down when they catch up. They're going to zoom right by and the United States fifty years from now will have half their per capita GNP.

DR. STEIN: I'm not sure of that at all. But I'm not willing to make a major change in the system on the bet that that is the case.

DR. THUROW: Let me ask you a question. Suppose you knew that it were true. Would you then be willing to change the system?

DR. STEIN: No.

DR. THUROW: You are saying that the system is more important than the result no matter how bad the result?

DR. STEIN: Well, you have to give me a little room about how bad the result is, but I mean—

DR. THUROW: I'll give you the result. Fifty years from now the American per capita GNP will be half that of the leading industrial country. Assume that were a fact. Would that then lead you to believe that we ought to change the system now?

DR. STEIN: No.[30]

And remember, when Thurow talks about changing the system, he is talking about nothing more than a modest list of industrial policies—not what Japan has, and nothing as extensive as a call for fundamental alterations in the architecture of our political institutions. Herbert Stein is no extremist. He speaks for the broad spectrum of opinion in the United States—the silent and the unsilent majority—when he rejects the use of state power to solve the serious problems Thurow presents.

As the severity of our economic problems deepens, demands for some type of action will intensify. But the odds strongly favor the muddling-through policies of the status quo. If effective industrial policies require strong and continuous government support, coupled with bureaucratic administration, then Americans don't want industrial policies. A minority of moderate Republicans and conservative Democrats would support limited efforts to institute various components of industrial policy, but that small and fragile center will make little headway against the mighty ideological redoubts on the right and the left. Thoroughly anti-statist, the right and the left are united only in their intense dislike and fear of state power, one reposing its trust in unrepentant individualism and the free-market arena, the other having unabashed faith in the cleansing power of a rising tide of democratic decision-making capable of reaching every economic and political crevice in American society. Either side has sufficient strength to uproot any attempt to implement industrial policy. Together they make the task virtually impossible.

Americans don't want industrial policy, either full-blown or patchwork, because they don't want the kind of political power required to secure its effective operation. We did not come on these convictions lightly or recently; they are buried within the national psyche as deeply as any set of beliefs can be. For more than 350 years, from the Puritans to George Bush, Americans have stayed the course, building on a uniquely American anti-statist tradition.

—

CONCLUSION

THINKING THE UNTHINKABLE

The owl of Minerva spreads its wings only at dusk.
—G. W. F. Hegel

In his sweeping study of world history, G. W. F. Hegel discovered that nations and civilizations have discerned the outlines of truth and reality only when their time is short, only when decline is well upon them. For the United States the years ahead will not be good ones. The easy prosperity and effortless superiority of the postwar years are now a distant memory. How far down the slippery slide of economic and political decline are we? Do we have hours of sunlight left, or are we quite close to dusk? These questions cannot be answered with any high degree of certainty, but it is clear that we are much worse off than a decade ago. And no evidence indicates that any reversal is under way.

Why did it happen? First let us summarize the argument again:

America faces economic decline and the loss of world economic and political leadership. The proximate causes of American economic decline are serious system-wide managerial, financial, and political shortcomings. Japan has undertaken a national effort to achieve global technological, economic, and perhaps even political dominance. Its success has been based on the comprehensive and system-wide use of industrial policy, which is defined as the state-induced willful shifting of the industrial structure toward high-technology, high-value-added industries. A strong central state and a top professional bureaucracy are essential preconditions for industrial policy. Japanese political institutions are European in origin and are replicated in most advanced industrial societies. America is totally lacking the statist traditions of Japan, Germany, and France. Our political development has been conditioned by an anti-statist tradition. American political institutions are utterly unique. The United States is the only advanced democratic society that lacks a strong central state and a top professional bureaucracy. The only way America can counter the Japanese challenge and regain world economic leadership is through the comprehensive use of industrial policy. Without a strong central state and a top professional bureaucracy—the two preconditions of industrial policy—America is doomed to economic decline. There is one way, only one way, out of our current predicament: fundamental institutional change.

It has been more than a decade since Ezra Vogel wrote *Japan as Number One*, subtitled "Lessons for America," and we have not learned those lessons. We stand listless, and in many areas Japan is now number one. The consequences of America's loss of world leadership will be enormous, touching every aspect of our lives. American economic decline will take a fearsome toll from all Americans.

The validity of the proposition that the American political system lies at the heart of the economic problems of the United States rests on three highly controversial and hotly contested assumptions:

1. That the United States will soon lose technological and economic leadership to Japan
2. That the United States can reverse its declining fortunes and compete

effectively with Japan only if it has a *comprehensive* industrial policy (a noncomprehensive industrial policy being worse than no industrial policy at all)

3. That without a strong central state and a higher-level bureaucracy, industrial policy is an impossibility in the United States

Because evidence accumulates monthly in favor of the first assumption, let us turn our attention to the second and the third.

In the late 1930s a noted American journalist told his U.S. audience: "The lights are going out all over Europe." As our major corporations are slowly but inexorably bested by their Japanese counterparts, the industrial lights are going out all over America. How long and how hard a beating do we have to take at the hands of the Japanese until we recognize that something is seriously wrong, until we understand that Japan has a superior economic system?

Under U.S. Trade Representative Carla Hills, American trade negotiators are hard at work, as they have been for at least twenty years, trying to get Japan to open its markets to U.S. products. The latest gambit is the Structural Impediments Initiative (SII), which the United States hopes to use to pry open Japan's markets—particularly those for high-technology products—by getting Japan to remove the many nontariff or "structural" barriers to the entry of U.S. goods.

It's unkind to cut short the suspense of this long-playing drama, but here's the way it ends: Japan is not going to open its markets to American high-technology products. Repeat: It simply is not going to do it. And Americans are incredibly naive to think that it will happen. Sure, Japan will go through the motions—let in a little more beef, a few more oranges, and one day perhaps even some rice—but in high-technology products, where it really counts, progress will be imperceptible. The SII is palpably nonsensical because the so-called "structural impediments" in Japan are actually some of the critical defining features of Japanese industrial policy. Ask Japan to eliminate structural impediments and you effectively ask Japan to change its economic system. No chance of that.

And if *you* were the Japanese, would you give up managed trade for the uncertainties of free trade? Would you begin to dismantle a system that has brought your country unprecedented well-being, a system that seems destined to carry your country to a position of world economic leadership? The answer must be a resounding no. The Japanese are riding a thirty-year winning streak. Why would they want to change?

Twenty and more years ago Japan wouldn't change, pleading weakness and vulnerability. The Japanese claimed they needed an edge in international competition, and we gave it to them. Today Japan is strong, and the United States doesn't have the power to compel it to change anymore. When we ask the Japanese to substitute free trade for managed trade, we are asking them to play by our rules. But they're now playing by their rules and winning the game. It is we who must change.

While the pro's and con's of the political and social fallout of Japan's industrial policy can be argued endlessly, as raw economic policy there is only one word to describe it: unbeatable. Call it managed trade, call it developmentalism, call it guided free enterprise, call it industrial policy, but above all call it unbeatable.

The Japanese must be amazed to see the United States continuing to lose ground competitively yet persisting in the same shopworn policies that led it to economic decline. A while back, the Japanese kept their amazement to themselves, but now, as witnessed by Akio Morita and Shintaro Ishihara's "The Japan That Can Say No," they are becoming more vocal and disdainful of America's tepid response to their continuing challenge.[1]

The laissez-faire free-trade policies of the Reagan and Bush administrations are not working. Today we ignore Japan at our own peril. Free trade? Forget it. Today's game is *managed trade*. Japan is not going to open its markets, not going to eliminate its trade surplus, not going to halt its pursuit of technological dominance. And Japan is not going to stop retaining the best and most expensive lobbyists in Washington to prevent any meaningful retaliation by our weak and fragmented economic policy-making apparatus.[2]

America must fight fire with fire. We can engage and contain the Japanese only by means of an American industrial policy. We can open Japan's markets only by means of managed trade. There are three alternatives: (1) continue the present policies of economic drift, (2) adopt a knee-jerk protectionism that has all the subtlety of smashing a Toshiba cassette player with a sledgehammer on the Capitol grounds, (3) successfully engage the Japanese by means of a comprehensive industrial policy. The rules of international trade and economic development in the late twentieth century have been set by Japan. The sooner we realize this the better.

An American industrial policy—what would it look like? Fortunately we don't have to invent industrial policy; Japan has already done that. We must simply establish a uniquely American version of the Japanese system and improve on it. Topping the list of elements comprising an American industrial policy would be a national commitment to make the United States the most technologically advanced nation in the world. That is saying a lot, but technology is indeed the key to political and economic strength in the years ahead. Technological leadership effectively guarantees economic and political preeminence.

Regaining technological leadership (which to all intents and purposes we have already lost to the Japanese) will not be easy for the United States. It will require sacrifice from numerous quarters. The first order of business is to identify strategic industries and, within them, certain critical industry segments. It doesn't take much imagination to begin the list with computers, consumer electronics, semiconductors, and telecommunications equipment. Investment in strategic industries would be encouraged by means of differential depreciation schedules, investment tax credits, export incentives, and tariff and nontariff barriers to threatening foreign competition, among other policies. The massive investments required to regain lost ground and reestablish world leadership would necessitate a redrafting of tax codes to penalize consumption and reward savings. To achieve the objectives, the U.S. savings rate must at the very least be doubled.

Would an American industrial policy be discriminatory? You bet it would. Varying depreciation schedules and selective tax credits are good examples. Make soap, dog food, and breakfast cereal, and you might be able to depreciate equipment over ten years, but if you manufacture computers and semiconductors, equipment write-offs could be in two years. An American industrial policy would not involve state ownership, outright subsidies, or micromanagement on the part of the president or Congress. The working definition of industrial policy as "the state-induced willful shifting of the industrial structure toward high-technology, high-value-added products" makes the objective and methods clear. Industrial policy provides broadly favorable incentives that channel the economy toward a high-technology future. Company and industry-segment success and failure would be left to the harsh discipline of the competitive market. Effective industrial policy is market-reinforcing, not market-thwarting.

The use of comprehensive or Japanese-style industrial policy does not mean intensifying the existing ad hoc interventionism of the U.S. government. The proposed remedy calls for an entirely different form of economic policy-making cast in a new political dimension. Comparisons to existing governmental ineptitude and bureaucratic bungling are wholly inappropriate.

The consumer electronics industry provides a good illustration of how an American industrial policy might work. The U.S. steel and automotive industries look positively robust compared with the virtually nonexistent consumer electronics industry. How can the United States go about reviving that moribund industry? Generous investment tax credits, rapid depreciation schedules, and gradually increased tariffs on imported products would offer real incentives for investments in what would now become a promising field. Given this kind of economic environment, AT&T, GE, IBM, or other corporate giants might find the consumer electronics industry attractive.

We can even picture the first American video cassette recorder. It would probably look like an electronic version of those funny little cars the Japanese shipped to the United States in the early 1960s. The quality of the new VCRs probably wouldn't measure up to Japanese standards, and Japan's consumer electronics giants might even dismiss us as a serious competitive threat. But now there is a big difference. The U.S. government and its newly revived consumer electronics industry is committed, so somehow we'd make them and sell them. When we brought out the second generation, the quality would be better and the price lower. With a little luck and a lot of hard work, our third-generation VCRs might be better than competing Japanese offerings, and they could be exported—perhaps to Japan.

Similar stories would be repeated in industry after industry with varying degrees of urgency, depending on the strategic importance of particular products and markets. The bootstrap efforts that would characterize U.S. industrial policy would be a long, slow, and very painful process.

Whether Americans have the courage and vision required for a national commitment of this type remains an unanswered question.

Having the courage and vision to adopt industrial policy is one thing, undertaking serious consideration of the political and institutional preconditions of industrial policy is quite another. It moves the industrial policy debate into an entirely different dimension.

The nature of Japan's economic and political institutions makes it clear that the institutional structure that must stand behind the formulation and implementation of industrial policy is critical. Industrial policy in Japan is designed and guided by a higher-level bureaucracy. It covers a lengthy time-span, requiring consistency over a ten- to twenty-year period. It demands consistency with respect to an internal vision of an economic future, and also continuity in terms of the people running it. Rapid turnover of political appointees at the upper levels of the executive branch, as is the case now in the United States, makes industrial policy impossible. You can't initiate industrial policy under the Democrats and repudiate it four years later under the Republicans.

To be successful, industrial policy must be insulated from the day-to-day winds of political change. Under no circumstances can it be the product of a legislative chamber, least of all the U.S. Congress. Of course, only the legislative branch as the fundamental repository of the democratic desires of the electorate can make the crucial decision to pursue a brighter economic future through the use of industrial policy. But once the initial commitment has been made, decided on by the electorate and ratified by the legislature, industrial policy can and must be a bureaucratic responsibility. Legislative meddling in the daily workings of industrial policy will quickly render it useless.

Industrial policy decisions are not easy decisions. They must inflict some pain on everyone, and slightly more on some groups than others. Successful industrial policy requires that the legislative and executive branches of the government stand together in support of industrial policy, in support of the public good, and against the vocal minorities that will inevitably attack it in the name of their particular parochial causes.

If you sat down to design a political system that was inherently and instinctively antithetical to the conduct of industrial policy, you could not come up with a better one than existing U.S. political institutions. American political institutions were created to stabilize, not to mobilize. The gross imbalance between the weak, short-term, and politically appointed upper reaches of the executive branch, and the overwhelming power of the U.S. Congress with its subset of thousands of "bureaucratically specialized" congressional staffers, is striking. The legislative branch should make the big decisions, and the bureaucracy the little ones. Under the current system, Congress attempts to make them all and nearly succeeds.

Once we understand the unbreakable link between industrial policy and its political prerequisites, the industrial policy debate assumes a new cast and enters a new political dimension. The debate should not be about establishing industrial policy in the absence of appropriate political preconditions, but rather about creating the political institutions industrial policy requires. Two factors help explain why the industrial policy debate has not gotten very far. First, industrial policy is anathema to the laissez-faire and hyperindividualistic political culture in America. Second, if by some chance the pro-industrial-policy forces begin to make some progress, they would soon run headlong into the hard truth that the United States simply does not have the type of political institutions necessary for industrial policy. The link between industrial policy and political institutions has not received sufficient attention, so it has yet to be established with convincing academic proof, but Japan's experience provides abundant evidence that such a link exists.

So how seriously should Americans consider institutional reform as a solution to the dire economic predicament of the United States? From the standpoint that our strong anti-statist tradition makes it highly unlikely that Americans will provide the changes necessary to give the government the power it needs to implement industrial policy, institutional reform could be dismissed out of hand. But when we consider the alternatives—continued economic decline, loss of global technological and economic leadership to the Japanese, loss of de facto political independence, and quite possibly loss of certain fundamental rights and freedoms—institutional reform deserves serious consideration. Those who appear to accept America's loss of world leadership so casually probably have not fully reflected on the enormity of the consequences.

This is an appropriate place to issue a cautionary note to the U.S. business community. Cut the average American CEO, manager, or independent businessman, and he bleeds free market, antigovernment, and anti-bureaucracy. So often we hear the refrain "If only the government would leave us alone we could do the job." And of course this is with good cause, because decades of sad experience have taught them to expect from Washington a steady stream of bureaucratic bungling and government ineptness. Unfortunately, their visceral distrust and disrespect for government economic policy has become a self-fulfilling prophecy. Convinced that the majority of federal initiatives hurt rather than help them, they instinctively fight government intervention of all stripes. Many industries in the United States have been almost fatally wounded by lack of cooperation from Washington. The steel and semiconductor industries are notable examples.

In Japan, however, it is altogether different. The extraordinary success of Japan's economic machine rests squarely on the bold, independent, and market-driven initiatives of Japanese business, operating in a domestic and international economic environment conditioned to the greatest extent possible by intelligent and consistent government policies. The cooperation, intimacy, mutual respect, and not infrequent constructive disagreement between business and government in Japan form the keystone of that country's economic strength.

American business ignores or fights the government only at its own peril. Without favorable and farsighted government economic policies, the United States cannot compete with Japan, so business must *engage* government with long-term, hard-fought efforts aimed at substantive government reform, particularly at the creation of a higher-level bureaucracy capable of generating the kind of comprehensive industrial policy that American business so desperately needs.

Don't expect any intelligent or coherent probusiness, procompetitiveness policy out of the U.S. government as it exists today—not under the Democrats, not under the Republicans. You are disappointed today, you have been disappointed in the past, and you will be disappointed in the future. Institutional reform or economic decline—that's what it comes down to.

Only a strong central state can produce the necessary simultaneous economic and political pressure at multiple points throughout American society. The number of things that must be changed is too great, and time is too short, for the country to stay on its present course. We should not seek institutional reform only because of a U.S. imperative toward economic or political world dominance, and we should not do it simply to beat the Japanese. We must do it to defend ourselves against a new form of economic competition that threatens not only our standard of living but also our entire way of life.

Considered in an international context, the creation of a modern state in America does not involve quite so deep a plunge into the political unknown as one might at first think. It does not require the force of political imagination that inspired the founders to create the world's first large-scale democracy. A modern democratic state is a strong central state with policy-making initiated and implemented by a top professional bureaucracy. It is the pattern state represented by Japan, Germany, and France, each of which has a constitutional model of the modern democratic state. All are of postwar vintage: Japan, 1947; West Germany, 1949; France, 1958. Has the art of constitution-writing not improved in the last two hundred years?

If more state is the answer, what about the Soviet Union? It has plenty of state, but as Gorbachev has freely admitted, their economy is a disaster. Obviously, the Soviets have too much state; in their command economy, the state allows little room for the necessary workings of the free market. The Soviet state stifles economic and social dynamism. If a choice must be made between too little state and too much state, the Soviet Union provides ample evidence that too little state is infinitely better than too much. But as the Japanese have so clearly demonstrated, the very best political arrangements call for a careful *balance* of state and market—an Aristotelian mean. The strong central state proposed as the only workable solution to American economic decline is not a Hegelian monstrosity run by half-crazed Nietzschean supermen. It is a stable democratic regime with the institutional capacity to formulate coherent policy. It is illustrated not only by Japan, Germany, and France, but also by many other advanced industrial societies.

Mindful that Japan is a more egalitarian society than the United States, we should not assume that modern political institutions imply a marked shift toward greater social inequities. Proposals for institutional reform relative to income distribution are not rightist or leftist, but centrist, politically neutral. Within stable democratic regimes, be it Japan or the United States, the political process will dictate varying degrees of egalitarianism.

At a time when the United States suffers from the weakness of its political institutions, we are not moving toward Japan's state/market mean. In fact, we are moving away from it. The forces of selfish and uncontrolled pursuit of private interest are steadily advancing against the weakened and demoralized defenders of institutional authority and the public good. The legal activism of recent years has served to further weaken the authority of the government in a nation already awash in hyperindividualism. Recent court decisions have created a lengthy new list of constitutional rights for individuals and groups against the government. When new rights cannot be legislated, they are now adjudicated.

The anti-statist tradition in America has made us reluctant to grasp the Promethean fire of state power. We continue to think of America as a nation set apart, a nation that does not require the political tools of lesser mortals. But it is now late in the day. It is time to set aside our idiosyncratic ways and return to the path of normalcy—to the path of modern state development. Eventually, increased political authority will come to the United States. It will come suddenly from unforeseen quarters, or it will come slowly and incrementally. Let us pray to God it comes slowly.

Institutional reform—how do we do it? As we have already covered too much ground, this question will be answered only in broadest outline. But the start of it all, the huge first step, is to think about it.

The replacement of 2,000 or so political appointees with a top professional bureaucracy would permit implementation of effective and coherent economic and political policies. A necessary corollary to establishing a top professional bureaucracy at the helm of the cabinet-level departments and major agencies would be reform of the committee system of the U.S. Congress. A drastic downsizing of the number and scope of congressional committees and subcommittees, along with an attendant reduction in the present army of congressional staffers, would permit Congress to focus on major issues. The details of policy-making would then find their rightful home in the hands of a top professional bureaucracy. All these reforms would pave the way for adoption of a comprehensive industrial policy.

Congress does have the power to effect these and other necessary institutional reforms, but under the present circumstances it is doubtful—to say the least—that the U.S. Congress would acquiesce in the transfer of a major portion of its policy-making capacity to the executive branch. It is more likely that fundamental institutional reforms might be necessary—in the form of constitutional revision.

This is not a book about constitution-making, constitutional engineering, or even bureaucratic reform, and it is certainly not about constitution-bashing. Awe and reverence must pervade and condition our thinking about the Constitution of the United States. It is the greatest constitution in history, the work of inspired genius. It was the political act that gave birth to modern democracy. But the U.S. Constitution was never intended for a life eternal. Imagine the founders brought to life in present-day America. They would doubtless be surprised, and perhaps dismayed, to see their constitutional handiwork still in use. Now, in the late twentieth century, in a world of infinite complexity, we are bound fast in the straitjacket of eighteenth-century political institutions.

Every story must have a villain, and the villain of this story is the U.S. Congress. The executive branch, fatally wounded by the lack of a higher professional bureaucracy, has been devoured by a swollen and omnivorous Congress. A government without a top professional bureaucracy is like a human body missing a vital organ—it cannot function effectively. The United States tries to do entirely with politicians what Japan, Germany, and France do with a delicate blend of politics and bureaucracy. Time and time again it has been proven that amateurs cannot beat the Japanese professionals.

The problem lies not with the dedicated and well-intentioned men and women of the U.S. Congress. In fact, Congress appears to have a better understanding of America's grave economic problems than the White House. But in the absence of a top professional bureaucracy, Congress lacks the institutional capacity to do the job.

The easiest answer to Japan's challenge is to deny there is a problem. There is a wide body of opinion that insists on doing just that. *Forbes* magazine, very much the prose poet laureate of the "Roaring Eighties," tells us to stay the course, that with a little more deregulation, a lot less government, and continued faith in the political wisdom of the free market everything will turn out all right.

The *Forbes* message does not fall on deaf ears. There is a lot of Texas in all of the United States. Many Americans—gunslingers at heart—are convinced we can "wing it," successfully pitting American individualism against Japanese organization. But the technological/industrial/economic scoreboard shows we are falling further and further behind.

Fortunately, month by month, year by year, there are more doubters. A thriving cottage industry of thoughtful and concerned writers releases book after book on the "Japanese question / decline of America problem." The growing acceptance of these books' argument that there is a serious problem requiring immediate action is a good first step. But so far the literature has not put the finger on the real problem. Pick up any of those books, turn to the last chapter, and you will find recommended in varying forms the same laundry list of policy initiatives to get America back on track:

- We must provide incentives for management to focus on long-term results and not quarterly earnings, put greater emphasis on personnel management and less on financial management, improve management/government relations, close the gap between management and labor, and adopt certain proven Japanese managerial techniques, such as "just in time" and "total quality control."

- We must get our financial house in order by balancing the budget, eliminating our trade deficit, achieving a positive trade balance in high-technology manufactured goods, strengthening the dollar, encouraging savings, providing incentives for investment, reducing reliance on short-term capital, reining in the current excesses of Wall Street—particularly the frenzy of merger and acquisition activity—seeking ways to lower the cost of capital in the United States, and strengthening the banking system by permitting the creation of truly global banks capable of competing internationally with the Japanese.

- We must radically alter our trade policies by conducting trade negotiations within a framework of far-reaching strategy, and not by knee-jerk reaction to a barrage of complaints charging injury, and by modifying our free-trade policies and philosophy. And because we cannot conduct trade policies effectively from a position of weakness, we must first set our economic house in order, then negotiate from strength, and when trade negotiations fail put teeth in U.S. policy with retaliatory action.

• We must begin confronting the Japanese in several areas, insisting that Japan open its markets to U.S. manufactured goods with special emphasis on high-technology products, calling on Japan to shoulder a greater portion of the free world's defense burden, pressuring Japan to increase its foreign aid programs, and demanding equal access to Japanese financial markets.

• We must come up with some political solutions by reforming our antitrust policies, developing a comprehensive energy policy, instituting a series of policies aimed at strengthening our high-technology sector, creating new high-technology cooperative efforts, such as the Sematech project for regaining semiconductor leadership, setting up mechanisms to speed dissemination of scientific knowledge into manufacturing and process technology, appointing an economic czar to pull together the often divergent efforts of the Treasury Department, the Commerce Department, the Council of Economic Advisors, the Office of Management and Budget, and the Office of the U.S. Trade Representative, creating a cabinet-level Department of Trade and Industry, and establishing a cadre of professional industry, trade, and finance experts akin to those in the military and foreign service.

• We must address the serious shortcomings of our educational system at the primary and secondary levels, we must radically increase the output of engineers by undergraduate and graduate schools, and we must do something substantive about the disgrace of our national drug problem.

• We must develop a broad consensus that many of these items must be placed on the national agenda.

This is, to say the least, a daunting and lengthy list, but the problem is more serious yet. Piecemeal solutions usually do more harm than good. To strengthen the dollar in the absence of tough new trade policies will widen, not narrow, the trade gap. Changing the focus of a firm from emphasis on quarterly earnings to an emphasis on long-term results might result in plunging stock values and takeover threats, given the powerful influence of today's equity markets. Thus, all these recommendations are interrelated and interconnected. Grab ahold of one, and several others must come along with it. We cannot build great companies in the absence of the proper financial and political environment, and without a trade policy in concert with certain long-term goals. Lacking a coordinated effort and a strategic vision, we will accomplish very little. A coherent and consistent policy that will stretch over several decades is desperately needed.

How do we meet Japan's challenge? Only by adopting an American version of Japanese industrial policy. We have no choice. And again, it must be stressed that the proper focus of the great debate over industrial policy is not how to establish an industrial policy in the absence of state power—which is impossible—but whether to create the state power necessary to conduct an effective industrial policy. An American system-wide response to Japan's system-wide challenge requires the creation of a modern state.

For Japan the great lesson of World War II was that there is an inextricable link between military superiority and industrial might. With a fraction of U.S. industrial production, Japan went to war convinced that strength of spirit alone would carry the day against America's material abundance and economic power—a replay of the Peloponnesian War, with Sparta defeating Athens. Spirit never failed the Japanese, but in retrospect they believed that America won the war as much on the factory floors of Pittsburgh, Detroit, and Chicago as on the bloody battlefields of the Pacific Islands.

A corollary to the proposition linking industrial and military power was that technological mastery creates industrial supremacy. The United States had not only more arms with which to assault Japan but also weapons of clear technological superiority—and in the case of the atomic bomb a product of an entirely different technological dimension. Japan saw American industrial superiority resting on a blend of abundant natural resources and more advanced technology. Japan's postwar economic prospects looked bleak. Woefully deficient in land and natural resources, and with its industrial infrastructure destroyed, Japan faced an America that was almost embarrassed by its riches.

But fortunately for Japan, the relationship between technology, natural resources, and industrial might was beginning to change. Whereas technology had in the past come in the wake of industrial growth, explosive technological change now made technology the driving force behind industrial strength. Technology could overcome factor endowment deficiencies, but it could also be used to create new and stronger factor endowments. Technology was open-ended. It was anybody's game, and the Japanese were determined to make it theirs. Japan began a comprehensive effort to capture the technological high ground. For the United States, technology is important, but for Japan it is critical. It is the whole game, a dead-serious game based on the premise that technological mastery creates economic superiority, which in turn may be used to establish political dominance.

Most Americans would reason that the appropriate causal chain of political dominance should run: technological, economic, military, and political. The Japanese, however, know that military superiority is no longer meaningful, that it does not have to be part of a geopolitical grand strategy in the late twentieth century. Nuclear stalemate and mutual assured destruction (MAD) make the military contest a zero-sum game. In retrospect, the cold war was like a struggle between two dinosaurs. It drew off vital resources needed for the real game of technological, economic, and political mastery. With arms reduction and economic reform the highest of priorities, Gorbachev's Soviet Union is now learning what the Japanese have learned from experience: pursuit of power by military means is a dead-end street, but the economic gambit offers interesting possibilities.

In the 1990s it is likely that the United States will see rapprochement with the Soviet Union and a disengagement from Japan. As national security increasingly comes to be framed in terms of economic and financial independence, a National Security Council of the future may be discussing new technologies and critical industries in lieu of armed forces and weapons. Japan already has just such an economic national security council, MITI, which is its economic general staff. The Japanese do not have to conquer the world if they can buy it.

What we are witnessing with the emergence of Japan and a lessening of military tensions with the Soviet Union is nothing less than a political-economic version of what Thomas Kuhn described as a "scientific revolution."[3] This ongoing shift in "shared paradigms" is to the political world what the revolutionary change from Newtonian mechanics to quantum physics represented to the world of science. The meaning of this move from military to economic paradigms as the defining dimension of global power is of monumental significance. It is the kind of thing that happens once or twice in a millennium.

Did the Japanese see it all from the beginning? Is there a master plan that is being carefully unfolded decade by decade? That is not likely. But at given times after 1945 their periodic visions of Japan's economic future stretched to the very bounds of disbelief. In the late 1940s the Japanese looked toward recovery and return to major power status. By 1960 they saw that their high-growth economy was capable of catching up with the United States. Their vision in 1975 stretched to the possibility of technological and economic world leadership. And given the stunning realization of their previous goals, what do they expect today? A vision of economic empire in a world controlled by Japan does not seem so wild a dream.

Those who don't like the idea of institutional reform, who even find the idea repugnant, need to know something they'll like much less, something America is dead on course for now. It's called Pax Nipponica.[4]

In some quarters it is fashionable to accept the fact of American economic decline and subsequent loss of world leadership to the Japanese. The argument is that Great Britain carried the torch of world leadership and then passed it on to the United States, and that now we shall pass it to Japan. But with the emergence of Pax Nipponica, the consequences for life in the United States will be enormous. As we have seen, the values embedded in Japan's economic, political, and social systems are altogether different from those of Americans. With Japan as the most powerful nation in the world, and with that power resting on Japan's de facto control of the American economic system, many of the freedoms we enjoy today are likely to vanish. Pax Nipponica will thrust the United States into an entirely different world. An estimated time-frame for the emergence of Pax Nipponica would be sometime between the year 2005 and the year 2015. Most of us will experience it. Let's take a quick look.

The time is circa 2015: With the advent of Pax Nipponica, Japan's continued high savings rate and dedication to technological leadership have given Japan uncontested dominance in every leading-edge industry—for example, computers, semiconductors, commercial aircraft, aerospace, pharmaceuticals, biogenetic engineering, nuclear power, and, not without great significance, defense. Japan's gross national product is twice that of the United States, and Japan's per capita GNP is four times ours. The world economy is now structured and hierarchical. What the Japanese failed to achieve by military means through the Greater East Asia Co-Prosperity Sphere in the 1940s they have now gained by economic means under Pax Nipponica in a Global Co-Prosperity Sphere. All roads now lead to Tokyo.

Japan, of course, is at the directing apex of the new world economy. The world's most sophisticated designing, engineering, and manufacturing are all done in Japan. Japan also controls the world economy because it is the world's financial center. Whether measured by commercial banks, investment banks, brokerage houses, financial transactions, or foreign currency reserves, Tokyo dominates global financial markets to an extent never approached by London or New York.

The second-tier nations are the East Asian states whose economies are most closely linked to that of Japan. The many high-technology manufacturing operations that cannot be accommodated within Japan proper—given its land and population constraints—are farmed out to Japan's Asian neighbors. Together with Japan, these nations constitute a manufacturing system that produces a high percentage of the world's most technically advanced goods.

The third-tier nations, which include the United States and the European community, may be classified as the world's great consuming nations. The manufacturing sectors of these economies are kept busy producing middle-technology products, such as appliances, automobiles, and consumer electronics, products that the Japanese regard as less critical to high-technology dominance than the advanced goods produced in the Japan / East Asia techno-industrial complex. As the Japanese see it, the primary function of the consuming nations is to provide a huge, stable, and profitable market for the ever-increasing flow of East Asian high-technology products.

The underdeveloped and developing nations of the fourth tier have not been neglected by the Japanese. Before the turn of the century, a financial crisis threw Mexico into the hands of Japan, its major creditor. Teams of

*high-level Japanese bureaucrats reformed both the Mexican national bu-
reaucracy and its educational system. Financial reforms, including import restrictions, currency controls, and forced draft savings and investments, began to push Mexico along the value-added chain toward
upscale manufactured products. By the year 2015 Mexico's per capita
gross national product is 75 percent of that in the United States. The
demonstration effect of what is called the "Mexican miracle" has been so
electric that Japan now has similar bureaucratic teams at work in more
than thirty nations around the world.*

*On the surface, at least, the United States appears to be faring quite
well under Pax Nipponica. Our foreign debt has been greatly reduced,
and we are running modest budget and trade surpluses. The American
educational system has been reformed, and the drug problem has been
nearly eliminated. Sharply lower defense spending has permitted the expansion of social services and environmental safeguards. As some argue,
America never had it so good.*

*The hard truth is that our economy is no longer mismanaged because
the Japanese are managing it for us. The Japanese now own over 40 percent of American manufacturing assets, an amount more than four times
that of all other foreign direct investments combined. Fifty percent of
American bank assets are now held by the Japanese. Through a combination of strategically placed manufacturing investments and overwhelming financial leverage, Japan is able to move the U.S. economy in
concert with Japan's strategic economic world vision.*

*Considerable basic and applied research is still done in the United
States, but it is controlled by the Japanese and the best of it appears first
in Japanese products. The chairman of the Federal Reserve Board has
little more power than a bureau chief in the Japanese Ministry of Finance.
In fact, the Federal Reserve and the U.S. Treasury Department are now
de facto colonial outposts of the Ministry of Finance, which is indisputably the most powerful bureaucratic agency in the world. Interest rates,
debt levels, and target currency exchange rates are all effectively set in
Tokyo.*

*Despite the pervasive and not too subtle economic and political con-
trol by the Japanese, there is surprisingly little backlash. Japan's economic power has generated numerous political IOU's from most of the
influential members of Congress. The Japanese lobby on Capitol Hill has*

awesome power. The media are no problem, as laws have been changed to permit the Japanese to amass extensive media holdings. The normally questioning and querulous academic community has been bought off by a steady and sizable flow of funds to most major universities. In fact, more than 50 percent of the endowments of Cal Tech, Carnegie Mellon University, and M.I.T. have been funded by the Japanese.

At least the United States can no longer complain that Japan is taking a free ride on defense. The Japanese constitution was amended in 1998 to permit Japan to have nuclear weapons. While the United States still spends slightly more on defense as a percentage of GNP than Japan, the huge disparity in favor of Japan, relative to absolute GNP, leaves that nation with a much larger defense budget. However, after years of slow incubation and many heated debates, the Strategic Defense Initiative— Reagan's Star Wars, now renamed "The Freedom Shield"—is at last a reality. Unfortunately, it stands guard over the Japanese home islands.

Preposterous? Off the wall? Insane? Couldn't happen? Well, let's imagine that it's 1955 and you had Ben Fairless of U.S. Steel, Ralph Cordiner of General Electric, and "Engine" Charlie Wilson of General Motors sitting down together. You tell them that within twenty-five years the Japanese steel industry will be the most powerful and technologically advanced in the world, Japan will totally dominate the U.S. consumer electronics market, and Japan will produce more passenger cars than the United States. Those three very able men would have told you in no uncertain terms that could never happen. But I submit that the Pax Nipponica of 2015 is far easier to envision in 1991 than the Japan of 1980 was in 1955.

A shift from the politics of plenty to the politics of economic decline will not be pleasant. Americans must harbor no illusions as to favorable prospects for institutional reform and economic revival in the face of the twin barriers of political recalcitrance and the almost universal mind-set of the anti-statist tradition. Things will no doubt get worse before they get better. It is often said that the American political system responds well only to a national crisis. The worsening situation of the United States will probably not result in a deep depression or an unsolvable financial crisis; the more likely course will be a gradual wasting away of our economic resources and national power. The drama will be played out in slow motion over decades. Before long, economic decline will begin to fit like an old shoe.

We need only look at the sad case of Great Britain to see how long and painful the slippery slide of economic decline can be. And Americans will probably not accept economic decline with the grace and civility the British showed; it will probably have an uglier face in the United States. When the mantle of leadership passed from England to America after World War I it was a family affair, like an inheritance left to a younger brother or eldest son. When the torch is passed to Japan, it will not be the same.

Twenty and more years ago, when the economic going in the United States was much better, Richard Hofstadter observed: "The nation seems to slouch onward toward its uncertain future like some huge inarticulate beast, too much attainted by wounds and ailments to be robust, but too strong and resourceful to succumb." When Hofstadter so eloquently caught the sense of the political drift in America, the danger from Japan was only a glimmer on the horizon. The Soviet Union challenged the United States militarily, but events later showed that the Soviet threat was merely a military Frankenstein bootstrapped up from a fatally deficient economic, political, and social base. At a fundamental level, then, the American system was not challenged. Americans could aimlessly roam the world secure in their might and moral right, convinced that their economic and political institutions were the best in the world. And in that world they probably were. But today Americans are challenged across the board by Japanese institutions of clearly demonstrable superiority.

Facing a darker future, the United States lives on imprisoned in the present. Business planning runs from quarter to quarter, and economic policy runs from election to election. Until our downwardly spiraling economic fortunes miraculously reverse, until the Japanese system seriously falters, or until somebody comes up with a better explanation for the present predicament of the United States, we ought to look more closely at the political roots of American economic decline.

And don't blame Japan. Yes, the Japanese have been aggressive, have cut a few corners, but that's what competition is all about. A comic-strip character called Pogo had an appropriate line for the current situation: "We have met the enemy and he is us." The Japanese are doing what they are doing because they haven't received an adequate, or even half-hearted, U.S. response to their powerful challenge. Japan has a superior economic system governed by a theory of industrial policy. Japan is winning and the United States is losing, yet we want Japan to drop its industrial policy and its state-market balance for the state-neutral free-market economic system of the United States. Would you change if you were the Japanese? Certainly not. And they're not going to change either.

The choice is ours. The United States must adopt the tools of industrial policy and respond to, or evade, the Japanese challenge. If we stay the course of state-neutral free-market economics, Americans will continue to suffer the consequences of economic decline. And if you believe that fundamental political reforms should not be undertaken just to reap the rewards of an ever-increasing GNP, then consider the fact that without such reforms the economic autonomy, political independence, and personal freedoms of all Americans will be at stake.

While in a large sense this book is a call to arms, it should not be labeled as part of the current genre of "Japan-bashing." Indeed, most Japan-bashers insist that Japan change to become more like the United States, while it is the settled opinion of this work that we must become more like Japan.

Japan's invention of industrial policy and the delicate balancing of state/market economic power stand as a monumental achievement. The Japanese, unlike any other nation, have seized on the importance of technology; they understand best the linkage between technology and economic growth. They are using the dynamics of advancing technology to fashion the world's premiere high-growth economy. In new inventions, new technology, and soon in basic scientific discoveries themselves, the Japanese are destined to be leaders.

When future historians list the honor roll of great nations that have made overgenerous contributions to the advance of civilization, Japan will be included with Greece, Rome, France, Germany, Great Britain, and the United States—among others. What the Japanese have accomplished has certainly accrued to their benefit, but their development of new principles of industrial and economic management constitute a gift to the entire world. In this sense the Japanese have made the world a better place in which to live. As beneficiaries, we in the United States, and all mankind, should be thankful for it.

Japan learned from, borrowed from, and copied wholesale from the West, especially the United States. It was never too proud to do so. Japan blended Western ideas with the unique qualities and capacities of its own people. It took what it thought best and ignored the rest. In 1854 it was challenged by Admiral Perry, the United States, and the West. It was challenged by demonstrably superior economic, political, and social institutions. Japan had to respond or perish as an independent nation, and it chose to respond.

Today, we are challenged by the Japanese. The challenge is more subtle and more difficult to understand than the stark economic and political gulf that separated mid-nineteenth-century Japan from the United States. But in countless ways the Japanese have demonstrated that they possess improved economic, political, and social institutions. It's not a clear-cut case of right or wrong. On the institutional scoreboard there are pluses and minuses, but Japan's pluses far outweigh the minuses. Like Japan in the past, we must study their institutions, and adopt what is appropriate while rejecting what is not useful.

The United States today is like an ostrich with its head in the sand. It steadfastly refuses to face reality. Americans ask: How can a nation that was utterly destroyed forty-five years ago rise up phoenix-like to challenge the mightiest nation on earth? The how of it is a very long story, but the important point is that it happened.

The Japanese are way out in front of the pack and are gaining ground daily. That's dangerous for us, and probably dangerous for them too. A serious U.S. response to their challenge would make our nation stronger and it would quicken their pace. The whole world would benefit. But as long as we remain obsessed with our hyperindividualism, anti-statism, and free-market absolutism, we're doomed to decline.

APPENDIXES

APPENDIX A:
STATE AND BUREAUCRACY
IN GERMANY

As the German Federal Republic (now a newly united Germany) moves into its fifth decade, the success of its political institutions is widely acknowledged. Whether measured by political stability, a fundamental commitment to democracy, or outstanding economic performance, the record is impressive. Germany's federal structure notwithstanding, state authority and a powerful bureaucracy at both the federal and the *Land* (state) level play a crucial role in the successful functioning of the German political system. A strong central state and a top professional bureaucracy characterize Germany, as well as Japan and France.

Prussian state-building since the seventeenth century was based on military strength and efficient bureaucratic administration. The state-building imperative in Prussia was stronger than in Japan or France. Japan's natural insularity and self-imposed isolation postponed demand for a strong central state until the second half of the nineteenth century. Japan's Meiji Constitution owes more to German influences than to those of any other nation. Secured by mountains and water on five of six sides, France was spared the constant threats that a host of potentially hostile neighbors posed to Prussia.

Frederick William I (reigning from 1713 to 1740) has been called the "greatest domestic king" in Prussian history. According to the noted German historian Hajo Holborn, it is he who is most deserving of the title "father of the Prussian bureaucracy."[1] While maintaining certain collegial and territorial institutions, Frederick William centralized and consolidated the bureaucracy, creating clear lines of authority from top to bottom. He reigned and ruled, but he also managed his administration. By vesting state servants with equal responsibility and authority, emphasizing strict execution of orders and stringent economy with public funds, he established a dedicated body of public servants. Prior to Frederick William's reforms, state offices had usually been benefices and sinecures used to raise money and placate aristocratic ambitions. Although the majority of those who held high office continued to be selected from the ranks of the aristocracy, examinations were initiated to eliminate the incompetent. By the end of Frederick William's reign, meritocratic principles had begun to override the traditional ascriptive nature of the royal administration.

State-building and bureaucratic development received major impetus as a result of Prussia's defeat at the hands of Napoleon. Soon after the disastrous loss at Jena, reforms were instituted by two remarkable prime ministers, Baron Heinrich von Stein and Prince Karl August von Hardenberg. Stein's signal accomplishments center on his pioneering but incomplete efforts to link centralized and responsible administration to a broad base of political support. Hardenberg moved decisively to strengthen the authority of the five functional ministries created by Stein, extending their scope of administration from provincial offices through a hierarchal chain culminating in the responsible minister.

The heritage of the Stein and Hardenberg reforms yielded a dedicated cadre of public servants. An increased percentage of top positions were held by university graduates, including modest numbers drawn from outside the ranks of the aristocracy. However, the top positions were essentially reserved for the landholding nobility, the Junkers. Any politically ambitious members of this class realized their aspirations through career channels provided by state service.

A majority of enlightened opinion in Prussia saw in the higher bureaucracy a form of national representation, in the words of Leopold von Ranke, "a selection of the ablest of the whole nation."[2] Unfortunately the legacy of Stein and Hardenberg registered a darker side. There was a price to be paid for bureaucratic development outrunning the restraining bonds of liberalism and constitutionalism. The inbred conviction that administrative guidance should remain unhampered by unenlightened public opinion tended to preserve the authoritarian and militaristic nature of the Prussian state.

The legacy of Otto von Bismarck with respect to the history of German bureaucratic administration is unquestionably negative. A rigid but effective Robert von Puttkammer was the principal architect of Bismarck's civil service program. Through his efforts, and only with the unswerving support of Bismarck, the civil service and the Ministry of Justice were purged of all elements that demonstrated any tendencies toward liberalism. The finished product of Puttkammer's "reforms" was a more powerful bureaucracy cast in a mold of ironbound conservatism finally broken only by the demonic fury of Hitler. Thus a pattern of misuse and abuse is part of the divided heritage of the German bureaucracy, taking its place alongside competence, dedication, and well-earned respect.

With the dynastic dreams of Imperial Germany dashed by defeat in 1918, the nation turned with equal measures of enthusiasm and reluctance toward liberal democracy. Because Bismarck and his successors had kept liberal democratic tendencies under wraps for so long, the tragedy of democracy under the Weimar Republic is a story of too much, too fast. The revolution of 1918 was by no means a genuine social revolution. While the dynastic head was lopped off, a substantial body of influential opinion was still sympathetic to the old order.

The forlorn hope that a newfound or feigned zeal for democratic institutions might soften the burden of the Allied peace terms ended in bitter disappointment. Before German democracy had a chance, the minds of many who were favorably disposed to a new political and social order were poisoned against the Weimar leadership. To an increasing number of people, it seemed that those Germans who had lost the war and also lost the peace were now ruling the nation.

The Weimar Constitution was one of the most democratic in the world. It introduced, in a single rush, universal suffrage, proportional representation, referendum, and recall. It might have worked with difficulty in the best of times, but faced with the burdens of indemnification and ravaged by virulent inflation, the Weimar Republic never had much of a chance. Its fourteen-year life span saw twenty-one governments, few lasting beyond six months.

Unfortunately, the democratic tide stopped short of much-needed civil service reforms. Given the anticipated uncertainty surrounding the performance of Germany's new democratic institutions, the Weimar Constitution hedged its bets. It effectively preserved the status quo of the old imperial civil service with a guarantee of "well-earned rights."[3] As a result of these shortcomings, successive Weimar governments were forced to deal with a civil service that was both deeply conservative and suspect of democracy. Fundamental attitudes within the bureaucracy had changed little since the time of Puttkammer and Bismarck.

The electoral system of proportional representation introduced under the Weimar Constitution gave every possible shade of political opinion a voice while permitting none a clear mandate. Fears of the revolving-door-style of French assembly politics, combined with nostalgia for the monarchy, produced in the office of president an ersatz kaiser and ultimately a lethal counterpoise to parliamentary power. In a nation unaccustomed to the give-and-take of partisan politics, German novelist Thomas Mann spoke for many Germans when he said: "I don't want the trafficking of Parliament and parties that leads to the infection of the whole body of the nation with the virus of politics. . . . I don't want politics. I want impartiality, order, and propriety."[4]

Unduly harsh peace terms, the racking economic dislocations of inflation and depression, and the inherent instability of the regime thrust a nation desperately searching for Mann's "impartiality and order" into the arms of Hitler. In the years following Hitler's assumption of dictatorial power by means of the March 1933 Enabling Act, there appeared throughout the villages and towns of Germany a framed lithograph showing in profile the heads of Frederick the Great, Bismarck, and Hitler. A product of Goebbels's Propaganda Ministry, the lithograph was intended to depict the rootless ahistorical Hitler as the product of a centuries-long process of German state-building.

Despite continued debate, informed historical opinion in Germany and the United

States comes down on the side of Hitler's distinct historical discontinuity.[5] In fact, Hitler was no product of a bureaucratic, statist, or monarchial tradition. When he assumed absolute power on the afternoon of March 23, 1933, he was "created by democracy and appointed by parliament."[6] Hitler's triumph represented a clear-cut victory of the forces of democratic radicalism over those of parliamentary liberalism.[7] His domination in Weber's typology was "charismatic" not "legal." Never before or after has the German civil service been "so much instrumentalized or played so subservient a role."[8] But despite the frightful price paid by the entire world for the Nazi madness, Hitler must stand as the major figure in the process of German modernization. In the creation and subsequent fall of the Nazi regime, he cleared away the thicket of historical impediments to the rise of liberal democracy. By 1945 the slate was wiped clean.

The Basic Law, originally the West German Constitution, can be understood only in terms of the disastrous history of Germany during the twenty-five years encompassing the Weimar and Nazi eras. Unlike the American founders, the framers of the Basic Law did not have to return to ancient Greece to find relevant examples of democratic excess and instability. Those conditions were living memories for most of the people gathered at the Bonn Parliamentary Council. The Basic Law, then, is a backward-looking document, the product of what Carl Friedrich called the "negative revolution" of the postwar era.[9] In this sense, it attempts to turn back the clock to 1919, rejecting both the democratic revolution of Weimar and the counterrevolution of a return to the imperial period. Instead of being a reflection of a keen enthusiasm for a better tomorrow, the Basic Law is tempered primarily by an instinctive revulsion against the horrors of the recent past.

Fearing the emotional undertow of mass democracy and reposing less than unbridled faith in the political capacities of the common man, the Basic Law exempted from popular election the chancellor, the president, and the upper house. It trusted selection of the head of government to the more considered judgment of the directly elected lower house. The popular will was to be adequately and fairly registered, but only through a process of institutional refinement. Institutional arrangements established by the Basic Law confined policy-making mainly to political interaction between interest group, party, and bureaucratic elites well insulated from direct popular pressure.

The Germans have never been unduly fearful about the political consequences of an administrative state. The framers of the Basic Law were far more frightened about their very real experience with the democratic excess of Weimar and the ultimate emergence of Hitler's "leader state." Political institutions that had adequate and healthy democratic controls yet were "administratively competent" seemed to be the favored model of the Parliamentary Council. In this vein, expressing concern that too much Rousseau and too little Hegel might leave the state with insufficient power, Theodore Heuss, West Germany's first president, observed: "Every State, even the democratic State, rests upon the power to command and the claim to obedience. The essence of the democratic State lies in the fact that it possesses a mandate to rule that has a limit and hence is revocable."[10]

Alone among the major European powers, Germany has rejected the unitary form of government in favor of a federal structure. On balance, German federalism has produced democracy and political stability in fair measure, without yielding such unfortunate by-products as political immobilism and democratic deadlock. German federalism is easily distinguished from the form of federalism practiced in the United States. The critical difference between the two federal forms is that U.S. federalism is based on essentially complete and independent sets of governing institutions at the state and federal level, while in Germany the division of powers is along functional lines, with the bulk of policy-making power concentrated at the national level, and the burdens of administration on the ten *Laender* (states). In Germany, then, the federal government assumes responsibility for most of the powers that the national and state governments in the United States share.

The consensus of German public opinion is that policy-making, whether in the parliamentary arena or the bureaucratic arena, is best left to experts. "In a society noted for the early development of a modern bureaucracy," observes political scientist Gerhard Loewenberg, "government is still widely regarded as a purely administrative matter." He continues: "From this it is an easy step to the conclusion that administrators are the best-qualified occupants of any governmental position, and that the parliamentary mandate is a type of administrative office."[11] Parliamentary leadership in Germany, and hence the leadership of the government, has been carefully placed in the hands of a small group of professionals. Bureaucratically organized interest groups bargain painstakingly over detailed issues with a bureaucratically organized parliament.

It is fair, then, to speak of a German "corporatist" political style, with interest groups and the government operating with a "client-broker" relationship. To a considerable degree, the "internal politics" of the bargaining in the Bundesrat (the German upper house) between federal and state authorities over administrative matters is mirrored by the no less internalized politics of the Bundestag (the lower house), where government and interest groups seek solutions to wider-ranging political questions. As Loewenberg has noted, "amateurism, common sense, publicity, and open competition for electoral support" have been willingly sacrificed for an administrative politics.[12] The melding of the political and the bureaucratic in Germany has paralleled developments in Japan and France.

In each German ministry only the top position is filled by a political appointee. Within Germany there is no counterpart for the hundreds of political appointees that dominate the top layers within U.S. cabinet departments. German ministers are vitally dependent on the top bureaucrats in their ministries to formulate policy. Their task is to react to the ministry's initiatives by steering legislative proposals through the cabinet, past the potential veto power of the Finance Ministry, and on to ultimate approval by the legislature. The responsibility of transforming ministerial proposals into legislative successes leaves ministers little time to replicate the tasks of their top bureaucrats. The remarkably long tenure of German ministers greatly facilitates the smooth meshing of bureaucratic and political gears at the ministerial interface. Ministers in Germany average five years in office, a full year longer than the legislative term.

With the possible exception of Japan, nowhere among the major advanced industrial societies is the bureaucrat accorded more respect than in Germany. The French—despite the unitary structure of their state, a bureaucratic tradition in the grand corps extending back beyond Napoleon, and a system of higher education dedicated to educating for service to the state—still have a love-hate relationship with the state and its bureaucratic corps. In Germany, however, with its centuries-long bureaucratic tradition in Prussia and the intellectual underpinnings of Hegel and Weber, state and bureaucracy are an integral part of the governing structure. And it is significant that the Japanese consciously modeled their political institutions after those of Imperial Germany.

After World War II, the German bureaucracy emerged largely intact, gaining relative strength with the elimination of the army and the Nazi political elite. Despite demands for a sweeping democratization of the civil service, economic recovery aimed at strengthening the anti-Communist West took precedence over further civil service reforms. In West Germany, events dictated the priority of political stability over continued democratic experimentation, very much as they did in Japan. The constitutional prerogatives attaching to civil service positions were firmly imbedded at several points within the Basic Law.

In 1989 employment within the twenty-odd federal ministries was about 20,000, of which somewhat less than 5,000 comprise the higher bureaucracy. This number does not differ materially from corresponding figures for Japan and France. The section head is the basic building block of bureaucratic administration within Germany, and there are approximately 1,600 sections. Says one observer, "They are the real 'powerhouses' of [German] administration, and as one frustrated reformer has put it, the section heads are the 'princes' of the policy-making process within the ministries." [13] Sections are small, comprising between three and eight members, with a section head, one or two assistants, and clerical personnel. Given the large number of sections and the slender supervisory structure above it, policy-making within the ministries is decentralized. Section autonomy is strengthened by the relative monopoly of the expert knowledge possessed by the individual sections.

What kinds of people occupy key bureaucratic positions? What are their social origins and educational backgrounds? How are they recruited and promoted? As one might expect, the majority of higher civil servants are from middle-class and upper-middle-class backgrounds. This middle-class orientation is derived primarily from the social selectivity inherent in the secondary educational system. It does not markedly distinguish the origins of German bureaucrats from those of their counterparts in France or Japan. The only noteworthy feature of this social profile is the consistently high percentage of top bureaucrats drawn from the families of former civil servants. Social scientist Ralf Dahrendorf has underscored "the overwhelming fact that in Imperial Germany, the Weimar Republic, and the Federal Republic about one half of all higher civil servants were recruited from the families of civil servants." He calls this "the real inner continuity of German officialdom." [14]

Training of the higher civil service traces its roots to the West German educational system. At the age of ten (after four years of common primary education) all students are divided into sharply differentiated educational paths. In the traditional "three-track system," a nonacademic track leads to general and vocational training, ending full-time education at fifteen or sixteen. A semi-academic course culminates in teachers' colleges and technical schools. The academic route followed by those aiming at university training (including virtually all future higher civil servants) provides nine years of "gymnasium," or academic high school. The gymnasium graduate is awarded the Abitur degree (equivalent to the U.S. junior college diploma) and the opportunity to enter a university. Less than 15 percent of all German students will enter a university.[15]

The educational background of tenured civil servants cannot be understood without some knowledge of the special and long-standing relationship between the German university and the state. Universities are controlled by the *Laender* (the constituent states comprising the Federal Republic). University professors and all academic personnel are employed by each *Land* as tenured civil servants. University budgets are subject to approval in detail by state legislatures, and academic appointments must win state acceptance. Finally, more than 50 percent of all university graduates find employment in the public service. The intimate nature of state/university relationships is graphically displayed in a statement by the *Land* of Baden-Württemberg:

> Universities are, . . . as state institutions, subject to the state's directives in such matters as personnel, finance and state examinations . . . as well as in the areas of student numbers and admissions. . . . [The state] scrutinizes and controls not only the legality of university decisions but also their appropriateness and their funding.[16]

All this notwithstanding, adequate safeguards are provided for academic freedom in teaching and research. The indissoluble links between state and university clearly identify the university as a key element of widespread societal support for the state.

For university students who aspire to the upper reaches of the federal bureaucracy, the study of law predominates over all possible alternatives. In Germany, approximately 65 percent of the higher bureaucracy are jurists.[17] As one proceeds upward within this group of 5,000, the percentage of jurists increases. Well back into the nineteenth century, administrative law in Germany supplanted the slowly evolving disciplines of economics and public administration as the favored language of administrative action.

Legal studies aim very much at the education of generalists rather than specialists. A fundamental grounding in the workings of administrative law enables the aspiring bureaucrat to be an upwardly mobile public servant, not a specialist confined to a particular niche. Administrative law at an elite university stamps its recipient with a degree of acceptance similar to that given by the arts and letters at Cambridge or Oxford.

In contrast to Japan and France, and undoubtedly due to Germany's unhappy authoritarian past, there has been a long-standing fear of excessive administrative discretion in Germany. The legislature, with the cooperation of the bureaucracy, attempts to confine administrative discretion to the greatest degree possible through the drafting of detailed and complex legislation. Given this mandate, it falls to the bureaucracy to translate carefully the desired administrative results into a practicable framework of legal language. The legal education of a jurist anticipating a bureaucratic career then involves the demanding task of learning the "legal consequences of an administrative act."

The legal education of the future high-level civil servant counts for more in career preparation than in academic training. Dahrendorf notes: "The law faculties of German universities accomplish for German society what the exclusive Public Schools do for the English, and the *grandes écoles* for the French. In them an elite receives its training." [18] The study of law is generally regarded by German students as "tedious and uninteresting." The crucial decision involved in the choice of a legal career is in one sense a rejection of more specialized and perhaps more interesting fields of study. By opting for a legal education, the law student makes a fundamental decision to aim for positions of authority both inside and outside the civil service. These positions are reserved mainly for those who have the skills of the generalist rather than the specialist.

Because the demands of legal study may be satisfied by the bright student with much less than maximum effort, considerable time is left for nonacademic activities. The situation in the leading German universities, then, bears some resemblance to that of the University of Tokyo. After one has overcome the extremely difficult admission requirements, the educational process itself is anticlimactic. Student activities and political groups, along with a heavy social schedule, are an important part of university life. In the law faculties of German universities, a future elite is not only educated but socialized. The resulting patterns of thinking and behavior may blunt creativity, but they help establish common commitment to the civil service and to the support of the state.

Recruitment into the higher civil service requires, in addition to a university degree, a preliminary entrance examination followed by two or three years of on-the-job training in the so-called "preparatory service." After the combination of theoretical learning and practical experience, a successful final examination results in the awarding of the coveted status of Beamter auf Lebenszeit (public official for life). [19]

While the bulk of German public servants are recruited for a specific position, members of the higher bureaucracy are recruited into careers within a ministry or functional category. Their preparatory training is aimed at providing them with the knowledge they need to fill a variety of positions within a given ministry. Intraministerial mobility is high, while interministerial mobility is relatively rare. Short of the very few slots at the upper reaches of the higher bureaucracy, political patronage has little effect on career advancement.

Career patterns for the higher civil service are conditioned by the division of the entire bureaucracy into service levels. Each service level constitutes a separate and distinct career ladder with a number of ranks designating career advancement. Entry into each service level normally occurs only at the lowest rung of the career ladder. Promotion, heavily influenced by seniority, moves the bureaucrat upward through his or her service level. Lateral entry into intermediate career ranks, or promotion from one service level to another, is rare. In the case of the higher bureaucracy, one begins the career ladder at the section level. Here again there is marked similarity to Japan as bureaucratic careers advance by seniority on one of several hierarchal career escalators.

Promotion is eagerly sought, because salary is adjusted to rank and not to position, so promotion is the only way to gain financial rewards. Advancement within the higher bureaucracy seldom leads to a political career. Although the Bundestag has a high percentage of existing or former bureaucrats, they do not come from the higher bureaucracy. Because the retirement age for the federal bureaucracy is much higher than in Japan, the phenomenon of former high-level bureaucrats sitting in the

Bundestag is relatively rare. The great majority finish their careers within the civil service.

The pinnacle of the federal bureaucracy is occupied by a limited number of bureaucrats designated "political officials." The core group of political officials includes twenty-four tenured state secretaries and 110 department heads or division heads who carry the title "ministerial director."[20] A typical ministry will have one or two state secretaries and four to eight department heads. As implied by the term "political officials," those who hold these positions, while tenured civil servants, are not bound to the instrumental approach of the stereotypical Weberian bureaucrat. As political officials, they are more in tune with the political objectives of the minister and the minister's government. At the department-head level they are generally civil servants promoted from the ranks of the higher service.

Political officials are distinguished from those below them in that they are subject to temporary retirement at the minister's discretion. This ministerial prerogative is not often used, save during a change of government, when the new minister will then seek to exercise control over the ministry through a body of political officials sympathetic to his views. During the 1970s and 1980s less than 25 percent of the political officials came from outside the federal bureaucracy, and many of these had civil service backgrounds. In contrast to Heclo's description of the U.S. government, this is no government of strangers. It falls to the 130-odd political officials to meld the political perspective skillfully from the top with expert bureaucratic opinion from below. The ground occupied by political officials represents a crucial nodal point in the German political system.

Until recently, high-level German civil servants have for the most part been perceived as classical Weberian bureaucrats. "Legalistic," "impartial," "obedient," and "impersonal" have been the words used most often to convey the instrumental notion of the bureaucracy expressed by the Weberian ideal type.[21] Under national socialism, bureaucratic traditions resting on the image of the bureaucrat as a powerful and independent champion of the public interest received a devastating blow from which they never recovered. At no other time before or after was the bureaucracy so totally instrumentalized and weakened as under Hitler. Utterly subservient to the Nazi party, the bureaucracy was effectively eliminated as a political force.[22] Although the bureaucracy has been restored along traditional lines, the vitality and power of the German party system has limited and modified its authority.

For the influential party leaders of the early postwar years, an independent and nonpartisan civil service meant at best a civil service neutral to the newly established democratic society, and at worst one opposed to it. The ascendancy of the parties signaled a diminution of bureaucratic power, achieved in part by political penetration of the once-monolithic bureaucratic structure. The political responsiveness of top bureaucrats doubtless owes a debt to the overwhelming acceptance of democratic politics at all levels of German society.

The changing role of the top bureaucracy within Germany will become more clear after we examine the critical role played by parties. For the moment, let us note that the major role played by parties within the German political system has at the very least changed the nature of the higher bureaucracy. But to speak of a blurring of distinctions between bureaucrats and politicians is to overstate the case. The structure and mind-set of the parties in Germany will indirectly tell us much about higher-level civil servants. Thus far there is little evidence that party influence has diminished the effectiveness of the bureaucracy.

Despite the tumultuous history of Germany in the twentieth century, including 1990's lightning reunification, the civil service in general and public officials in particular still enjoy great prestige and substantive authority not unlike that of their Japanese and French counterparts. Higher civil servants today, as in times past, are perceived by the public as defending the general interest against the more narrow claims of parties and interest groups. The Germans draw a "qualitative" distinction between state civil servants and functionaries of interest groups or parties very much to the advantage of the former.[23] While the higher civil service has long since ceased to be the exclusive preserve of an aristocracy, the popular image of these positions still retains the cachet of high social status. In Germany, wealth does not provide the convenient shortcut to the attainment of policy-making positions that it does in the United States. It is very difficult to avoid the painstaking career ladders that are within both the bureaucracy and the party hierarchy.

Both law and custom wrap public officials securely with the mantle of state authority. Article 33 of the Basic Law restored to the bureaucracy many of the prerogatives that had been part of its long tradition. Even today, the "common code of administrative practice," a slight revision of a 1926 code, part office manual and part a manual on bureaucratic etiquette, governs much of the procedures and behavior of the federal bureaucracy.[24]

All this is not to deny a host of negatives that might easily be cataloged in any fair assessment of the German higher civil service. Here our argument only goes so far as to demonstrate the powerful position of the federal bureaucracy within the German political system. Says one observer: "Given these structural features and the fact that the political executive (not parliament) plays the dominant role in policy development, policy making in Germany is and indeed must be the responsibility of higher civil servants in the federal bureaucracy."[25] Any adequate understanding of the workings of the German political system must include the federal bureaucracy's rule as central and critical.

Political parties in Germany occupy an extremely important position. In most political systems of advanced industrial societies, organized politics emerged within an existing institutional framework, but Germany provides a notable exception to this rule. Because parties were outlawed by the Nazi regime in 1933, they were the one political force untainted by the Nazi experience. When the allied powers sanctioned active party participation in government at the *Land* level as early as 1945, the parties moved quickly to establish their preeminence in the emerging postwar political system. As influential authors of the Basic Law, they helped insert unusual language giving constitutional support to their position. Article 21 of the Basic Law states: "The parties participate in the forming of the political will of the people." In fact, Section 2 of the same article empowers the constitutional court to outlaw extremist parties: "Parties which, by reason of their aims or the behavior of their adherents, seek to impair or abolish the free democratic basic order or to endanger the existence of the Federal Republic of Germany shall be unconstitutional."[26]

Party discipline within the Bundestag adds strength to the parties. Under the standing rules of the Federal Parliament, all legislative assignments and committee posts are made through the leadership of the ruling party. Not only do parties control the recruitment of elected officials, but through their influence on the political level of the federal bureaucracy they exercise de facto veto power over the appointment of political officials.

Because parties are the only vehicle for the meaningful expression of voter will, party leaders at the state and federal level occupy positions of considerable strength. Lacking primary elections, the nominating process of the party is largely in the hands of its leading professionals. Political amateurs, independents, or renegades are rare or nonexistent.

A still vital "state tradition" in Germany, coupled with the new preeminence of political parties, has led several political scientists to describe Germany as a party state (*Parteienstaat*). The so-called "party state" of today may be contrasted with the bureaucratically dominated "administrative state" of the German Reich, the "interest-group state" of Weimar, and the "leader state" of national socialism.[27]

Germany provides a model of organized interest groups bargaining with a strong state. The resulting politics—a blend of politicized bureaucracy and a bureaucratized politics—tends to be incremental and characterized by development in preconceived and well-understood directions.[28]

The idea of the state is fundamental to an understanding of politics and society in Germany. Dahrendorf has termed the state "an abstraction that has played a great role in German political theory."[29] Today, as under the more authoritarian regimes of the past, there is general acceptance of the idea that the state bears ultimate responsibility for the social welfare of its citizens. In sharp contrast to the Anglo-American democracies, where the public interest is seen as no more than the sum of individual interest or wills, the public interest in Germany receives thorough and authoritative definition through the medium of the state.

The successful functioning of German democratic institutions over the past forty years has demythologized the idea of the transcendental state. And the statist tradition of Germany's unhappy past has transmitted to the contemporary state a moral sense registered in a deep commitment to and responsibility for the public welfare. The notion that political and administrative acts carry a moral function is one that is easily accepted by most Germans. The tacit acceptance and endorsement of state activity in Germany on a number of levels is in sharp contrast to government involvement in the United States, which is all too often erratic, highly politicized, and predictably controversial.

In the economic sphere, the idea of the neutral state has been emphatically rejected. This explicit rejection of strict laissez-faire brings the German state squarely in line with Japanese and French conceptions of the role of the state in economic matters. There is in Germany a pronounced intellectual tradition of political economy that specifies a central position for the state. Adequate state regulation of private interest aims at the enhancement of the public welfare, and consequently economic performance. In Germany, as in Japan and France, due respect is given to the crucial input of free-market forces. This blending of politics and economics, of state and market, mandates for the state a framing role rather than a directing role in the economy. Says one observer, "In an era when rational efficiency, effective economic management, and apolitical domestic stability have become the bases for national economic and political power . . . [Germany appears to be] in an ideal position."[30]

During a period when it is fashionable to speak of a serious case of overload facing the world's liberal democracies, the German political system may present an interesting alternative. With the complexities of economic and social problems increasing yearly, political arenas such as the British Parliament or the U.S. Congress appear to have inherent problems producing effective policy outputs. With public acceptance of state authority, a policy-making administrative structure peopled by a self-confident and capable bureaucracy, and a vigorous party system transmitting broad democratic mandates, Germany may serve as a helpful model. Rather than attempting to eradicate bureaucratic and statist traditions by an overgenerous dose of Anglo-American democracy, the Germans, by fusing politics and bureaucracy, may have become politically "supermodern" and stumbled on a political system better suited for the age to come.[31]

APPENDIX B:
STATE AND BUREAUCRACY
IN FRANCE

France was among the first European nations to unify and centralize. It was also the first to develop a powerful civil service to achieve those ends. Seventeenth- and eighteenth-century monarchs paid close attention to the advice Cardinal Richelieu (whom Hegel called the architect of modern France) offered Louis XIII in 1629: "Reduce and restrict those bodies which, because of pretensions to sovereignty, always oppose the good of the realm. Ensure that your majesty is absolutely obeyed by great and small."[1]

A few decades later, Louis XIV could rightfully declare, "L'état c'est moi," but the absolutist state encompassed far more than the person of the ruler. Staffed by large bureaucracies, state institutions collected taxes, extended and defended national borders, conducted diplomatic relations, maintained public order, and regulated the economic life of prerevolutionary France. Although acting in the name of the king, this vast and durable administrative machine developed an institutional identity apart from that of the monarch. By the time of the revolution, the state rather than the king had become the locus of absolute power.[2]

Effective state centralization and a meritocratic civil service were products of the French Revolution. In the words of de Tocqueville,

> [The revolution] sought to increase the power and jurisdiction of the central authority. . . . The chief permanent achievement of the French Revolution was the suppression of those political institutions, commonly described as feudal, which for many centuries had held unquestioned sway in most European countries.[3]

On August 4, 1789, the selling of offices was abolished. As stated in the Declaration of Rights of 1791, no "other distinction than that of their virtues and their talents" should serve as the basis for the selection of civil servants. The creation of modern, specialized ministries with clearly defined spheres of competence was also to be one of the lasting accomplishments of the French Revolution.[4] And what the revolution had begun, Napoleon would complete. Under his direction a centralized and efficient administrative structure was firmly established. It provided an institutional legacy that has survived, intact in many respects, for two centuries.

To enable the central government to impose a uniform system of rules on the entire nation, the territory of France was divided into eighty-three *départements,* each headed by prefects appointed by and directly answerable to Napoleon (who called them "mes petits empereurs"). This new hierarchy of prefects, subprefects, and centrally appointed mayors resulted in greater control and bureaucratic responsiveness than existed under the Old Regime. Virtually all aspects of life throughout France were now controlled by officials who answered only to the central government.[5]

The choice of the individuals who were to serve as the top administrators of the state was a matter of great concern to Napoleon. A military or civil service position was accorded great honor; to be a servant of the state was (and remains today) widely regarded as the most illustrious of careers. Comprising the agents of the state would be a meritorious corporate body composed, Napoleon proclaimed, "not of Jesuits who have their sovereign in Rome, but of Jesuits who have no other ambition than that of being useful, and no other interest but the public interest."[6]

The importance Napoleon placed on recruitment and education of these state elites led him to establish highly selective schools of higher education. These so-called *grandes écoles* were to train and imbue future civil servants with a strong sense of loyalty to the state. A few grandes écoles had been created in the aftermath of the revolution, and some even existed under the Old Regime, but it was Napoleon who made the grandes écoles the pinnacle of an elite educational system consciously designed to produce a central state administration managed by patriots of outstanding ability. The grandes écoles, and in turn the state bureaucracy, admitted individuals on the basis of merit rather than birth, wealth, or nepotism. Thus Napoleon could proudly claim that the education and selection of state administrators exemplified both the egalitarian tenets of the revolution and the principle of meritocracy.

By the early nineteenth century France had a powerful, centralized administrative system staffed by a highly qualified and greatly esteemed national bureaucracy. Recruited (increasingly from the growing ranks of the bourgeoisie) on the basis of talent, the bureaucracy was socialized in the principles of service to the nation, neutrality, equality of treatment, and uniformity of rule application. Centralized state control and direction (*étatisme* and *dirigisme*) continued as major facets of French political and economic life. And because the Bonapartist tradition held that the administrative apparatus served the interests of the state and that the state in turn was the defender of the public interest, there was also a moral justification for centralized state control.

The centralized administrative structure Napoleon had so thoroughly integrated and streamlined was to prove far more enduring than the political institutions of postrevolutionary France. Against a dizzying succession of monarchist, republican, and imperial regimes, the central bureaucratic apparatus, in the words of de Tocqueville, "stood firm amid the debacles of political systems,"[7] providing an anchor of administrative stability amid political fluctuations.

Throughout the Third and Fourth Republics, the pattern of executive impotence was broken only during times of crises, when Parliament would temporarily yield power to the "savior" governments of such national heroes as Georges Clemenceau and Raymond Poincaré. The Fifth Republic was born out of just such a major crisis—Algeria—as once more the legislature relinquished its cherished sovereignty to a man on horseback, this time in an attempt to avoid civil war. But the deputies were not to regain the powers they had so jealously guarded during the previous eight decades. Charles de Gaulle made it a condition of his return from self-imposed political exile that his government be granted the power to draft a new constitution. And the new Gaullist constitution was light years removed from the republican sentiments of legislative sovereignty.

In a speech at Bayeux in 1946, de Gaulle delivered what was to be in essence a blueprint for the constitution of the Fifth Republic. The state must be "safeguarded in its rights, its dignity, its authority," he declared, adding that its sanctity could be guaranteed only if the government of France depended not on Parliament for its executive power but on a "national arbiter," a "head of state, placed above the parties. . . ."[8] And to ensure that the new constitution would institutionalize de Gaulle's ideas, its drafting was entrusted not to an elected assembly but to an appointed committee headed by his close associate, Michel Debré, who would serve as the Fifth Republic's first prime minister.

Both Debré and de Gaulle claimed that only a "true" parliamentary regime (rather than what they scornfully termed the system of "government by assembly" of the Third and Fourth Republics) could bring effective governance to France. In such a regime, de Gaulle said in a 1958 speech, Parliament would act to "represent the political will of the nation, to enact laws, and to control the executive," but it would have to do so "without venturing to overstep its role."[9] To help keep the legislature from infringing on the executive, de Gaulle's notion of a strong and autonomous chief of state was incorporated into the new constitution. What emerged on paper was a hybrid presidential-parliamentary system that in practice assigned the central political role to the executive and not to Parliament. The prerogatives of Parliament were sharply limited, while those of the executive were strengthened.

In the Fifth Republic, ministers and junior ministers hold office on the basis of political appointment, as do their immediate subordinates, the 140 departmental directors; each ministry thus averages three to five political appointees. But the majority of all such appointees are top-ranking civil servants. As a result, the political echelon, which is non-civil-service and changes when a new party or minister comes in, averages no more than one hundred people.[10] Although ministers are not required by law to do so, they select their directors almost exclusively from the ranks of upper-level civil servants. Hence, senior career bureaucrats hold almost all departmental line positions below that of minister, resulting in far greater administrative continuity than in the United States.

Within the French executive, top-ranking bureaucrats have maintained a preeminent position as key players in both the formulation and execution of policy. De Gaulle and his followers recognized that bureaucratic cooperation was absolutely essential in meeting their goals of state-initiated economic change and modernization. The Gaullist constitution sought to terminate undue parliamentary influence over the bureaucracy and to bring the administrative system more securely under executive control. Senior bureaucrats were also brought into the government itself, as ministers and members of ministerial and presidential cabinets. Thus, individuals who were well versed in the operation of administrative machinery were placed in top government positions. As in Japan, the higher bureaucracy in France wields vast political as well as administrative power and influence, and its members have increasingly great influence in the private sector. It is therefore no exaggeration to say that top professional bureaucrats now constitute the core of France's political, administrative, and industrial elite.

And who are these senior civil servants, the so-called mandarins of modern France, and by what paths do they attain their positions? Like the top members of the French civil service since the days of the First Empire, they have been educated at the highly restrictive and competitive *grandes écoles*. These specialized, state-run institutions train the most intellectually qualified candidates for a higher civil service career and impart to them a strong sense of allegiance to the state. Although selected solely on the basis of academic merit, the social origins of these civil service careerists are generally upper-middle-class and Parisian; many are the children of top civil servants. Like their Japanese counterparts, they are accorded high status and respect by the rest of society.

Since the reign of Napoleon, education has been *the* path to the ranks of the senior bureaucracy. Napoleon instituted a centralized and uniform public school system (the Imperial University) whose function was both political and vocational: to teach the "national doctrine" to the many and to train a select few as the future elite administrators of the state. The educational system was rigidly stratified, with only upper-middle-class and upper-class males progressing beyond the primary level to the secondary *lycées*. Nor were all lycées equal in rank. The most prestigious were located in Paris, and their graduates were the most likely to gain entrance to the pinnacle of the Napoleonic educational system, the grandes écoles.

Through World War II, French secondary and higher education remained almost the exclusive province of the bourgeoisie, but under the Fifth Republic the educational system has been restructured and democratized. Compulsory attendance has been raised to age sixteen. All students are required to attend elementary school for six years and then to progress to four years of study at a middle school, or *collège,* where everyone receives two years of common liberal arts education, *la culture générale.*

During their final two years, after eight years of common schooling, students are slotted into one of three distinct educational tracks, according to academic ability. The shortest of the three educational ladders culminates in a terminal degree on completion of the final two years of the middle school. These students enter the work force at age sixteen, after ten years of schooling. After middle school, the second track leads to two years of technical study at an upper secondary school of professional education.

The highest academic track leads to three years of humanistic or scientific study at a lycée. On graduation from the lycée, after thirteen years of education, the holder of the lycée baccalaureate degree (attained by about one-fourth of all eighteen-year-olds) is automatically eligible to enter one of France's seventy-three universities. The open admissions policy instituted in the wake of the 1968 student upheavals has increased university enrollment dramatically, to close to one million.[11]

At the apex of France's educational system, largely untouched by the waves of postwar educational reforms, stand the grandes écoles. These venerable institutions remain the exclusive training ground for top French bureaucrats. There are today nearly one hundred grandes écoles providing undergraduate and graduate education in very specialized fields such as statistics, taxes, social security administration, and public health administration, along with more general administrative and technical training.

Unlike the universities, which are all controlled by the Ministry of Education, the grandes écoles are attached to and run by the ministries closest to their field of specialization. They are by design much smaller in size (total enrollment is around 70,000, only about 8 percent of all postsecondary students) and far more selective than the universities (fewer than 10 percent of all applicants are accepted to the top-ranking grandes écoles).[12] Universities are required to admit all lycée graduates, but entrance to an undergraduate grande école requires at least two years of preparation beyond the baccalaureate degree, plus successful completion of a grueling written examination, the *concours*. Graduate-level grandes écoles are equally selective.

Because of their greater prestige and more stringent standards, the grandes écoles draw the best students in France. Admission is all the more desirable because students at the grandes écoles receive stipends for the duration of their studies and are assured of employment in the state administration upon graduation.[13] No such privileges are accorded university students. France thus possesses a dual system of higher education, with the grandes écoles standing above the universities. Over the decades, those in positions of power, both on the left and the right, have defended this system because it guarantees that the state will always have its pick of the best talent in France. And since the days of Napoleon, many of the most capable French students have regarded state service as the career of choice.

The most distinguished undergraduate grande école is the École Polytechnique, founded by Napoleon as a school for the training of military officers and engineers. Now controlled by the Ministry of Defense, it trains technical administrators and engineers as well as military officers at the undergraduate level. Known colloquially as "X," the École Polytechnique has been aptly described as a cross between West Point and M.I.T. Admission is extremely selective (the size of the entering class is around 300), and only the very best science students from the top Parisian lycées can hope to gain a place. For advanced training in engineering, Polytechnicians choose among a number of postgraduate grandes écoles (*écoles d'application*) affiliated with the technical ministries of Industry, Public Works, and so on. Graduates of the École Polytechnique lay claim to the most prestigious positions in the technical and defense ministries as well as to top positions in nationalized and private industries.

Members of the nontechnical administrative elite are now trained at the preeminent graduate-level grande école, the École Nationale d'Administration (ENA). Founded in 1945 and placed under the direct control of the prime minister's office, the ENA provides uniform training for future upper-level administrative generalists. It too is extremely selective, admitting only about 150 students a year. Successful entrants are usually top-ranking, upper-middle-class Parisian graduates of the highly selective Institut d'Études Politiques in Paris who have also performed well on the ENA's demanding *concours*. *Enarques* (as ENA graduates are called) have the inside track to the best general administrative positions. The top graduates of the ENA also experience great career mobility outside as well as within the central administration.

The program of study at the grandes écoles is intensive and rigorous. Competition is fierce, because the best positions go to graduates who rank highest in their class. The three-year training period at the ENA begins with a year-long internship (*stage*), usually in a provincial administrative office. The next year is spent in programs of seminars at the school itself, taught by a rotating faculty of ENA graduates who have pursued successful administrative, political, and/or corporate careers. The course of study emphasizes administrative and judicial matters, economics, international and domestic politics, and social problems. The final year consists of further on-the-job training in the particular ministry the student hopes to enter. In a similar fashion, study at the École Polytechnique and its specialized postgraduate schools emphasizes hands-on training in the public and/or private sector as much as formal classroom work in the sciences. The *stage* provides an introduction to the subtleties of high-level decision-making; such generalized and applied knowledge is seen as more important to a student's future career than formal training in a narrow area.[14]

Formal and applied academic training is not the only objective of the grandes écoles. These institutions also instill in their students the importance and prestige of a public service career, the ideals of political neutrality, a disdain for "political" solutions to public issues, and a reliance on technocratic approaches to problem-solving. These goals were forcefully expressed by the ENA's creator, Michel Debré, at the time of the school's founding:

> The training—one need not hide this—also has a moral objective. It is not one of the missions of the school to play politics or to impose a particular doctrine. But the school must also teach its future civil servants "*le sens de l'état,*" it must make them understand the responsibilities of the Administration, make them taste the grandeur and accept the servitudes of the *métier.*[15]

In addition, the grandes écoles infuse their students with a commitment to serve the national interest. Today that means support of the goals of economic growth, modernization, and efficiency—in a word, competitiveness. Nothing less than an initiating leadership is expected of the state in achieving these ends.[16]

Graduates of each grande école develop a sense of common identity and purpose, a feeling of camaraderie usually accompanied by a certain intellectual arrogance.

These individuals have met exacting academic criteria and are well aware of their considerable talents. They have been socialized to think that they alone truly understand and represent the national interest.[17] Such sentiments of inherent superiority are summed up well in the following statement by Georges Pompidou, who graduated from the École Normale Supérieure, the distinguished Parisian grande école established by Napoleon to train secondary teachers: "One is a *normalien* as one is a prince by blood."[18] In fact, Pompidou first came on the national scene when the imperious de Gaulle demanded: "Get me a *normalien* who can write."

At the upper reaches of the French civil service are the members of the twenty-odd *grands corps*. The 7,000 or so members of the grands corps constitute an administrative oligarchy that has a monopoly on the highest positions in the central administration. They are the top professional bureaucracy in France.

Every grand corps has its own sphere of activity, organization, sense of mission, identity, and esprit de corps. The grands corps are independent institutions that carry out certain important functions on behalf of the state and recruit their own members. One remains a member of a grand corps for life, and the corps functions as an exclusive club, providing camaraderie and an effective job network. Because each grand corps attempts to enhance its prestige by securing the most influential positions for its members, rivalries among them abound.[19] Some grands corps are more prominent than others. The leading grands corps include the Inspectorate of Finance (the corps of financial inspectors and auditors), the Council of State (the corps of administrative lawyers), the Court of Accounts (the corps of public accountants), the diplomatic corps, the prefectural corps, and the technical Corps of Mines and the Corps of Bridges and Highways.

The route to the grands corps is a highly circumscribed one. To enter a grand corps, one must be a graduate of a grande école. The most prestigious grands corps select their recruits solely from the top graduates of the leading grandes écoles. Thus, to be admitted to membership in the Inspectorate of Finance or the Court of Accounts, one would have to be in the top 15 to 20 percent of the graduating class of the ENA or, for the technical Corps of Mines, one of the top graduates of the École Polytechnique. Only these highly qualified graduates of the most prominent grandes écoles will have the opportunity to become part of the top French bureaucracy.

For those fortunate few ENA or Polytechnique graduates who do make it to the top of their graduating class and then into the highest echelons of a grand corps, the professional rewards are great. Each grand corps is affiliated with one of the leading ministries or an important state agency, and initial appointments are to upper-level line positions within that ministry or agency. For members of the Inspectorate of Finance, for example, this would mean an appointment within the Ministry of Economy and Finance; those recruited into the diplomatic corps would enter the Ministry of Foreign Affairs.

But entrance into the leading corps in no way restricts one's career to a line position within that ministry. In fact the cream of the bureaucratic crop experience tremendous career mobility within the government. They may serve as members of ministerial and presidential cabinets and perhaps even as a minister, and in the semipublic and private sectors of the economy as presidents or directors of nationalized industries and large private enterprises. For example, as many as 90 or more percent of inspectors of finance have been employed outside their "home ministry."[20] Such mobility is facilitated by a system of "detached" service whereby higher civil servants can temporarily leave the administration without giving up their administrative careers. Members of the grands corps always maintain membership in their corps.

We cannot overemphasize the mobility that exists within the upper reaches of the French administrative system. Within several years of graduation from the ENA or the École Polytechnique, administrators on the "fast track" can look forward to an appointment to a ministerial *cabinet*. After serving for several years in this political capacity, cabinet members can expect either to return to the departmental line hierarchy (as senior officials, perhaps department directors) or to be appointed to a top managerial post in another public enterprise or nationalized industry. They may also decide to seek elected office or to move into an executive position in the private sector, a practice commonly referred to as *pantouflage*. This movement of former French bureaucrats into politics and industry is remarkably similar to the phenomenon of *amakudari* in Japan.[21]

Because senior bureaucrats staff most of the top positions within each ministry, an incoming government does not need to look outside the higher civil service for the several political appointments it makes within the administration. This is a dramatic departure from the practice in the United States, and one that leads to far greater coherence in policy-making. At one point, for example, half the French cabinet ministers were ENA graduates, as were thirteen of the ministers in the Chirac government. Nor did the Socialists exclude the top bureaucracy from decision-making and advisory roles. The ministerial staffs of Socialist ministers have been liberally peppered with members of the higher civil service, and most of Mitterand's key advisers are top bureaucrats. The French system thus permits the appointment of persons of great intellect, expertise, and experience, and with a minimum dislocation of top decision-makers. It also maintains a high level of morale among the top ranks of the bureaucracy.[22]

Top French bureaucrats rapidly become administrative and political generalists. They quickly develop what political scientist Ezra Suleiman calls generalized or "polyvalent" skills that allow them to move freely among a variety of institutional settings. And among this group, the importance of being a generalist is universally recognized.[23] Because they occupy diverse posts, members of the grands corps perceive themselves as more able than line bureaucrats to be thoroughly objective and to offer disinterested advice to the various ministers they serve. Researchers have found that they have a broader outlook than those whose careers are confined to the line bureaucracy of a single ministry, that they tend to be more innovative, and that they have acted as the major agents of change in France.[24]

It has become increasingly common for the higher bureaucracy to seek election to the French Parliament, a move made all the easier because they may temporarily detach from their civil service positions. These so-called "deputy bureaucrats," who number more than 20 percent of the total membership, tend to be among Parliament's most influential members, sitting on and frequently chairing major committees, acting as the rapporteurs of important bills, and leading parliamentary debates in their area of specialization. Their style has been described as "[a mixture of] technical expertise [and] a certain intellectual flair, quite typical of the top-flight administrator in France."[25]

The usual pattern in a parliamentary regime is for the legislature to supervise the bureaucracy by placing members of Parliament in the executive. In the Fifth Republic, this situation has been reversed: members of the senior bureaucracy are now "colonizing" the legislature.[26] In the United States, political appointees come from outside the bureaucracy, and the movement is from the corporate or academic world into government. In France, just the opposite occurs. The managers of large corporations tend now to come from the upper-level bureaucracy. And rarely would a person without a high-level administrative background be appointed to a top political post.

The career of the former prime minister Jacques Chirac illustrates well the educational pedigree and political mobility of an ambitious top civil servant. A graduate of the Institut d'Études Politiques in Paris and of the ENA in 1959, Chirac entered the grand corps of auditors, the Court of Accounts. But his stay in the central administration was brief, and in the early 1960s he was appointed a member of Prime Minister Georges Pompidou's ministerial staff. In 1967 he was elected a Gaullist deputy to the National Assembly. He was then nominated to a cabinet post and held the positions of minister of agriculture and of the interior under the Pompidou presidency. In 1974, at the age of forty-two, he was appointed prime minister by Giscard d'Estaing and at the same time became the leader of the Gaullist party. In 1976 he resigned as prime minister and was elected mayor of Paris in 1977, a post he still held when appointed prime minister by François Mitterrand in 1986 (Michel Rocard succeeded Chirac).

Valéry Giscard d'Estaing is another member of the grands corps who experienced a meteoric rise to political power. A top graduate of both the École Polytechnique and the ENA, Giscard entered the Inspectorate of Finance, but soon left the ranks of administration for greener political fields. Elected to the National Assembly while simultaneously holding positions in local government and founding a new centrist-right political party, he was appointed to his first cabinet post at the age of thirty-two. Several years later, he was appointed minister of finance by de Gaulle, a position he retained under Pompidou's presidency. In 1974 he was elected president of the Republic and held that position until he was defeated by Mitterrand in 1981.

Although they have scaled great political heights, the political career paths of Giscard and Chirac are far from unique. Top bureaucrats often penetrate the highest levels of the French political system. Prime Ministers Debré, Couve de Murville, Messmer, and Fabius were all high-ranking civil servants, as were many of their cabinet ministers. And the ever more common phenomenon of *pantouflage* means that greater numbers of upper-level executives in business, banking, and industry have a civil service background. One study found that 43 percent of the presidents of the one hundred most important business firms in France came from the senior civil service, and that 12 percent of those top executives came from just two grands corps: the Inspectorate of Finance and the Council of State.[27]

The same situation applies in France's numerous public enterprises, as members of the grands corps (particularly the Inspectorate of Finance and the technical corps) serve as the directors and general managers of the public corporations. A report to the National Assembly in 1972 called the public enterprises "private game-parks for the major corps." It is little wonder that scholars and other observers now speak of a "fusion" of elites in the upper ranks of the public and private sectors. A small and very select group shares a common social origin, training, and outlook and holds a significant number of the top positions in French administration, politics, and business.[28] The widespread influence of top bureaucrats in France is quite similar to the Japanese case.

In addition to increasing France's political stability, the constitutional reforms of the Fifth Republic and the changes in party behavior have dramatically enhanced the effectiveness of the regime. The *immobilisme* of the Third and Fourth Republics has all but disappeared, as the government is free to pursue its initiatives without undue parliamentary harassment. Parliament still retains, as it must in a democracy, the ability to scrutinize and even improve legislation, but its power to impede the government has been greatly limited.[29]

Within the executive, the power of the higher bureaucracy has increased relative to that of politicians. Top bureaucrats are the highly qualified experts who draft the legislation, help usher its passage through Parliament, and then implement it. These so-called technocrats have become major lawmakers in contemporary France. In contrast to Germany, but like Japan, the upper levels of the bureaucracy also wield significant discretionary power in the implementation of legislation. Parliament generally determines only the general principles of legislation, leaving the details to the administration. And of course there is tremendous bureaucratic latitude when Parliament enables the government to act by ordinance or when the subject of legislation falls under the category of government regulation. The central lawmaking role of the senior bureaucracy is evidenced by the fact that major interest groups concentrate more of their lobbying efforts on the upper-level administrators in the ministries and in the ministerial cabinets than on the members of parliamentary committees.[30]

Throughout this review of the French political system, we have noted the power of the state. As far back as the eighteenth century, as de Tocqueville reminds us, the central state "was accepted as being the only source of energy for the maintenance of the social system, and as such, indispensable to the life of the nation."[31] From the mercantilist policies of Colbert to the contemporary combination of liberalism and *dirigisme* known as the mixed economy, the French state has been the guiding force in establishing the economic priorities of the nation. Such state activism has been supported by a long tradition of *étatisme*, a conception of the state as the guardian of the national interest, the manifestation of the general will, the protector of individual liberties, and the guarantor of equality. This statist conception has been eloquently expressed by Georges Pompidou:

> For more than a thousand years . . . there has been a France only because there was a State, the State to keep it together, to organize it, to make it grow, to defend it not only against external threats but also against collective egotism, the rivalry of groups. Today, more than ever, the State's force is indispensable not only to assure the nation's future and its security, but also to assure the individual his liberty.[32]

Since the days of Napoleon, the French state has been institutionalized in a powerful central administration whose members firmly adhere to *étatist* goals. The caliber of those who choose a career in the bureaucracy and the esteem in which a civil service career is held by the rest of French society are indicative of the strength of the statist tradition.

NOTES

CHAPTER 1

1. See Steven Schlossstein, *Trade War: Greed, Power, and Industrial Policy on Opposite Sides of the Pacific* (New York: Congdon and Weed, 1984), p. 148; Organisation for Economic Co-Operation and Development (OECD), *Historical Statistics* (Paris, 1990), p. 41, table 2.11; ibid., p. 69, table 6.8; ibid., p. 73, table 6.16; Bureau of Labor Statistics, *Monthly Labor Review,* October 1990, p. 98, table 50; National Science Board, *Science and Engineering Indicators, 1989* (Washington, D.C., 1989), pp. 3–4; and Kevin Phillips, *The Politics of Rich and Poor: Wealth and the American Electorate in the Reagan Aftermath* (New York: Random House, 1990), pp. 132, 137.

2. Charles McMillion, quoted in Chriss Swaney, "Speaker Says U.S. Losing World Clout," *Wall Street Journal,* March 21–27, 1988.

3. Alfred L. Malabre Jr., *Beyond Our Means: How America's Long Years of Debt, Deficits, and Reckless Borrowing Now Threaten to Overwhelm Us* (New York: Random House, 1987), p. 38.

4. Theodore H. White, "The Danger from Japan," *New York Times Magazine,* July 28, 1985, p. 21.

5. Michael Stewart, *The Age of Interdependence: Economic Policy in a Shrinking World* (Cambridge: M.I.T. Press, 1984), p. 19.

6. Ira C. Magaziner and Robert B. Reich, *Minding America's Business: The Decline and Rise of the American Economy* (New York: Harcourt Brace Jovanovich, 1982), p. 375.

7. Theodore Levitt, "The Globalization of Markets," *Harvard Business Review* 61 (May–June 1983): 94.

8. Ibid.

9. See OECD, *Historical Statistics,* p. 94, table 9.2; ibid., p. 41, table 2.11; and Schlossstein, *Trade War,* pp. 6–7.

10. Peter G. Peterson (interviewed by D. N. Dickson and G. E. Willigan), "The Peterson Prescription," *Harvard Business Review* 62 (May–June 1984): 68.

11. The sharp devaluation of the dollar since 1986 has eliminated this problem, but during the period of overvaluation great damage was inflicted on the U.S. manufacturing sector by artificially cheap imports. The steel, automotive, and machine tool industries have never recovered from that devastating onslaught.

12. Otto Eckstein, Christopher Caton, Roger Brinner, and Peter Duprey, *The DRI Report on U.S. Manufacturing Industries* (New York: McGraw-Hill Book Company, 1984), p. 3.

13. William J. Abernathy, Kim B. Clark, and Alan M. Kantrow, "The New Industrial Competition," *Harvard Business Review* 59 (September–October 1981): 74.

14. See Daniel Bell, *The Coming of Post-Industrial Society: A Venture in Social Forecasting* (New York: Basic Books, 1973).

15. Office of the U.S. Trade Representative, "Annual Report of the President of the United States on the Trade Agreements Program, 1984–1985," issue 28, February 1986, p. 43; New York Stock Exchange, "U.S. International Competitiveness: Perception and Reality," August 1984, p. 32; Gary S. Becker, "The Prophets of Doom Have a Dismal Record," *Business Week,* January 27, 1986, p. 22.

16. For further discussion, see Stephen S. Cohen and John Zysman, *Manufacturing Matters: The Myth of the Post-Industrial Economy* (New York: Basic Books, 1987).

17. Eckstein et al., *DRI Report,* p. 80.

18. For an extended discussion of the importance of manufacturing, see again Cohen and Zysman, *Manufacturing Matters.*

19. Donald F. Barnett and Louis Schorsch, *Steel: Upheaval in a Basic Industry* (Cambridge, Mass.: Ballinger Publishing Company, 1983), pp. 27, 18, 79, 49, 44, 53, respectively.

20. Ibid., p. 28.

21. Ibid., pp. 18, 79.

22. See American Iron and Steel Institute, *Annual Statistical Report* (various years), for world production in steel. See also D. Barnett and R. Crandall, *Up from the Ashes: The Rise of the Steel Minimill in the United States* (Washington, D.C.: The Brookings Institution, 1986).

23. Refers only to firms comprising two-thirds of each nation's steel capacity.

24. Barnett and Schorsch, *Steel,* pp. 44, 53; *American Metal Market,* June 14, 1990; United Nations, *Statistics of World Trade in Steel,* various years.

25. Auto industry data here from Michael S. Salter, Alan M. Webber, and Davis Dyer, "Lessons from the Auto Industry," in Bruce R. Scott and George C. Lodge, eds., *U.S. Competitiveness in the World Economy* (Boston: Harvard Business School Press, 1985), p. 185; and William J. Abernathy, Kim B. Clark, and Alan M. Kantrow, *Industrial Renaissance: Producing a Competitive Future for America* (New York: Basic Books, 1983), p. 13.

26. Auto industry data here from Abernathy et al., *Industrial Renaissance,* p. 46, and from Salter et al., "Lessons from the Auto Industry," pp. 192, 196.

27. Data from Salter et al., "Lessons from the Auto Industry," pp. 192, 207.

28. Interview with General Motors official.

29. Donald E. Petersen in Michael L. Wachter and Susan M. Wachter, eds., *Toward a New U.S. Industrial Policy?* (Philadelphia: University of Pennsylvania Press, 1983), p. 419.

30. "Losing Control," *Wall Street Journal,* February 16, 1990, p. A1.

31. Ibid.

32. John Zysman and Laura Tyson, eds., *American Industry in International Competition: Government Policies and Corporate Strategies* (Ithaca, N.Y.: Cornell University Press, 1983), p. 112.

33. Ibid., p. 107.

34. *Business Week,* October 7, 1985, p. 94.

35. William F. Finan and Annette M. LaMond, "Sustaining U.S. Competitiveness in Microelectronics," in Scott and Lodge, *U.S. Competitiveness,* p. 161.

CHAPTER 2

1. Amitai Etzioni, *An Immodest Agenda: Rebuilding America Before the Twenty-First Century* (New York: McGraw-Hill Book Company, 1983), p. 259.

2. Ibid., p. 285.

3. See Robert B. Reich, *The Next American Frontier* (New York: Times Books, 1983), pp. 158–159. For a greater understanding of the adverse implications of a financial orientation as against manufacturing dominance, see David Halberstam, *The Reckoning* (New York: William Morrow and Company, 1986).

4. Robert H. Hayes and William J. Abernathy, "Managing Our Way to Economic Decline," *Harvard Business Review* 58 (July–August 1980): 67.

5. Robert H. Hayes and Steven C. Wheelwright, *Restoring Our Competitive Edge: Competing Through Manufacturing* (New York: John Wiley and Sons, 1984), pp. 9–13.

6. Joseph A. Schumpeter, *Capitalism, Socialism, and Democracy* (New York: Harper and Row Publishers, 1975), p. 81.

7. Reich, *The Next American Frontier,* pp. 140–141.

8. George C. Lodge, *The American Disease* (New York: Alfred A. Knopf, 1984), p. 75.

9. Hiroyuki Itami, "The Firm and the Market in Japan," in Lester C. Thurow, ed., *The Management Challenge: Japanese Views* (Cambridge: M.I.T. Press, 1985), p. 75.

10. Richard J. Schonberger, *Japanese Manufacturing Techniques: Nine Hidden Lessons in Simplicity* (New York: The Free Press, 1982).

11. OECD, *Historical Statistics.*

12. Bruce R. Scott, "National Strategies: Key to International Competition," in Scott and Lodge, *U.S. Competitiveness,* p. 118.

13. Lodge, *The American Disease,* pp. 32, 36.

14. See Introduction, Scott and Lodge, *U.S. Competitiveness,* p. 6; Wellons, "The

Role of the U.S. Financial System," in ibid., p. 360; and Eckstein et al., *DRI Report,* p. 30.

15. See Philip A. Wellons, "The Role of the U.S. Financial System," in Scott and Lodge, *U.S. Competitiveness,* pp. 373, 376. Financial intermediaries include commercial banks, savings and loan associations and other savings institutions, insurance companies, private pension funds, state and local retirement funds, finance companies, and investment companies.

16. Ranking varies according to the dollar-yen relationship at a particular point in time.

17. Itami, "The Firm and the Market in Japan," p. 71.

18. Shoichi Royama, "The Japanese Financial System: Past, Present, and Future," in Thurow, *The Management Challenge,* pp. 101–102.

19. Lodge, *The American Disease,* p. 69; Lester C. Thurow, *The Zero-Sum Society: Distribution and the Possibilities for Economic Change* (New York: Basic Books, 1980), p. 8.

20. For a further discussion of the developmental state as it has been conceptualized in Japan, see Chalmers Johnson, *MITI and the Japanese Miracle: The Growth of Industrial Policy, 1925–1975* (Stanford, Calif.: Stanford University Press, 1982). While Johnson did not coin the term, his pioneering effort linking state and industrial growth best defines developmentalism.

21. See Merrill D. Peterson, ed., *The Portable Thomas Jefferson* (New York: Penguin Books, 1975), p. 293.

22. Samuel P. Huntington, *American Politics: The Promise of Disharmony* (Cambridge: Harvard University Press, Belknap Press, 1981), p. 39.

23. See Peter W. Huber, *Liability: The Legal Revolution and Its Consequences* (New York: Basic Books, 1988), esp. p. 6.

24. Ibid., p. 78.

25. Ibid., pp. 166–167.

26. Quoted in James Reston, "Discussing the Bugs in the Machinery, Q & A: David A. Stockman," *New York Times,* April 12, 1984.

27. Thurow, *The Zero-Sum Society,* p. 18.

CHAPTER 3

1. Schumpeter, *Capitalism, Socialism, and Democracy,* p. 84.

2. Kenichi Ohmae, *Triad Power: The Coming Shape of Global Competition* (New York: The Free Press, 1985), p. 9.

3. Jared Taylor, *Shadows of the Rising Sun: A Critical View of the "Japanese Miracle"* (New York: William Morrow and Company, 1983), p. 87.

4. Johnson, *MITI and the Japanese Miracle,* p. 241.

5. On the developmental state, see Johnson, *MITI and the Japanese Miracle.*

6. Peter F. Drucker, "Behind Japan's Success: Defining Rules for Managing in a Pluralist Society," *Harvard Business Review* 59 (January–February 1981): 87.

7. E. Herbert Norman, *Japan's Emergence as a Modern State: Political and Economic Problems of the Meiji Period* (Westport, Conn.: Greenwood Press, 1973), p.

194; see also Julian Gresser, *Partners in Prosperity: Strategic Industries for the United States and Japan* (New York: McGraw-Hill Book Company, 1984), p. 91.

8. Kiyohiko Fukushima, "Public Use of Private Interests: Japan's Industrial Policy," in Robert E. Driscoll and Jack N. Behrman, eds., *National Industrial Policies* (Weston, Mass.: Oelgeschlager, Gunn, and Hain, 1984), p. 78.

9. Zysman and Tyson, in *American Industry in International Competition,* chap. 1, pp. 31–33.

10. William H. Davidson, *The Amazing Race: Winning the Technorivalry with Japan* (New York: John Wiley and Sons, 1984), p. 14.

11. See Lawrence G. Franko, *The Threat of Japanese Multinationals: How the West Can Respond* (New York: John Wiley and Sons, 1983), pp. 35–36.

12. Ibid., p. viii.

13. Ibid., p. 35; Franko cites La Documentation Française, Commissariat Général du Plan, *La Specialisation international des industries à l'horizon 1985* (1978). See also Lawrence G. Franko, "British Industry, the International Dimension," in C. L. Suzman et al., *Foreign Direct Investment in the Southeast United States* (Atlanta: The Southern Center, January 1979).

14. Franko, *The Threat of Japanese Multinationals,* p. 45.

15. Toyohiro Kono, *Strategy and Structure of Japanese Enterprises* (London: Macmillan and Company, 1984), p. 50.

16. Ibid.

17. Ira C. Magaziner and Thomas M. Hout, *Japanese Industrial Policy* (Berkeley and Los Angeles: University of California Press, 1981), p. 5.

18. Ibid., p. 254.

CHAPTER 4

1. Chie Nakane, *Japanese Society* (Berkeley and Los Angeles: University of California Press, 1970), p. 2.

2. Edwin O. Reischauer, *The Japanese* (Cambridge: Harvard University Press, Belknap Press, 1977), p. 131.

3. Ruth Benedict, *The Chrysanthemum and the Sword: Patterns of Japanese Culture* (New York: New American Library, 1946), p. 43.

4. Nakane, *Japanese Society,* p. 26; Benedict, *Chrysanthemum and the Sword,* p. 95.

5. Nakane, *Japanese Society,* p. 87.

6. Edwin O. Reischauer, *The Japanese Today: Change and Continuity* (Cambridge: Harvard University Press, Belknap Press, 1988), p. 152.

7. Ibid., p. 166.

8. Ezra F. Vogel, *Japan as Number One: Lessons for America* (Cambridge: Harvard University Press, 1979), p. 167.

9. Reischauer, *The Japanese,* p. 171.

10. Ronald P. Dore, *The Diploma Disease* (Berkeley and Los Angeles: University of California Press, 1976), p. 50.

11. T. J. Pempel, *Policy and Politics in Japan: Creative Conservatism* (Philadelphia: Temple University Press, 1982), p. 173.

12. Drucker, "Behind Japan's Success," p. 86.

13. Kono, *Strategy and Structure of Japanese Enterprises,* pp. 126–127, 139.

14. Thurow, *The Management Challenge,* p. 114.

15. Robert H. Hayes, "Why Japanese Factories Work," *Harvard Business Review* 59 (July–August 1981): 61.

16. Richard Tanner Pascale and Anthony G. Athos, *The Art of Japanese Management: Applications for American Executives* (New York: Warner Books, 1981), p. 125.

17. Ronald Dore, *British Factory, Japanese Factory: The Origins of National Diversity in Industrial Relations* (Berkeley and Los Angeles: University of California Press, 1973), p. 52.

18. Kono, *Strategy and Structure,* p. 36.

19. Thurow, *The Management Challenge,* p. 115.

20. Dore, *British Factory, Japanese Factory,* p. 211.

21. Robert E. Cole, *Japanese Blue Collar: The Changing Tradition* (Berkeley and Los Angeles: University of California Press, 1971), p. 225; Kazuo Kawai, *Japan's American Interlude* (Chicago: University of Chicago Press, 1960), pp. 160–161.

22. Dore, *British Factory, Japanese Factory,* p. 197.

23. Schonberger, *Japanese Manufacturing Techniques,* p. 121.

24. Ibid., p. 44.

25. Abernathy et al., *Industrial Renaissance,* p. 85.

26. Philip B. Crosby, *Quality Is Free: The Art of Making Quality Certain* (New York: New American Library, 1979), p. 49.

27. See Daniel Burstein, *Yen! Japan's New Financial Empire and Its Threat to America* (New York: Simon and Schuster, 1988), p. 114.

28. Wellons, "The Role of the U.S. Financial System," p. 363.

29. Ibid., p. 367; Thurow, *The Management Challenge,* pp. 83, 85.

30. Wellons, "The Role of the U.S. Financial System," p. 392. With the great economic progress of Japan in the last ten years, debt/equity ratios of Japan's major corporations have been notably reduced. At the same time, with the recent surge of leveraged buyouts and acquisitions, debt/equity ratios of U.S. corporations are now on the rise.

31. Johnson, *MITI and the Japanese Miracle,* p. 10.

32. George Orwell, *Animal Farm* (New York: Harcourt Brace Jovanovich, 1946), p. 123.

CHAPTER 5

1. Ito Hirobumi, "Some Reminiscences of the Grant of the New Constitution," in S. Okuma, ed., *Fifty Years of New Japan,* 2 vols. (London, 1910), 1:127.

2. Harold S. Quigley, *Japanese Government and Politics* (New York: Century Company, 1932), p. 44.

3. Yoshinore Ide and Takeshi Ishida, "The Education and Recruitment of Gov-

erning Elites in Modern Japan," in Rupert Wilkinson, ed., *Governing Elites: Studies in Training and Selection* (New York: Oxford University Press, 1969), p. 122.

4. Ibid., p. 124.

5. Quoted in ibid.

6. December 13, 1971. Quoted in Chalmers Johnson, "Japan: Who Governs? An Essay on Official Bureaucracy," *Journal of Japanese Studies* 2 (Autumn 1975): 6.

7. Quoted in Robert E. Ward, *Japan's Political System* (Englewood Cliffs, N.J.: Prentice-Hall, 1967), app. 5, p. 229.

8. The Ministry of Finance, MITI, and the Ministry of Agriculture have two parliamentary vice-ministers each.

9. Akira Kubota, *Higher Civil Servants in Postwar Japan: Their Social Origins, Educational Backgrounds, and Career Patterns* (Princeton: Princeton University Press, 1969), p. 53.

10. J. A. A. Stockwin, *Japan: Divided Politics in a Growth Economy* (New York: W. W. Norton and Company, 1975), p. 132.

11. Reischauer, *The Japanese*, pp. 259–260.

12. Johnson, "Japan: Who Governs?" p. 25.

13. Chalmers Johnson, "The Reemployment of Retired Government Bureaucrats in Japanese Big Business," *Asian Survey* 14 (July–December 1974): 956.

14. Ibid., p. 964.

15. Johnson, *MITI and the Japanese Miracle*, p. 49.

16. Pempel, *Policy and Politics in Japan*, p. 24.

17. Quoted in Albert M. Craig, "Functional and Dysfunctional Aspects of Government Bureaucracy," in Ezra Vogel, ed., *Modern Japanese Organization and Decision Making* (Berkeley and Los Angeles: University of California Press, 1975).

18. Masuda Yoneji, quoted in ibid., pp. 8–9.

19. Johnson, *MITI and the Japanese Miracle*, p. 114.

20. Shinji Yoshino, *Nihon Kogyo Seisaku: Japan's Industrial Policy* (1935), as quoted in Johnson, *MITI and the Japanese Miracle*, p. 108.

21. Johnson, *MITI and the Japanese Miracle*, p. 240.

22. Takashi Kakuma, *Documentary on MITI, I: The Era of the "New Bureaucrats"* (1979), quoted in Johnson, *MITI and the Japanese Miracle*, p. 26.

23. Ezra F. Vogel, *Japan as Number One: Lessons for America* (Cambridge: Harvard University Press, 1979), p. 70.

24. Kawai, *Japan's American Interlude* (Midway Reprint, 1979), p. 57.

25. Vogel, *Japan as Number One*, p. 5.

26. At this juncture the attentive reader might ask, What about the British political system—will it be considered? Great Britain has a top professional bureaucracy and a parliamentary system; in these respects it resembles our pattern European state. And certainly the economic performance of Britain has been much worse than that of the United States. But no, we will not consider Britain. It would only complicate an already complex subject. Two comments, however, are in order. Because Great Britain lacks a statist tradition in the continental sense, its bureaucracy has been instrumentalized and constrained to an extent that is unknown in Japan, Germany, and France. Most important, however, is the fact that there was never an English social revolution that finally and irrevocably destroyed the aristocracy. This alone makes the British case unique and incomparable.

27. In France the number of appointed officials in a ministry may range upward of five, but 75 percent of those appointed are tenured bureaucrats.

28. The comparison of bureaucratic influence in the legislature holds more true for Japan and France than it does for Germany. Most of the numerous bureaucrats in the Bundestag are mid-level, not top-level, bureaucrats.

29. Of course, France has taken a tougher stand than Germany, where the Erhardian legacy of the "absolute" free market will die somewhat harder, but nonetheless die.

CHAPTER 6

1. Quoted in Richard Hofstadter, *Anti-Intellectualism in American Life* (New York: Alfred A. Knopf, 1969), p. 49.

2. Quoted in Richard Hofstadter, *The Progressive Historians: Turner, Beard, Parrington* (New York: Alfred A. Knopf, 1968), p. 127.

3. Ibid., p. 122.

4. Quoted in Hofstadter, *Anti-Intellectualism,* p. 273.

5. Quoted in Louis Hartz, *The Liberal Tradition in America: An Interpretation of American Political Thought Since the Revolution* (New York: Harcourt Brace Jovanovich, 1955), epigraph.

6. Hartz, *The Liberal Tradition in America,* p. 43.

7. Quoted in ibid., p. 61.

8. Hartz, *The Liberal Tradition in America,* p. 10.

9. Quoted in Nathan Glazer and Irving Kristol, eds., *The American Commonwealth, 1976* (New York: Basic Books, 1976), p. 143.

10. Quoted in Perry Miller, *The American Puritans: Their Prose and Poetry* (Garden City, N.Y.: Doubleday and Company, Anchor Books, 1956), p. 86.

11. Alexis de Tocqueville, *Democracy in America,* ed. J. P. Mayer and Max Lerner, trans. George Lawrence (New York: Harper and Row Publishers, 1966), p. 29.

12. H. G. Wells, "The Future in America," quoted in Herbert Croly, *The Promise of American Life* (New York: Macmillan Publishing Company, 1914), p. 4.

13. Quoted in Vernon L. Parrington, *The Colonial Mind, 1620–1800,* vol. 1 of *Main Currents in American Thought* (New York: Harcourt Brace Jovanovich, 1927), p. 303.

14. Quoted in George A. Peek Jr., *The Political Writings of John Adams: Representative Selections* (Indianapolis: Bobbs-Merrill Educational Publishing, 1954), p. xiv.

15. Federalist Paper No. 55, *The Federalist Papers,* with introduction by Clinton Rossiter (New York: New American Library of World Literature, 1961), p. 346.

16. Ibid., Federalist Paper No. 39, p. 241.

17. Quoted in Peek, *Political Writings of John Adams,* p. xviii.

18. Quoted in Edward McNall Burns, *James Madison: Philosopher of the Constitution* (New York: Octagon Books, 1968), p. 43.

19. Federalist Paper No. 51, in *The Federalist Papers,* p. 322.

20. Burns, *Madison,* pp. 122–123.

21. Federalist Paper No. 37, in *The Federalist Papers,* p. 227.

22. Quoted in Peek, *Political Writings of John Adams,* p. 121.

23. Hartz, *The Liberal Tradition in America,* p. 86.

CHAPTER 7

1. Clinton Rossiter, *Alexander Hamilton and the Constitution* (New York: Harcourt, Brace, and World, 1964), p. viii.

2. Quoted in ibid., p. 21.

3. Quoted in ibid., pp. 142, 143.

4. Ibid., p. 190.

5. Ibid., p. 237.

6. Ibid., p. 230.

7. Ibid., p. 233.

8. Parrington, *The Colonial Mind,* pp. 305–306.

9. Carl Becker, *The Declaration of Independence: A Study in the History of Political Ideas* (New York: Alfred A. Knopf, 1942), p. 27.

10. Peterson, *The Portable Jefferson,* p. 292.

11. Ibid., p. 293.

12. Thomas Jefferson, *Notes on the State of Virginia,* quoted in Richard Hofstadter, *The American Political Tradition and the Men Who Made It* (New York: Alfred A. Knopf, 1948), p. 27.

13. Peterson, *The Portable Jefferson,* p. 549.

14. Quoted in Charles M. Wiltse, *The Jeffersonian Tradition in American Democracy* (New York: Hill and Wang, 1935), pp. 81, 84.

15. Merrill D. Peterson, *Adams and Jefferson: A Revolutionary Dialogue,* Mercer University Lamar Memorial Lectures 19 (Athens: University of Georgia Press, 1976), p. 20.

16. Hofstadter, *Anti-Intellectualism,* p. 155.

17. Peterson, *The Portable Jefferson,* p. 417.

18. Ibid., p. 445.

19. Hofstadter, *American Political Tradition,* p. 42.

20. Quoted in Merrill D. Peterson, *The Jefferson Image in the American Mind* (New York: Oxford University Press, 1960), p. 8.

21. Quoted in Hofstadter, *American Political Tradition,* p. 33.

22. Ibid., p. 42.

23. Quoted in ibid., pp. 337–338.

24. See Peterson, *The Portable Jefferson,* p. 415.

25. Quoted in Hofstadter, *American Political Tradition,* p. 50.

26. Ibid., p. 60.

27. Ibid., p. 104.

28. Ibid., p. 109.

29. See ibid., p. 124.

30. Ibid., p. 101.

31. See Peterson, *The Jefferson Image,* p. 221.

32. Ibid., pp. 221, 222.

33. Quoted in Hofstadter, *American Political Tradition,* p. 188.

34. Ibid., p. 190.

35. Ibid., p. 223.

CHAPTER 8

1. Joel Aberbach et al., *Bureaucrats and Politicians in Western Democracies* (Cambridge: Harvard University Press, 1981). Political appointees fill the important positions held by senior bureaucrats in the other major Western democracies.

2. Hugh Heclo, *A Government of Strangers* (Washington, D.C.: The Brookings Institution, 1977), p. 103.

3. See Francis Rourke, "Bureaucracy in the American Constitutional Order," *Political Science Quarterly* 102 (Summer 1987): 217–218.

4. Ibid., p. 229. See also Michael Nelson, "The Irony of American Bureaucracy," in *Bureaucratic Power in National Policy Making,* ed. Francis Rourke, 4th ed. (Boston: Little, Brown, and Company, 1986), p. 186.

5. Richard Neustadt, *Presidential Power: The Politics of Leadership from FDR to Carter* (New York: John Wiley and Sons, 1980), p. 26.

6. Peter Woll, *American Bureaucracy,* 2d ed. (New York: W. W. Norton and Company, 1977), p. 64.

7. Ibid., pp. 62–63.

8. All quoted in Hofstadter, *Anti-Intellectualism,* pp. 180, 181–182, 183, 184.

9. Ibid., p. 185.

10. Hugh Heclo, "In Search of a Role: America's Higher Civil Service," in *Bureaucrats and Policymaking,* ed. Ezra Suleiman (New York: Holmes and Meier Publishers, 1984), p. 12.

11. Woll, *American Bureaucracy,* p. 39.

12. Ibid., pp. 43–47.

13. Franklin D. Roosevelt, "First Inaugural Address," March 4, 1933, *Congressional Record,* 73d Cong., special session, p. 5.

14. President's Committee on Administrative Management, *Administrative Management in the Government of the United States* (Washington, D.C.: U.S. Government Printing Office, 1937), pp. 3–5.

15. Ibid., p. iv.

16. Quoted in James A. Morone, *The Democratic Wish: Popular Participation and the Limits of American Government* (New York: Basic Books, 1990), p. 138.

17. Neustadt, *Presidential Power,* pp. 115–116; Stephen Hess, *Organizing the Presidency* (Washington, D.C.: The Brookings Institution, 1976), p. 36.

18. Heclo, "In Search of a Role," p. 13.

19. Ibid., p. 15.

20. James Fesler, "Politics, Policy, and Bureaucracy at the Top," *Annals of the American Academy of Political and Social Science* 466 (March 1983): 37.

21. Heclo, *A Government of Strangers,* p. 118; Lawrence Dodd and Richard

Schott, *Congress and the Administrative State* (New York: John Wiley and Sons, 1979), p. 50.

22. Heclo, *A Government of Strangers*, p. 154.

23. Ibid., p. 116.

24. Ibid., pp. 143–144.

25. Calvin Mackenzie, "The Paradox of Presidential Personnel Management," in *The Illusion of Presidential Government*, ed. Hugh Heclo and Lester Salamon (Boulder, Colo.: Westview Press, 1981), p. 124.

26. There is some tendency toward specialization among Japanese politicians, although it is less pronounced than in the U.S. Congress. It stems not from membership on parliamentary committees but from service on the LDP's internal policy-making body, the Policy Affairs Research Council.

27. Paula Dwyer and Douglas Harbrecht, "Congress: It Doesn't Work. Let's Fix It," *Business Week*, April 16, 1990, pp. 58–59; Norman Ornstein et al., *Vital Statistics on Congress, 1984–1985* (Washington, D.C.: American Enterprise Institute, 1984), pp. 120–127; Randall B. Ripley, *Congress: Process and Policy*, 3d ed. (New York: W. W. Norton and Company, 1983).

28. Herbert Kaufman, *The Administrative Behavior of Federal Bureau Chiefs* (Washington, D.C.: The Brookings Institution, 1981), pp. 164–165.

29. R. Douglas Arnold, *Congress and the Bureaucracy* (New Haven: Yale University Press, 1979).

30. Ibid., pp. 35–36.

31. Morris Fiorina, "Congressional Control of the Bureaucracy: A Mismatch of Incentives and Capabilities," in *Congress Reconsidered*, ed. Lawrence Dodd and Bruce Oppenheimer, 2d ed. (Washington, D.C.: Congressional Quarterly, 1981), p. 337. See also Morris Fiorina, *Congress: Keystone of the Washington Establishment*, 2d ed. (New Haven: Yale University Press, 1989).

32. Heclo, "In Search of a Role," p. 21.

33. Quoted in David Rosenbloom, "The Judicial Response to the Bureaucratic State," in *Bureaucratic Power in National Policy Making*, ed. Rourke, p. 234.

34. Quoted in ibid., p. 232.

35. See ibid., pp. 237–254; and Richard Stillman, *The American Bureaucracy* (Chicago: Nelson-Hall, 1987), pp. 105–106, 218–219.

36. Fesler, "Politics, Policy, and Bureaucracy," p. 36.

37. Ibid., pp. 27–28.

38. Ibid., p. 28.

39. Bruce L. R. Smith, "The U.S. Civil Service in Comparative Perspective," in *The Higher Civil Service in Europe and Canada: Lessons for the United States*, ed. Bruce L. R. Smith (Washington, D.C.: The Brookings Institution, 1984), pp. 8–9; James Fesler, "The Higher Civil Service in Europe and the United States," in Smith, *Higher Civil Service*, p. 89.

40. Fesler, "Politics, Policy, and Bureaucracy," p. 24.

41. Ibid., p. 31; Heclo, "In Search of a Role," p. 101.

42. Fesler, "Politics, Policy, and Bureaucracy," p. 32; Heclo, *A Government of Strangers*, pp. 1, 104.

43. John Hart, *The Presidential Branch* (New York: Pergamon Press, 1987), p. 49.

44. Ibid., pp. 49, 96.

45. Fesler, "Politics, Power, and Bureaucracy," p. 26.

46. Ibid., p. 25.

47. Quotations from presidents and Ehrlichman are from Richard Nathan, *The Administrative Presidency* (New York: John Wiley and Sons, 1983), pp. 1, 2, 100, 53, 30.

48. John Macy et al., *America's Unelected Government: Appointing the President's Team* (Cambridge, Mass.: Ballinger Publishing Company, 1983), p. 17.

49. Richard Rose, "Governments Against Subgovernments: A European Perspective on Washington," in *Presidents and Prime Ministers,* ed. Richard Rose and Ezra Suleiman (Washington, D.C.: American Enterprise Institute, 1980), p. 337.

50. National Academy of Public Administration, *Leadership in Jeopardy: The Fraying of the Presidential Appointments System* (Washington, D.C.: National Academy of Public Administration, 1985), p. 19.

51. Quoted in Fesler, "Politics, Power, and Bureaucracy," p. 32.

52. *Leadership in Jeopardy,* pp. 4–5.

53. Fesler, "Politics, Power, and Bureaucracy," pp. 25, 39; Fesler, "The Higher Civil Service in Europe and the United States," p. 89.

54. *Leadership in Jeopardy,* pp. 9, 7.

55. Ibid., p. 11.

56. Nelson Polsby, "Some Landmarks in Modern Presidential-Congressional Relations," in *Both Ends of the Avenue: The Presidency, the Executive Branch, and Congress in the 1980s,* ed. Anthony King (Washington, D.C.: American Enterprise Institute, 1983), p. 20.

57. Quoted in Rose, "Governments Against Subgovernments," p. 339.

58. Hugh Heclo, "One Executive Branch or Many?" in King, *Both Ends of the Avenue,* p. 32; *Leadership in Jeopardy,* p. 8.

CHAPTER 9

1. Andrew Shonfield, *In Defense of the Mixed Economy,* ed. Zuzanna Shonfield (New York: Oxford University Press, 1984), p. 20.

2. See Andrew Shonfield, *The Use of Public Power,* ed. Zuzanna Shonfield (New York: Oxford University Press, 1982), p. iii.

3. Jack H. Behrman, "Industrial Strategies in the United States," in Driscoll and Behrman, *National Industrial Policies,* p. 227.

4. Quoted in Schlossstein, *Trade War,* p. 9.

5. David Yoffie, *Power and Protectionism: Strategies of the Newly Industrializing Countries* (New York: Columbia University Press, 1983), p. 4.

6. Brenton R. Schlender and Stephen Kreider Yoder, "Chip Makers See New Threat from Japanese Firms," *Wall Street Journal,* October 27, 1986, p. 6.

7. John Diebold, *Making the Future Work: Unleashing Our Powers of Innovation for the Decades Ahead* (New York: Simon and Schuster, 1984), p. 128.

8. Steve Coll, *The Deal of the Century: The Breakup of AT&T* (New York: Atheneum Publishers, 1986), p. 369.

9. Quoted in Robert B. Reich and John D. Donahue, *New Deals: The Chrysler Revival and the American System* (New York: Times Books, 1985), p. 133.

10. Lee Iacocca (with William Novak), *Iacocca: An Autobiography* (New York: Bantam Books, 1984), pp. 220–221.

11. Diebold, *Making the Future Work,* pp. 328–329.

12. Lester C. Thurow, *The Zero-Sum Solution: Building a World-Class American Economy* (New York: Simon and Schuster, 1985), p. 295.

13. George F. Will, *Statecraft as Soulcraft: What Government Does* (New York: Simon and Schuster, 1983), p. 38.

14. For an elaboration of this argument, see Mancur Olson, *The Rise and Decline of Nations* (New Haven: Yale University Press, 1982).

CHAPTER 10

1. See Robert Z. Lawrence, *Can America Compete?* (Washington, D.C.: The Brookings Institution, 1984), pp. 94–95.

2. Reich, *The Next American Frontier,* p. 232.

3. Shonfield, *The Use of Public Power,* pp. 92–93.

4. *Economist,* May 22, 1982, p. 25.

5. Thurow, *The Zero-Sum Solution,* p. 30.

6. Kevin P. Phillips, *Staying on Top: The Business Case for a National Industrial Strategy* (New York: Random House, 1984), p. 112. Phillips is also the author of *The Emerging Republican Majority* (1969).

7. Ibid., pp. 83, 84, 98.

8. Gresser, *Partners in Prosperity,* p. 300.

9. For a thorough discussion of the logic driving industrial enterprise toward increasing size, see Alfred D. Chandler Jr., *Scale and Scope: The Dynamics of Industrial Capitalism* (Cambridge: Harvard University Press, 1990). Chandler decisively and authoritatively puts to rest some of the more egregious claims, by George Gilder and others, on behalf of entrepreneurialism as a cure-all for U.S. economic shortcomings.

10. Don Gevirtz, *Business Plan for America: An Entrepreneur's Manifesto* (New York: G. P. Putnam's Sons, 1984), p. 177; quotation from Louis Kehoe, "The Chips Are Down in California," *Financial Times,* February 5, 1982, as cited in ibid.

11. George Gilder, *The Spirit of Enterprise* (New York: Simon and Schuster, 1984), p. 217.

12. Felix G. Rohatyn, *The Twenty-Year Century: Essays on Economics and Public Finance* (New York: Random House, 1980), pp. 133–134.

13. Ibid., p. 134.

14. Ibid., p. 150.

15. Thurow, *The Zero-Sum Solution,* pp. 13, 124.

16. Thurow, *The Zero-Sum Society,* p. 150.

17. Thurow, *The Zero-Sum Solution,* p. 263.

18. See Alan M. Kantrow, "The Political Realities of Industrial Policy," *Harvard Business Review* 61 (September–October 1983): 83.

19. Thurow, *The Zero-Sum Society,* p. 201.

20. Quoted in Kantrow, "Political Realities," p. 79.

21. Reich, *The Next American Frontier,* p. 276.

22. Ibid., p. 134.

23. Ibid., pp. 246, 248.

24. See Kantrow, "Political Realities," p. 82.

25. Reich, *The Next American Frontier,* p. 277.

26. Tom Hayden, *The American Future: New Visions Beyond Old Frontiers* (Boston: South End Press, 1980).

27. Barry Bluestone and Bennett Harrison, *The Deindustrialization of America: Plant Closings, Community Abandonment, and the Dismantling of Basic Industry* (New York: Basic Books, 1982), p. 245. Emphasis in the original.

28. Michael Walzer, *Radical Principles: Reflections of an Unreconstructed Democrat* (New York: Basic Books, 1980), p. 46.

29. In Introduction to Chalmers Johnson, ed., *The Industrial Policy Debate* (San Francisco: ICS Press, 1984), p. 16.

30. Quoted in Thurow, *The Zero-Sum Solution,* p. 383, from "Do Modern Times Call for an Industrial Policy?" *Public Opinion,* August–September 1983, p. 2. The quotation comes from the initial transcript of the conversation.

CHAPTER 11

1. Akio Morita and Shintaro Ishihara's "The Japan That Can Say No" has not been published in the United States as of this writing.

2. See Pat Choate, *Agents of Influence* (New York: Random House, 1990).

3. Thomas S. Kuhn, *The Structure of Scientific Revolutions,* vol. 2, no. 2, 2d ed. enl. (Chicago: University of Chicago Press, 1970).

4. Steven Schlossstein, *The End of the American Century* (New York: Congdon and Weed, 1989). Schlossstein's chapter entitled "Pax Nipponica" provided the initial inspiration for the look into the future below. His characterization of the "second-tier" East Asian economies as the high-tech workshop of the world and the "third-tier" economies of the United States and the EEC as "consumption economies" was incorporated into my vision of a Japanese-dominated world economy circa 2015. Also, his mention of bureaucratically led Japanese political and economic reform in Mexico triggered my paragraph on the "Mexican miracle."

APPENDIX A

1. Hajo Holborn, *A History of Modern Germany, 1648–1840* (New York: Alfred A. Knopf, 1964), p. 196.

2. Ibid., p. 460.

3. Article 129, par. 1.

4. Thomas Mann, *Betrachtungen eines Unpolitischen* (1918), quoted in Gordon Craig, *Germany, 1866–1945* (New York: Oxford University Press, 1978), p. 415.

5. See Gerhard A. Ritter, "Historical Foundations of the Rise of National Socialism," in *The Third Reich International Council for Philosophy and Humanistic Studies* (London, 1955). National socialism in no way signaled a return to the absolutism of Bismarck and William II, but rather resulted in a disintegration of the administrative state. Political power rested on personality and not with office (see Craig, *Germany*).

6. Konrad Heiden, *Der Fuehrer: Hitler's Rise to Power*, trans. Ralph Manheim (Boston: Houghton Mifflin Company, 1944), p. 579.

7. See Ritter, "Historical Foundations."

8. Renate Mayntz, "German Federal Bureaucrats: As Functional Elite Between Politics and Administration," in Suleiman, *Bureaucrats and Policymaking*, p. 177.

9. Peter H. Merkl, *The Origin of the West German Republic* (New York: Oxford University Press, 1963), p. 176.

10. Quoted in Gordon A. Craig, *The Germans* (New York: G. P. Putnam's Sons, 1982), p. 40.

11. Gerhard Loewenberg, *Parliament in the German Political System* (Ithaca, N.Y.: Cornell University Press, 1966), p. 46.

12. Ibid., p. 435.

13. David P. Conradt, *The German Polity* (New York: Longman, 1978), pp. 163–164.

14. Ralf Dahrendorf, *Society and Democracy in Germany* (New York: W. W. Norton and Company, 1979), p. 240.

15. Conradt, *The German Polity*, p. 38.

16. Quoted in Roger Tilford, "The State, University Reform, and the 'Berufsverbot,'" *West European Politics* 4 (May 1981): 158.

17. See Renate Mayntz, "The Higher Civil Service of the Federal Republic of Germany," in Smith, *Higher Civil Service*, pp. 57–58.

18. Dahrendorf, *Society and Democracy in Germany*, p. 225.

19. Conradt, *The German Polity*, p. 167.

20. Mayntz, "Higher Civil Service," p. 63.

21. Renate Mayntz and Fritz W. Scharpf, *Policy-Making in the German Federal Bureaucracy* (New York: Elsevier, 1975), p. 58.

22. Mayntz, "German Federal Bureaucrats," p. 177.

23. Lewis J. Edinger, *Politics in West Germany*, 2d ed., revision of *Politics in Germany* (Boston: Little, Brown, and Company, 1977), pp. 102–103.

24. Conradt, *The German Polity*, p. 167.

25. Mayntz, "Higher Civil Service," p. 57.

26. Conradt, *The German Polity*, p. 79.

27. Edinger, *Politics in West Germany*, p. 168.

28. Gordon Smith, "Does West German Democracy Have an 'Efficient Secret'?" *West European Politics* 4 (May 1981): 174.

29. Dahrendorf, *Society and Democracy in Germany*, p. 240.

30. Robert A. Isaak, *European Politics: Political Economy and Policy Making in Western Democracies* (New York: St. Martin's Press, 1980), p. 38.

31. Tilford, "The State, University Reform, and the 'Berufsverbot,'" p. 163.

APPENDIX B

1. Quoted in Gianfranco Poggi, *The Development of the Modern State* (Stanford: Stanford University Press, 1978), p. 62.

2. Bertrand Badie and Pierre Birnbaum, *The Sociology of the State* (Chicago: University of Chicago Press, 1983), pp. 108–109; Pierre Birnbaum, "State, Centre, and Bureaucracy," *Government and Opposition* 16 (Winter 1981): 62–63.

3. Alexis de Tocqueville, *The Old Regime and the French Revolution,* trans. Stuart Gilbert (New York: Doubleday and Company, Anchor Books, 1955), pp. 19–20.

4. Wolfram Fischer and Peter Lundgren, "The Recruitment and Training of Administrative and Technical Personnel," in *The Formation of National States in Western Europe,* ed. Charles Tilly (Princeton: Princeton University Press, 1975), p. 508; Otto Hintze, "The Emergence of the Democratic Nation-State," in *The Development of the Modern State,* ed. Heinz Lubasz (New York: Macmillan Publishing Company, 1964), p. 67.

5. Douglas Ashford, *Policy and Politics in France* (Philadelphia: Temple University Press, 1982), p. 13; Badie and Birnbaum, *The Sociology of the State,* pp. 109–110; Birnbaum, "State, Centre, and Bureaucracy," pp. 64–65.

6. Quoted in Ezra Suleiman, *Elites in French Society* (Princeton: Princeton University Press, 1978), p. 19.

7. De Tocqueville, *The Old Regime,* p. 202.

8. Quoted in David Thomson, *Democracy in France Since 1870,* 5th ed. (London: Oxford University Press, 1969), pp. 317–318.

9. Quoted in Henry Ehrmann, *Politics in France,* 4th ed. (Boston: Little, Brown, and Company, 1983), p. 301.

10. James Fesler, "The Higher Public Service in Western Europe," in *A Centennial History of the American Administrative State,* ed. Ralph Chandler (New York: The Free Press, 1987), p. 513.

11. Ehrmann, *Politics in France,* pp. 87–88; William Safran, *The French Polity,* 2d ed. (New York: Longman, 1985), p. 43; Paul Gagnon, "The Fifth Republic and Education: Modernity, Democracy, Culture," in *The Impact of the Fifth Republic on France,* ed. William G. Andrews and Stanley Hoffmann (Albany: State University of New York Press, 1981), pp. 223–225.

12. Ehrmann, *Politics in France,* p. 92.

13. Suleiman, *Elites in French Society,* p. 87; Ezra Suleiman, "From Right to Left: Bureaucracy and Politics in France," in Suleiman, *Bureaucrats and Policymaking,* p. 116.

14. Suleiman, *Elites in French Society,* p. 164.

15. Quoted in ibid., p. 41.

16. Ibid., pp. 265, 271.

17. Ibid., pp. 134–136.

18. Ibid., p. 37.

19. Ezra Suleiman, *Politics, Power, and Bureaucracy in France* (Princeton: Princeton University Press, 1974), pp. 241–244; Suleiman, *Elites in French Society,* p. 29; John A. Armstrong, *The European Administrative Elite* (Princeton: Princeton University Press, 1973), pp. 24, 213–214.

20. Bernard Gournay, "The Higher Civil Service of France," in Smith, *Higher Civil Service in Europe and Canada,* p. 78.

21. There is, however, a difference in timing. *Amakudari* takes place toward the end of a bureaucratic career, while *pantouflage* is a mid-career or earlier move.

22. Ashford, *Policy and Politics in France,* chap. 2; Suleiman, "From Right to Left," p. 117; Gournay, "The Higher Civil Service of France," pp. 83–84.

23. Suleiman, *Elites in French Society,* pp. 174–175.

24. Ehrmann, *Politics in France,* p. 170; Ashford, *Politics and Policy in France,* p. 69; Michael Crozier, *The Bureaucratic Phenomenon* (Chicago: University of Chicago Press, 1964), p. 309.

25. Ehrmann, *Politics in France,* pp. 161–162.

26. Stanley Hoffmann, "The Fifth Republic at Twenty," in Andrews and Hoffmann, *Impact of the Fifth Republic on France,* p. 306.

27. Ehrmann, *Politics in France,* p. 173.

28. Ibid., p. 174.

29. John Frears, "Parliament in the Fifth Republic," in Andrews and Hoffmann, *Impact of the Fifth Republic on France,* pp. 47, 54.

30. Ehrmann, *Politics in France,* pp. 204–206.

31. De Tocqueville, *The Old Regime,* p. 68.

32. Cited in Suleiman, *Politics, Power, and Bureaucracy,* p. 25.

SELECTED BIBLIOGRAPHY

Abegglen, James C., and Thomas M. Hout. "Facing Up to the Trade Gap with Japan." *Foreign Affairs* 57 (Fall 1978): 146–168.

Aberbach, Joel, Robert D. Putnam, Bert A. Rockman, et al. *Bureaucrats and Politicians in Western Democracies*. Cambridge: Harvard University Press, 1981.

Abernathy, William J., Kim B. Clark, and Alan M. Kantrow. *Industrial Renaissance: Producing as Competitive Future for America*. New York: Basic Books, 1983.

———. "The New Industrial Competition." *Harvard Business Review* 59 (September–October 1981): 68–81.

Adams, Walter, and James W. Brock. *Dangerous Pursuits: Mergers and Acquisitions in the Age of Wall Street*. New York: Pantheon Books, 1989.

Almond, Gabriel A., and Sidney Verba, eds. *The Civic Culture Revisited*. Boston: Little, Brown, and Company, 1980.

Alperovitz, Gar, and Jeff Faux. *Rebuilding America*. New York: Pantheon Books, 1984.

Armstrong, John A. *The European Administrative Elite*. Princeton: Princeton University Press, 1973.

Arndt, Hans-Joachim. *West Germany: Politics of Non-Planning*. Preface by Bertram M. Gross. Syracuse, N.Y.: Syracuse University Press, 1966.

Arnold, R. Douglas. *Congress and the Bureaucracy*. New Haven: Yale University Press, 1979.

Aron, Raymond. *Main Currents in Sociological Thought: Durkheim, Pareto, Weber*. Volume 2. Translated by Richard Howard and Helen Weaver. Garden City, N.Y.: Doubleday and Company, Anchor Books, 1970.

Ashford, Douglas. *Policy and Politics in France.* Philadelphia: Temple University Press, 1982.

Avineri, Shlomo. *Hegel's Theory of the Modern State.* London: Cambridge University Press, 1972.

Badaracco, Joseph L. Jr., and David B. Yoffie. "'Industrial Policy': It Can't Happen Here." *Harvard Business Review* 61 (November–December 1983): 97–105.

Badie, Bertrand, and Pierre Birnbaum. *The Sociology of the State.* Chicago: University of Chicago Press, 1983.

Baker, Kendall L., Russell J. Dalton, and Kai Hildebrandt. *Germany Transformed: Political Culture and the New Politics.* Cambridge: Harvard University Press, 1981.

Barnett, Donald F., and Robert W. Crandall. *Up from the Ashes: The Rise of the Steel Minimill in the United States.* Washington, D.C.: The Brookings Institution, 1986.

Barnett, Donald F., and Louis Schorsch. *Steel: Upheaval in a Basic Industry.* Cambridge, Mass.: Ballinger Publishing Company, 1983.

Batra, Dr. Ravi. *The Great Depression of 1990.* New York: Simon and Schuster, 1987.

Beasley, W. G. *The Modern History of Japan.* 2d ed. 1973. Reprint. New York: Praeger Publishers, 1974.

Becker, Carl. *The Declaration of Independence: A Study in the History of Political Ideas.* New York: Alfred A. Knopf, 1942.

Beenstock, Michael. *The World Economy in Transition.* London: George Allen and Unwin, 1983.

Bell, Daniel. *The Coming of Post-Industrial Society: A Venture in Social Forecasting.* New York: Basic Books, 1973.

Bendix, Reinhard. *Max Weber: An Intellectual Portrait.* Garden City, N.Y.: Doubleday and Company, 1960.

Benedict, Ruth. *The Chrysanthemum and the Sword: Patterns of Japanese Culture.* New York: New American Library, 1946.

Berger, Suzanne. *The French Political System.* New York: Random House, 1974.

Beyme, Klaus Von, and Manfred G. Schmidt. *Policy and Politics in the Federal Republic of Germany.* Translated by Eileen Martin. New York: St. Martin's Press, 1985.

Billington, Ray Allen. *Frederick Jackson Turner: Historian, Scholar, Teacher.* New York: Oxford University Press, 1973.

Birnbaum, Pierre. "State, Centre, and Bureaucracy." *Government and Opposition* 16 (Winter 1981): 62–63.

Bluestone, Barry, and Bennett Harrison. *The Deindustrialization of America: Plant Closings, Community Abandonment, and the Dismantling of Basic Industry.* New York: Basic Books, 1982.

Bolling, Richard, and John Bowles. *America's Competitive Edge: How to Get Our Country Moving Again.* New York: McGraw-Hill Book Company, 1982.

Borrus, Michael G. *Competing for Control: America's Stake in Microelectronics.* Cambridge, Mass.: Ballinger Publishing Company, 1988.

Bowers, Claude G. *Jefferson and Hamilton: The Struggle for Democracy in America.* Boston: Houghton Mifflin Company, 1925.

Breen, T. H. *The Character of the Good Ruler: A Study of Puritan Political Ideas in New England, 1630–1730.* New Haven: Yale University Press, 1970.

Brzezinski, Zbigniew, and Samuel P. Huntington. *Political Power: USA/USSR.* New York: Viking Press, 1965.

Burks, Ardath W. *The Government of Japan.* London: University Paperbacks, 1966.

Burns, Edward McNall. *James Madison: Philosopher of the Constitution.* New York: Octagon Books, 1968.

Burstein, Daniel. *Yen! Japan's New Financial Empire and Its Threat to America.* New York: Simon and Schuster, 1988.

Calleo, David P. *The Imperious Economy.* Cambridge: Harvard University Press, 1982.

Campbell, John Creighton. *Contemporary Japanese Budget Politics.* Berkeley and Los Angeles: University of California Press, 1977.

Carmines, Edward, and Lawrence Dodd. "Bicameralism in Congress: The Changing Partnership." In *Congress Reconsidered,* edited by Lawrence Dodd and Bruce Oppenheimer, 3d ed. Washington, D.C.: Congressional Quarterly, 1985.

Carnoy, Martin, Derek Shearer, and Russell Rumberger. *A New Social Contract: The Economy and Government After Reagan.* New York: Harper and Row Publishers, 1983.

Chandler, Alfred D. Jr. *Scale and Scope: The Dynamics of Industrial Capitalism.* Cambridge: Harvard University Press, Belknap Press, 1990.

Choate, Pat. *Agents of Influence.* New York: Random House, 1990.

Churchill, Winston. *A History of the English-Speaking Peoples.* 1st ed. New York: Dodd, Mead, and Company, 1956.

Cohen, Stephen S., and John Zysman. *Manufacturing Matters: The Myth of the Post-Industrial Economy.* New York: Basic Books, 1987.

Cole, Richard, and David Caputo. "Presidential Control of the Senior Civil Service: Assessing the Strategies of the Nixon Years." *American Political Science Review* 73 (June 1979): 399–412.

Cole, Robert E. *Japanese Blue Collar: The Changing Tradition.* Berkeley and Los Angeles: University of California Press, 1971.

Coll, Steve. *The Deal of the Century: The Breakup of AT&T.* New York: Atheneum Publishers, 1986.

Commager, Henry Steele. *The American Mind: An Interpretation of American Thought and Character Since the 1880s.* New Haven: Yale University Press, 1950.

"Competitiveness Survey: HBR Readers Respond." *Harvard Business Review* 65 (September–October 1987): 8–12.

Conradt, David P. *The German Polity.* New York: Longman, 1978.

———. "Political Culture, Legitimacy, and Participation." *West European Politics* 4 (May 1981): 18–34.

Craig, Albert M. "Functional and Dysfunctional Aspects of Government Bureaucracy." In *Modern Japanese Organization and Decision Making,* edited by Ezra Vogel. Berkeley and Los Angeles: University of California Press, 1975.

Craig, Gordon A. *The Germans.* New York: G. P. Putnam's Sons, 1982.

———. *Germany, 1866–1945.* New York: Oxford University Press, 1978.

Croly, Herbert. *The Promise of American Life*. New York: Macmillan Publishing Company, 1914.

Crosby, Philip B. *Quality Is Free: The Art of Making Quality Certain*. New York: New American Library, 1979.

Crozier, Michel. *The Bureaucratic Phenomenon*. Chicago: University of Chicago Press, 1964.

———. *The Trouble with America*. Translated by Peter Heinegg. Foreword by David Riesman. Berkeley and Los Angeles: University of California Press, 1984.

Crozier, Michel, Samuel P. Huntington, and Joji Watanuki. *The Crisis of Democracy: Report on the Governability of Democracies to the Trilateral Commission*. New York: New York University Press, 1975.

Dahrendorf, Ralf. *Society and Democracy in Germany*. New York: W. W. Norton and Company, 1979. Originally published as *Gesellschaft und Demokratie in Deutschland* (Munich: R. Piper, 1965).

Davidson, William H. *The Amazing Race: Winning the Technorivalry with Japan*. New York: John Wiley and Sons, 1984.

Debre, Michel. "The Constitution of 1958: Its Raison d'Être and How It Evolved." In *The Impact of the Fifth Republic on France*, edited by William Andrews and Stanley Hoffmann. Albany: State University of New York Press, 1981.

Derivry, Daniel. "The Managers of Public Enterprises in France." In *The Mandarins of Western Europe*, edited by Mattei Dogan. New York: Halsted Press, 1975.

Dertouzos, Michael L., Richard K. Lester, Robert M. Solow, and M.I.T. Commission on Industrial Productivity. *Made in America: Regaining the Productive Edge*. Cambridge: M.I.T. Press, 1989.

Dewar, Margaret E., and Harlan Cleveland. *Industry Vitalization: Toward a National Industrial Policy*. New York: Pergamon Press, 1982.

Diebold, John. *Making the Future Work: Unleashing Our Powers of Innovation for the Decades Ahead*. New York: Simon and Schuster, 1984.

Dodd, Lawrence, and Richard Schott. *Congress and the Administrative State*. New York: John Wiley and Sons, 1979.

Dogan, Mattei, ed. *The Mandarins of Western Europe*. New York: John Wiley and Sons, 1975.

Dore, Ronald P. *British Factory, Japanese Factory: The Origins of National Diversity in Industrial Relations*. Berkeley and Los Angeles: University of California Press, 1973.

———. *The Diploma Disease: Education, Qualification, and Development*. Berkeley and Los Angeles: University of California Press, 1976.

Dragnich, Alex, and Jorgen Rasmussen. *Major European Governments*. 7th ed. Chicago: Dorsey Press, 1986.

Driscoll, Robert E., and Jack N. Behrman, eds. *National Industrial Policies*. Weston, Mass.: Oelgeschlager, Gunn, and Hain, 1984.

Drucker, Peter F. "Behind Japan's Success: Defining Rules for Managing in a Pluralist Society." *Harvard Business Review* 59 (January–February 1981): 87.

Dyson, Kenneth. "The Ambiguous Politics of Western Germany: Politicization in a 'State' Society." *European Journal of Political Research* 7 (December 1979): 375–396.

———. *Party, State, and Bureaucracy in Western Germany*. Beverly Hills, Calif.: Sage Publications, 1977.

———. "Planning and the Federal Chancellor's Office in the West German Federal Government." *Political Studies* 21 (September 1973): 348–362.

———. "The Politics of Corporate Crises in West Germany." *West European Politics* 7 (January 1984): 24–46.

———. "The Politics of Economic Management in West Germany." *West European Politics* 4 (May 1981): 35–55.

Eckstein, Otto, Christopher Caton, Roger Brinner, and Peter Duprey. *The DRI Report on U.S. Manufacturing Industries*. New York: McGraw-Hill Book Company, 1984.

Edinger, Lewis J. *Politics in West Germany*. 2d ed. Revision of *Politics in Germany*. Boston: Little, Brown, and Company, 1977.

Ehrmann, Henry. *Politics in France*. 4th ed. Boston: Little, Brown, and Company, 1983.

Epstein, David F. *The Political Theory of "The Federalist."* Chicago: University of Chicago Press, 1984.

Etzioni, Amitai. *An Immodest Agenda: Rebuilding America Before the Twenty-First Century*. New York: McGraw-Hill Book Company, 1983.

———. *The Moral Dimension: Toward a New Economics*. New York: The Free Press, 1988.

Evans, Richard J. "Rethinking the German Past." *West European Politics* 4 (May 1981): 134–148.

Fallows, James. *More Like Us: Making America Great Again*. Boston: Houghton Mifflin Company, 1989.

Feigenbaum, Edward A., and Pamela McCorduck. *The Fifth Generation: Artificial Intelligence and Japan's Computer Challenge to the World*. London: Addison-Wesley Publishing Company, 1983.

Fesler, James. "The Higher Civil Service in Europe and the United States." In *The Higher Civil Service in Europe and Canada: Lessons for the United States*, edited by Bruce L. R. Smith. Washington, D.C.: The Brookings Institution, 1984.

———. "The Higher Public Service in Western Europe." In *A Centennial History of the American Administrative State*, edited by Ralph C. Chandler. New York: The Free Press, 1987.

———. "Politics, Policy, and Bureaucracy at the Top." *Annals of the American Academy of Political and Social Science* 466 (March 1983): 23–41.

Fiorina, Morris. *Congress: Keystone of the Washington Establishment*. 2d ed. New Haven: Yale University Press, 1989.

———. "Congressional Control of the Bureaucracy: A Mismatch of Incentives and Capabilities." In *Congress Reconsidered*, edited by Lawrence Dodd and Bruce Oppenheimer. 3d ed. Washington, D.C.: Congressional Quarterly, 1981.

Fischer, Wolfram, and Peter Lundgren. "The Recruitment and Training of Administrative and Technical Personnel." In *The Formation of National States in Western Europe*, edited by Charles Tilly. Princeton: Princeton University Press, 1975.

Fisher, Louis. *President and Congress: Power and Policy.* New York: The Free Press, 1972.

"A Forum on National Industrial Policy." Special Report. *The Best of Business* 6 (Spring 1984): 47–61.

Franko, Lawrence G. *The Threat of Japanese Multinationals: How the West Can Respond.* New York: John Wiley and Sons, 1983.

Frears, John. "Parliament in the Fifth Republic." In *The Impact of the Fifth Republic on France,* edited by William G. Andrews and Stanley Hoffmann. Albany: State University of New York Press, 1981.

Friedman, Benjamin. *Day of Reckoning: The Consequences of American Economic Policy Under Reagan and After.* New York: Random House, 1988.

Gagnon, Paul. "The Fifth Republic and Education: Modernity, Democracy, Culture." In *The Impact of the Fifth Republic on France,* edited by William G. Andrews and Stanley Hoffmann. Albany: State University of New York Press, 1981.

Gevirtz, Don. *Business Plan for America: An Entrepreneur's Manifesto.* New York: G. P. Putnam's Sons, 1984.

Gilder, George. *Microcosm: The Quantum Revolution in Economics and Technology.* New York: Simon and Schuster, 1989.

———. *The Spirit of Enterprise.* New York: Simon and Schuster, 1984.

———. *Wealth and Poverty.* New York: Basic Books, 1981.

Gillis, John R. "Germany." In *Crises of Political Development in Europe and the United States.* Princeton: Princeton University Press, 1978.

Glazer, Nathan, and Irving Kristol, eds. *The American Commonwealth, 1976.* New York: Basic Books, 1976.

Glickman, Norman J., and Douglas P. Woodward. *The New Competitors: How Foreign Investors Are Changing the U.S. Economy.* New York: Basic Books, 1989.

Goldman, Eric F. *Rendezvous with Destiny: A History of Modern American Reform.* Revised and abridged. New York: Vintage Books, 1956.

Gournay, Bernard. "The Higher Civil Service of France." In *The Higher Civil Service in Europe and Canada,* edited by Bruce Smith. Washington, D.C.: The Brookings Institution, 1984.

Grayson, C. Jackson Jr., and Carla O'Dell. *American Business—A Two-Minute Warning: Ten Changes Managers Must Make to Survive into the 21st Century.* New York: The Free Press, 1988.

Gresser, Julian. *Partners in Prosperity: Strategic Industries for the United States and Japan.* New York: McGraw-Hill Book Company, 1984.

Gross, Bertram. *Friendly Fascism: The New Face of Power in America.* New York: M. Evans and Company, 1980.

Gunlicks, Arthur B. "Administrative Centralization and Decentralization in the Making and Remaking of Modern Germany." *Review of Politics* 46 (July 1984): 323–345.

Halberstam, David. *The Reckoning.* New York: William Morrow and Company, 1986.

Hamilton, Alexander, James Madison, and John Jay. *The Federalist Papers.* Introduction by Clinton Rossiter. New York: New American Library of World Literature, 1961.

Hardach, Karl. *The Political Economy of Germany in the Twentieth Century.* Berkeley and Los Angeles: University of California Press, 1980.

Harrison, Bennett, and Barry Bluestone. *The Great U-Turn: Corporate Restructuring and the Polarizing of America.* New York: Basic Books, 1988.

Hart, John. *The Presidential Branch.* New York: Pergamon Press, 1987.

Hartz, Louis. *The Liberal Tradition in America: An Interpretation of American Political Thought Since the Revolution.* New York: Harcourt Brace Jovanovich, 1955.

Hayden, Tom. *The American Future: New Visions Beyond Old Frontiers.* Boston: South End Press, 1980.

Hayes, Robert H. "Why Japanese Factories Work." *Harvard Business Review* 59 (July–August): 61.

Hayes, Robert H., and William J. Abernathy. "Managing Our Way to Economic Decline." *Harvard Business Review* 58 (July–August 1980): 77.

Hayes, Robert H., and Steven C. Wheelwright. *Restoring Our Competitive Edge: Competing Through Manufacturing.* New York: John Wiley and Sons, 1984.

Hayward, Jack. *The One and Indivisible French Republic.* New York: W. W. Norton and Company, 1973.

Heclo, Hugh. *A Government of Strangers.* Washington, D.C.: The Brookings Institution, 1977.

———. "In Search of a Role: America's Higher Civil Service." In *Bureaucrats and Policymakers,* edited by Ezra Suleiman. New York: Holmes and Meier Publishers, 1984.

———. "One Executive Branch or Many?" *Both Ends of the Avenue: The Presidency, the Executive Branch, and Congress in the 1980s,* edited by Anthony King. Washington, D.C.: American Enterprise Institute, 1983.

Heidenheimer, Arnold J. "The Politics of Educational Reform: Explaining Different Outcomes of School Comprehensivization Attempts in Sweden and West Germany." *Comparative Education Review* 18 (October 1974): 388–410.

Heisler, Martin O., ed. *Politics in Europe: Structures and Processes in Some Postindustrial Democracies.* New York: David McKay Company, 1974.

Hess, Stephen. *Organizing the Presidency.* Washington, D.C.: The Brookings Institution, 1976.

Hintze, Otto. "The Emergence of the Democratic Nation-State." In *The Development of the Modern State,* edited by Heinz Lubasz. New York: Macmillan Publishing Company, 1964.

Hochmuth, Milton, and William Davidson, eds. *Revitalizing American Industry: Lessons from Our Competitors.* Cambridge, Mass.: Ballinger Publishing Company, 1985.

Hoffmann, Stanley. "The Fifth Republic at Twenty." In *The Impact of the Fifth Republic on France,* edited by William G. Andrews and Stanley Hoffmann. Albany: State University of New York Press, 1981.

Hofheinz, Roy Jr., and Kent E. Calder. *The Eastasia Edge.* New York: Basic Books, 1982.

Hofstadter, Richard. *The Age of Reform: From Bryan to F.D.R.* New York: Alfred A. Knopf, 1955.

———. *America at 1750: A Social Portrait.* New York: Alfred A. Knopf, 1971.

———. *The American Political Tradition and the Men Who Made It.* New York: Alfred A. Knopf, 1948.

———. *Anti-Intellectualism in American Life.* New York: Alfred A. Knopf, 1969.

———. *The Paranoid Style in American Politics and Other Essays.* New York: Alfred A. Knopf, 1965.

———. *The Progressive Historians: Turner, Beard, Parrington.* New York: Alfred A. Knopf, 1968.

———. *Social Darwinism in American Thought.* Revised edition. Boston: Beacon Press, 1955.

Holborn, Hajo. *A History of Modern Germany.* New York: Alfred A. Knopf, 1969.

———. *A History of Modern Germany, 1648–1840.* New York: Alfred A. Knopf, 1964.

Holland, Max. *When the Machine Stopped: A Cautionary Tale from Industrial America.* Boston: Harvard Business School Press, 1989.

Howe, John R. Jr., ed. *The Role of Ideology in the American Revolution.* New York: Holt, Rinehart, and Winston, 1970.

Huber, Peter W. *Liability: The Legal Revolution and Its Consequences.* New York: Basic Books, 1988.

Huntington, Samuel P. *American Politics: The Promise of Disharmony.* Cambridge: Harvard University Press, Belknap Press, 1981.

———. *Political Order in Changing Societies.* New Haven: Yale University Press, 1968.

Iacocca, Lee, with William Novak. *Iacocca: An Autobiography.* New York: Bantam Books, 1984.

Ike, Nobutaka. *Japanese Politics.* New York: Alfred A. Knopf, 1957.

———. *Japanese Politics: Patron-Client Democracy.* New York: Alfred A. Knopf, 1972.

Imai, Masaaki. *Kaizen: The Key to Japan's Competitive Success.* New York: Random House, 1986.

Isaak, Robert A. *European Politics: Political Economy and Policy Making in Western Democracies.* New York: St. Martin's Press, 1980.

Ishida, Takeshi, and Ellis S. Krauss, eds. *Democracy in Japan.* Pittsburgh: University of Pittsburgh Press, 1989.

Jacob, Herbert. *German Administration Since Bismarck: Central Authority Versus Local Autonomy.* 1963. Reprint. Westport, Conn.: Greenwood Press, 1974.

Jochimsen, Reimut. "Aims and Objectives of German Vocational and Professional Education in the Present European Context." *Comparative Education* 14 (October 1978): 199–209.

Johnson, Chalmers, ed. *The Industrial Policy Debate.* San Francisco: Institute for Contemporary Studies Press, 1984.

———. "Japan: Who Governs? An Essay on Official Bureaucracy." *Journal of Japanese Studies* 2 (Autumn 1975): 1–28.

———. *Japan's Public Policy Companies.* Washington, D.C.: American Enterprise Institute for Public Policy Research, 1978.

———. *MITI and the Japanese Miracle: The Growth of Industrial Policy, 1925–1975.* Stanford, Calif.: Stanford University Press, 1982.

———. "The Reemployment of Retired Government Bureaucrats in Japanese Big Business." *Asian Survey* 14 (July–December 1974): 953–965.

Kahn, Herman. *The Emerging Japanese Superstate: Challenge and Response.* Englewood Cliffs, N.J.: Prentice-Hall, 1970.

Kahn, Herman, and Thomas Pepper. *The Japanese Challenge: The Success and Failure of Economic Success.* London: Harper and Row Publishers, 1978.

Kamasta, Satoshi. *Japan in the Passing Lane: An Insider's Account of Life in a Japanese Auto Factory.* Translated and edited by Tatsuru Akimoto. Introduction by Ronald Dore. New York: Pantheon Books, 1982.

Kantrow, Alan M. "The Political Realities of Industrial Policy." *Harvard Business Review* 61 (September–October 1983): 76–86.

Katzenstein, Peter J. *Between Power and Plenty: Foreign Economic Policies and Advanced Industrial States.* Madison: University of Wisconsin Press, 1978.

Kaufman, Herbert. *The Administrative Behavior of Federal Bureau Chiefs.* Washington, D.C.: The Brookings Institution, 1981.

Kawai, Kazuo. *Japan's American Interlude.* Chicago: University of Chicago Press, 1960; Midway Reprint, 1979.

Kissinger, Henry A. "The White Revolutionary: Reflections on Bismarck." *Daedalus Journal of the American Academy of Arts and Sciences* 97 (Summer 1968): 888–924.

Kobayashi, Tetsuya. *Society, Schools, and Progress in Japan.* New York: Pergamon Press, 1976.

Koch, Adrienne. *The Philosophy of Thomas Jefferson.* Columbia Studies in American Culture, 14. New York: Columbia University Press, 1943.

Koch, Adrienne, and William Peden, eds. *The Life and Selected Writings of Thomas Jefferson.* New York: Random House, Modern Library, 1944.

Kono, Toyohiro. *Strategy and Structure of Japanese Enterprises.* London: Macmillan and Company, 1984.

Kotkin, Joel, and Yoriko Kishimoto. 1988. *The Third Century: America's Resurgence in the Asian Era.* New York: Crown Publishers, 1988.

Kristol, Irving. *On the Democratic Idea in America.* New York: Harper and Row Publishers, 1972.

Kubota, Akira. *Higher Civil Servants in Postwar Japan: Their Social Origins, Educational Backgrounds, and Career Patterns.* Princeton: Princeton University Press, 1969.

Kuhn, Thomas S. *The Structure of Scientific Revolutions.* 2d ed. enl. Volume 2, no. 2. Chicago: University of Chicago Press, 1970.

Kuisel, Richard. *Capitalism and the State in Modern France.* Cambridge: Cambridge University Press, 1981.

Landfried, Christine. "The Impact of the German Federal Constitutional Court on Politics and Policy Output." *Government and Opposition* 20 (Fall 1985): 522–541.

Lawrence, Paul R., and Davis Dyer. *Renewing American Industry.* New York: The Free Press, 1983.

Lawrence, Robert Z. *Can America Compete?* Washington, D.C.: The Brookings Institution, 1984.

Leone, Robert A., and Stephen P. Bradley. "Toward an Effective Industrial Policy." *Harvard Business Review* 59 (November–December 1981): 91–97.

Levitt, Theodore. "The Globalization of Markets." *Harvard Business Review* 61 (May–June 1983): 94.

Lijphart, Arend. *Democracy in Plural Societies: A Comparative Exploration.* New Haven: Yale University Press, 1977.

Lindblom, Charles E. *Politics and Markets: The World's Political Economic Systems.* New York: Basic Books, 1977.

Linder, Staffan Burenstam. *The Pacific Century: Economic and Political Consequences of Asian-Pacific Dynamism.* Stanford, Calif.: Stanford University Press, 1986.

Lodge, George C. *The American Disease.* New York: Alfred A. Knopf, 1984.

Lodge, George C., and Ezra F. Vogel, eds. *Ideology and National Competitiveness: An Analysis of Nine Countries.* Boston: Harvard Business School Press, 1987.

Loewenberg, Gerhard. *Parliament in the German Political System.* Ithaca, N.Y.: Cornell University Press, 1966.

Lord, Guy. *The French Budgetary Process.* Berkeley and Los Angeles: University of California Press, 1973.

Lowi, Theodore. *The Personal President.* Ithaca, N.Y.: Cornell University Press, 1985.

MacDonald, Hugh H., and Milton J. Esman. "The Japanese Civil Service." *Public Personnel Review,* no. 7 (October 1946): 213–224.

Mackenzie, Calvin. "The Paradox of Presidential Personnel Management." In *The Illusion of Presidential Government,* edited by Hugh Heclo and Lester Salamon. Boulder, Colo.: Westview Press, 1981.

Macy, John, et al. *America's Unelected Government: Appointing the President's Team.* Cambridge, Mass.: Ballinger Publishing Company, 1983.

Magaziner, Ira C., and Thomas M. Hout. *Japanese Industrial Policy.* Berkeley and Los Angeles: University of California, 1981.

Magaziner, Ira C., and Robert B. Reich. *Minding America's Business: The Decline and Rise of the American Economy.* New York: Harcourt Brace Jovanovich, 1982.

Malabre, Alfred L. Jr. *Beyond Our Means: How America's Long Years of Debt, Deficits, and Reckless Borrowing Now Threaten to Overwhelm Us.* New York: Random House, 1987.

Mayntz, Renate. "Executive Leadership in Germany: Dispersion of Power or 'Kanzlerdemokratie'?" In *Presidents and Prime Ministers,* edited by Richard Rose and Ezra Suleiman. Washington, D.C.: American Enterprise Institution, 1980.

———. "German Federal Bureaucrats: As Functional Elite Between Politics and Administration." In *Bureaucrats and Policymaking: A Comparative Overview,* edited by Ezra Suleiman. New York: Holmes and Meier Publishers, 1984.

———. "The Higher Civil Service of the Federal Republic of Germany." In *The Higher Civil Service in Europe and Canada,* edited by Bruce Smith. Washington, D.C.: The Brookings Institution, 1984.

Mayntz, Renate, and Fritz W. Scharpf. *Policy-Making in the German Federal Bureaucracy.* Amsterdam: Elsevier, 1975.

McLaren, Walter Wallace. *A Political History of Japan During the Meiji Era.* New York: Russell and Russell Publishers, 1965.

McNelly, Theodore. *Politics and Government in Japan.* Boston: Houghton Mifflin Company, 1963.

Merkl, Peter H. *The Origin of the West German Republic.* New York: Oxford University Press, 1963.

Merritt, Richard L., Ellen P. Flerlage, and Anna J. Merritt. "Political Man in Postwar West German Education." *Comparative Education Review* 15 (October 1971): 346–361.

Miller, Perry. *The American Puritans: Their Prose and Poetry.* Garden City, N.Y.: Doubleday and Company, Anchor Books, 1956.

Monden, Yasuhiro. *The Toyota Production System: Practical Approach to Production Management.* Norcross, Ga.: Institute of Engineering and Management Press, Institute of Industrial Engineers, 1983.

Morita, Akio, et al. *Made in Japan: Akio Morita and Sony.* New York: E. P. Dutton, 1986.

Morone, James A. *The Democratic Wish: Popular Participation and the Limits of American Government.* New York: Basic Books, 1990.

Moynihan, Daniel Patrick. *Family and Nation:* New York: Harcourt Brace Jovanovich, 1986.

Muller, Ronald E. *Revitalizing America: Politics for Prosperity.* New York: Simon and Schuster, 1980.

Muramatsu, Michio, and Ellis S. Krauss. "Bureaucrats and Politicians in Policymaking: The Case of Japan." *American Political Science Review* 78 (March 1984): 126–146.

Nakane, Chie. *Japanese Society.* Berkeley and Los Angeles: University of California Press, 1970.

Nathan, Richard. *The Administrative Presidency.* New York: John Wiley and Sons, 1983.

National Academy of Public Administration. *Leadership in Jeopardy: The Fraying of the Presidential Appointments System.* Washington, D.C.: National Academy of Public Administration, 1985.

Nelson, Michael. "The Irony of American Bureaucracy." In *Bureaucratic Power in National Policy Making,* edited by Francis Rourke, 4th ed. Boston: Little, Brown, and Company, 1986.

Neustadt, Richard. *Presidential Power: The Politics of Leadership from FDR to Carter.* New York: John Wiley and Sons, 1980.

Norman, E. Herbert. *Japan's Emergence as a Modern State: Political and Economic Problems of the Meiji Period.* 1940. Reprint. Westport, Conn.: Greenwood Press, 1973.

Ohmae, Kenichi. *Triad Power: The Coming Shape of Global Competition.* New York: The Free Press, 1985.

Okimoto, Daniel I., Takuo Sugano, and Franklin B. Winstein, eds. *Competitive Edge: The Semiconductor Industry in the U.S. and Japan.* Stanford, Calif.: Stanford University Press, 1984.

Olson, Mancur. *The Rise and Decline of Nations: Economic Growth, Stagflation, and Social Rigidities*. New Haven: Yale University Press, 1982.

O'Neill, Gerard K. *The Technology Edge: Opportunities for America in World Competition*. New York: Simon and Schuster, 1983.

Ornstein, Norman, et al. *Vital Statistics on Congress, 1984–1985 Edition*. Washington, D.C.: American Enterprise Institute, 1984.

Orwell, George. *Animal Farm*. Introduction by C. M. Woodhouse. New York: Harcourt Brace Jovanovich, 1946.

Ouchi, William G. *Theory Z: How American Business Can Meet the Japanese Challenge*. Reading, Mass.: Addison-Wesley Publishing Company, 1981.

Parrington, Vernon Louis. *The Beginnings of Critical Realism in America, 1860–1920*. Vol. 3 of *Main Currents in American Thought*. New York: Harcourt Brace Jovanovich, 1927.

———. *The Colonial Mind, 1620–1800*. Vol. 1 of *Main Currents in American Thought*. New York: Harcourt Brace Jovanovich, 1927.

———. *The Romantic Revolution in America, 1800–1860*. Vol. 2 of *Main Currents in American Thought*. New York: Harcourt Brace Jovanovich, 1927.

Pascale, Richard Tanner, and Anthony G. Athos. *The Art of Japanese Management: Applications for American Executives*. New York: Warner Books, 1981.

Paterson, William E. "The Chancellor and His Party: Political Leadership in the Federal Republic." *West European Politics* 4 (May 1981): 3–17.

Patrick, Hugh, ed., with Larry Meissner. *Japan's High Technology Industries: Lessons and Limitations of Industrial Policy*. Seattle: University of Washington Press, 1986.

Peek, George A. Jr., ed. *The Political Writings of John Adams: Representative Selections*. Indianapolis: Bobbs-Merrill Educational Publishing, 1954.

Pempel, T. J. "The Bureaucratization of Policymaking in Postwar Japan." *Journal of Political Science* 18 (1974): 647–664.

———. *Policy and Politics in Japan: Creative Conservatism*. Philadelphia: Temple University Press, 1982.

Peterson, Merrill D. *Adams and Jefferson: A Revolutionary Dialogue*. Mercer University Lamar Memorial Lectures 19. Athens: University of Georgia Press, 1976.

———. *The Jefferson Image in the American Mind*. New York: Oxford University Press, 1960.

Peterson, Merrill D., ed. *The Portable Thomas Jefferson*. New York: Penguin Books, 1975.

Peterson, Peter G. "The Peterson Prescription." *Harvard Business Review* 62 (May–June 1984): 66–77.

Peterson, Peter G., and Neil Howe. *On Borrowed Time: How the Growth in Entitlement Spending Threatens America's Future*. San Francisco: ICS Press, 1988.

Pfaff, William. *Barbarian Sentiments: How the American Century Ends*. New York: Hill and Wang, 1989.

Phillips, Kevin. *The Politics of Rich and Poor: Wealth and the American Electorate in the Reagan Aftermath*. New York: Random House, 1990.

———. *Staying on Top: The Business Case for a National Industrial Strategy*. New York: Random House, 1984.

Pinney, Edward L. *Federalism, Bureaucracy, and Party Politics in Western Germany*.

Chapel Hill: University of North Carolina Press, 1963.

Piore, Michael J., and Charles F. Sabel. *The Second Industrial Divide: Possibilities for Prosperity.* New York: Basic Books, 1984.

Poggi, Gianfranco. *The Development of the Modern State.* Stanford, Calif.: Stanford University Press, 1978.

Polsby, Nelson. "Some Landmarks in Modern Presidential-Congressional Relations." In *Both Ends of the Avenue: The Presidency, the Executive Branch, and Congress in the 1980s,* edited by Anthony King. Washington, D.C.: American Enterprise Institute, 1983.

Porter, Michael E. *Competitive Advantage: Creating and Sustaining Superior Performance.* New York: The Free Press, 1985.

Potter, David M. *People of Plenty: Economic Abundance and the American Character.* Chicago: University of Chicago Press, 1954.

President's Committee on Administrative Management. *Administrative Management in the Government of the United States.* Washington, D.C.: U.S. Government Printing Office, 1937.

Prestowitz, Clyde V. Jr. *Trading Places: How We Allowed Japan to Take the Lead.* New York: Basic Books, 1988.

Pridham, Geoffrey. "The 1980 Bundestag Election: A Case of 'Normality.'" *West European Politics* 4 (May 1981): 112–123.

Quigley, Harold S. *Japanese Government and Politics.* New York: Century Company, 1932.

Reich, Robert B. "Making Industrial Policy." *Foreign Affairs* 60 (Spring 1982): 852–881.

———. *The Next American Frontier.* New York: Times Books, 1983.

———. *The Resurgent Liberal (And Other Unfashionable Prophecies).* New York: Times Books, 1989.

———. *Tales of a New America.* New York: Times Books, 1987.

———. "Why the U.S. Needs an Industrial Policy." *Harvard Business Review* 60 (January–February 1982): 74–81.

Reich, Robert B., and John D. Donahue. *New Deals: The Chrysler Revival and the American System.* New York: Times Books, 1985.

Reischauer, Edwin O. *The Japanese.* Cambridge: Harvard University Press, Belknap Press, 1977.

———. *The Japanese Today: Change and Continuity.* Cambridge: Harvard University Press, Belknap Press, 1988.

Reischauer, Robert Karl. *Japan: Government, Politics.* New York: Thomas Nelson and Sons, 1939.

Ridley, F., and J. Blondel. *Public Administration in France.* New York: Barnes and Noble Books, 1964.

Ripley, Randall B. *Congress: Process and Policy.* 3d ed. New York: W. W. Norton and Company, 1983.

Rohatyn, Felix G. *The Twenty-Year Century: Essays on Economics and Public Finance.* New York: Random House, 1980.

Rohlen, Thomas P. "Why Japanese Education Works." *Harvard Business Review* 65 (September 1987): 42–47.

Rose, Richard. "Governments Against Subgovernments: A European Perspective on Washington." In *Presidents and Prime Ministers,* edited by Richard Rose and

Ezra Suleiman. Washington, D.C.: American Enterprise Institute, 1980.

Rosenberg, Hans. *Bureaucracy, Aristocracy, and Autocracy: The Prussian Experience, 1660–1815.* Cambridge: Harvard University Press, 1958.

Rosenbloom, David. "The Judicial Response to the Bureaucratic State." In *Bureaucratic Power in National Policy Making,* edited by Francis Rourke, 4th ed. Boston: Little, Brown, and Company, 1986.

Rossiter, Clinton. *Alexander Hamilton and the Constitution.* New York: Harcourt, Brace, and World, 1964.

———. *Conservatism in America: The Thankless Persuasion.* New York: Random House, Vintage Books, 1955.

———. "The Constitutional Significance of the Executive Office of the President." *American Political Science Review* 43 (1949): 1206–1217.

Rourke, Francis. "Bureaucracy in the American Constitutional Order." *Political Science Quarterly* 102 (Summer 1987): 217–232.

Rutledge, John, and Deborah Allen. *Rust to Riches: The Coming of the Second Industrial Revolution.* New York: Harper and Row Publishers, 1989.

Safran, William. *The French Polity.* 2d ed. New York: Longman, 1985.

Samuels, Richard J. *The Business of the Japanese State: Energy Markets in Comparative and Historical Perspective.* Ithaca, N.Y.: Cornell University Press, 1987.

Schlossstein, Steven. *The End of the American Century.* New York: Congdon and Weed, 1989.

———. *Trade War: Greed, Power, and Industrial Policy on Opposite Sides of the Pacific.* New York: Congdon and Weed, 1984.

Schonberger, Richard J. *Japanese Manufacturing Techniques: Nine Hidden Lessons in Simplicity.* New York: The Free Press, 1982.

Schumpeter, Joseph A. *Capitalism, Socialism, and Democracy.* New York: Harper and Row Publishers, 1975.

Scott, Bruce R. "National Strategy for Stronger U.S. Competitiveness." *Harvard Business Review* 62 (March–April 1984): 77–91.

Scott, Bruce R., and George C. Lodge, eds. *U.S. Competitiveness in the World Economy.* Boston: Harvard Business School Press, 1985.

Shapiro, Irving S., with Carl B. Kaufmann. *America's Third Revolution: Public Interest and the Private Role.* New York: Harper and Row Publishers, 1984.

Shingo, Shigeo. *A Revolution in Manufacturing: The SMED System.* Translated by Andrew P. Dillon. Cambridge, Mass.: Productivity Press, 1985.

Shonfield, Andrew. *In Defense of the Mixed Economy.* Edited by Zuzanna Shonfield. New York: Oxford University Press, 1984.

———. *Modern Capitalism: The Changing Balance of Public and Private Power.* London: Oxford University Press, 1969.

———. *The Use of Public Power.* Edited with introduction by Zuzanna Shonfield. Oxford: Oxford University Press, 1982.

Skinner, Wickham. *Manufacturing: The Formidable Competitive Weapon.* New York: John Wiley and Sons, 1985.

Smith, Bruce L. R. "The U.S. Higher Civil Service in Comparative Perspective." In *The Higher Civil Service in Europe and Canada: Lessons for the United States,* edited by Bruce L. R. Smith. Washington, D.C.: The Brookings Institution, 1984.

Smith, Gordon. "Does West German Democracy Have an 'Efficient Secret'?" *West*

European Politics 4 (May 1981): 166–176.

Stewart, Michael. *The Age of Interdependence: Economic Policy in a Shrinking World.* Cambridge: M.I.T. Press, 1984.

Stillman, Richard. *The American Bureaucracy.* Chicago: Nelson-Hall, 1987.

Stockwin, J. A. A. *Japan: Divided Politics in a Growth Economy.* New York: W. W. Norton and Company, 1975.

Stoffaes, Christian. "Industrial Policy in the High Technology Industries." In *French Industrial Policy,* edited by William J. Adams and Christian Stoffaes. Washington, D.C.: The Brookings Institution, 1986.

Stokes, William S. Jr. "Emancipation: The Politics of West German Education." *Review of Politics* 42 (April 1980): 191–215.

Suleiman, Ezra. *Elites in French Society.* Princeton: Princeton University Press, 1978.

———. *Politics, Power, and Bureaucracy in France.* Princeton: Princeton University Press, 1974.

Suleiman, Ezra, ed. *Bureaucrats and Policymaking: A Comparative Overview.* New York: Holmes and Meier Publishers, 1984.

Sundquist, James. *The Decline and Resurgence of Congress.* Washington, D.C.: The Brookings Institution, 1981.

Takeuchi, Tatsuji. *War and Diplomacy in the Japanese Empire.* Chicago: University of Chicago Press, 1935.

Taylor, Jared. *Shadows of the Rising Sun: A Critical View of the "Japanese Miracle."* New York: William Morrow and Company, 1983.

Thayer, Nathaniel B. *How the Conservatives Rule Japan.* Princeton: Princeton University Press, 1969.

Thomson, David. *Democracy in France Since 1870.* 5th ed. Oxford: Oxford University Press, 1969.

Thurow, Lester C., ed. *The Management Challenge: Japanese Views.* Cambridge: M.I.T. Press, 1985.

———. *The Zero-Sum Society: Distribution and the Possibilities for Economic Change.* New York: Basic Books, 1980.

———. *The Zero-Sum Solution: Building a World-Class American Economy.* New York: Simon and Schuster, 1985.

Tilford, Roger. "The State, University Reform, and the 'Berufsverbot.'" *West European Politics* 4 (May 1981): 149–165.

Tilly, Charles, ed. *The Formation of National States in Western Europe.* Princeton: Princeton University Press, 1975.

Tocqueville, Alexis de. *Democracy in America.* Edited by J. P. Mayer and Max Lerner. Translated by George Lawrence. New York: Harper and Row Publishers, 1966.

———. *The Old Regime and the French Revolution.* Translated by Stuart Gilbert. New York: Doubleday and Company, Anchor Books, 1955.

Van Riper, Paul. "The American Administrative State: Wilson and the Founders." In *A Centennial History of the American Administrative State,* edited by Ralph Chandler. New York: The Free Press, 1987.

Vaughan, Alden T., ed. *The Puritan Tradition in America, 1620–1730.* New York: Harper and Row Publishers, 1972.

Vogel, Ezra F. "Guided Free Enterprise in Japan." *Harvard Business Review* 56 (May–June 1978): 161–170.

————. *Japan as Number One: Lessons for America.* Cambridge: Harvard University Press, 1979.

Vogel, Ezra F., ed. *Modern Japanese Organization and Decision Making.* Berkeley and Los Angeles: University of California Press, 1975.

Wachter, Michael L., and Susan M. Wachter, eds. *Toward a New U.S. Industrial Policy?* Philadelphia: University of Pennsylvania Press, 1983.

Walzer, Michael. *Radical Principles: Reflections of an Unreconstructed Democrat.* New York: Basic Books, 1980.

Ward, Robert E. *Japan's Political System.* Englewood Cliffs, N.J.: Prentice-Hall, 1967.

Ward, Robert E., ed. *Political Development in Modern Japan.* Princeton: Princeton University Press, 1968.

Watanuki, Joji. *Politics in Postwar Japanese Society.* Tokyo: University of Tokyo Press, 1977.

Weiss, Andrew. "Simple Truths of Japanese Manufacturing." *Harvard Business Review* 62 (July–August 1984): 119–125.

Wheelwright, Steven C. "Japan—Where Operations Really Are Strategic." *Harvard Business Review* 59 (July–August 1981): 67–74.

Wilkinson, Rupert, ed. *Governing Elites: Studies in Training and Selection.* New York: Oxford University Press, 1969.

Will, George F. *Statecraft as Soulcraft: What Government Does.* New York: Simon and Schuster, 1983.

Williams, Philip. *The French Parliament.* Westport, Conn.: Greenwood Press, 1977.

Wilson, James Q. "The Rise of the Bureaucratic State." *The Public Interest,* no. 41 (Fall 1975): 77–103.

Wilson, John Oliver. *The Power Economy: Building an Economy That Works.* Boston, Mass.: Little, Brown, and Company, 1985.

Wiltse, Charles Maurice. *The Jeffersonian Tradition in American Democracy.* New York: Hill and Wang, 1935.

Wolferen, Karel van. *The Enigma of Japanese Power: People and Politics in a Stateless Nation.* New York: Alfred A. Knopf, 1989.

Wolin, Sheldon S. *Politics and Vision: Continuity and Innovation in Western Political Thought.* Boston: Little, Brown, and Company, 1960.

Woll, Peter. *American Bureaucracy.* 2d ed. New York: W. W. Norton and Company, 1977.

Wright, Gordon. *France in Modern Times.* 3d ed. New York: W. W. Norton and Company, 1981.

Yates, Brock. *The Decline and Fall of the American Automobile Industry.* New York: Vintage Books, 1984.

Yoffie, David B. *Power and Protectionism: Strategies of the Newly Industrializing Countries.* New York: Columbia University Press, 1983.

Zimmerman, Mark. *How to Do Business with the Japanese.* New York: Random House, 1985.

Zysman, John. *Governments, Markets, and Growth: Financial Systems and the Politics of Industrial Change.* Ithaca, N.Y.: Cornell University Press, 1983.

Zysman, John, and Laura Tyson, eds. *American Industry in International Competition: Government Policies and Corporate Strategies.* Ithaca, N.Y.: Cornell University Press, 1983.

INDEX

DATE DUE

DEMCO, INC. 38-3011